# HISTORICAL DICTIONARIES
## OF RELIGIONS, PHILOSOPHIES, AND MOVEMENTS
### Jon Woronoff, Series Editor

1. *Buddhism*, by Charles S. Prebish, 1993.
2. *Mormonism*, by Davis Bitton, 1994. *Out of print. See no. 32.*
3. *Ecumenical Christianity*, by Ans Joachim van der Bent, 1994.
4. *Terrorism*, by Sean Anderson and Stephen Sloan, 1995. *Out of print. See no. 41.*
5. *Sikhism*, by W. H. McLeod, 1995. *Out of print. See no. 59.*
6. *Feminism*, by Janet K. Boles and Diane Long Hoeveler, 1995. *Out of print. See no. 52.*
7. *Olympic Movement*, by Ian Buchanan and Bill Mallon, 1995. *Out of print. See no. 39.*
8. *Methodism*, by Charles Yrigoyen Jr. and Susan E. Warrick, 1996. *Out of print. See no. 57.*
9. *Orthodox Church*, by Michael Prokurat, Alexander Golitzin, and Michael D. Peterson, 1996.
10. *Organized Labor*, by James C. Docherty, 1996. *Out of print. See no. 50.*
11. *Civil Rights Movement*, by Ralph E. Luker, 1997.
12. *Catholicism*, by William J. Collinge, 1997.
13. *Hinduism*, by Bruce M. Sullivan, 1997.
14. *North American Environmentalism*, by Edward R. Wells and Alan M. Schwartz, 1997.
15. *Welfare State*, by Bent Greve, 1998. *Out of print. See no. 63.*
16. *Socialism*, by James C. Docherty, 1997. *Out of print. See no. 73.*
17. *Bahá'í Faith*, by Hugh C. Adamson and Philip Hainsworth, 1998. *Out of print. See no. 71.*
18. *Taoism*, by Julian F. Pas in cooperation with Man Kam Leung, 1998.
19. *Judaism*, by Norman Solomon, 1998. *Out of print. See no. 69.*
20. *Green Movement*, by Elim Papadakis, 1998. *Out of print. See no. 80.*
21. *Nietzscheanism*, by Carol Diethe, 1999. *Out of print. See no. 75.*
22. *Gay Liberation Movement*, by Ronald J. Hunt, 1999.
23. *Islamic Fundamentalist Movements in the Arab World, Iran, and Turkey*, by Ahmad S. Moussalli, 1999.

24. *Reformed Churches*, by Robert Benedetto, Darrell L. Guder, and Donald K. McKim, 1999.
25. *Baptists*, by William H. Brackney, 1999. *Out of print. See no. 92.*
26. *Cooperative Movement*, by Jack Shaffer, 1999.
27. *Reformation and Counter-Reformation*, by Hans J. Hillerbrand, 2000.
28. *Shakers*, by Holley Gene Duffield, 2000.
29. *United States Political Parties*, by Harold F. Bass Jr., 2000.
30. *Heidegger's Philosophy*, by Alfred Denker, 2000.
31. *Zionism*, by Rafael Medoff and Chaim I. Waxman, 2000. *Out of print. See no. 83.*
32. *Mormonism*, 2nd ed., by Davis Bitton, 2000. *Out of print. See no. 89.*
33. *Kierkegaard's Philosophy*, by Julia Watkin, 2001.
34. *Hegelian Philosophy*, by John W. Burbidge, 2001. *Out of print. See no. 90.*
35. *Lutheranism*, by Günther Gassmann in cooperation with Duane H. Larson and Mark W. Oldenburg, 2001.
36. *Holiness Movement*, by William Kostlevy, 2001.
37. *Islam*, by Ludwig W. Adamec, 2001.
38. *Shinto*, by Stuart D. B. Picken, 2002.
39. *Olympic Movement*, 2nd ed., by Ian Buchanan and Bill Mallon, 2001. *Out of print. See no. 61.*
40. *Slavery and Abolition*, by Martin A. Klein, 2002.
41. *Terrorism*, 2nd ed., by Sean Anderson and Stephen Sloan, 2002.
42. *New Religious Movements*, by George D. Chryssides, 2001.
43. *Prophets in Islam and Judaism*, by Scott B. Noegel and Brannon M. Wheeler, 2002.
44. *The Friends (Quakers)*, by Margery Post Abbott, Mary Ellen Chijioke, Pink Dandelion, and John William Oliver Jr., 2003.
45. *Lesbian Liberation Movement: Still the Rage*, by JoAnne Myers, 2003.
46. *Descartes and Cartesian Philosophy*, by Roger Ariew, Dennis Des Chene, Douglas M. Jesseph, Tad M. Schmaltz, and Theo Verbeek, 2003.
47. *Witchcraft*, by Michael D. Bailey, 2003.
48. *Unitarian Universalism*, by Mark W. Harris, 2004.
49. *New Age Movements*, by Michael York, 2004.

# Historical Dictionary of Environmentalism

Peter Dauvergne

*Historical Dictionaries of Religions,
Philosophies, and Movements, No. 92*

The Scarecrow Press, Inc.
Lanham, Maryland • Toronto • Plymouth, UK
2009

SCARECROW PRESS, INC.

Published in the United States of America
by Scarecrow Press, Inc.
A wholly owned subsidiary of
The Rowman & Littlefield Publishing Group, Inc.
4501 Forbes Boulevard, Suite 200, Lanham, Maryland 20706
www.scarecrowpress.com

Estover Road
Plymouth PL6 7PY
United Kingdom

British Library Cataloguing in Publication Information Available

**Library of Congress Cataloging-in-Publication Data**
Dauvergne, Peter.
   Historical dictionary of environmentalism / Peter Dauvergne.
      p. cm. — (Historical dictionaries of religions, philosophies, and movements ;
no. 92)
   Includes bibliographical references.
   ISBN-13: 978-0-8108-5804-6 (cloth : alk. paper)
   ISBN-10: 0-8108-5804-5 (cloth : alk. paper)
   ISBN-13: 978-0-8108-6290-6 (ebook)
   ISBN-10: 0-8108-6290-5 (ebook)
   1. Environmentalism–History–Dictionaries. I. Title.
   GE195.D358 2009
   333.7209–dc22                                           2008037837

# Contents

# Editor's Foreword

There are few topics that are more important for all of us than the environment, since we are among the many creatures who live in it and will be seriously affected by any problems, let alone major disasters, it encounters. So it is definitely a plus that this series now has a major work on the environment, one that considers its many different aspects, looks at the situation in many different places, and shows the numerous efforts that are being made to resolve problems and avoid disasters. This volume includes information on the pioneers—those who wrote about the environment well before the subject was popular or even had a name—and it looks at the most recent state of knowledge on the environment, while in passing tracing the efforts of those who study it and recommend practices that will hopefully be in humanity's best interest. Inevitably, this text also examines many of the issues that have cropped up (and keep on coming fast and furious) and the infrequent disasters, although worse can be expected if we do not get things right.

Many of the volumes in this particular series of historical dictionaries deal with controversial topics. But one might—perhaps naively—think that environmentalism would not be among those since we all presumably want life on "spaceship earth" to be as congenial as possible and to avoid any nasty bumps, let alone a crash. Nonetheless, there is controversy over virtually every aspect, from causes to solutions, let alone apportioning blame, and all too many of the spokespeople assume that they hold the "right" views while varying ones are hopelessly "wrong." It is therefore to be welcomed that this book is broad enough to span opinions on all sides of each question while introducing and examining a bevy of issues that seem to get more intractable with the passing years. This includes those who insist that time is running out and we must act immediately, as well as some who fear that precipitate action could be dangerous and others who think that the whole issue is overblown and that perhaps doing nothing or just letting things sort themselves out would be best. This volume even shows the increasingly positive role being played by the apparent villains—big government and big business.

This historical dictionary tackles its topic, as usual, in several interrelated sections. The list of acronyms is quite long this time, as not knowing the acronyms could leave you lost in trying to follow the debates. The chronology then traces the more significant events, relatively few and sporadic a few centuries back, but coming fast and furious in recent decades (which already says something about the situation). The introduction takes a broader view, showing the different and sometimes cooperative efforts of the various players—scholars, governments, nongovernmental organizations (which is not quite equivalent to the "people"), and corporations—and what has been achieved so far. But the most important section is once again a substantial dictionary with specific entries on, among other things, issues, problems and disasters, conferences, conventions, organizations, and notable individuals as well as some key countries. Obviously, there is so much to say about environmentalism that any serious reader will want to refer to some of the more detailed sources and also look more closely into some specific aspects. This justifies an impressively long and well-structured bibliography, which readers should certainly consult.

This *Historical Dictionary of Environmentalism* was written by Peter Dauvergne, who is a professor of political science at the University of British Columbia, where he also served as director of the Environment Program at the Liu Institute for Global Issues and more recently as associate dean in the Faculty of Arts and at present as senior advisor to the university president. In addition, he is the Canada Research Chair in Global Environmental Politics. Dr. Dauvergne's research interests include critical global change theory and environmental theory in international relations. These have given him considerable insight into a broad range of issues, both practical and theoretical. He has published extensively, with many books and shorter works. Among his books, most deal with one aspect or another of political economy, including consumption and its impacts, logging in the Asia Pacific, and more generally global environmental politics. This experience has made him an unusually skilled guide to the very complex and, as noted, controversial field of environmentalism and certainly makes this volume an excellent starting point for those who want to know more.

Jon Woronoff
Series Editor

# Acknowledgments

I would like to thank the Social Sciences and Humanities Research Council of Canada and the Canada Research Chairs Program for their funding, which supported a team of graduate students who for several years methodically collected research for this book. My special thanks to Kaija Belfry for coordinating this project and to the team of adept researchers under her guidance: Nicolas Dragojlovic, Josh Gordon, Talusier Arbour LaSalle, Jane Lister, Vanessa Meadu, Nicolas Sternsdorff, and Colin Trehearne. I am also indebted to Kate Neville for fact-checking and assistance with dictionary entries (especially the country entries) and to Sharon Goad for editorial support and assistance with the bibliography. My thanks as well to Jon Woronoff for his helpful advice and support throughout.

# Acronyms and Abbreviations

| | |
|---|---|
| AA | AccountAbility |
| ABN | L'Autorité du Bassin du Niger (Niger Basin Authority) |
| ACF | Australian Conservation Foundation |
| ADEME | Agence de l'Environnement et de la Maîtrise de l'Energie (Environment and Energy Efficiency Agency) (France) |
| AEPS | Arctic Environmental Protection Strategy |
| AIA | Advance informed agreement |
| ARPA | Programa Áreas Protegidas da Amazônia (Amazon Protected Areas Programme) |
| ASEAN | Association of Southeast Asian Nations |
| ASEM | Asia-Europe Meeting |
| AZAP | Arid Zone Afforestation Project (Nigeria) |
| BAPA | Bangladesh Poribesh Andolon (Bangladesh Environment Movement) |
| BCSD | Business Council for Sustainable Development |
| BEN | Bangladesh Environment Network |
| BIO | Biotechnology Industry Organization |
| BPA | Bisphenol A |
| CASBEE | Comprehensive Assessment System for Building Environmental Efficiency (Japan) |
| CBD | Convention on Biological Diversity |
| CCAMLR | Convention on the Conservation of Antarctic Marine Living Resources |
| CCP | Cities for Climate Protection |
| CDM | Clean Development Mechanism |
| CELA | Canadian Environmental Law Association |
| CEN | Coalition of Environmental NGOs (Bangladesh) |
| CERES | Coalition for Environmentally Responsible Economies |

| CFCs | Chlorofluorocarbons |
|------|---------------------|
| CFN | Commission du Fleuve Niger (Niger River Commission) |
| CI | Conservation International |
| CIEL | Center for International Environmental Law |
| CITES | Convention on International Trade in Endangered Species of Wild Fauna and Flora |
| CLRTAP | Convention on Long-Range Transboundary Air Pollution |
| COAG | Council of Australian Governments |
| COFEMA | Consejo Federal de Medio Ambiente (Federal Council of the Environment) (Argentina) |
| CONAMA | Comisión Nacional del Medio Ambiente (National Commission for the Environment) (Chile) |
| COP | Conference of the Parties |
| COPUOS | Committee on the Peaceful Uses of Outer Space (in the United Nations) |
| COSEWIC | Committee on the Status of Endangered Wildlife in Canada |
| CRT | Cathode ray tube |
| CSA | Canadian Standards Association |
| CSE | Centre for Science and Environment (India) |
| CSR | Corporate social responsibility |
| DDT | Dichlorodiphenyltrichloroethane |
| Defra | Department for Environment, Food and Rural Affairs (Great Britain) |
| DPRK | Democratic People's Republic of Korea (North Korea) |
| ECO | Environmental Challenge Organisation (Singapore) |
| EDF | Environmental Defense Fund (United States) |
| EEZ | Exclusive Economic Zone |
| EIA | Environmental Investigation Agency |
| EKC | Environmental Kuznets Curve |
| ELF | Earth Liberation Front |
| EMAS | Eco-management and audit scheme |
| EMS | Environmental management system (of the ISO) |
| ENB | *Earth Negotiations Bulletin* |
| EPA | Environmental Protection Agency |
| EPFIs | Equator Principles Financial Institutions |

| | |
|---|---|
| EPR | Extended producer/product responsibility |
| ETC | Erosion, Technology and Concentration (Action Group on) |
| EU | European Union |
| FAO | Food and Agriculture Organization |
| FBI | Federal Bureau of Investigations (United States) |
| FERN | Forests and the European Union Resource Network |
| FLO | Fairtrade Labelling Organizations International |
| FOEI | Friends of the Earth International |
| FSC | Forest Stewardship Council |
| FUNAM | Fundación para la defensa del ambiente (Environment defense foundation) (Argentina) |
| FUNBIO | Fundo Brasileiro para a Biodiversidade (Brazilian Biodiversity Fund) |
| GDP | Gross domestic product |
| GEF | Global Environment Facility |
| GEN | Global Ecolabelling Network |
| GM | Genetically modified |
| GMO | Genetically modified organisms |
| GNP | Gross national product |
| GRAIN | Genetic Action Resources International |
| GRI | Global Reporting Initiative |
| GROZA | Zelenaya Alternativa (Green Alternative) (Russia) |
| GW | Gigawatts |
| HCB | Hexachlorobenzene |
| HCFCs | Hydrochlorofluorocarbons |
| HELCOM | Helsinki Commission (Finland) |
| HFCs | Hydrofluorocarbons |
| HIV/AIDS | Human Immunodeficiency Virus/Acquired Immunodeficiency Syndrome |
| IBAMA | Instituto Brasileiro do Meio Ambiente e dos Recursos Naturais Renováveis (Brazilian Institute of Environment and Renewable Natural Resources) |
| IBDF | Instituto Brasileiro de Desenvolvimento Florestal (Brazilian Institute of Forestry Development) |
| IBF | International Biofuels Forum |
| ICC | Inuit Circumpolar Conference |
| ICED | International Center for Environment and Development |

| ICLEI | Local Governments for Sustainability |
| ICMM | International Council on Mining and Metals |
| IFAT | International Fair Trade Association |
| IFAW | International Fund for Animal Welfare |
| IIED | International Institute for Environment and Development |
| IISD | International Institute for Sustainable Development |
| IMF | International Monetary Fund |
| IMO | International Maritime Organization |
| INBio | Instituto Nacional de Biodiversidad (National Biodiversity Institute) (Costa Rica) |
| INCR | Investor Network on Climate Risk |
| INRIC | International Network of Resource Information Centers |
| IPAM | Instituto de Pesquisa Ambiental da Amazônia (Institute for Environmental Research in Brazil) |
| IPCC | Intergovernmental Panel on Climate Change |
| ISA | Instituto Socioambiental (an institute in Brazil to promote social and environmental rights) |
| ISEE | International Society for Ecological Economics |
| ISEW | Index of Sustainable Economic Welfare |
| ISO | International Organization for Standardization |
| IUCN | International Union for Conservation of Nature |
| IWC | International Whaling Commission |
| LEED | Leadership in Energy and Environmental Design |
| LVEMP | Lake Victoria Environmental Management Project (Africa) |
| MEWR | Ministry of the Environment and Water Resources (Singapore) |
| MINAE | Ministerio de Ambiente y Energía (Ministry of the Environment and Energy) (Costa Rica) |
| MoE | Ministry of Environment (South Korea) |
| MoEF | Ministry of Environment and Forests (Bangladesh) |
| MOEF | Ministry of Environment and Forests (India) |
| MOSOP | Movement for the Survival of the Ogoni People (Nigeria) |
| MNC | Multinational corporation |
| MSC | Marine Stewardship Council |

| | |
|---|---|
| MV SZOPK | Slovensky Zvaz Ochrancov Prirodky a Krajiny (Slovak Association of Protectors of Nature and Landscape) |
| MW | Megawatts |
| NASA | National Aeronautics and Space Administration |
| NCEP | National Committee on Environmental Planning (India) |
| NEPA | National Environmental Policy Act (United States) |
| NEWS! | Network of European Worldshops |
| NFZT | Nuclear Free Zone Treaty (South Pacific) |
| NIMBY | Not in my backyard |
| NGO | Nongovernmental organization |
| NRDC | Natural Resources Defense Council |
| ODA | Official Development Assistance |
| OECD | Organisation for Economic Co-operation and Development |
| OPEC | Organization of the Petroleum Exporting Countries |
| PBDE | Polybrominated diphenyl ethers |
| PCB | Polychlorinated biphenyl |
| PCSD | Philippine Council for Sustainable Development |
| PEFC | Programme for the Endorsement of Forest Certification |
| PIROP | Pacific Islands Regional Ocean Policy |
| POPs | Persistent organic pollutants |
| PRA | Participatory rural appraisal |
| PVC | Polyvinyl chloride |
| RAN | Rainforest Action Network |
| RCMS® | Responsible Care Management System® |
| REDD | Reduced Emissions through Avoided Deforestation and Degradation |
| RENOVE | Rede Nacional de Organizações da Sociedade Civil para as Energias Renováveis (a network of NGOs to promote renewable energy in Brazil) |
| RFF | Resources for the Future |
| RTS | Reclaim the Streets |
| SARA | Species at Risk Act (Canada) |
| SCAR | Scientific Committee on Antarctic Research |
| SEC | Singapore Environment Council |

| | |
|---|---|
| SEDUE | Secretaría de Desarrollo Urbano y Ecología (Secretariat of Urban Development and Ecology) (Mexico) |
| SEMA | Secretaria Especial do Meio Ambiente (secretariat for the environment under the jurisdiction of the Minister of the Interior in Brazil) |
| SEPA | State Environmental Protection Administration (China) |
| SFI | Sustainable Forestry Initiative |
| SGLS | Singapore Green Labelling Scheme |
| SINAC | Sistema Nacional de Áreas de Conservación de Costa Rica (National Conservation Areas System of Costa Rica) |
| SNUC | Sistema Nacional de Unidades de Conservação (National System of Conservation Units in Brazil) |
| SPREP | South Pacific Regional Environment Programme |
| TACIS | Technical Assistance to the Commonwealth of Independent States (a program of the European Commission) |
| TAMAR | Tartarugas Marinhas (Sea Turtles, a Brazilian NGO) |
| TIS | Svaz Pro Ochranu Přírody a Krajiny (Yew Tree, the Union for the Protection of Nature and Landscape) (Czechoslovakia) |
| TRAFFIC | Trade Records Analysis of Fauna and Flora in Commerce |
| TWN | Third World Network |
| UN | United Nations |
| UNCCD | United Nations Convention to Combat Desertification |
| UNCED | United Nations Conference on Environment and Development |
| UNCLOS | United Nations Convention on the Law of the Sea |
| UNCSD | United Nations Commission on Sustainable Development |
| UNDP | United Nations Development Programme |
| UNEP | United Nations Environment Programme |
| UNESCO | United Nations Educational, Scientific and Cultural Organization |
| UNFCCC | United Nations Framework Convention on Climate Change |
| UNFPA | United Nations Fund for Population Activities |

| | |
|---|---|
| UNOOSA | United Nations Office for Outer Space Affairs |
| U.S. | United States |
| USAID | United States Agency for International Development |
| USSR | Union of Soviet Socialist Republics |
| UTG | United Tasmania Group (Australia) |
| WALHI | Wahana Lingkungan Hidup Indonesia (Indonesian Forum for Environment) |
| WBCSD | World Business Council for Sustainable Development |
| WMO | World Meteorological Organization |
| WRI | World Resources Institute |
| WWF | World Wide Fund for Nature/World Wildlife Fund |

# Chronology

**1601  Russia:** One of the worst famines in Russia's history begins, lasting until 1603 and killing up to one third of the population.

**1626  United States:** Plymouth Colony passes an ordinance for cutting and selling timber.

**1642  China:** Near the end of the Ming dynasty (1368–1644), General Gao Mingheng breaches dikes to fight a peasant uprising, one of the first recorded uses of water as a military tool.

**1666  Japan:** Tokugawa Shogunate takes control of logging and promotes tree planting to reduce soil erosion and flooding.

**1669  France:** Forest Code is established to regulate wood production for the navy.

**1681  Mauritius:** Last Mauritius dodo (*Raphus cucullatus*) dies. **United States:** Proprietor of Pennsylvania, William Penn, decrees that one acre (0.4 hectares) of old-growth forest must remain for every five cleared.

**1710  United States:** Massachusetts protects waterfowl in coastal regions.

**1722  Easter Island:** Dutch explorer Jacob Roggeveen visits on Easter Sunday, surprised to find an ecological wasteland littered with majestic stone monuments.

**1730  India:** More than 300 Bishnois in what is now the state of Rajasthan are killed trying to prevent logging.

**1798  Great Britain:** Thomas Malthus' *An Essay on the Principle of Population* is published.

**1804** **International:** World population reaches 1 billion.

**1829** **France:** Statute to protect fish is enacted (still in effect).

**1845** **Prussia (present-day Germany):** Regulations for industrial air pollution are introduced.

**1859** **South Africa:** Cape Colony government passes Forest Protection Act.

**1861** **Mexico:** Forest Service and forest ranger corps are established.

**1862** **France/Vietnam:** First of a series of French ordinances to create forest reserves in Cochinchina (Vietnam) is enacted.

**1864** **India:** Forest Service is founded. **United States:** George Perkins Marsh's *Man and Nature* is published, a foundational study of scientific conservation.

**1865** **Great Britain:** First private group for environmental protection forms the Open Spaces Society. **India:** First Indian Forest Act is passed. **Java (controlled by the Netherlands):** Forest legislation is passed.

**1866** **Germany:** Ernst Haeckel coins the term *ecology*.

**1869** **Egypt:** Suez Canal opens, creating the first saltwater passage between the Mediterranean Sea and Red Sea; species previously blocked by hypersaline lakes begin to move between the seas, with the Mediterranean especially invaded by Red Sea species.

**1871** **United States:** *American Sportsman* becomes the first publication to weave together the topics of conservation, hunting, fishing, and natural history.

**1872** **United States:** Yellowstone National Park becomes the world's first national park (March). Nebraska sets aside 10 April as a holiday to plant trees (which in 1885 becomes a legal holiday, with the date now 22 April).

**1873** **Australia:** Forest Tree Act passes in South Australia.

**1879** **Australia:** First national park is established: Royal National Park in New South Wales.

**1885** **Canada:** Banff National Park is established.

**1892  United States:** John Muir cofounds the Sierra Club.

**1894  New Zealand:** Tongariro National Park is established.

**1895  United States:** Wildlife Conservation Society is founded with headquarters at the Bronx Zoo in New York City.

**1897  Thailand:** Royal Forest Department is set up to manage revenue from teak forests.

**1899  Thailand:** All forests in Thailand are declared government property.

**1900  International:** First "international" conference on the environment is held in London in order to protect African wildlife. Parties adopt the Convention for the Preservation of Animals, Birds and Fish in Africa (May).

**1905  Great Britain:** In a London newspaper Dr. Henry Antoine Des Voeux describes the London Fog as "smog" (combining "smoke" and "fog"), popularizing the term. **United States:** National Audubon Society is established from local Audubon clubs set up in the late 1800s.

**1906  Mexico/United States:** Mexico and the United States sign the Convention on the Equitable Distribution of the Waters of the Rio Grande (for irrigation purposes), one of the first international environmental agreements (May).

**1908  United States:** President Theodore Roosevelt hosts a conference on conservation that leads to the formation of 38 state conservation commissions.

**1914  United States:** Once the most common bird in eastern North America, the last passenger pigeon dies in a Cincinnati zoo.

**1916  International:** Convention for the Protection of Migratory Birds concludes (August).

**1921  United States:** Thomas Midgley Jr. discovers that adding tetraethyl lead to gasoline can reduce engine knock, the beginning of the leaded gasoline industry.

**1926  South Africa:** National Parks Act is enacted.

**1927 International:** World population reaches 2 billion. **France:** French scientist and explorer Louis Lavauden coins the term *desertification.*

**1928 United States:** Thomas Midgley Jr. discovers chlorofluorocarbons (CFCs), later sold under the trademark Freon to cool refrigerators.

**1933 International:** Convention Relative to the Preservation of Fauna and Flora in their Natural State opens for signature (November).

**1934 Argentina:** A National Parks system is established.

**1935 United States:** Wilderness Society is founded.

**1939 Switzerland:** Paul Hermann Müller (1899–1965) discovers the "high efficiency" of dichlorodiphenyltrichloroethane (DDT) as an insecticide (for which he receives a Nobel Prize in 1948).

**1946 International:** International Convention for the Regulation of Whaling opens for signature (December). **Bikini Atoll:** Atomic bomb is tested in July, the first of over 20 in Micronesia over the next 12 years; nuclear fallout leaves behind a devastating toll, convincing many to oppose nuclear tests on ecological grounds.

**1948 International:** International Union for Conservation of Nature (IUCN) is founded. **Great Britain:** Six hundred die in London from fog laced with particulate matter and sulphuric acid. **India:** Mohandas Karamchand (Mahatma) Gandhi (1869–1948) is assassinated.

**1949 United States:** Aldo Leopold's *A Sand County Almanac* is published, which would shape the environmental movement into the 1950s and 1960s.

**1950 Bangladesh:** Government begins to manage fish resources under the Protection and Conservation of Fish Act.

**1951 International:** International Plant Protection Convention opens for signature (December). **Czechoslovakia:** Communist Party forcibly disbands all "decorative" clubs, including organizations concerned with landscape preservation that—as part of the nascent preservationist movement prior to World War I—had approximately 50,000 members in 378 clubs. **Iran:** Government nationalizes oil, straining relations with Great Britain and the United States. **United States:** Nature Conservancy is founded, although roots go back to 1915.

**1952   Great Britain:** "Killer fog" contributes to 4,000–7,000 deaths in London (December). **United States:** Resources for the Future is founded, the first think tank in the United States to focus solely on energy, environmental issues, and natural resources.

**1954   International:** International Convention on Pollution of the Sea by Oil opens for signature (May). **United States:** Bell Laboratories develops a silicon photovoltaic cell able to convert enough sunlight to power electrical equipment.

**1955   Israel:** Wildlife Protection Law is enacted.

**1956   China:** The first nature reserve is established. **Great Britain:** Clean Air Act is passed. **Japan:** Minamata disease, a neurological condition, is officially "discovered" in villagers living upstream from Minamata Bay (linked in 1959 to methyl mercury from the Chisso industrial plant).

**1958   International:** Convention on the Continental Shelf, the Convention on the Territorial Sea and Contiguous Zone, and the Geneva Convention on Fishing and Conservation of the Living Resources of the High Seas open for signature (April). **Czechoslovakia:** Yew Tree, the Union for the Protection of Nature and Landscape (TIS)—the first conservation group—is formed; it is not completely independent, however, as it works within the state apparatus and, thus, supports the Soviet regime.

**1959   International:** Main international organization for space law, the United Nations and its Committee on the Peaceful Uses of Outer Space (COPUOS), becomes a permanent body of the General Assembly. Antarctic Treaty opens for signature (December). **Vietnam:** Vietnam War (1959–1975) begins, causing widespread environmental damage over the next decade and a half as the United States sprays herbicides, such as the dioxin-containing Agent Orange, to defoliate forests.

**1960   International:** World population reaches 3 billion. Paris Convention on Third Party Liability in the Field of Nuclear Energy opens for signature (July).

**1961   International:** World Wildlife Fund is founded (today known simply as WWF). **South Korea:** Government enacts a new Forest Law to promote reforestation, the country's first environmental law.

**1962   United States:** Rachel Carson's *Silent Spring* is published, which for many marks the start of the modern environmental movement.

**1963** **International:** Berne Convention on the International Commission for the Protection of the Rhine against Pollution opens for signature (April). Vienna Convention on Civil Liability in the Field of Nuclear Energy opens for signature (May). **Israel:** Government passes first law for national parks. **Soviet Union:** *Oktiabr* publishes the most famous of the essays related to Lake Baikal, "Luminous Eye of Siberia," by Vladimir Chivilikhin.

**1964** **International:** Convention for the International Council for the Exploration of the Sea opens for signature (September).

**1966** **International:** International Convention for the Conservation of Atlantic Tunas opens for signature (May). **South Korea:** Protests in Pusan against air pollution from an oil-fired power station spur emerging environmental citizen activism. **United States:** Scientists concerned about the effects of dichlorodiphenyltrichloroethane (DDT) establish the Environmental Defense Fund (which incorporates the following year). Kenneth Boulding publishes "The Economics of the Coming Spaceship Earth."

**1967** **Great Britain:** *Torrey Canyon* sinks off the coast of England, spilling over 30 million gallons of crude oil.

**1968** **International:** African Convention on the Conservation of Nature and Natural Resources opens for signature (September). **United States:** Paul Ehrlich publishes *The Population Bomb*. Garrett Hardin publishes in the journal *Science* what would become one of the most cited articles of all time, "The Tragedy of the Commons."

**1969** **International:** United Nations establishes the Fund for Population Activities (UNFPA). **Canada:** Don't Make a Wave Committee forms in Vancouver, the beginning of what later becomes Greenpeace. **Czechoslovakia:** Yew Tree, the Union for the Protection of Nature and Landscape (TIS)—the first conservation group—splits in two, giving rise to the Slovak Union of Nature Conservationists (with the original organization continuing in some areas). **United States:** David Brower founds Friends of the Earth after resigning as executive director of the Sierra Club.

**1970** **International:** United Nations General Assembly adopts the Declaration of Principles Governing the Seabed and the Ocean Floor, and the Subsoil Thereof, beyond the Limits of National Jurisdiction (December). **Germany:** Paul Crutzen of the Max Planck Institute for Chemistry in Mainz raises the possibility that nitrogen oxides from fertilizers and supersonic aircraft could be damaging the ozone layer. **Japan:** The Diet holds a special session that passes 14 new laws to regulate pollution. **United States:** First Earth Day held on 22 April. Group of law students and attorneys founds the Natural Resources Defense Council to influence environmental laws. Environmental Protection Agency (EPA) is established.

**1971   International:** Ramsar Convention on Wetlands of International Importance Especially as Waterfowl Habitat opens for signature (February). International Institute for Environment and Development is founded with a base in London. **Brazil:** Economist Jose Lutzemberger founds Gaucho Association for the Protection of the Natural Environment. **Canada:** Department of Environment is established. Group of activists founds Greenpeace in Vancouver. **France:** Environment Ministry is established. **Great Britain:** World Wide Opportunities on Organic Farms begins, eventually evolving into a worldwide network of national organizations to link travelers wanting to volunteer (in exchange for food and accommodation) on organic farms.

**1972   International:** United Nations Conference on the Human Environment is held in Stockholm (June). Convention on the Prevention of Pollution by Dumping of Wastes and Other Matter (London Convention) opens for signature (November). Club of Rome authors publish *The Limits to Growth*. United Nations Environment Programme is established with its headquarters in Nairobi, Kenya. United Nations establishes World Environment Day to be held every year on 5 June. **Australia:** United Tasmania Group (UTG) forms, which some environmental historians consider the world's first green party. **Singapore:** A Ministry of the Environment is created. **United States:** Pesticide dichlorodiphenyltrichloroethane (DDT) is banned.

**1973   International:** Convention on International Trade in Endangered Species of Wild Fauna and Flora opens for signature (March). International Convention for the Prevention of Pollution from Ships opens for signature (November). **Bangladesh:** Wild Life (Preservation) Order is enacted. **Great Britain:** E. F. Schumacher publishes *Small Is*

*Beautiful.* Under the name PEOPLE, Europe's first green party is founded (renamed the Ecology Party in 1975 and the Green Party in 1985). **India:** Chipko movement emerges when villagers in the Himalayan mountains start hugging trees to stop logging. **Israel:** Environmental Protection Service is established. **Norway:** Arne Naess publishes "The Shallow and the Deep, Long-Range Ecology Movements" in *Inquiry*, coining the phrase *deep ecology*. **United States:** Endangered Species Act is enacted.

**1974 International:** World population reaches 4 billion. **Finland:** Helsinki Convention (Convention on the Protection of the Marine Environment of the Baltic Sea Area) is adopted (replaced in 1992 by a new Helsinki Convention). **France:** Françoise d'Eaubonne coins the term *ecofeminism*, merging environmentalism and feminism into a new intellectual movement. René Dumont contests the French presidential elections with an environmental platform. **Germany:** Federal Environmental Agency is established. **Mexico:** Symposium on development and environment is held at Cocoyoc, hosted by the United Nations Environment Programme and the United Nations Conference on Trade and Development (October). The Cocoyoc Declaration represents one of the earliest uses of the phrase *sustainable development*. **United States:** Lester Brown founds the Worldwatch Institute (based in Washington, D.C.). Mario J. Molina and F. Sherwood Rowland publish an article hypothesizing that chlorofluorocarbons (CFCs) might be destroying the ozone layer.

**1975 International:** Convention on Registration of Objects Launched into Outer Space opens for signature (January). **Australia:** Peter Singer publishes *Animal Liberation*, a highly influential book within the animal rights movement. **Bikini Atoll:** People of Bikini file first of many lawsuits against the United States for the environmental and health consequences of nuclear testing in the region. **New Zealand:** Plan to clear-cut 340,000 hectares of forest in South Island is abandoned after widespread public opposition.

**1976 International:** Convention on International Trade in Endangered Species of Wild Fauna and Flora (CITES) lists Asian elephants as a species threatened with extinction, thus banning commercial trade internationally. **Australia:** Tasmania Wilderness Society is founded, changing its name in 1984 to the Wilderness Society. **France:** Conservation Act creates a legal foundation for protecting the natural environment, although implementation proves difficult. **Nigeria:** Government begins the Arid Zone Afforestation Project.

**1977 International:** United Nations Conference on Desertification is held in Nairobi, Kenya (August–September). **Argentina:** Wildlife Foundation established to protect biodiversity. **Bangladesh:** Department of Environment is established. **Canada:** Paul Watson founds the Earthforce Society in Vancouver (which is incorporated in the United States as the Sea Shepherd Conservation Society in 1981). **Germany:** First eco-labeling scheme is launched: the "Blue Angel" program. **Kenya:** Wangari Maathai founds the Green Belt Movement. **South Korea:** Government passes an Environmental Preservation Act, the first attempt to develop comprehensive environmental legislation. **United States:** Herman Daly publishes one of his most influential books, *Steady-State Economics*.

**1978 Argentina:** Local office of Greenpeace opens. **Malaysia:** Sahabat Alam Malaysia (Friends of the Earth Malaysia) is established. **United States:** Government evacuates the first homeowners from Love Canal in Niagara Falls, New York, following a grassroots campaign to expose poisons leaking into yards and basements. **West Germany:** Environmentalists in local elections present candidates under a "Green List" (*Grüne Liste Umweltschutz*), the first use of the term *green* to describe a political party.

**1979 International:** Geneva Convention on Long-range Transboundary Air Pollution opens for signature (November). Convention on the Conservation of Migratory Species of Wild Animals opens for signature (June). Greenpeace International is officially founded to connect a half-dozen loosely affiliated groups. **China:** Government puts in place its One Child Policy. Government enacts its first major environmental legislation, the Environmental Protection Law for Trial Implementation. **Great Britain:** James Lovelock publishes *Gaia: A New Look at Life on Earth*, popularizing his Gaia hypothesis. **Taiwan:** Environmental Protection Bureau forms out of the Department of Environmental Health. **United States:** Three Mile Island nuclear facility accident (a core meltdown of one of two reactors). The name "Earth First!" appears to describe a new radical environmental group willing to take direct action to "protect" the environment. **West Germany:** Green Party is founded.

**1980 International:** Convention on the Conservation of Antarctic Marine Living Resources opens for signature (May). **Brazil:** The nongovernmental organization Projeto TAMAR (Projeto Tartarugas Marinhas, or Sea Turtles Project) is founded to protect sea turtles and promote marine conservation. **India:** Prime Minister Indira Ghandi orders a 15-year ban on logging in the Himalayan forests, a victory for the Chipko Movement. **Indonesia:** Indonesian Forum for Environment (Wahana Lingkungan Hidup Indonesia, WALHI) is established as a network of nongovernmental and community-based organizations. **United States:** First ecofeminist conference takes place in Amherst, Massachusetts.

**1981 Ireland:** The Ecology Party is established. **South Africa:** National Conservation Strategy is implemented. **Sweden:** Green Party, Miljöpartiet de Gröna, is founded. **United States:** Julian Simon publishes *The Ultimate Resource*, challenging the intellectual foundation of environmentalism. Donella and Dennis Meadows found the International Network of Resource Information Centers (INRIC) to advance systems-oriented analysis and activism. New administration of Ronald Reagan cuts the budget of the Environmental Protection Agency.

**1982 International:** United Nations General Assembly adopts a World Charter for Nature (October). United Nations Convention on the Law of the Sea opens for signature (December). International Whaling Commission declares a moratorium on commercial whaling. **Argentina:** Environmentalists found the Fundación para la Defensa del Ambiente (FUNAM, or Environment Defense Foundation). **India:** Vandana Shiva establishes the Research Foundation for Science, Technology and Ecology. **Mexico:** The government establishes a Secretariat of Urban Development and Ecology (SEDUE). **Soviet Union:** Two feeder rivers, Amu Darya and Syr Darya, stop emptying into the Aral Sea. **United States:** World Resources Institute is founded to produce independent and scientific policy research and analysis on environmental issues. Amory Lovins founds the Rocky Mountain Institute as an entrepreneurial nonprofit organization to advance environmental efficiencies.

**1983 International:** United Nations General Assembly forms the World Commission on Environment and Development, which meets for the first time the following year. **Canada:** Green Party is established. **European Community:** Following a global environmental campaign, a two-year ban is imposed on the import of whitecoat harp seals, leading to a collapse in prices and markets that in effect ends Canada's commercial seal hunt. **Germany:** German Green Party becomes the first new party to enter the German Parliament in 60 years. **India:** Appiko Movement, following in the tradition of the Chipko Movement, begins a nonviolent struggle to save trees by hugging them. **Iran:** Government restricts traffic in the city center to combat air pollution. **United States:** Seven million tires burn in Virginia.

**1984 International:** Environmental Investigation Agency, with offices in London and Washington, D.C., is founded to investigate "crimes" against the environment. **Chile:** President Augusto Pinochet establishes a National Commission for Ecology to draft a national environmental framework (although it never completes its task). **Europe:** Green parties capture 12 seats in the European Parliament. **France:** The political party *Les Verts* (the Greens) is formed. **India:** Toxic gas leak kills thousands in Bhopal (December). **Malaysia:** Third World Network, an international network of nongovernmental organizations across developing countries, is founded with an international secretariat in Penang. Swiss activist Bruno Manser moves to Sarawak where he lives with the Penan people and helps to organize local resistance to logging. **Spain:** Confederation of the Greens is founded. **United States:** Green Party is founded.

**1985 International:** International Tropical Timber Agreement opens for signature (April). Vienna Convention for the Protection of the Ozone Layer opens for signature (March). Randall Hayes establishes the Rainforest Action Network (with offices in San Francisco and Tokyo) to protect rainforests and the rights of indigenous peoples living in these forests. **Brazil:** Chico Mendes founds the National Council of Rubber Tappers. **Canada:** The Canadian Chemical Producers' Association launch Responsible Care®, an environmental management system for chemicals. **New Zealand:** French agents sink the Greenpeace ship, *Rainbow Warrior*.

**1986 International:** Convention for the Protection of the Natural Resources and Environment of the South Pacific Region opens for signature

(November). **Brazil:** The nongovernmental organization Pro-Natura is founded to promote better environmental management. **Soviet Union:** Nuclear disaster occurs at Chernobyl, Ukraine. **Switzerland:** National Swiss Green Party (Grüne Partei der Schweiz) forms.

**1987    International:** Montreal Protocol on Substances That Deplete the Ozone Layer opens for signature (September). World Commission on Environment and Development releases *Our Common Future* containing the now widely accepted definition of sustainable development. World population reaches 5 billion. **Bolivia:** Conservation International brokers an exchange of US$650,000 in debt relief for an agreement with the government to conserve 1.5 million hectares of tropical forests, the world's first debt-for-nature swap. **Czechoslovakia:** Environmental group, MV SZOPK (Slovensky Zvaz Ochrancov Prirodky a Krajiny, or Slovak Association of Protectors of Nature and Landscape), releases a damning report titled *Bratislava Nahlas* (Bratislava Aloud)—the government responds harshly, bringing the editor of the report up on criminal charges. **United States:** Conservation International, a nongovernmental organization working to conserve worldwide biodiversity, is founded.

**1988    International:** First genetically modified plants are grown. The World Meteorological Organization and the United Nations Environment Programme establish the Intergovernmental Panel on Climate Change (IPCC). **Brazil:** Chico Mendes, leader of Brazil's rubber tappers, is murdered. **Philippines:** Philippines becomes the first country in Asia to participate in a WWF debt-for-nature swap. **Sweden:** Green Party, Miljöpartiet de Gröna, becomes the first new political party in 70 years to win a seat in the Swedish Parliament.

**1989    International:** Basel Convention on the Control of Transboundary Movements of Hazardous Wastes and Their Disposal opens for signature (March). Wellington Convention for the Prohibition of Fishing with Long Driftnets in the South Pacific opens for signature (November). Convention on International Trade in Endangered Species of Wild Fauna and Flora prohibits the international trade in ivory. International Society for Ecological Economics is founded. **Canada:** Kalle Lasn and Bill Schmalz found Adbusters Media Foundation as an anticorporate and anticonsumption movement. **Europe:** Green parties win 32 seats in the European Parliament, the most to date. **Philippines:** Government bans timber exports following floods, although illegal logging and deforestation continue. **Thailand:** Government bans commercial logging in natural forests. **United States:** Oil tanker *Exxon Valdez* spills over 40 million liters of crude oil into Prince William Sound off the coast of Alaska.

**1990 International:** An international association of local governments called the International Council of Local Environmental Initiatives is established (now called ICLEI: Local Governments for Sustainability). **Argentina:** Federal government creates the Consejo Federal de Medio Ambiente (COFEMA, or Federal Council of the Environment) to manage and coordinate environmental protection. **Canada:** International Institute for Sustainable Development is established in Winnipeg to promote sustainable development worldwide. **Malaysia:** Bruno Manser, now a well-known environmental activist fighting for the rights of the Penan people, goes missing in the rainforests of Sarawak. **United States:** Clean Air Act Amendments establish a sulphur dioxide cap-and-trade program. Goldman Environmental Prize is established to honor grassroots environmentalists in Africa, Asia, Europe, Islands and Island Nations, North America, and South and Central America.

**1991 International:** Bamako Convention on the Ban of Import into Africa and the Control of Transboundary Movement and Management of Hazardous Wastes within Africa opens for signature (January). Protocol on Environmental Protection to the Antarctic Treaty opens for signature (October). Global Environment Facility is piloted to provide environmental project grants to developing countries. United Nations General Assembly passes a moratorium on high seas driftnet fishing. Swiss industrialist Stephan Schmidheiny founds the Business Council for Sustainable Development (BCSD) to participate in the 1992 United Nations Conference on Environment and Development. **Great Britain:** Protest group Reclaim the Streets emerges in London as part of a direct-action movement against automobiles. **Russia/Soviet Union:** End of the Soviet Union contributes to an economic crisis in the Russian Federation, further straining environmental conditions. **Sweden:** Government imposes a carbon tax on oil, coal, and natural gas to promote renewable energy. **United States:** David Foreman, cofounder of Earth First!, publishes *Confessions of an Eco-Warrior*. Greens/Green Party

USA forms, emerging from a group called the Green Committees of Correspondence.

**1992 International:** Framework Convention on Climate Change opens for signature (May). Convention on Biological Diversity opens for signature (June). United Nations Conference on Environment and Development (also known as the Earth Summit and Rio Summit) held in Rio de Janeiro (June). Newly independent countries bordering the Aral Sea sign the first of a series of agreements to manage the Aral Basin. **Bangladesh:** Environmental Lawyers Association is founded. **Germany:** Petra Kelly, a founder of the West German Green Party, is murdered. **Great Britain:** Earth Liberation Front (ELF) emerges as a "leaderless" global resistance to capitalism and environmental destruction. **Singapore:** Ministry of the Environment establishes a Green Labelling Scheme.

**1993 International:** With funding from the WWF, the Forest Stewardship Council is established to support certification of sustainable forest practices. **China:** Plans to construct the world's largest hydroelectric dam, the Three Gorges Dam on the Yangtze River, move ahead, despite opposition from many human rights activists and environmentalists. **European Union:** Eco-management and audit scheme, or EMAS, is introduced as a voluntary program to audit an organization's environmental impacts.

**1994 International:** Convention on Nuclear Safety opens for signature (June). United Nations Convention to Combat Desertification in Countries Experiencing Serious Drought and/or Desertification, Particularly in Africa opens for signature (October). Mostafa Kamal Tolba, former head of the United Nations Environment Programme, founds the nonprofit International Center for Environment and Development (ICED) to finance environmental projects in developing countries. **Chile:** A general environmental framework is enacted. **China:** Government begins to implement the China Action Plan for Biodiversity Conservation. Construction begins on the Three Gorges Dam. First formal environmental nongovernmental organization is established (Friends of Nature, initially called the Academy for Green Culture). **Germany:** Constitution of the Federal Republic of Germany is amended to include environmental protection. **Great Britain:** Reclaim the Streets emerges to protest the M11 highway through Claremont Road, London, becoming one of the main organizations in the antiroad/anticar movement. **United States:** American Forest and Paper Association establishes the Sustainable Forestry Initiative as a voluntary certification standard to promote sustainable management and responsible purchasing practices.

**1995   International:** Straddling Stocks Convention opens for signature (December). Kenya, Uganda, and Tanzania establish the Lake Victoria Environmental Management Project to manage the lake basin. **Brazil:** Nongovernmental Brazilian Biodiversity Fund is established. **Costa Rica:** Government creates a Ministry of the Environment and Energy and passes an overarching environmental law. **European Union:** Environmental auditing scheme EMAS opens for participation. **Great Britain:** Shell's plan to decommission and sink a facility for storing and loading oil in the North Sea (the Brent Spar) causes a global controversy. **Nigeria:** Military regime hangs Ken Saro-Wiwa with eight others after trumped up charges follow protests against Shell's environmental impact in Ogoni Territory. **Southeast Asia:** Cambodia, Lao PDR, Thailand, and Vietnam establish the Mekong River Commission to manage river development (April).

**1996   International:** Comprehensive Nuclear Test Ban Treaty opens for signature (although still not in force) (September). **Arctic:** Arctic Council is formed to coordinate nonmilitary matters, support environmental strategies, and promote sustainable development. **Australia:** Australian Greens formed. **China:** "Green Lights" program is set up to promote energy-efficient lighting. **Cuba:** Havana passes bylaws so the city only produces organic food. **Great Britain:** Institute for Social and Ethical AccountAbility is founded (now called AccountAbility) to support socially accountable business practices. **South Africa:** Government puts in place a new constitution that includes the right to water in its Bill of Rights.

**1997   International:** Convention on the Law of the Non-navigational Uses of International Watercourses opens for signature (May). Convention on Supplementary Compensation for Nuclear Damage opens for signature (September). Kyoto Protocol to the United Nations Framework Convention on Climate Change opens for signature (December). Marine Stewardship Council, a nonprofit international organization dedicated to the sustainable use of marine fisheries, is founded. Global Reporting Initiative is launched as a joint project between the Coalition for Environmentally Responsible Economies (CERES) and the United Nations Environment Programme to strengthen corporate reporting on sustainability. **China:** Energy Conservation Law is passed. **Cuba:** National Environmental Strategy is put in place. **Indonesia:** Forest fires sweep across the islands of Sumatra and Borneo. Asian financial crisis adds to the country's (and Southeast Asia's) environmental woes. **Japan:** The hybrid Toyota Prius is launched. **Mexico:** Ecologist Green Party wins a seat in the national Senate.

**1998   International:** Convention on Access to Information, Public Participation in Decision Making, and Access to Justice in Environmental Matters opens for signature (June). Protocol on Heavy Metals opens for signature (June). Protocol on Persistent Organic Pollutants opens for signature (June). Rotterdam Convention on the Prior Informed Consent Procedure for Certain Hazardous Chemicals and Pesticides in International Trade opens for signature (September). **Africa:** Federation of Green Parties is established. **North Korea:** Government enacts the National Biodiversity Strategy and Action Plan to protect biodiversity.

**1999   International:** World population reaches 6 billion. An umbrella organization for national forest certification schemes, the Programme for the Endorsement of Forest Certification (PEFC), is launched to promote sustainable forest management. **Great Britain:** For the first time the Green Party wins a seat in the European Parliament. **India:** National Green Party registers as a political party. **South Africa:** The Green Party of South Africa forms. **Switzerland/Malaysia:** Swiss environmentalist Bruno Manser paraglides onto the front lawn of the chief minister of Sarawak to protest logging. **United States:** After living for 738 days in a giant California Redwood tree, Julia Butterfly Hill comes down after the company Pacific Lumber agrees to preserve the tree. Antiglobalization protestors disrupt meetings of the World Trade Organization and International Monetary Fund in Seattle, drawing global publicity to the anger among activists over the economic inequalities and environmental injustices of the global trading system.

**2000   International:** Cartagena Protocol on Biosafety to the Convention on Biological Diversity opens for signature (January). United Nations launches the Global Compact (July). United Nations hosts the Millennium Summit, which produces eight Millennium Development Goals, including achieving environmental sustainability. **Brazil:** Brazilian Network of Civil Organizations for Renewable Energy is founded to promote renewable energy. **Great Britain:** Hundreds of guerrilla gardeners plant flowers and vegetables in London's Parliament Square on May Day (1 May).

**2001 International:** Stockholm Convention on Persistent Organic Pollutants opens for signature (May). Global Greens established. **Denmark:** Bjørn Lomborg publishes an English translation of his book *The Skeptical Environmentalist*, which would go on to become a bestseller with some seeing it as "proof" environmental activists were exaggerating environmental problems with false statistics. **United States:** New administration of George W. Bush withdraws from the Kyoto Protocol, a decision most analysts see as effectively ending its chances of ever entering into force. Green Party of the United States (not to be confused with the Greens/Green Party USA) is created out of the Association of State Green Parties (1996–2001). September 11 terrorist attacks on the World Trade Center and Pentagon profoundly alter global politics.

**2002 Africa:** World Summit on Sustainable Development held in Johannesburg, South Africa. South Africa, Mozambique, and Zimbabwe establish the Great Limpopo Transfrontier Park—linking South Africa's Kruger National Park, Mozambique's Limpopo National Park, and Zimbabwe's Gonarezhou National Park—creating the largest park in Africa and one of the largest cross-border conservation areas in the world. **Antarctica:** Larsen B ice shelf, 200 meters thick with a surface area of over 3,000 square kilometers, breaks apart, a result, most scientists agree, of warmer temperatures from climate change. **Brazil:** Government establishes the Amazon Protected Areas Programme to protect millions of hectares of forests (with the goal of protecting 50 million hectares in the Amazon by 2012). Tumucumaque National Park is created as the world's most extensive tropical forest park. **Pakistan:** Green Party is established. **Vietnam:** Government creates a Ministry of Natural Resources and develops a National Strategy for Environmental Protection.

**2003 International:** Equator Principles, a voluntary initiative by leading financial institutions with support from the World Bank, is launched.

It establishes principles to raise the standard of social and environmental risk assessment in major project financing. **Canada:** Species at Risk Act (SARA) is enacted. **China:** Government establishes Cleaner Production Promotion Law and the Environment Impact Assessment Law. Filling begins for the huge reservoir for the Three Gorges Dam. **Japan:** Japan hosts the Third World Water Forum in Kyoto. **Philippines:** To address worsening air pollution, the government sets hydrocarbon emission standards for motorcycles and tricycles and requires emissions testing to register motor vehicles. **Sweden:** Government introduces Tradeable Green Certificates to promote renewable electricity production.

**2004 International:** Parties to the Convention on International Trade in Endangered Species of Wild Fauna and Flora (CITES) agree to act against the unregulated trade in African ivory. Tsunami devastates many coastal and island communities in the Asia-Pacific region. **Arctic:** Arctic Council publishes the Arctic Climate Impact Assessment, predicting devastating consequences of climate change for life in the Arctic. **Bangladesh:** Green Party founded. **Europe:** European Green Party forms. **Kenya:** Wangari Maathai wins the Nobel Peace Prize for the Green Belt Movement, providing recognition of the growing global consensus about the importance of environmental stability for world peace. **Latvia:** Founder of the Latvian Green Party, Indulus Emsis, becomes the world's first "green" prime minister. **South Korea:** Political party Korea Greens is launched.

**2005 International:** Initiated by the United States, the Asia-Pacific Partnership on Clean Development and Climate is launched as an alternative approach to the Kyoto Protocol for addressing climate change (besides the United States, the group includes Australia, China, India, Japan, and South Korea). Year ends as the warmest in over a century. **Arctic:** Ayles ice shelf off the northern coast of Ellesmere Island (800 kilometers south of the North Pole) breaks off and floats to sea. **Bangladesh:** Government establishes the Sundarban Tiger Project to protect wild tigers. **Bolivia:** Noel Kempff Climate Action Project becomes the world's first project to use a third party to certify "avoided deforestation." **Europe:** An Emissions Trading Scheme for greenhouse gases becomes operational (covering almost half the European Union's emissions of carbon dioxide). **France:** Parliament ratifies an environmental charter, making the French Constitution the first to include the precautionary principle. **Russia:** Government ratifies the Kyoto Protocol, allowing the Protocol to enter into force without the United States (the rules required at least 55 countries contributing at least 55 percent of 1990 greenhouse gas emissions). **Spain:** The government allows commercial genetically modified (GM) corn imports, making it the only country in the European Union to allow imports of GM crops.

**2006   International:** United Nations declares it the *International Year of Deserts and Desertification.* **Canada:** Green Party wins 4.5 percent of the popular vote in the federal election. **China:** Scientists, searching the Yangtze River, are unable to find any Yangtze dolphins and declare the species "likely extinct," making it the first extinction of a large vertebrate in more than 50 years, for many in China and abroad a shocking end to one of the world's oldest animals (scientists estimate the species was more than 20 million years old). **Sub-Saharan Africa:** Region completes a phaseout of leaded gasoline, making it the first developing region to do so.

**2007   International:** Brazil, China, the European Commission, India, South Africa, and the United States launch the International Biofuels Forum (IBF) to advance biofuels markets. **Australia:** Just hours after being sworn in as Prime Minister, Kevin Rudd of the Labour Party ratifies the Kyoto Protocol (3 December) and creates a new Department of Climate Change. **Costa Rica:** The government announces plans to become the first carbon-neutral country (aiming for 2021). **Israel:** An explosion at the Makhteshim Agan chemical plant in Ramat Hovav releases hazardous waste into the surrounding area. **Russia:** National park is created to protect the Siberian tiger. **United States:** Al Gore, along with the Intergovernmental Panel on Climate Change, wins the Nobel Peace Prize. His film, *An Inconvenient Truth*, wins two Academy Awards, including best documentary film.

**2008   International:** Oil prices go over US$100 a barrel, spurring along efforts to increase energy efficiencies and dampening interest in gas-guzzling automobiles. Global food crisis develops, and United Nations Secretary-General Ban Ki-moon establishes a Task Force on the Global Food Security Crisis. **Canada:** Stores pull products with bisphenol A (such as some plastic water bottles) after Health Canada becomes the world's first government agency to issue an alert about its dangers.

**China:** Ministry of Environmental Protection replaces the State Environmental Protection Administration. Lead-up to the 2008 Olympics in Beijing draws global attention to China's urban environmental record. Work on the Three Gorges Dam continues, with the aim of finishing in 2009. **Poland:** Country hosts an international conference on climate change with the aim of moving toward negotiations in 2009. **United States:** With its habitat disappearing as sea ice melts, the polar bear is listed as a threatened species under the Endangered Species Act.

# Introduction

The history of environmentalism is woven into the history of global ecological change. Before the 1960s, the word *environment*, in the relatively rare instances when it appeared in print, referred primarily to the home or work environment, not to nature, ecosystems, or the earth. Efforts to balance human societies with nature's capacity to adapt certainly has a much longer history than the more modern meaning of the word *environment*, extending back to when nomadic hunters and gatherers were allowing animals and plants to regenerate, settled indigenous communities were developing cultural practices of living *within* nature, and ancient Greek and Roman philosophers were reflecting on the consequences of different political and social orders for the natural world. By the time of at least the 17th century, various scholars and state officials were already calling for greater efforts to preserve, conserve, and manage natural systems. By the 19th and early 20th centuries, as consumption of natural resources began to rise alongside industrial production and growing populations, more and more governments, including some colonizers, began to implement "scientific" management of resources (such as sustained yield management for timber) to try to ensure more efficient use of natural resources and lessen unnecessary degradation and unwanted consequences (such as soil erosion and flooding). Some governments, writers, and ordinary citizens began to worry, too, about the quality of air and unsanitary conditions in industrializing cities. Many began to advocate for measures to preserve the "countryside" and "nature" by, for example, establishing national parks to preserve scenic beauty or species for viewing (e.g., birds) or hunting (e.g., bears) in natural settings.

Still, the word *environment* only began to take on its more modern political, social, ecological, and global meaning during the 1960s and early 1970s, as public demands for cleaner and safer living conditions became more vocal, as newly formed nongovernmental groups began to lobby governments and campaign to influence consumers and corporations, and as global-scale problems began to move up national and international political agendas. Today, the concept of "the environment" is highly political, with definitions varying across and within societies. Some see the word *environment* as shorthand for *natural ecosystem*—for rainforests, oceans, deserts, and wetlands, as well as the atmosphere, climate, and ozone layer. For them, protecting the global environment is about protecting the earth itself *from* growing numbers of people. For others, the word *environment* includes, or is more about, the living spaces for humans: the air in towns and cities, the garbage in streets, the rats and disease in dirty cities, the sewage in canals and oceans, and the industrial poisons in wells and lakes. Thus, "managing" the environment is more about making the spaces where people reside cleaner, safer, and more pleasant; preserving "natural" beauty for hikers and birdwatchers; and ensuring efficient economic growth and sufficient resources for future generations.

The understanding of environmental*ism* is even more contested. Most would agree the "ism" connotes a movement advocating for change to reduce the impact of humans on the environment (with its multiple definitions). But who are the legitimate environmental*ists*? Most would agree that ideas like "sustainable development" and the "precautionary principle"—as well as knowledge of the causes and consequences of escalating problems (deforestation, desertification, biodiversity loss, ozone depletion, climate change)—infuse environmentalism with beliefs and values, shaping arguments and prescriptions. And most, too, would agree that an environmentalist, by definition, believes environmental problems are real and that some action is necessary (or, at least, potentially beneficial).

But what action? Here, little consensus exists among environmentalists on the best path forward. Some stress the need for better science and technologies, more trade, and more investment to reduce poverty and ensure more efficient production and distribution of environmental resources. Others emphasize the need for stronger international laws and state regulations. Still others stress the need to reform the globalizing capitalist world order to eliminate South-North inequalities, foreign debts, and exploitative multinational corporations. And still others see the only way for lasting change to occur is to shift global consciousness to alter lifestyles, reduce human populations, and decrease consumption.

To capture this diversity within environmentalism, this dictionary takes a global tack with a focus on ideas, events, institutions, initiatives, and green movements since the 1960s. It strives to avoid a common error in many histories of environmentalism: to exaggerate the input of the wealthy countries of Europe and North America and understate the influence of Africa, Asia, South and Central America, Eastern Europe, and the polar regions. It aims as well for a more comprehensive analysis than most histories of the modern environmental movement, understanding environmentalism as emerging not only from grassroots and formal nongovernmental associations, but also from corporate, governmental, and intergovernmental organizations and initiatives. This assumes the ideas and energy infusing environmentalism with political purpose arise from hundreds of thousands of sources: from corporate boardrooms to bureaucratic policies to international negotiations to activists. Thus, environmentalists are not only indigenous people blocking a logging road, Greenpeace activists protesting a seal hunt, or green candidates contesting an election; an equal or larger number of environmentalists are working within the Japanese bureaucracy to implement environmental policies, within the World Bank to assess the environmental impacts of loans, within Wal-Mart to green its purchasing practices, or within intergovernmental forums to negotiate international environmental agreements.

Understanding environmentalism in this way reveals that, unlike in the 1960s, as a movement it is no longer on the political fringes but is now a driving global force reforming state policies, international law, business practices, and community life everywhere. To chart the contours of this powerful movement, and to provide necessary background for the dictionary entries, this introduction divides environmentalism into four categories that, although overlapping slightly, are in significant ways distinctive: scholarly environmentalism, governmental environmentalism, nongovernmental environmentalism, and commercial environmentalism.

## SCHOLARLY ENVIRONMENTALISM

Environmentalism, more so than in the case of other social and political movements, can suddenly shift and reorient in unexpected directions following groundbreaking scientific research or new ways of understanding from the social sciences and humanities. Other new ideas have taken root following a bestselling book or popular essay. One of the most influential essays in the intellectual history of environmentalism goes back to 1798 when Thomas Malthus published the first edition of *An Essay on the Principle of Population*, which predicted that a worldwide famine would one day ensue because population, left unchecked, rises exponentially while food production can only increase arithmetically. One of the most influential books was Rachel Carson's *Silent Spring* (1962), which many people believe ushered in modern environmentalism by raising American (and over time global) consciousness of the environmental dangers of chemicals such as dichlorodiphenyltrichloroethane (DDT). But many other books and essays have shaped environmentalism, too.

Before Carson, books such as Aldo Leopold's *A Sand County Almanac* (1949) were influencing the emerging environmental movement in the United States. Numerous bestselling books and popular articles would also follow Carson's *Silent Spring*, with many of the authors inspired by a belief that environmentalists must reach a global audience to bring about necessary reforms. One particularly influential book from the late 1960s was Paul Ehrlich's *The Population Bomb* (1968), with its metaphor of the earth bombed by an exploding human population, leaving it no longer able to feed the starving survivors. One of the most cited academic articles of all time came out in the same year: Garrett Hardin's article, "The Tragedy of the Commons," which sees the history of access and collapse of the English commons as an analogy to access and collapse of shared environments in modern times. The idea of a global environment began to emerge around this time as well, reinforced as astronauts took stunning pictures of a fragile and borderless earth from space, an image that soon became a symbol of global environmentalism (and common on book covers). This image also reinforced a growing sense in both the First and Third Worlds of mutual vulnerability of increasingly entwined economies and ecosystems.

Three especially influential books in the 1970s were *The Limits to Growth* (1972) by Donella Meadows, Dennis Meadows, Jørgen Randers, and William Behrens III; *Small Is Beautiful* (1973) by E. F. Schumacher; and *Steady-State Economics* (1977) by Herman Daly. *The Limits to Growth*, using groundbreaking computer simulations to argue that economies would one day crash into the earth's finite resources, convinced many people to question the value of unrestrained economic growth. *Small Is Beautiful* took these critiques further and proposed reforming the global economy to decentralize and democratize decision making and ensure appropriate technology scaled for a quality community life. *Steady-State Economics* added further to a growing vision among some environmentalists about how to manage economic life sustainably, and became a foundational text for the emerging field of ecological economics.

Some influential books were also written by politicians, such as Petra Kelly's *Fighting for Hope* (1984) (she was one of the founders of the West German Green Party). Other influential books and articles came out of governmental forums. The World Commission on Environment and Development, set up by the United Nations in 1983 to develop ideas for bringing together the goals of development with the values of environmentalism, published a report in 1987 called *Our Common Future* that included a definition of sustainable development that to this day continues to guide most governments and many nongovernmental organizations (NGOs): "development that meets the needs of the present without compromising the ability of future generations to meet their own needs."

Although rarer, corporate leaders have also authored influential books, such as *Changing Course* (1992) by Swiss industrialist Stephan Schmidheiny, who founded the Business Council for Sustainable Development (BCSD) in 1991. More common is for books to receive a significant boost in publicity as business leaders praise it. One example is economist Julian Simon's *The Ultimate Resource* (1981). Another is journalist Gregg Easterbrook's bestseller *A Moment on the Earth* (1995). An even more dramatic example is the bestselling translation of Danish political scientist's Bjørn Lomborg's *The Skeptical Environmentalist* (2001), a Cambridge University Press book with more than 3,000 footnotes. Bestselling books critical of environmentalism, however, remain much less common than ones about the global environmental "crisis" or ones calling for global reforms to "save" the planet from humanity. The list of influential books in this category is long: three examples are Herman Daly's *Beyond Growth* (1996), Jared Diamond's *Collapse* (2005), and Bill McKibbin's *Deep Economy* (2007). A few environmental movies, too, have been highly influential in shaping public debates and global consciousness: one of the best known is Al Gore's documentary film *An Inconvenient Truth* (2006), which won two Academy Awards and was one of the reasons Gore won the 2007 Nobel Peace Prize.

## GOVERNMENTAL ENVIRONMENTALISM

Collective efforts to control nature started in earnest 8,000 to 15,000 years ago as nomadic hunters and gatherers began turning to settled agriculture. Large civilizations emerged as inventions like the animal-drawn plow, the wheel, numbers, and writing began to change political and social life. Often, these same civilizations began to clear forests, degrade land, and pollute local waters. Environmental collapse even toppled a few great civilizations, such as Mesopotamia (a land between the Tigris and Euphrates Rivers, part of contemporary Iraq), where a badly designed irrigation system slowly poisoned the land with salt. Until some 200–300 years ago, however, environmental problems were primarily local; only with the industrial revolution did human activities start to cause noticeable regional and global environmental damage.

One reason for the increasing global damage was the rise in the production and the burning of fossil fuels (such as coal). Another was the growing global population, which jumped from 1 billion people in the early 1800s to over 2 billion by the end of the 1920s. A third reason was the rising consumption of natural resources from places far from producers and consumers (with colonial administrations often facilitating this "trade"). The evidence of severe damage was already clear by the late 19th and early 20th centuries. On some days smog in cities like London and New York became thick enough to kill. Once abundant species, such as the Plains bison of North America, were brought to near extinction; a few, such as the passenger pigeon, even went extinct (in 1914). By then, some governments were starting to respond by passing new national and regional policies to promote conservation of wildlife and better resource management. Canada and the United States, for example, signed the Migratory Birds Treaty in 1918.

State environmentalism began to take off after the late 1960s, however, as more and more people (especially in wealthy countries) began to demand better living conditions and as "global" environmental problems began to emerge. By the beginning of the 1970s various governments were establishing environmental departments and agencies. The United States, for example, created the Environmental Protection Agency (EPA) in 1970. The following year Canada set up its Department of the Environment and France established its Environment Ministry. A year later Singapore established a Ministry of the Environment. By this time many governments were also putting together negotiating teams to participate in international environmental negotiations. One outcome was the United Nations Conference on the Human Environment, held in June 1972 in Stockholm, Sweden.

The Stockholm conference was the first international United Nations conference for state officials on the environment and a sign of the growing importance of environmentalism for governments worldwide. The only heads of state to attend were Swedish Prime Minister Olof Palme and Indian Prime Minister Indira Gandhi; still, the turnout was impressive, with about 1,200 delegates from over a hundred countries attending (although, disappointedly for the organizers, Russia and the Communist bloc countries boycotted the conference to protest the exclusion of East Germany). The conference revealed, however, some fundamental differences in how governmental environmentalism was emerging in developed and developing countries. Delegates from wealthier states tended to stress issues such as industrial pollution, nature conservation, and population growth. Delegates from poorer states tended to stress the need for development, arguing rich conservationists should not deny the world's poor the benefits of economic growth. Sharp differences emerged as well over who was responsible for solving (and thus financing the solutions to) global environmental problems. Many delegates from the Third World saw global capitalism as a cause of poverty and a core reason for the pressures on natural environments, especially with global economic institutions such as the World Bank and the International Monetary Fund pressuring developing countries to export natural resources on declining terms of trade. These delegates coined the phrase *the pollution of poverty* to express the idea that the greatest global environmental threat was in fact poverty and that the only solution for poverty was international economic reforms.

In the end, the official conference documents—the nonbinding Declaration on the Human Environment (with 26 principles), the Action Plan for the Human Environment (with 109 recommendations), and the

Resolution on Institutional and Financial Arrangements—did not stress these calls to reform the global economy. The conference did, however, raise the profile of global environmental issues within states as well as reveal the complexity and diversity of worldviews about the causes and consequences of global environmental change. It also led to the creation of the United Nations Environment Programme (UNEP), officially launched in 1973 with its headquarters in Nairobi, Kenya, and with Canada's Maurice Strong as the first executive director. It was not designed as a strong institution—more a coordinating program than a specialized agency with a significant budget. Both the First and Third Worlds supported this. The First World did not want to fund a large institution; the Third World did not want an institution able to interfere with development goals.

After the Stockholm Conference, rising oil prices in 1973–1974 rocked the global economy: inflation soared, economic growth slowed, and foreign debt increased in many Third World countries, particularly in Latin America and Africa. Such turbulence deflated some of the more ambitious environmental plans after Stockholm, especially in countries with heavy debts and weak economies. Still, governmental environmentalism continued to strengthen. In 1973 the United States passed the Endangered Species Act and Bangladesh enacted the Wild Life (Preservation) Order. In 1974 Germany set up its federal Environment Agency and Mexico hosted a symposium on development and environment in Cocoyoc, formulating some of the earliest conceptions of sustainable development. Just after Stockholm, states also signed some noteworthy international environmental treaties, including the Convention on the Prevention of Marine Pollution by Dumping of Wastes and Other Matter (the London Convention of 1972, which entered into force in 1975), and the Convention on International Trade in Endangered Species of Wild Fauna and Flora (CITES, 1973, which entered into force in 1975).

In the second half of the 1970s and first half of the 1980s, conservative governments more hostile to environmentalism came to power in the United States and Great Britain, and many developing economies fell further into debt. Nevertheless, governmental environmentalism was continuing to strengthen, partly because of advances in scientific understanding (such as the dangers of chlorofluorocarbons [CFCs] for the ozone layer and the link to skin cancer), partly because of disasters such as the 1979 U.S. nuclear accident at Three Mile Island and the

1984 Union Carbide chemical leak in Bhopal, India, and partly because of increasing pressure from grassroots and nongovernmental environmentalism (and thus, in democracies, pressure from voters). More and more states established environmental agencies, including increasingly in the developing world (for example, Bangladesh established its Department of Environment in 1977 and Taiwan created its Environmental Protection Bureau in 1979). States also continued to sign and ratify international environmental agreements, such as the 1979 Convention on the Conservation of Migratory Species of Wild Animals (which entered into force in 1983), the 1979 Convention on Long-range Transboundary Air Pollution (which entered into force in 1983), and the 1980 Convention on the Conservation of Antarctic Marine Living Resources (which entered into force in 1982).

Global environmental issues began to move up the list of government priorities in the second half of the 1980s. States continued to negotiate and sign international environmental treaties, including the 1985 Vienna Convention for the Protection of the Ozone Layer, the 1987 Montreal Protocol on Substances That Deplete the Ozone Layer, and the 1989 Basel Convention on the Control of Transboundary Movements of Hazardous Wastes and Their Disposal. By the end of the 1980s, the debate was centering on the concept of sustainable development, drawing on the definition from the 1987 report by the World Commission on Environment and Development, *Our Common Future*.

This report, commonly called the Brundtland report after its chair Gro Harlem Brundtland, was an ingenious compromise between those wanting more development and those wanting more environmental protection. It did not assume any necessary limits to growth, and it saw industrialization and natural resource production, under correct management, as suitable, even essential, for some countries. The report saw poverty as a core cause of unsustainable development. Thus, the only way forward was to stimulate—not slow—economic growth, although not the unchecked growth of the 1960s and 1970s but growth arising from sustainable development. It called for developed countries to transfer more environmental technologies and economic assistance to the Third World. It also recommended better education and food security as well as more controls on population growth.

The growing consensus around the Brundtland concept of sustainable development culminated in a 1989 United Nations General Assembly resolution to hold the first summit of world leaders on the global environment: what became the 1992 United Nations Conference on Environment and Development (UNCED), held in Rio de Janeiro, Brazil. Popularly called the Rio or Earth Summit, this was the largest conference ever held by the United Nations, with 117 heads of state participating and 178 national delegations. The official conference also included thousands of NGO representatives; thousands more also attended a parallel NGO forum. Most state delegates endorsed the Brundtland definition of sustainable development, although many from developing countries also called for far more economic assistance and technology transfers from the First World to balance the additional costs of green growth.

The Rio Summit reinforced the view among state leaders that more economic growth was necessary for a healthy global environment. It produced several important consensus documents: the Rio Declaration on Environment and Development (a set of 27 principles on the rights and responsibilities of states for environment and development), and Agenda 21 (a 300-page action program to promote sustainable development). It also produced the Non-legally Binding Authoritative Statement of Principles for a Global Consensus on the Management, Conservation and Sustainable Development of All Types of Forests, as well as opened two conventions for signature: the United Nations Framework Convention on Climate Change and the Convention on Biological Diversity.

The decade after the Rio Summit saw environmental issues again slide down the list of state priorities as threats of terrorism, chemical and biological warfare, and a financial crisis in Asia took center stage. State negotiators nevertheless kept signing and ratifying environmental treaties. The Convention on Biological Diversity entered into force in 1993. The United Nations Convention on the Law of the Sea, first opened for signature in 1982, entered into force in 1994. The United Nations Convention to Combat Desertification in Countries Experiencing Serious Drought and/or Desertification, Particularly in Africa was opened for signature in 1994 (and entered into force in 1996). The Kyoto Protocol to the United Nations Framework Convention on Climate Change was opened for signature in 1998. And the Stockholm Convention on Persistent Organic Pollutants (POPs) was opened for signature in 2001. State negotiators also continued to review the progress of

Agenda 21 and the implementation of sustainable development, including a 1997 special session of the United Nations General Assembly (commonly called the Earth Summit +5) that paved the way for the 2002 World Summit on Sustainable Development in Johannesburg, South Africa.

The Johannesburg Summit, also called Rio +10, was designed to evaluate the progress toward sustainable development, establish mechanisms to implement the Rio goal, and develop a global strategy to reach the United Nations' Millennium Development Goals. Global environmental change was no longer at the top of global agenda (the terrorist attack on the World Trade Center and Pentagon on 11 September 2001 profoundly changed foreign policy priorities worldwide). Still, the Johannesburg Summit was a landmark event reaffirming the importance of governmental environmentalism: although fewer heads of state attended (about 100) than in the case of the Rio Summit, overall the conference was even larger than Rio, with more than 10,000 delegates from more than 180 countries; at least 8,000 civil society representatives; and about 4,000 members of the press. The official documents from the Johannesburg Summit were similar to the Rio Summit in terms of their broad support for sustainable development. The two most significant ones were the Johannesburg Declaration on Sustainable Development, a list of nonbinding challenges and commitments, and the Johannesburg Plan of Implementation. Like the Rio Summit, the Johannesburg Summit added yet another layer to environmentalism. It further raised the profile of environmental issues among world leaders and within state bureaucracies. It cemented sustainable development as the core organizing concept for governmental environmentalism. And it brought many nongovernmental organizations and community groups into partnerships with business and governments to implement policies to promote sustainable development.

## NONGOVERNMENTAL ENVIRONMENTALISM

Among ordinary citizens, concern over deteriorating local and global environmental conditions began to increase in the late 1960s and early 1970s. Symbolic of this was the first Earth Day in April 1970, which saw some 20 million people rally at one of the largest organized demonstrations ever held in the United States. At the same time more and more environmental activists were creating national and transnational organizations to lobby governments and corporations and rally public support. The World Wildlife Fund (WWF, later the World Wide Fund for Nature), which started in 1961 with fundraising headquarters in Switzerland, was evolving into an international network of national offices. By the early 1970s it had already established a US$10 million trust fund to cover administrative expenses. Greenpeace was also beginning to take shape after a group of activists set sail in 1971 from Vancouver for Amchitka, an island off Alaska, to "bear witness" to U.S. nuclear testing. The same year four groups—from England, France, Sweden, and the United States—founded Friends of the Earth International to coordinate environmental campaigns.

Over the next decade networks of environmental activism began to deepen. Greenpeace, for example, evolved into a multinational enterprise as more than 20 groups in North America, Europe, Australia, and New Zealand adopted the name Greenpeace. In 1979 the Canadian Greenpeace Foundation, facing financial and organizational difficulties, agreed to create a new international organization called Greenpeace International (with its headquarters in Amsterdam). By the 1980s this new structure was allowing Greenpeace to coordinate campaigns and fundraising in ways not unlike the advertising and sales strategies of a multinational corporation. Some Greenpeace activists stole a page from advertisers, using daring stunts to reach front pages and primetime, repeating messages and images to embed new meanings and emotions into the public psyche. There were many successes. For example, whales became "majestic" and seals "cuddly," and whaling and sealing were recast in the minds of many people as senseless slaughters.

Friends of the Earth International (FOEI) was continuing to grow and evolve over this time as well. In the second half the 1970s, the number of national offices in the federation increased (primarily in developed countries). Such expansion began to necessitate more organizational capacity. The federation decided to set up a small international secretariat in 1981 (rotating from country to country) to assist with coordinating and running the increasingly large annual meetings. Two years later the number of groups in the federation reached 25—and the members decided to elect an executive committee to oversee the issues dealt with at the annual meetings. Two years after this the European members decided to create the first regional coordinating office in Brussels. The number of national offices in the federation was continuing to grow, with more joining through the 1980s from Africa, Asia, and Latin America. The first Eastern European member—Poland's Polski Klub Ekologiczny—joined in 1985. A year later the number of members was at 31—and for the first time a national office in the developing world hosted the annual meeting (Sahabat Alam Malaysia, or Friends of the Earth Malaysia). The mandate was expanding with more national offices from developing countries, and by the mid-1980s FOEI was campaigning to protect tropical rainforests and indigenous forest dwellers.

The increase in the number of WWF projects and campaigns is yet another typical example of the growth of many nongovernmental environmental organizations from the mid-1970s to the mid-1980s. In 1973 the WWF launched Project Tiger (with the Indian government) to try to save India's endangered tigers. Its first worldwide tropical rainforest campaign—covering Africa, Latin America, and Southeast Asia—began two years later. In 1976 the WWF launched an ambitious marine campaign—called The Seas Must Live—to establish sanctuaries for dolphins, seals, turtles, and whales. The WWF was focusing more as well on monitoring and strengthening controls on trade in animals and plants (including ivory and rhino horn). It cooperated with the International Union for Conservation of Nature (IUCN) to create a new organization in 1976 called TRAFFIC (Trade Records Analysis of Fauna and Flora in Commerce). The end of the decade saw the WWF raise over US$1 million in a campaign to "Save the Rhino" from poachers.

By then the WWF was a truly international institution with a mandate well beyond its original focus on endangered species and habitat loss—one that many within the organization now felt required more cooperation with governments to integrate conservation into development strategies. The WWF was also emerging as an actor in more formal international structures—for example, cooperating with the IUCN and the UNEP to launch in 1980 a World Conservation Strategy endorsed by the United Nations. Meanwhile, its number of regular supporters was continuing to grow—sitting at about 1 million by the early 1980s.

Since the 1980s the capacity of environmental activists to influence governments, public attitudes, and corporations has continued to expand. Today, thousands of groups—big and small—form networks advocating for change. These can include celebrity consumer advocates like Ralph Nader. They can include innovative NGOs like Adbusters that practice "culture jamming," running spoof ads and counter-ads to encourage people to *not* consume. They can include grassroots movements like the Green Belt Movement in Kenya, which under the leadership of Wangari Maathai (winner of the 2004 Nobel Peace Prize) was able to plant some 30 million trees in Africa. And they can include local groups of just a couple of people working to protect a patch of land in a village. A few environmental groups, however—ones like Greenpeace, Friends of the Earth, and the WWF—now sit as big multinational players in this thicket of diverse environmental voices. Greenpeace International now has millions of contributors and offices in dozens of countries. Friends of the Earth also has millions of members and supporters, with over 70 national groups and over 5,000 local ones. And the WWF now has close to 5 million regular supporters, operating in over 100 countries and funding more than 2,000 conservation projects.

Over the last decade more of these activists have been cooperating with governments to achieve "mutual" goals. For groups like the WWF this strategy has resulted in many successful projects. In recent years, for example, the WWF has been able to assist with establishing millions of hectares of protected forests. This includes, for example, in 2006 convincing Brunei Darussalam, Indonesia, and Malaysia to commit to the WWF's Heart of Borneo initiative to protect the biological diversity of 220,000 square kilometers of forests on the island of Borneo. The WWF has also been cooperating with governments to strengthen environmentalism in local communities as well—such as working with the Malagasy government on an environmental syllabus for primary schools, training locals as wildlife scouts in Zambia, and training gold miners in Suriname. It is collaborating as well with scientists to conduct research—on occasion making original discoveries, such as when a team of WWF divers found a new coral reef off the coast of Thailand in 2006.

The WWF is also partnering with many companies. "The WWF sees a future in which the private sector makes a positive contribution to the well-being of the planet," explains a website pamphlet called *The Nature of Business*. "To achieve this, WWF engages in challenging and innovative partnerships with business to drive change." A few examples show the diversity and range of activities. WWF-Sweden has worked with the food company Tetra Pak to establish policies for responsible wood purchases and to mitigate climate change. WWF-India has worked with the Austrian crystal firm Swarovski to establish a wetlands visitor center in India's Keoladeo National Park. And WWF-Denmark has worked with the pharmaceutical firm Novo Nordisk on a policy to reduce the firm's carbon dioxide emissions. The WWF has also been partnering with many firms on policies to reduce greenhouse gases—including multinationals such IBM, Johnson & Johnson, Nike, and Polaroid.

NGOs such as the WWF have been especially eager to develop partnerships for eco-labeling programs. Two of the most influential programs are the Forest Stewardship Council (FSC) and the Marine Stewardship Council (MSC). Today, the FSC, founded in 1993 primarily using WWF funds, is the world's most recognizable logo for sustainable forest management, with retailers like Home Depot relying on FSC-certified wood to market sustainable timber. The MSC, founded in 1996 by the WWF and the Unilever food conglomerate, is now the most recognizable international eco-labeling program for sustainable seafood, gaining worldwide publicity in 2006 when Wal-Mart—the world's biggest retailer—pledged to only buy wild seafood from fisheries meeting MSC standards. The partnering of some NGOs with governments and firms does not mean activists are no longer challenging from the periphery of power. If anything, there are more activists than ever before, in part because the Internet allows for a cheap and easy global presence. Still, the trend in recent years has been toward more partnerships and a more commercial focus to all environmentalism.

## COMMERCIAL ENVIRONMENTALISM

Corporations in a few sectors, such as forestry, have long histories of working toward "environmental" objectives such as sustainable yields; the purpose, however, was primarily about improving efficiency, reducing waste, and managing long-term risks to profits, not conservation or environmental protection. As governmental and nongovernmental environmentalism was strengthening and spreading during the 1960s and 1970s, most corporations in most sectors tried to block, stall, and counteract environmental regulations and criticisms. Tactics varied across cultures and economic settings, but the core objective—to stop environmentalism from cutting into profits—was the same. In countries like the United States business executives financed political parties, deployed industry scientists to create uncertainty, lobbied politicians, and sued government departments such as the Environmental Protection Agency. In countries like the Philippines and Indonesia, multinational and local corporations funded military operations, bribed enforcement officers, and gave millions of dollars to politicians and their families.

The corporate approach to the challenges of environmentalism started to change in the 1980s. This was occurring partly because government regulations and civil society pressures were forcing corporations in many countries to alter practices. And it was happening partly because more and more firms began to see opportunities to gain competitive advantages and increase efficiencies by engaging with, rather than opposing, environmentalism. One example is Responsible Care®, which began in 1985 as a voluntary commitment by the chemical industry to improve the health, safety, and environmental performance of chemical operations. By the end of the 1980s, multinational corporations were working toward developing a more constructive role in international environmental negotiations. The willingness of DuPont (the chemical company) to develop substitutes for CFCs, for example, was instrumental in moving along the international agreement to phase out ozone-depleting substances. By 1991, Swiss industrialist Stephan Schmidheiny had founded the Business Council for Sustainable Development to participate more effectively in the upcoming 1992 United Nations Conference on Environment and Development, as well as facilitate business efforts to achieve sustainable development and develop a green image.

Since this conference, just about every multinational corporation (MNC) has now created an environment section and put in place internal guidelines to advance sustainable development. Programs similar to Responsible Care® are now common, and their reach is extending. Responsible Care®, for example, is now operating in over 50 countries, with more expected after the International Council of Chemical Associations passed a Responsible Care® Global Charter in 2005 that encourages adoption of national Responsible Care® programs. Together, "corporate environmentalists" advocate a business approach to environmentalism: policies such as eco-efficiency (a business strategy to maximize resource efficiencies and minimize ecological impacts to produce more with less), market liberalization, industry self-regulation, corporate codes of conduct, and voluntary eco-labeling and certification schemes. They participate in international meetings and "partnerships" with governments, communities, and NGOs (especially with more moderate groups such as WWF). They have also become increasingly active in developing international environmental policy, such as the Kyoto Protocol, advocating for flexible, voluntary, trade- and market-based instruments.

A common business label for this approach to environmentalism is corporate social responsibility—or, what is now commonly called CSR. Often, corporate brochures describe this as meeting a "triple bottom line": economic, social, and environmental. Such an approach requires companies to be diligent producers, sometimes even going "beyond compliance" with existing environmental regulations (especially in poorer countries with relatively low standards). The phrase *corporate social responsibility* first began to spread in the 1970s and 1980s in response to calls from nongovernmental groups and some states for stricter national and international regulations (including an initiative to develop a United Nations code of conduct) for multinational corporations. In the 1990s CSR began to take hold as a standard policy for MNCs, and today just about every MNC is using the phrase to frame its approach toward, and input into, national and international environmental policy.

Supporters of corporate environmentalism see these contributions as a practical and effective way to advance sustainable development. For some it is a way for MNCs to raise environmental standards in developing countries, such as the policy of the Swedish firm Electrolux to require suppliers and contractors in developing countries to follow its code of conduct. For other supporters it is a way to expand niche eco-markets into profitable global ones. Corporate environmentalism is, they argue, currently encouraging many markets to grow, such as for wind and solar power, organic foods, fair trade coffee, and sustainable timber. For them the case of fair trade coffee is indicative. For decades this was a tiny market prodded along by the energy of international activists and farmers in the developing world; but today it is expanding quickly as big coffee chains like Starbucks purchase more as part of their policies of corporate social responsibility. Another revealing trend for supporters of corporate environmentalism is the growth of forest certification schemes, which now cover hundreds of millions of hectares of forests.

Not everyone is enthusiastic about the growing strength of corporate environmentalism. Critics see many of these initiatives as disingenuous public relations—what some call greenwash—to conceal business as usual: that is, more profits from more production and more consumption, all of which requires more natural resources and generates more waste. Some critics, too, are increasingly worried that corporate environmentalism is undermining the radicalism of grassroots, nongovernmental, and Third World environmentalism as more and more groups and community leaders join corporate partnerships in an effort to achieve concrete changes without disrupting the economic growth arising from corporate investment and trade.

## THE FUTURE OF ENVIRONMENTALISM

Environmentalism, then, involves hundreds of international environmental groups, thousands of national groups, and tens of thousands of local ones. It also includes hundreds of international agreements, hundreds of national environmental agencies, and countless environmental sections in other organizations—from ones in MNCs to ones in regional and international organizations. Environmental concepts such as sustainable development, the precautionary principle, corporate social responsibility, and eco-labeling percolate from all of these sources. Every year new ideas, refinements, policies, institutions, markets, and problems continue to enter into environmental debates and discourses—so many from so many different sources one dictionary could not possibly capture all of it. Thus, this book strategically skips across issues, concepts, time, organizations, and cultures, not with any pretense of producing a definitive dictionary, but rather with the aim of producing an inclusive, wide-ranging, and global history of environmentalism.

# The Dictionary

## – A –

**ACCOUNTABILITY (AA).** Founded in 1996 as the Institute for Social and Ethical AccountAbility, AccountAbility, or AA, promotes socially accountable business practices, including increasing the credibility of sustainability reports. Its 350 members include private firms, civil society organizations, and research bodies. AA first published its AA1000 Framework in 1999 as a principles-based standard applicable to any sector of any size in any region. It is designed to help organizations strengthen accountability and social responsibility through superior social and ethical accounting, auditing, and reporting. Through systematic engagement of stakeholders, AA is supposed to increase transparency and improve organizational performance. There are four parts: AA1000 Purpose and Principles; AA1000 Framework for Integration; AA1000 Assurance Standard; and AA1000 Stakeholder Engagement Standard. In 2008, over 150 organizations were using or referring to the AA1000 Assurance Standard as part of strategies to advance **corporate social responsibility**.

**ACID RAIN.** Scottish chemist Robert Angus Smith coined the term *acid rain* in the mid-1800s after speculating that emissions from local **coal**-burning factories were making rainfall in Manchester unusually acidic. The main pollutants producing acid rain are sulphur dioxide and nitrogen oxides, which are released into the atmosphere as by-products of industrial processes and transportation, especially from burning fossil fuels. Smokestacks can contribute to acid rain by spewing pollutants above the inversion layer, which reduces local **pollution** but can cause pollution to travel as much as 1,000 kilometers on higher winds. Acid rain creates many problems, including

1

acidification of lakes; harming aquatic life; damaging terrestrial plants and forests; harming human health; and damaging buildings and monuments.

Controlling acid rain requires transboundary cooperation. Acid deposition is particularly bad in Asia, partly because **China** relies heavily on burning coal for energy; if trends continue, by 2025 China will produce more sulfur dioxide than the **United States, Canada,** and **Japan** combined. Efforts to promote transboundary cooperation on acid rain and air pollution include the **Convention on Long-range Transboundary Air Pollution (CLRTAP)**; and the Protocol to the 1979 Convention on Long-range Transboundary Air Pollution on the Reduction of Sulphur Emissions or their Transboundary Fluxes by at least 30 percent (Sulphur Emissions Reduction Protocol). *See also* SWEDEN.

**ADAPTIVE MANAGEMENT.** Adaptive management takes a holistic and systems approach in an effort to manage resources in complex ecosystems, emphasizing ongoing experimentation and continual learning. Since developing in the early 1970s, it has been defined in various ways across different jurisdictions and ecosystems. Generally, its practices resemble scientific methods, although some key differences do exist. Adaptive management integrates uncertainty: specifically, it assumes that ecosystems evolve with multiple equilibriums. Its methods of experimentation also differ. In particular, it is done at a management scale (thousands of hectares) without strict controls, rather than within a controlled experiment of, say, a few square meters. Adaptive management assumes ecological and economic systems are integrated and coevolve. This requires decision makers to remain open and flexible—to receive, understand, and respond to positive or negative signals in the physical and social environment and to change management responses accordingly.

Adaptive management is most commonly employed as a way to oversee ecosystems such as fisheries, forests, and wildlife. The concept was first developed by **C. S. Holling** and Carl J. Walters at the University of British Columbia (**Canada**) in the 1970s; later, it was further developed at the International Institute for Applied Systems Analysis in Vienna, Austria, while Holling was director of the institute.

**ADBUSTERS.** Adbusters Media Foundation is a nonprofit activist network cofounded in Vancouver, **Canada**, in 1989 by Kalle Lasn (a documentary filmmaker) and Bill Schmalz (a wilderness filmmaker and photographer). Adbusters sees itself as an anticorporate social movement, using a method of social change it calls "culture jamming," defined by bestselling Canadian author Naomi Klein as "the practice of parodying advertisements and hijacking billboards in order to drastically alter their messages."

The network's primary means of communication is its *Adbusters* magazine, which, after starting in 1989 with 5,000 copies, has grown into a bimonthly magazine with a circulation of 120,000. The magazine has subscribers from around 60 countries, although two thirds live in the **United States**. The foundation also operates a website (www.adbusters.org) and runs its own advocacy advertising agency, PowerShift, which offers creative services to environmental campaigns and produces "uncommercials" and "subvertisements." In recent years, Adbusters has pulled off some high-profile campaigns, including buying space on CNN to advertise TV Turnoff Week and Buy Nothing Day and purchasing a full-page advertisement in the *New York Times* for its Unbrand America campaign.

**AFFORESTATION.** *See* REFORESTATION.

**AFRICA.** *See* KENYA; NIGERIA; SOUTH AFRICA; SUB-SAHARAN AFRICA; UNITED NATIONS CONVENTION TO COMBAT DESERTIFICATION IN COUNTRIES EXPERIENCING SERIOUS DROUGHT AND/OR DESERTIFICATION, PARTICULARLY IN AFRICA.

**AGENDA 21.** Agenda 21, a document arising from the 1992 **United Nations Conference on Environment and Development**, is a nonbinding plan to achieve **sustainable development** for the 21st century. The result of years of preparatory meetings, it reflected the emerging consensus among state negotiators that global environmental sustainability would require cooperation and partnerships across developed and developing countries. The specifics of how to share the financing of sustainable development—by far the most contentious topic at the 1992 conference—were never resolved, although

Agenda 21 does call for more Official Development Assistance (ODA).

**ALTERNATIVE ENERGY.** *See* RENEWABLE ENERGY.

**AMAZON.** The Amazon Basin covers roughly 7 million square kilometers—nearly 5 percent of the world's land surface—and contains about 5.5 million square kilometers of tropical rainforest. Close to two-thirds of the Amazon is in **Brazil**; the rest is in **Bolivia**, Colombia, Ecuador, French Guiana, Guyana, Peru, Suriname, and Venezuela. It is a rich source of **biodiversity**, by some estimates containing, for example, around 30 percent of all plant species. Approximately 20 million people reside in the Amazon, including over 200,000 indigenous people. Since the 1980s a global environmental movement has been campaigning to protect the Amazon—in particular the old-growth forests of the Brazilian Amazon. **Chico Mendes**, a Brazilian rubber tapper, was one of the best known activists until his assassination in 1988. This diverse movement has managed to advance research and spotlight many injustices and environmental disasters; however, in terms of slowing **deforestation**, it has been less effective. The Brazilian Amazon, for example, lost over 17 million hectares of forest in the 1990s alone—an area the size of Uruguay. The total deforested area had reached nearly 60 million hectares by the beginning of the 21st century. Since then deforestation has continued to escalate as cattle ranchers convert forests into pasture to supply a surging export market for beef and, to a lesser extent, as farmers burn logged forests to grow crops such as soybeans (burning is a cheap and quick way to clear land and fertilize soil). *See also* GOLDMAN ENVIRONMENTAL PRIZE; ILLEGAL LOGGING.

**ANIMAL RIGHTS.** *See* SINGER, PETER.

**ANTARCTICA.** The Antarctic accounts for 10 percent of the earth's total land surface, roughly equal in size to Europe and the **United States** combined. The southern circumpolar seas also comprise nearly 10 percent of the world's oceans. The Antarctic continent is home to more than 800 species of plant life (approximately 350 are lichens), 8 types of seals, 12 cetacean species, and about 45 different species of birds. It is the only continent without trees; only two flowering plants have been discovered. Antarctica's ice sheet contains 70–75 percent of the world's freshwater reserves and 90 percent of the earth's ice. On average, the ice sheet is about 2,000 meters thick: if all of this ice were to melt, global sea levels would rise by 60 meters or so.

Extreme weather conditions mean the ecosystems in Antarctica are especially fragile and vulnerable to any disturbance. The lowest temperature ever recorded on earth was near the South Pole on 21 July 1983, at the Soviet Vostok station (-89.2 Celsius, or -128.6 Fahrenheit). Antarctica is also one of the world's driest places, receiving less precipitation than the Sahara desert.

Antarctica, except for the indirect effects of **greenhouse gases** and **ozone depletion**, suffers from little atmospheric **pollution**. Trawlers have exploited some **fishing** grounds and several species are close to commercial collapse. **Whaling** also put some species at risk prior to the moratorium on commercial whale hunting by the International Whaling Commission (IWC) in the mid-1980s.

The Southern Ocean and boundless ice were too rough for early explorers, and until the 19th century most states ignored Antarctica (considered *terra nullius*, or belonging to nobody). **Great Britain** was the first country to claim sovereignty over Antarctica in 1908. **New Zealand**, **Australia**, Norway, **France**, **Argentina**, and **Chile** would later claim sovereignty to various parts (some overlap, notably the claims by Great Britain, Argentina, and Chile). The Antarctic treaty was signed in 1959 and it came into force in 1961. The treaty forbade new sovereignty claims, while neither recognizing nor delegitimizing existing ones. The treaty only allows nonmilitary research (and bans nuclear weapons testing). Initially, it did not include environmental protection clauses. However, in 1964 the Antarctic Treaty Consultative Parties passed the Agreed Measures for the Conservation of the Antarctic Fauna and Flora. Since then the parties to the treaty have negotiated other conventions as well, including the Conservation of Antarctic Seals (1972) and the **Convention on the Conservation of Antarctic Marine Living Resources** (1980). In 1991, the parties agreed to halt all **oil** and mineral exploration and/or exploitation for another 50 years, an amendment called the Environmental Protocol to the Antarctic Treaty, or the Madrid Protocol (which came into force in 1998). *See also* ARCTIC; SEALING.

**APPIKO MOVEMENT.** *See* INDIA.

**ARAL SEA.** The Aral Sea, in Central Asia, was once the world's fourth largest lake. In just three decades, as governments and industry diverted its inflows for agriculture and hydroelectricity, its surface area shrank by half and its level fell by 15 meters, leaving this saline lake almost as salty as an ocean by the early 1990s. **Desertification** in the region increased; soil quality deteriorated. The remaining water became increasingly polluted from sewage waste and rising use of pesticides and herbicides to maintain agricultural output, leaving it unsafe for human consumption. Local fish could not adapt, and commercial **fishing** ended.

Authorities in the **Soviet Union** declared the region an ecological catastrophe at the tail end of the Communist regime. After the breakup of the Soviet Union in the early 1990s, degradation of the Aral Sea turned into an international problem involving the new nations of Kazakhstan, Kyrgyzstan, Tajikistan, Turkmenistan, and Uzbekistan. In February 1992, the new states signed the first of a series of agreements to manage the Aral Basin. The **Global Environment Facility**, together with the World Bank, ran a project between 1998 and 2003 to improve water management, collect data, raise awareness, and restore wetlands in the region. Some progress is occurring in terms of improving environmental management; nevertheless, the Aral Sea is continuing to contract.

**ARBOR DAY.** *See* MARSH, GEORGE PERKINS.

**ARCTIC.** The Arctic is located around the North Pole. Countries with sovereignty over areas of the Arctic are **Canada**, Greenland (territory of Denmark), **Russia**, the **United States**, Iceland, Norway, **Sweden**, and **Finland**. Little international effort was made to conserve the Arctic environment before the 1970s, with a 1973 agreement to preserve polar bears as one of the first attempts. The first form of air **pollution** in the Arctic was called "Arctic haze" and was seen by airplane pilots in the mid-1950s; it was also seen by indigenous people. Not until the 1980s did scientists confirm the haze was a result of aerosols of sulphate and black carbon particles traveling over the Arctic from industrial Europe and Russia.

Notably, for most of the Cold War states did not account for environmental impacts. In contrast to **Antarctica**, where the Scientific Committee on Antarctic Research (SCAR) was set up to coordinate efforts, nothing equivalent was put in place for the Arctic. There was the Arctic Ocean Sciences Board and the Comité Arctique International (International Arctic Committee), but the **Soviet Union** did not participate and the organizations did not have the means to coordinate large-scale research. In October 1987, however, with the Arctic now containing ships, weapons, nuclear fuel, and radioactive waste, Mikhail Gorbachev did call for environmental cooperation.

In the late 1980s a number of treaties were negotiated to better manage the Arctic environment. In August 1990, the scientific organizations of the eight Arctic states agreed to form the International Arctic Science Committee as an international **nongovernmental organization**. In 1991, the environment ministers of the eight Arctic nations issued the Rovaniemi Declaration, which outlined an Arctic Environmental Protection Strategy (AEPS). They identified six critical problems: **persistent organic pollutants (POPs)**, radionuclides, heavy metals, **oil**, acidification, and noise. In 1996 the Arctic Council was formed to coordinate nonmilitary matters and AEPS among Arctic states, as well as promote **sustainable development** and promote interest in the Arctic. In November 2004, the Arctic Council published the Arctic Climate Impact Assessment, which predicts severe impacts of **climate change** on the Arctic. While the Arctic Council is an intergovernmental organization, indigenous groups, such as the Inuit Circumpolar Conference (ICC), have permanent participant status. The ICC, formed in 1977, has been critical of AEPS for focusing too much on conservation and not enough on how to ensure livelihoods in Arctic communities. *See also* STOCKHOLM CONVENTION ON PERSISTENT ORGANIC POLLUTANTS.

**ARGENTINA.** Argentina's landscape is diverse. It contains the fifth largest desert in the world (the Patagonian desert), the Andes Mountains, subtropical rainforests, scrubland, as well as substantial agriculture (with products such as soy and vegetable oil accounting for 10 percent of gross domestic product in 2007). It is also a major exporter of **oil** and **natural gas**; **mining** for gold, zinc, silver, magnesium, and copper is also increasingly important.

The 1970s and 1980s saw the founding of several influential environmental **nongovernmental organizations**. The Wildlife Foundation was set up in 1977 to protect **biodiversity**; a branch of **Greenpeace** opened in 1978. The Fundación para la Defensa del Ambiente (FUNAM, or the Environment Defense Foundation) was set up in 1982; an influential founding member was Raúl Montenegro, an Argentinean biologist, environmentalist, and activist who won the Right Livelihood Award in 2004 (often described as the Alternative Nobel Prize, it is awarded for work on ecology and poverty alleviation). The Federación Amigos de la Tierra Argentina was founded in 1984 (joining **Friends of the Earth** International in 1985). The group Environment and Natural Resources was created in 1985 (with a specialty in legal services); City Foundation was established in 1995 to promote civic participation.

In 1990 the government established the Consejo Federal de Medio Ambiente, or Federal Council of the Environment (COFEMA), a federal agency tasked with environmental protection, including helping to coordinate provincial level efforts. In 2002 the government passed a general law on the environment. Argentina also has a long history of **national parks**, creating a National Parks system in 1934, a process that began in 1903 with donation of land in the Andes that later became part of a larger protected area. Today, there are 29 national parks; the country also has 13 **United Nations Educational, Scientific and Cultural Organization (UNESCO)** World Biosphere Reserves and eight World Heritage Sites.

**AUSTRALIA.** Environmental management in Australia involves several levels of government; the peak coordinating body is the Council of Australian Governments (COAG), an intergovernmental forum including the prime minister, state premiers, territory chief ministers, and the president of the Australian Local Government Association.

Two major environmental **nongovernmental organizations** in the country are the Australian Conservation Foundation (ACF), established in 1966, and the **Wilderness Society**, established in 1976 under the name Tasmania Wilderness Society. Some environmental historians consider the United Tasmania Group (UTG), which arose in 1972 as part of a campaign to save Lake Pedder in Tasmania from plans to develop hydroelectricity, as the world's first **green party** (it was at least one of the world's first green political organizations to compete in elections). The green movement would strengthen and develop out of various forest campaigns across Australia in the 1980s; in 1992, the Australian Greens, a confederation of eight state and territory Greens, was formally established as a national party.

Invasive species have been a particularly grave threat to Australia's **biodiversity**. Australia was active in negotiating the **Convention on Biological Diversity**, signing and ratifying the agreement in 1992. It established the National Environment Protection Council Act in 1994, a National Reserve System Programme in 1996 under the National Strategy for the Conservation of Australia's Biodiversity, the National Environment Protection Measures (Implementation) Act in 1998, and its main environmental legislation—the Environment Protection and Biodiversity Conservation Act—in 1999.

Australia is the world's driest inhabited continent and water has been a long-standing environmental issue. Numerous regional and basin-specific water agreements have been created, including the 1965 Western Australia (South-West Region Water Supplies) Agreement Act; the 1968 and 1980 Western Australia Agreement (Ord River Irrigation) Acts; the Dartmouth Reservoir Agreement Act; and the 1993 Murray-Darling Basin Act. Joint efforts of national, state, and territorial governments to create a more comprehensive framework for water management led to the adoption of the National Action Plan for Salinity and Water Quality in 2000 and the National Water Initiative in 2004, the creation of the National Water Commission in 2004, and the passing of the 2007 Water Act.

Although Australia's **Cities for Climate Protection** program has been supporting local action to reduce **greenhouse gases** since 1997, Australia—like the **United States**—was notably absent from the **Kyoto Protocol** until 2007. The transition in 2007 from John Howard's conservative government to the Labor Party, under Kevin Rudd, brought with it Australia's ratification of the Kyoto Protocol and the creation of its Department of Climate Change.

**AUTOMOBILES.** A mere handful of wealthy citizens in wealthy countries owned automobiles at the beginning of the 20th century. Today, there are more than 850 million cars and commercial vehicles emitting significant amounts of **greenhouse gases**. Globally, automobiles account for about one-fifth of carbon dioxide emissions related to energy and cause many premature deaths—about 1.2 million people die every year in traffic collisions—with especially high death rates in the Third World.

Still, the number of motor vehicles keeps rising as automakers roll out over 80 million a year; if trends continue, the total number of vehicles will reach 2 billion by the middle of this century. Some jurisdictions—such as London and **Singapore**—do attempt to reduce traffic congestion with financial incentives and penalties, and a rare few, such as Toronto Island, ban automobiles. However, in the vast majority of places environmental campaigns to ban or restrict automobiles have failed. There is also no effort to negotiate an international environmental agreement for automobiles. Instead, governments and **nongovernmental organizations** tend to rely on technological advances (such as catalytic converters, fuel injection, and seat belts), education campaigns, and international trade to improve the safety and environmental efficiency of automobiles. *See also* CRITICAL MASS; HYBRID AUTOMOBILES; LEADED GASOLINE; RECLAIM THE STREETS; TIRES.

## – B –

**BANGLADESH.** The first environmental legislation in Bangladesh was put in place during British colonial rule, including public parks, agricultural regulations, and sanitation laws in the early 20th century. After partition and prior to independence from Pakistan in 1971, Bangladesh's forests were administered under the Provincial Forest Department and the Bangladesh Forest Industries Development Corporation (the Bangladesh Forest Research Institute was also created in the mid-1950s). During this time, fisheries resource management began with the 1950 Protection and Conservation of Fish Act. Forests were transferred to the jurisdiction of the Ministry of Agriculture in 1971. Postindependence also saw the government establish further measures such as the 1973 Bangladesh Wild Life (Preservation) Order and the 1983 Marine Fisheries Ordinance.

The Department of Environment was formed in 1977 and replaced by the Ministry of Environment and Forests (MoEF) in 1989. Further development of environmental planning occurred during the early 1990s, with the MoEF creating the National Environment Management Action Plan in 1992, the Forestry Master Plan in 1993, and the Bangladesh Environment Conservation Act in 1995. The Forest Department is involved in conservation efforts and in 2005 started the Sundarban Tiger Project to protect wild tigers.

Advocates work from within the country and abroad to promote environmental action. The Bangladesh Environmental Lawyers Association was created in 1992 to advocate for environmental legislation, while in 1998 nonresident Bangladeshis formed the Bangladesh Environment Network (BEN) to facilitate environmental communication. BEN helped to initiate the International Conference on Bangladesh Environment in 2000, which sparked the formation of the nongovernmental environmental network Bangladesh Poribesh Andolon (BAPA). The Coalition of Environmental NGOs (CEN) performs a similar role as an umbrella group for a network of over 100 **nongovernmental organizations**.

One of the more serious environmental and public health issues confronting Bangladesh is arsenic in drinking water, especially in shallow wells (called tubewells), which is exposing millions of people to arsenic levels in water above what the World Health Organization considers safe.

**BASEL CONVENTION ON THE CONTROL OF TRANS-BOUNDARY MOVEMENTS OF HAZARDOUS WASTES AND THEIR DISPOSAL.** The Basel Convention was concluded in Basel, Switzerland, in 1989 and entered into force in 1992. This international treaty is designed to protect the environment and human health from the creation, movement, and disposal of **hazardous wastes**. By 2008, there were 170 parties to the agreement, including all countries in the Organisation for Economic Co-operation and Development (OECD) except for the **United States**, which has signed but not ratified the agreement.

The agreement is an example of the influence of several emerging principles of global environmentalism. To some extent it integrates the principles of "duty of care" and "polluter pays": that waste producers have a duty, as well as the legal and financial responsibility, to dispose of their waste safely. The agreement reflects a belief in the "proximity principle": that the disposal of waste should be as close as possible to the source of origin, taking into account the availability of environmentally sound disposal sites.

The Basel Convention also reflects some of values of the **environmental justice** movement. In particular, it aims to prevent wealthier states from transferring hazardous wastes to poorer ones (an increasingly common practice in the 1980s). Many environmental groups—and some states—seeing such practices as morally wrong and unsustainable called for a total ban on transboundary movements of hazardous wastes. In the end the Basel Convention did not ban such movements outright, instead setting limits and regulating transport. However, to address some of the ethical concerns around trading waste, it did establish a principle of ensuring "prior informed consent" from those at risk. A 1995 amendment to the convention, called the Basel Ban Amendment, goes further and prohibits to a far greater extent the export of hazardous waste from developed to developing countries. It is, however, not yet in force in international law, although many signatories do abide by it. *See also* POLLUTER PAYS PRINCIPLE.

**BHOPAL GAS LEAK.** A toxic gas leak in December 1984 at a pesticide plant in the city of Bhopal, **India**, is often called the world's worst industrial disaster. The plant was run by Union Carbide India, a subsidiary of the U.S. parent company, Union Carbide Company (now owned by Dow Chemical Company). After investigating, Union Carbide claimed the cause of the "accident" was employee sabotage. Activists discounted this "story," instead seeing the "disaster" as evidence of the grave dangers for workers and ecologies of producing chemicals without adequate safety measures or staff training, where multinational corporations set up shop in the world's poorest regions to exploit low standards and cut costs. Estimates of casualties vary, generally from 2,000–20,000 people dead (with higher estimates including cases of related illnesses, like cancer) and 50,000–70,000 poisoned and/or left with disabilities (such as scarred lungs, blindness, and loss of speech and memory). The nongovernmental Bhopal Medical Appeal estimates that half a million people were exposed to the gas methyl isocyanate and at least 100,000 still suffer from the consequences today.

Union Carbide, in a 1989 out-of-court settlement, agreed to pay US$470 million to the Bhopal victims. The company has also taken other small measures to assist with cleanup and compensation. Human rights and environmental groups, however, widely see these efforts and monies as utterly inadequate.

**BIKINI ATOLL.** The history of Bikini Atoll after World War II brought the dangers of nuclear testing to the attention of the environmental movement. Bikini is one of 29 atolls and five islands comprising the Marshall Islands in Micronesia. The **United States** chose to locate its nuclear testing program at Bikini because it was away from regular air and sea routes. In March 1946, the United States began to relocate the 167 inhabitants of Bikini "temporarily" to Rongerik Atoll, 125 miles away. In July 1946, the United States detonated the fourth atomic bomb ever (after Los Alamos, Hiroshima, and Nagasaki) in the Bikini Atoll. Over the next 12 years, as the people of Bikini suffered terrible hardships, the United States tested over 20 atomic and hydrogen bombs in this region. The United States allowed a small number of people to return to Bikini in the late 1960s. As the long-term environmental effects of radiation became clearer, however, the United States again relocated the locals in 1978.

The people of Bikini filed the first of many lawsuits against the U.S. government in 1975. Since then, a series of successful suits created a relocation and resettlement fund as well as a trust fund. Seeking further reparations, the people of Bikini launched another lawsuit in 2006. The United States completed its cleanup of the region in 1980. Even today many scientists do not consider it safe for permanent settlement, however, and most of the Bikini people continue to live on the Marshall Islands, although a tourist industry for diving and **fishing** does exist now on Bikini Atoll.

**BIODIVERSITY.** Scientists have now described some 1.8 million species of animals, plants, fungi, protists, and bacteria. The total number of species is likely somewhere between 10–30 million, although some put the number as high as 100 million.

Processes such as **deforestation**, **desertification**, and **climate change** are contributing to the death of 30–140 species every day. Much of this loss of biological diversity, or biodiversity (a word coined by Harvard biologist **Edward O. Wilson** in his 1988 edited book *Biodiversity*), involves microscopic organisms deep in oceans and forests. Still, even animal and plant species are going extinct—over 1,000 since the beginning of the 17th century—at rates 50–100 times higher than natural ones (assuming average life spans of 5 to 10 million years for a species).

At the global level, the **Convention on Biological Diversity (CBD)** functions as an umbrella agreement to protect biodiversity. Many other multilateral agreements are also now in place to protect biodiversity, including, for example, the **Convention on International Trade in Endangered Species of Wild Fauna and Flora (CITES)** and the **Convention on Wetlands of International Importance Especially as Waterfowl Habitat**. *See also* ANTARCTICA; AUSTRALIA; COSTA RICA; NATURE CONSERVANCY; PHILIPPINES, THE.

**BIOFUELS.** The definitions and categories of biofuels are not always consistent, but generally include biomass, biogas, bioethanol, and biodiesel. Primary biofuels rely on unprocessed organic material, such as the direct combustion of wood; secondary biofuels tend to be agrofuels (derived from agricultural products) and are processed. First generation biofuels, mainly biodiesel and bioethanol, are made directly from food crops by fermenting plant-derived sugars to produce ethanol. In contrast, second generation fuels are predominantly made from the residual nonfood parts of crops, such as the stems and leaves, or from things like wood chips or the leftover skins from fruit pressing. Second generation biofuels are not yet commercially viable on a large scale.

Many advocates of biofuels see them as an environmentally friendly alternative to fossil fuels as an energy source, particularly for transportation. Unlike fossil fuels, which produce large amounts of **greenhouse gases** from underground stores, in theory biofuels are carbon neutral because any carbon relased while using them as fuel is carbon the plants or trees absorbed during growth. Any reduction in net emissions, however, also depends in part on the environmental impact of the production cycle.

Worldwide, the use of biofuels for transportation is still relatively low, but many are predicting an explosive increase in consumption in the near future. **Brazil** and the **United States** are currently global leaders in biofuel production, and many countries, including within the European Union, have, or are now contemplating, mandatory inclusion of biofuels in their energy policies and **climate change** strategies. In recent years, however, a growing number of groups are calling for moratoriums on biofuels in light of ecological and social concerns. Most analysts agree that biofuels can diversify energy sources while enhancing rural economic development. Yet, critics argue, producing enough to meet the demand from global automobile and industrial markets has the potential to cause a global food shortage for the world's poor as prices for crops like corn rise. Critics worry, too, that biofuel markets will create even more incentives for developing countries to turn forests and farms into industrial plantations. At a minimum, many environmentalists are now calling for life-cycle analysis of the costs and benefits to account for impacts on water, energy, **biodiversity**, land degradation, climate change, and social and economic development. *See also* OIL; PEAK OIL.

**BIOPIRACY.** *See* SHIVA, VANDANA.

**BIOTECHNOLOGY.** The term *biotechnology* fuses the words *biology* and *technology* to describe the use of living organisms and biological systems to create or modify products or technological processes (such as genetically modifying agricultural crops). Biotechnology is growing in importance as a force of global change; the term also now appears in international agreements, such as the **United Nations Convention on Biological Diversity**. For advocates, biotechnology can produce many benefits: everything from improving food yields to preventing the spread of diseases. For opponents, it is one of the most dangerous of all technologies, as altering life forms brings with it the potential for unpredictable and uncontrollable spillover effects across food chains, ecosystems, and human health. *See also* GENETICALLY MODIFIED ORGANISMS.

**BISHNOIS OF RAJASTHAN.** The Bishnois of the Indian state of Rajasthan are renowned worldwide for their commitment to environmentalism and nature. A community of Hinduism, their history goes back to the followers of Jambaji or Jambeshwar Bhagavan

(1451–1537). Jambaji asked his followers to adopt 29 principles: two principal tenets forbid the cutting down of trees and the killing of animals. He also called for compassion for all living things, nonviolence, truth, vegetarianism, and no intoxicants. Bishnois derive their name from this list of principles, with *bis[h]* meaning "twenty" and *no/noi/nou* meaning "nine": thus, followers are sometimes called "twenty-niners." In one often-recounted story, over 300 Bishnois were killed in 1730 while attempting to stop the felling of trees around their village. Some see the Bishnois ethic, including the idea of hugging trees to protect them, as a significant predecessor of, and influence on, modern environmental movements such as the **Chipko Movement**. *See also* INDIA.

**BISPHENOL A (BPA).** Bisphenol A, or BPA, is a synthetic petrochemical and a core ingredient in polycarbonate **plastic**. It is one of the latest in a long list of chemicals—from **dichlorodiphenyltrichloroethane (DDT)** to **chlorofluorocarbons (CFCs)**—that environmentalists have campaigned to ban for health and ecological reasons. Volumes of BPA have been rising since the 1950s (with major producers including Bayer, Dow Chemical, GE Plastics, and Sunoco). Today, it is one of the most common chemicals, present in hard, clear plastic water and baby bottles; microwavable plastics; dental sealants; compact disks; sports helmets; and canned foods.

Trace amounts of BPA, which can mimic the female hormone estrogen, are migrating into the environment and into people. Scientists at Stanford University, trying to figure out what was interfering with their tests on the estrogen properties of yeast in the early 1990s, were the first to discover BPA was leaching into water from plastic polycarbonate flasks. Since then the chemical industry continues to assert it is safe, but hundreds of experiments over the last decade have found possible links to cancer, low sperm counts, and the early onset of puberty. The first class action lawsuit to draw on this research was against five manufacturers of baby bottles, filed in Los Angeles in March 2007. In 2008, Health **Canada** became the first government agency to alert the public it was getting ready to list BPA as a toxic substance; stores across the country immediately pulled products containing BPA from the shelves.

**BLUE ANGEL PROGRAM.** *See* ECO-LABELING.

**BOLIVIA.** Despite substantial natural resources, Bolivia is one of the poorest countries in South America and is part of the Heavily Indebted Poor Countries debt relief initiative of the World Bank and International Monetary Fund. To build the economy, the government, under the leadership of Gonzalo Sánchez de Lozada, adopted a contentious strategy of partial privatization of state enterprises. In 2000, large protests and riots erupted over a public-private partnership between the city of Cochabamba and a subsidiary of Bechtel Corporation for water provision in the city. Violent police responses, resulting in the deaths of several protestors, led to international headlines of "water wars," and the Bolivian government withdrew the contract. Protests in 2003 and 2005 over the privatization of **natural gas** resources also led to violent strikes and roadblocks, contributing to the resignation of Sánchez de Lozada and his successor, Carlos Mesa. In 2006, Evo Morales was elected president, with a platform including the "re-nationalization of gas."

Bolivia has participated in some innovative environmental programs. It was the site of the world's first debt-for-nature swap. In 1987, **Conservation International** brokered an exchange of US$650,000 in debt relief for an agreement by the Bolivian government to protect 1.5 million hectares of tropical lowlands. In 2005, the Noel Kempff Climate Action Project—started in 1997 by the **Nature Conservancy**, the Fundación Amigos de la Naturaleza (Friends of Nature Foundation, a **nongovernmental organization** started in 1988), the Bolivian government, and three energy companies—became the world's first project to use third-party international standards to certify "avoided **deforestation**."

**BOULDING, KENNETH E. (1910–1993).** Born in Liverpool, England, Kenneth Boulding was a professor at the University of Michigan (1949–1967) and at the University of Colorado at Boulder (until he retired). Influential in the field of **ecological economics**, he is credited in particular with developing the interdisciplinary field of systems theory for the study of nature, science, and society. He was also a founding thinker in evolutionary economics, which brings together the study of economics and biological evolution. His 1966 essay "The Economics of the Coming Spaceship Earth" also helped to popularize the metaphor of "**spaceship earth**," although the idea was in usage by then (including, for example, in a 1963 book titled *Operating Manual for Spaceship Earth*).

**BOVÉ, JOSÉ (1953–).** A sheep farmer and trade unionist, Joseph (José) Bové has gained international fame as an "alter-globalization" activist opposing industrial agriculture and **genetically modified organisms (GMOs)**. Born in Talence, France, he won 1.32 percent of the vote in the first round of the 2007 French presidential elections, running on a leftist platform promoting international integration that places human rights, social justice, environmental protection, and democracy above economic interests.

Bové's participation in environmental and social movements ranges from official political action to more radical civil disobedience and activism. He helped to found the agricultural union Confédération Paysanne (Peasant Confederation) in 1987 to promote organic farming and oppose industrial agriculture. In the late 1980s and early 1990s, Bové led protests against agricultural land use regulations and held hunger strikes to demand more government support for farmers. He served time in prison in 1976 for destroying military documents as part of a protest against a plan to displace sheep farms with an expanded military camp (the plan was eventually cancelled). He again served prison time in 2002 for damaging a McDonald's franchise to protest the chain's use of hormone-treated beef, as well as in 2003 and 2005 for destroying genetically modified crops. Bové has participated in **Greenpeace** protests, including on the *Rainbow Warrior* to oppose nuclear weapons testing, and attended the anti-globalization protests at the World Trade Organization meeting in Seattle in 1999. Today, Bové is active in La Via Campesina (International Peasant Movement), which started in 1993 to promote small and medium-sized agriculture; a fair economy; gender parity; social justice; and sustainable food, land, and resource use.

**BRAZIL.** Since the 1960s the Brazilian government—with many setbacks along the way—has been expanding its capacity to manage the environment. In 1962 it created a Fisheries Ministry; in 1965, it put in place a new forestry code, followed in 1967 by the Instituto Brasileiro de Desenvolvimento Florestal (IBDF, or Brazilian Institute of Forestry Development). Efforts have continued as well into the 1970s and 1980s. For example, in 1973 the government set up a special secretariat for the environment under the jurisdiction of the Minister of the Interior (Secretaria Especial do Meio Ambiente, or SEMA). In 1985 the government created a Ministry of Urban Development and the Environment (Ministério do Desenvolvimento Urbano e Meio Ambiente). In 1998 the National Congress approved the Environmental Crimes Act, restructuring the previous legislation dealing with environmental crimes and damage.

Many environmental **nongovernmental organizations (NGOs)** have also been established in Brazil over the last few decades. For example, in 1980 Projeto TAMAR (Tartarugas Marinhas, or Sea Turtles) was created, an NGO for sea turtle and marine protection and conservation. In 1986 Pro-Natura was founded, an NGO more broadly addressing **sustainable development** in Brazil before becoming international after the 1992 Rio Earth Summit. (That year a **green party** [the Partido Verde] also formed.) In 1988 **Conservation International** set up a project in Brazil; a Brazilian chapter was officially launched two years later. In anticipation of the Earth Summit, a group of NGOs also created the Brazilian NGO and Social Movements Forum, an umbrella organization for a network of environmental activists. Other NGOs also continued to form. For example, in 1994 the Institute for Social and Environmental Studies in Southern Bahia formed to promote conservation of the Atlantic Coastal Forest. In the same year the Instituto Socioambiental (ISA) was created to promote social and environmental rights. The following year the Instituto de Pesquisa Ambiental da Amazônia (IPAM, or Amazon Institute for Environmental Research), an organization to protect the **Amazon**, was set up. In 2000 the Rede Nacional de Organizações da Sociedade Civil para as Energias Renováveis (RENOVE, or Brazilian Network of Civil Organizations for Renewable Energy) was also established as a network of NGOs striving to promote **renewable energy** in Brazil's sustainable development plans.

In the 1970s the government began to invest in **biofuels**, in 1975 establishing Proálcool, a national ethanol program. Today, Brazil is a global leader in biofuels. For example, in 2007 Brazil—in partnership with **China**, the European Commission, **India**, **South Africa**, and the **United States**—launched the International Biofuels Forum (IBF) to support biofuels markets.

Over the last few decades **deforestation** in the Brazilian Amazon—one of the world's richest sources of **biodiversity**—has attracted intense global criticism. The 1988 murder of **Chico Mendes**, a well-known activist and rubber tapper, also brought worldwide condemnation. This has done little to slow deforestation rates. Recently, Brazil has been losing more forest than any other country—around 3 million hectares (7 million acres) a year, well ahead of **Indonesia** at about 2 million hectares (5 million acres). A major cause of deforestation in the Amazon region is cattle ranching, currently a booming industry as beef exports soar (ranchers often burn down logged forests as a cheap way to clear land for pastures).

The government did establish the Programa Áreas Protegidas da Amazônia (ARPA, or Amazon Protected Areas Programme) in 2002, which by 2006 had set aside 18 million hectares of protected areas. Its goal is to protect 50 million hectares in the Amazon by 2012—thus expanding and maintaining the Sistema Nacional de Unidades de Conservação (SNUC, or National System of Conservation Units). It is run by Brazil's national environmental protection agency, the Instituto Brasileiro do Meio Ambiente e dos Recursos Naturais Renováveis (IBAMA, or the Brazilian Institute of Environment and Renewable Natural Resources), supported by the **Global Environment Facility**, the World Bank, the **World Wide Fund for Nature/World Wildlife Fund (WWF)**, Fundo Brasileiro para a Biodiversidade (FUNBIO, or the Brazilian Biodiversity Fund, a nonprofit and nongovernmental association founded in 1995), the German government's Cooperation Bank, the German Cooperation Agency, and civil society organizations.

In May 2008, Marina Osmarina Silva Souza resigned as minister of the environment. Silva, an environmental activist who worked with Chico Mendes in the Association of Rubber Tree Tappers in the 1980s, was reportedly frustrated by internal squabbling within and between government departments over how to best pursue sustainable development. This squabbling may have partly been a result of the decision in 2007 by President Lula da Silva to divide IBAMA into two agencies, leading to a strike by IBAMA, which saw this move as a way to circumvent rigorous **environmental impact assessments** of hydroelectric projects. Silva was replaced by Carlos Minc, who helped to found the Green Party of Brazil.

**BRENT SPAR.** The plan by the **oil** company Shell UK to decommission and sink the Brent Spar, a facility for storing and loading oil in the North Sea off the coast of Scotland, created a storm of controversy in 1995 as **Greenpeace** took its case against the sinking to the global media. Activists and journalists occupied the Spar, video recorders in hand, protesting the lack of disclosure and the risk of toxic contamination. Greenpeace worried, too, that sinking the Brent Spar would set a precedent for other deep-sea dumping of oil facilities. Drivers boycotted Shell service stations throughout Europe; a few activists even vandalized Shell property. Throughout, Shell UK continued to maintain that its research showed deep-sea disposal was a sound environmental option. Greenpeace countered with evidence that the Brent Spar contained far more oil and toxic waste than Shell was revealing. After investigating, independent researchers concluded that at least some of Greenpeace's data were inaccurate, overestimating the environmental risk.

Nevertheless, confronting a global outcry and a critical popular press, Shell decided to rescind its decision and agreed to reevaluate its options. Greenpeace, meanwhile, retracted its estimate of the amount of oil left on the Brent Spar, stating its initial calculations involved an inadvertent error. Shell then initiated a two-year process of stakeholder consultation, eventually deciding in 1998 to reuse the Spar as a ferry quay in Norway. This outcome was part of a more general shift in the direction of global environmentalism during this period, as many other corporations and nongovernmental groups also began to shift strategies away from confrontation and toward more constructive dialogue with stakeholders.

**BROWER, DAVID (1912–2000).** David Brower was executive director of the **Sierra Club** from 1952 until 1969, when he left to found **Friends of the Earth**. He founded or helped to launch numerous other environmental bodies and conferences as well, including the Earth Island Institute, the League of Conservation Voters, and the Brower Fund.

Brower and others proposed the creation of the United Nations World Heritage Site to protect **biodiversity**, ecosystems, and the geological importance of key places. In 2000 he resigned from the board of the Sierra Club because he felt the organization was not treating overpopulation and immigration as serious environmental problems.

**BRUNDTLAND, GRO HARLEM (1939–).** Brundtland was one of the world's most influential leaders behind the strengthening of global environmental institutions in the 1980s and 1990s. Born in Norway, she began her career as a medical doctor before entering politics as a member of the Norwegian Labour Party. Brundtland became minister of the environment in 1974; then, seven years later, at the age of 41, she was elected as the youngest, and first female, prime minister of Norway. Over the next decade and a half Brundtland won three elections, serving as prime minister for a total of about 10 years. Her most significant impact on the evolution of global environmentalism came when she served as chair of the 1983–1987 **World Commission on Environment and Development**, the group responsible for defining the concept of **sustainable development** as well as developing a consensus for holding the 1992 **United Nations Conference on Environment and Development**. The commission's report, formally called *Our Common Future*, is frequently referred to as the Brundtland Report. From 1998 to 2003 Brundtland also served as director-general of the World Health Organization, moving the organization in many innovative directions, including more focus on the links between environmental change and health.

**BUBONIC PLAGUE.** The bubonic plague is one of three plague forms, along with septicaemic and pneumonic. It is thought to be responsible for three pandemics: the plague of Justinian (approximately 541 AD to 760 AD) in the Mediterranean basin and perhaps as far as England and Northern Europe; the Black Death (approximately 1347–1352) in Medieval Europe, which killed a third to half of the European population; and the plague of Asia (approximately 1898–1948), killing millions in **China**, Southeast Asia, Hong Kong, and **India**. Some in the environmental movement worry a new disease will soon strike humans once again, sweeping across a globalized world of industrial farms with even greater intensity and speed than the bubonic plagues of the past (one example is the Bird Flu).

**BUTTERFLY HILL, JULIA (1974–).** In the late 1990s Julia Butterfly Hill gained worldwide publicity after living for 738 days in a giant California Redwood tree (which she called Luna) to stop loggers from cutting it down. Initially, she did this on her own, although groups like **Earth First!** later supported her. In 1999 the company Pacific Lumber agreed to preserve Luna; in exchange, Hill agreed to vacate the tree. Today, her courage, spirit, and commitment to save California's redwood forest continue to inspire other environmental activists and tree-sitting campaigns.

# – C –

**CANADA.** In 1971 the Canadian government established a department called Environment Canada to manage and regulate environmental matters, although the departments of Natural Resources Canada and Fisheries and Oceans Canada play key roles, too. Canada has also passed new and stronger environmental regulations over the last four decades, including the Canada Water Act in 1970, the Canada Forestry Act in 1989, and the Canadian Environmental Protection Act—a central piece of environmental legislation—in 1999. In 1994, the government created the Canadian Environmental Assessment Agency to promote sustainability and public participation in development projects.

Other important environmental initiatives include establishing its Committee on the Status of Endangered Wildlife in Canada (COSEWIC) in 1977, which acts as an advisory board to the Species at Risk Act (SARA), enacted in 2003. **National parks** were first managed through the Dominion Parks Branch, created in 1911. This later became the National Parks Branch, Canadian Parks Service, Parks Canada, and then the Parks Canada Agency. The Canada National Parks Act, passed in 1930, was amended in 2000. Environment Canada created the Environmental Choice Program in 1988, as an **eco-labeling** program using the EcoLogo certification. The program also helped to found the Global Ecolabelling Network in 1994.

Canada has put in place many regulations around fisheries, although its record includes some spectacular failures, such as the collapse of the Atlantic cod industry in the early 1990s. This breakdown led to a two-year moratorium on cod **fishing**, followed by an extension of the moratorium and additional fisheries restrictions in 1994, limited re-openings in 1999, and subsequent reclosures in 2003.

Canada and Canadians have been active in advancing environmentalism in the international sphere. **Maurice Strong** has been one of the most influential individuals. He was secretary-general of the 1972 **United Nations Conference on the Human Environment**, the first executive director of **United Nations Environment Programme**, and the secretary-general of the 1992 Earth Summit. Canada hosted meetings to negotiate the reduction of ozone-depleting substances and signed the **Montreal Protocol** in 1987. It ratified the **Kyoto Protocol** in 2002 and hosted the 2005 United Nations Framework Convention on Climate Change Conference (UNFCCC COP11/Kyoto Protocol MOP1) in Montreal. Sheila Watt-Cloutier, an Inuit environmental activist and spokesperson, is another Canadian with considerable influence over the course of global environmentalism. She became the international chair of the Inuit Circumpolar Conference in 2002 and has been especially active on the **Stockholm Convention on Persistent Organic Pollutants** and on **climate change**. Canada's reputation as an international environmental leader has gone down considerably in recent years, however, with other states and **nongovernmental organizations (NGOs)** widely critical of decisions such as the one in 2006 to back out of Kyoto commitments and replace these with a "made-in-Canada" plan.

Canada has a vibrant history of environmental activism. Vancouver was the birthplace of **Greenpeace** in the early 1970s, leading to the founding of Greenpeace International in 1979. The Canadian Environmental Law Association (CELA) was founded in 1970 to advocate for environmental law reforms and enforcement; in 1984 the Canadian Environmental Defence Fund, later known as Environmental Defence, was created to provide support (legal, scientific, and organizational) to citizens and grassroots groups. In 1963 environmentalists in British Columbia aligned themselves with the **Sierra Club** of the **United States**; eventually, in 1989, a Canadian national office was established in Ottawa (which was legally incorporated in 1992).

The Canadian Environmental Network was established in 1977 to support NGO participation in consultations with government. In 1990, the David Suzuki Foundation was created.

The **Green Party** of Canada was established in 1983, running 60 candidates in the federal election in 1984. It won 6.7 percent of the popular vote in the 2008 election, leaving it as the largest party in Canada without a seat in the federal Parliament. Elizabeth May, a former executive director of the Sierra Club of Canada, became the Green Party leader in 2006.

**CANADIAN STANDARDS ASSOCIATION, CSA Z809.** An example of the global trend toward environmental certification, CSA Z809 (together with CSA Z808) provides a framework for voluntary forestry management design, implementation, and registration in **Canada**. Published by the Canadian Standards Association (a not-for-profit private sector organization), approved by the Standards Council of Canada, and developed by consensus among various stakeholders (although unanimity was not required), these criteria were originally published in 1996 and then updated in 2003. Participants included industry, individual owners, governments, academics, scientists, technical experts, aboriginal peoples, trade unions, consumer groups, conservationists, and environmental and social organizations. Certification requires an initial (and later periodic) third-party independent audit performed by an auditor certified by the Standards Council of Canada. Among sustainable forestry certification schemes, CSA Z809 has one of the highest requirements for public participation. *See also* ECO-CERTIFICATION; SUSTAINABLE FOREST MANAGEMENT.

**CAP-AND-TRADE.** *See* EMISSIONS TRADING.

**CARBON TAX.** A carbon tax is a tax on carbon dioxide emissions. It can take many forms; a common one is a direct levy on carbon-based fuels; another, less common, is a tax based on total carbon dioxide emissions of a corporation. Supporters see "green taxes" as a straightforward and effective way to change consumer and corporate behavior by internalizing the costs of **pollution** into production and prices. Advocates also see these as a way to finance government and societal efforts to comply with national regulations and international agreements (such as the emission targets under the **Kyoto Protocol**). Critics worry carbon taxes cause inflation with unequal effects and unclear consequences; some argue these are little more than government revenue grabs on the back of environmentalism. *See also* EMISSIONS TRADING.

**CARRYING CAPACITY.** The idea of carrying capacity is at the core of many debates in environmentalism, although definitions differ across disciplines. In ecology, a common focus is on the number of individuals of a given species that an ecosystem can support over the long term without damaging the ecosystem. This assumes resources (water, land, food) limit population growth; that is, when a species exceeds the available resources, the population will die back to a natural sustainable level. Defining carrying capactity in this way makes its application to humans a bit tricky, as factors such as technology, morality, or consumption patterns can alter its utility. Malthusians and ecological economists do tend to use the concept in this way, especially to analyze the limits of the earth's capacity to support life. Among Malthusians and neo-Malthusians, a common example of humans exceeding carrying capacity is **Easter Island**. However, for humans, many environmentalists also use the idea of carrying capacity to focus more on how much consumption and waste is safe and possible within ecosystems (which may include built systems, such as for water and sewage). *See also* ECOLOGICAL ECONOMICS; MALTHUS, THOMAS.

**CARSON, RACHEL (1907–1964).** Born in Pennsylvania, Carson graduated in 1932 with a master's in zoology from Johns Hopkins University in Maryland. She joined the U.S. Bureau of Fisheries (now the Fish and Wildlife Service) as a scriptwriter for science radio shows, eventually rising to become chief editor of publications in 1949. In 1951 Carson published *The Sea around Us*, winner of the U.S. National Book Award for nonfiction. In 1952 she left the Fish and Wildlife Service to write full time. Many consider the public outcry following her 1962 book, *Silent Spring*, the beginning of modern environmentalism. In that text, Carson elegantly asks, "Can anyone believe it is possible to lay down such a barrage of poisons on the surface of the earth without making it unfit for all life?" The book's critique of the deadly effects of **dichlorodiphenyltrichloroethane (DDT)** influenced **United States** President John F. Kennedy to ask his Scientific Advisory Committee to investigate, leading to a 1963 report highly critical of the impact of pesticides on human health and the environment. Carson was diagnosed with breast cancer in 1960, but continued to work on *Silent Spring* even after the cancer spread to her lymph nodes and bones. She succumbed to cancer less than two years after the publication of *Silent Spring*.

**CARTAGENA PROTOCOL ON BIOSAFETY.** *See* CONVENTION ON BIOLOGICAL DIVERSITY.

**CENTER FOR INTERNATIONAL ENVIRONMENTAL LAW (CIEL).** The Center for International Environmental Law is a nonprofit organization. It aims to use international law and institutions to protect the environment, enhance human health, and promote justice and sustainability. It works as well to incorporate the principles of ecology and justice into international law. Its offices are located in Washington, D.C., and in Geneva, Switzerland, although the center covers issues in over 60 countries. CIEL is an example of the increasing importance of **nongovernmental organizations** that focus on strengthening the legal aspects of global environmentalism.

**CFCs.** *See* CHLOROFLUOROCARBONS (CFCs).

**CHERNOBYL NUCLEAR MELTDOWN.** On 26 April 1986, a reactor core exploded at the Chernobyl Nuclear Power Plant in the Ukraine (then part of the **Soviet Union**), with fires and further explosions continuing into early May. By then, this had become the world's worst nuclear power accident, releasing at least six times more radioactivity than the 1979 accident at **Three Mile Island** (in the **United States**). A radioactive cloud floated over a large part of Europe and the Soviet Union. Authorities evacuated over 100,000 people around the power plant during the meltdown; over 200,000 more were relocated in subsequent years. This accident, along with many years of media stories about the long-term environmental and health consequences at the Chernobyl site and within surrounding regions, gave further impetus to a growing movement against nuclear power in the 1980s and 1990s. Today, tens of thousands of people still suffer from illnesses linked to radiation exposure; over 5 million people continue to live in contaminated areas that authorities now consider safe.

**CHILE.** Stretching along the Pacific Coast of the lower part of South America, Chile is home to the world's driest desert, the Atacama Desert, located in northern Chile. The central and southern regions contain vast temperate forests and agricultural lands, while the southern tip in Patagonia has ice fields. Chile also claims a section of **Antarctica.** Chile's economy depends on natural resources, with 80–90 percent of its exports coming from mineral (especially copper), agricultural, forestry, and fishery products.

Responding to political pressure, President Augusto Pinochet created the National Commission for Ecology in 1984, with the mission to draft a national environmental framework. It never accomplished this task, however. In 1994, Chile enacted into law a general environmental framework, which aimed to prevent further environmental degradation by making environmental assessment reports mandatory for new investments. Alongside, the government created the Comisión Nacional del Medio Ambiente (CONAMA, or National Commission for the Environment), the environmental agency in charge of enforcing the new law. CONAMA does not, however, have enough funding or staff to enforce the new regulatory framework. A grassroots environmental movement also exists in Chile, but a general lack of civic participation after the end of the Pinochet dictatorship in 1990 has left it with inconsistent influence over public policy.

Major environmental issues for Chile include **deforestation**, **mining**, and **fishing**. In the case of fishing, for example, most estimates put the annual catch well over the maximum **sustainable yield**. The industry has tended to go through repeated boom-and-bust cycles, turning to new species after each bust. Chile is also developing into a leading producer of farmed fish, with salmon aquaculture in the south now a booming business. Some ecologists are critical of the large amounts of waste and the large amounts of antibiotics; others, though, see this as a way to alleviate commercial pressure on the natural fish populations.

Some cities in Chile also suffer from extreme air **pollution**. On bad days in Santiago, for example, pollution can exceed 500 micrograms per cubic meter. Pollution has climbed to as high as 900 micrograms. In comparison, the **United States** Environmental Protection Agency estimates anything above 150 micrograms is unhealthy.

**CHINA, PEOPLE'S REPUBLIC OF.** Rapid economic growth over the last few decades is contributing to many environmental problems in China, including water **pollution**, scarcity, and flooding; natural disasters (droughts, floods, and landslides); **desertification**; **deforestation**; **hazardous waste**; **biodiversity** loss; air pollution; and **acid rain**. The government has passed many environmental laws, but often economic priorities prevail or enforcement is poor. The close ties between environmental management and economics in China is evident even in its international activities: for example, the Ministry of Finance is the focal point for the **Global Environment Facility** in China and works closely with the Ministry of Environmental Protection. In some cases, however, enforcement is much stronger than in other developing countries. For example, China, through its One Child Policy, has been strictly controlling population growth since 1979.

The government established the Environmental Protection Leadership Group in 1973. Later, this became the State Environmental Protection Administration (SEPA), which in 2008 was replaced by the Ministry of Environmental Protection. The first major environmental legislation was the Environmental Protection Law for Trial Implementation, created in 1979; a formal law for Environmental Protection was established 10 years later. The government created the Law on Protection of the Ocean Environment in 1982 (with amendments in 1999); the State Environmental Protection Committee and the Water Pollution Prevention and Control Law in 1984; the Air Pollution Prevention and Control Law in 1987; and the Water and Soil Conservation Law in 1991. The China Environmental Culture Promotion Association was created by SEPA in 1992, and the Environmental Resources Committee was created in 1993.

China created its first nature reserve in 1956; by the end of 2004, nearly 2,200 reserves were in place, covering close to 150 million hectares (almost 15 percent of China's total land area). In 1992,

China joined the Ramsar Convention on Wetlands, and today has over 500 natural wetland reserves. China also started the National Plan for Wetland Protection Actions in 2000, and approved the National Program for Wetland Protection Engineering in 2003. The **United Nations Educational, Scientific and Cultural Organization (UNESCO)** currently designates 27 reserves in China as World Biosphere Reserves.

In 1994, the government implemented the China Action Plan for Biodiversity Conservation. It is also party to the **Convention on Biological Diversity** and has set up wildlife breeding centers and protection projects for species such as the red ibis and the giant panda. In 2003, China also established a National Expert Commission on the Protection of Biological Species Resources. Still, many species remain under severe threat: for example, in 2006, the **International Union for Conservation of Nature (IUCN)** declared the Yangtze River dolphin critically endangered, a species now considered to be functionally extinct. China also participates in regional environmental management. In 1996, China became a dialogue partner of the Association of Southeast Asian Nations (ASEAN), and in 2007 added "environment" to their priority areas of cooperation. China also became a dialogue partner of the Mekong River Commission in 1996 and now provides information to assist with flood control in downstream states.

China's approach to resource management, especially water, has included large-scale engineering projects. In 1994, construction began on the **Three Gorges Dam** on the Yangtze River with the plan to develop the world's largest hydroelectric power source. Early planning stages involved advising from the **United States**, but the United States withdrew in 1993 following an increasingly vocal international outcry over the environmental impacts and violations of human rights.

Recently, the government has adopted a new focus on environmental issues, with a "green strategy" that includes developing a "revolving economy," clean production methods, green consumption, new energy resources, and increasing resource-use efficiency. It started the Green Lights program in 1996 to promote energy-efficient lighting and passed the Energy Conservation Law in 1997. It is working to reduce the costs of pollution from production, promoting more ecological processes for industry. It is developing "eco-areas" to promote regional **sustainable development** and integrate economic growth, social progress, and environmental management. The implementation of a program for prevention and control of water pollution was started in 2001. In 2003, new environmental legislation included the Cleaner Production Promotion Law and the Environmental Impact Assessment Law. That year also saw the Regulations on Conversion of Farmlands to Forest (to promote **reforestation**) enter into force; it was also the first year the government required annual reporting on pollution control in key watersheds. In 2004, SEPA concluded 12 international environmental protocols and multilateral environmental negotiations, including the ratification of the **Stockholm Convention**. The government has since launched the EPA-China Environmental Law Initiative to encourage dialogue with the United States on environmental regulations.

China's first formal environmental **nongovernmental organization**, Friends of Nature (initially Academy for Green Culture), was founded in 1994. Many have been set up since then (some estimates suggest there are now more than 2,000), such as the Global Village of Beijing in 1996. The lead-up to the 2008 Olympics in Beijing brought further focus on environmental issues, especially air quality in Beijing, as well as intense scrutiny from international environmental and human rights groups.

**CHIPKO MOVEMENT.** The Chipko Movement emerged in 1973 when a small number of female villagers in the Himalayan mountains of **India**, following a Gandhian philosophy of nonviolent resistance, began to hug trees in an effort to save them from loggers and thus protect the culture and survival of the village. In 1980, with the movement now extending (without any formal organization or ties between groups) to other Himalayan villages (and including some men), Indian Prime Minister Indira Gandhi ordered a 15-year ban on logging in the Himalayan forests. Since then, this grassroots movement has spontaneously spread across India, inspiring villagers who hope to prevent the loss of traditional land and forest rights without resorting to violence.

**CHLOROFLUOROCARBONS (CFCs).** Searching in 1928 for a safer way to cool refrigerators, **Thomas Midgley Jr.** took just three days to discover chlorofluorocarbons (CFCs): a stable, odorless, non-toxic, and nonflammable compound, later sold by DuPont and General Motors under the trademark Freon. The new compound seemed totally safe: so safe, as Midgley demonstrated at the 1930 American Chemical Society meeting, it was possible to breathe it in and blow out a candle. Soon, companies everywhere were using similar compounds in the class of CFCs, not only to cool refrigerators, freezers, and air conditioners, but also to make foams and insulations as well as propel aerosols and fire extinguishers. It would take over four decades before Mario J. Molina and F. Sherwood Rowland (in a 1974 article in the journal *Nature*) put forth the startling theory that CFCs, with millions of tons now in use, might be leaking from consumer products and drifting into the stratosphere, then splitting apart and triggering a chain reaction that was destroying the ozone layer. This theory, which won Molina and Rowland the 1995 Nobel Prize in Chemistry, changed global environmental relations, leading eventually to a series of international agreements to phase out the production and consumption of CFCs (most notably, the 1987 **Montreal Protocol on Substances That Deplete the Ozone Layer**). *See also* OZONE DEPLETION.

**CITIES FOR CLIMATE PROTECTION.** A campaign by **ICLEI: Local Governments for Sustainability**, Cities for Climate Protection (CCP) supports cities to adopt policies and implement changes to decrease local emissions of **greenhouse gases** and improve air quality; it also assists with efforts to advance urban sustainability. Over 650 local governments now participate in CCP, from **Australia** to **Japan** to **Mexico** to the **United States**. The ICLEI reports the actions of local governments through forums such as the **United Nations** conferences on **climate change**. Goals include, for example, working toward becoming carbon-neutral communities; concrete measures include, for example, developing more sustainable street lighting.

**CLIMATE CHANGE.** Of all the global environmental problems, climate change is arguably the most far-reaching, as well as the most difficult to solve. It is sometimes called global warming since the stimulus for climate change is rising average temperatures on the earth's surface, but this is a less precise term because shifting ocean currents and weather patterns mean some areas may become colder. Over the 20th century the average surface temperature increased by roughly 0.6 degrees Celsius, making it the warmest century of the last millennium. Most scientists now agree this is occurring because the atmosphere is trapping more heat, a process analogous to rolling up a car window on a hot day. The main reason this is happening is the increase in **greenhouse gases**—in particular carbon dioxide, methane, and nitrous oxide—from human activities. Just about every aspect of modern life seems to add greenhouse gases, including manufacturing, cattle, **automobiles**, and energy (such as burning **coal**, **oil**, and **natural gas**). Other environmental problems, such as **deforestation**, are also leaving the atmosphere with higher concentrations of carbon dioxide.

A primary scientific source for understanding climate change is the Intergovernmental Panel on Climate Change (IPCC), established in 1988 by the World Meteorological Organization (WMO) and the **United Nations Environment Programme (UNEP)**. So far, it has published four comprehensive assessment reports (1990, 1995, 2001, and 2007), contributing to a growing consensus that climate change is real, with the potential for great harm.

These reports show the problem of rising temperatures appears to be worsening. The 1990s was the warmest decade since instrumental measuring began in 1861, while 2005 was the warmest year. The decade from 1996–2006 saw many records set. According to the National Aeronautics and Space Administration (NASA), there is a tie for the second warmest year on record, between 1998 (mostly because of the warming effects of a strong tropical El Niño) and 2007. The year 2002 is now in fourth place (a year with a weak El Niño effect), followed by 2003 and 2006.

The IPCC expects the 21st century to get even warmer, with average surface temperatures rising by as much as 6.4 degrees Celsius above the 1980–1999 average. Many models now predict this century will see the fastest rate of change of the last 10,000 years or so. A rise of 3–5 degrees Celsius would, most scientists now agree, profoundly alter wind, rain, and snow patterns. One possible consequence is an increase in the magnitude and frequency of severe weather—such as hurricanes, tornados, hailstorms, and droughts. Another possible consequence is a rise in sea levels, which could displace millions of people living in low-lying coastal areas in places like **Bangladesh** or submerge low-lying countries like the Marshall Islands and the Maldives. Such changes would impact nearly every ecological issue, from melting ice caps in the **Arctic**, to deforestation, to **desertification**, to **biodiversity**, to the extinction of **endangered species**.

Developing countries tend to see the First World as primarily responsible for climate change, as developed countries accounted for the majority of greenhouse gas emissions during the 20th century. Political leaders in the First World, however, commonly stress the need for a global effort to tackle climate change, especially with greenhouse gas emissions from developing countries now edging toward levels found in the rest of the world. Still, governmental positions regarding climate change do not split cleanly along North-South lines. The European Union, **Japan**, and **Canada**, for example, have supported an international treaty to address climate change while the **United States** and **Australia** (until 2007) have been far more skeptical of the value, at times even questioning the science of climate change. Meanwhile, in the developing world the states in the Organization of Petroleum Exporting Countries (OPEC) oppose efforts to reduce oil consumption while the 30 countries in the Alliance of Small Island States support such efforts in the hopes of slowing the rise in sea levels.

The 1997 **Kyoto Protocol to the United Nations Framework Convention on Climate Change** is the main international agreement to slow greenhouse gas emissions. Many environmental groups see such efforts as insufficient and instead call for sweeping changes to the global economy. Some worry the process of climate change will soon reach a "**tipping point**," spiraling into a catastrophic ecological collapse. Others, such as environmental skeptic **Bjørn Lomborg** in his 2007 book *Cool It*, argue such scenarios exaggerate the probable consequences of warmer average temperatures. *See also* ANTARCTICA; COALITION FOR ENVIRONMENTALLY RESPONSIBLE ECONOMIES.

**COAL.** Coal, along with **oil** and **natural gas**, is one of the world's three main fossil fuels. It is primarily used to generate electricity at large utilities or for energy-intensive industries like cement manufacturing.

Worldwide, it is the largest source of fuel for electricity generation. It is the world's second largest source of primary energy needs, behind oil. Over 100 countries mine coal. The largest known reserves are in the **United States**, **Russia**, and **China**. Other major producers include **India**, **Australia**, and **South Africa**. Australia is by far the world's largest coal exporter. China is the largest consumer as coal-fired power stations fuel rapid economic growth.

Environmentalists have long challenged the cost-benefit calculations of relying on coal to generate electricity. It is the "dirtiest" of the fossil fuels, polluting air with particulates, spewing sulphur (a cause of **acid rain**), and emitting carbon dioxide into the atmosphere (a cause of **climate change**). Open pit coal **mining** also scars local landscapes. Many governments have implemented measures to mitigate the environmental effects of coal use, such as the U.S. Clean Air Act Amendments of 1990 that created a sulphur dioxide cap-and-trade program. Firms have also put in place clean coal technologies—sometimes because of legislation, sometimes voluntarily—to reduce, for example, the emissions of sulphur, nitrogen oxides, and mercury. Nevertheless, coal-fired power plants remain one of the world's major sources of **pollution**.

**COALITION FOR ENVIRONMENTALLY RESPONSIBLE ECONOMIES (CERES).** Founded in 1989, CERES promotes environmental and social responsibility among corporations and within capital markets from its office in Boston, Massachusetts. One of its most significant accomplishments was the founding in 1997 of the **Global Reporting Initiative (GRI)**, a joint initiative with the **United Nations Environment Programme** to develop global guidelines for reporting on the economic, social, and environmental performance of corporations, governments, and **nongovernmental organizations**. In 2002, the GRI became an independent international body; now based in Amsterdam, it is used by more than 1,200 companies as an international standard for reporting environmental, economic, and social performance.

Another major accomplishment is the Investor Network on Climate Risk (INCR), which CERES launched in 2003 at the first Institutional Investor Summit on Climate Risk at the **United Nations**. INCR began with 10 investors managing US$600 billion in assets;

today it includes more than 60 investors (such as asset managers, pension funds, and foundations) with over US$4 trillion of assets. INCR promotes improved disclosure and better practices on managing the business risks and opportunities arising from **climate change**. *See also* CORPORATE SOCIAL RESPONSIBILITY (CSR).

**COCOYOC DECLARATION.** *See* SUSTAINABLE DEVELOPMENT.

**COFFEE.** Coffee is one of the world's top-ten legal export crops by value. For many centuries growing coffee involved intercropping, with farmers planting trees for shade, soil balance, and homes for birds (which eat insects that harm coffee plants). Today, many plantations grow coffee directly under the sun, producing as much as six times more coffee per hectare than more traditional methods, but requiring intensive use of fertilizers and pesticides that can pollute waterways and degrade soils. Movements to promote sustainability and **fair trade** in the coffee sector became popular in the 1990s (although in Europe the first attempts to promote fair trade were appearing as far back as the 1950s). The core idea of **fair trade coffee** is for consumers to pay a premium to guarantee a minimum price for farmers even in periods of low world-market prices (and thus promote social stability and sustainable production). Today, many certified fair trade farms also produce organic, or shade, coffee, and although these still comprise a small percentage of global output, sales are slowly increasing. *See also* ECO-CERTIFICATION.

**CONSERVATION INTERNATIONAL (CI).** Founded in 1987 and based in the **United States**, the nonprofit organization Conservation International (CI) works to conserve natural ecosystems and global **biodiversity**. To achieve this goal, CI relies on a mix of science, economics, policy, and community participation. The focus is on biodiversity hotspots, high-biodiversity wilderness and marine regions. CI employs more than 900 people and operates in more than 40 countries, mostly developing ones. CI also funds more than 1,000 conservation partners (accounting for about one-quarter of its total budget). *See also* BOLIVIA.

**CONVENTION ON BIOLOGICAL DIVERSITY.** The Convention on Biological Diversity was opened for signature at the **United Nations Conference on Environment and Development (UNCED)** in 1992 and entered into force the following year. Most of the world has joined this international treaty—with 191 parties to the agreement as of 2008. The primary objective is to conserve biological diversity (**biodiversity**) and promote sustainable use of biological resources. The task is formidable. So far scientists have been able to identify about 1.8 million species of plants, animals, insects, and microorganisms. A common scientific estimate of the total number of species is 13 million, but some put the number as low as 2 million and as high as 100 million. Preserving biodiversity includes protecting this diversity of species as well as the genetic differences within each species. It includes, too, protecting the variety of ecosystems occurring in, for example, forests, deserts, mountains, wetlands, lakes, rivers, oceans, and agricultural landscapes. Two binding provisions of the convention (articles 6 and 20) include measures to conserve biodiversity through sustainable use, research and training, public education, impact assessments, technology transfers, and financing.

In 2000, the Conference of Parties to the Convention on Biological Diversity adopted a supplementary agreement called the Cartagena Protocol on Biosafety (named after Cartagena, Colombia). It aims to protect biological diversity from the possible threat posed by living organisms modified through **biotechnology**. It draws on a **precautionary approach** as defined in the Rio Declaration from the 1992 UNCED to establish an advance informed agreement (AIA) procedure to ensure governments receive sufficient information to make informed decisions before agreeing to import modified organisms. It also created a Biosafety Clearing-House to exchange information on living modified organisms and help countries implement the Cartagena Protocol. There were 147 parties as of 2008.

The Convention on Biological Diversity and the Cartagena Protocol on Biosafety both facilitate international dialogues on preserving the biodiversity of the earth as whole, the value of which is now a foundational principle of global environmentalism.

**CONVENTION ON INTERNATIONAL TRADE IN ENDANGERED SPECIES OF WILD FAUNA AND FLORA (CITES).** The text for the Convention on International Trade in Endangered Species of Wild Fauna and Flora—more commonly called CITES—was agreed upon in 1973. This international treaty entered into force in 1975 and as of 2008 had 173 parties (states that have ratified the convention). CITES is designed to safeguard wild plants and animals that are, or may be, threatened with extinction as a result of international trade. It provides a framework for parties to adopt appropriate domestic legislation and enforcement procedures. In this way, to varying degrees, it protects over 30,000 species of animals and plants, from live specimens to dried herbs.

Appendixes I and II are especially important. Appendix I of CITES lists species threatened with extinction. The rules prohibit international trade of these species for commercial purposes. Trade for noncommercial purposes requires the permission from both the exporting and importing countries. Examples on this list include apes, giant pandas, cheetahs, leopards, tigers, elephants, and rhinoceroses, as well as some mussels, orchids, and cacti. Appendix II includes species that are not immediately under threat of extinction but may become so unless trade is controlled, as well as some species similar in appearance to the ones in Appendix I (to make it harder for smugglers and illegal loggers to deceive authorities by claiming Appendix I species are similar-looking Appendix II species). Trade in the appendix II species only requires an export permit, which authorities can issue as long as the trade will not harm the survival of the species.

For the evolution of global environmentalism, CITES has set important precedents for the need—at least in circumstances where ecologies or species are nearing collapse—to restrict or even ban international trade. *See also* BIODIVERSITY; ENDANGERED SPECIES; IVORY TRADE.

**CONVENTION ON LONG-RANGE TRANSBOUNDARY AIR POLLUTION (CLRTAP).** The Convention on Long-range Transboundary Air Pollution, or CLRTAP, was responding in part to a growing scientific consensus of the acidification of Scandinavian lakes from sulphur emissions in continental Europe, thus confirming the need for international cooperation to address the ability of air pollutants to damage environments thousands of kilometers away. Signed in 1979 in Geneva, Switzerland, CLRTAP entered into force in 1983. Eight protocols have subsequently been added to address monitoring and evaluation of air pollutant transmission; sulphur emissions; nitrogen oxides; volatile organic compounds; **persistent organic pollutants**; heavy metals (especially cadmium, lead, and mercury); and acidification, eutrophication, and ground-level ozone. As of 2008, 51 countries were party to CLRTAP. A related agreement is the 2000 **Stockholm Convention on Persistent Organic Pollutants**. *See also* ACID RAIN.

**CONVENTION ON THE CONSERVATION OF ANTARCTIC MARINE LIVING RESOURCES (CCAMLR).** The Antarctic Treaty System is a series of agreements, including the 1980 Convention on the Conservation of Antarctic Marine Living Resources (CCAMLR), created to regulate relations among states in the Antarctic. The Antarctic Treaty, signed in 1959 and in force from 1961, is designed to promote scientific research and maintain peaceful relations among states in **Antarctica**; thus it puts territorial claims in abeyance and forbids military activity, except to support scientific research, as well as prohibits nuclear tests and the disposal of nuclear waste. In addition to the CCAMLR, the Antarctic Treaty System also includes the Protocol on Environmental Protection to the Antarctic Treaty (1991) and the Convention on the Conservation of Antarctic Seals (1972).

The CCAMLR, which entered into force in 1982, was negotiated primarily to improve the management of krill catches and other marine life in the Southern Ocean. The Convention adopts a **precautionary approach** to reduce risks from high uncertainty in the understanding of conservation in Antarctica. The Secretariat of the Commission for the Convention on the Conservation of Antarctic Marine Living Resources is located in **Australia**. The Commission monitors compliance with the Convention. Significant challenges, however, confront this mandate, including the sheer size and harsh conditions of the Southern Ocean, which make it very difficult, for example, to monitor and control illegal **fishing**.

**CONVENTION ON THE PREVENTION OF MARINE POLLUTION BY DUMPING OF WASTES AND OTHER MATTER.** The Convention on the Prevention of Marine Pollution by Dumping of Wastes and Other Matter—commonly called the London

Convention—was signed in 1972 in London, entering into force in 1975. It was amended in 1978, 1980, 1989, 1993, 1996 (with a protocol designed to replace the 1972 convention), and 2006 with an amendment to the protocol. The International Maritime Organization (IMO) administers the provisions of the convention and protocol. There were 83 parties to the convention in 2008.

The London Convention codifies a general prohibition against deliberate dumping of wastes and "other matter" (other than standard operational discharges) by vessels and aircraft at sea. Different substances face different restrictions, depending on factors like persistence, degradability, tendency to bioaccumulate, and toxicity. It also allows some exceptions for safety and emergencies. The 1972 London Convention bans the dumping of substances listed in Annex I (the black list): mostly toxic chemicals and some synthetics. Meanwhile, dumping substances listed in Annex II (the gray list) requires a "special permit." The 1996 protocol, which entered into force in 2006, is more restrictive than the 1972 convention. It restructured the 1972 convention to create a "reverse list," so parties are not allowed to dump any waste or other matter not listed in Annex I (rather than ones listed). It also links more effectively to other international environmental agreements, such as the **Basel Convention on the Control of Transboundary Movements of Hazardous Wastes and Their Disposal**. Significantly, it invokes the **precautionary approach**, requiring shipowners to take appropriate measures if harm from dumping wastes is deemed likely, even if there is no conclusive scientific proof of a direct causal link between the discharge of wastes and harm to the marine environment. It further invokes the **polluter pays principle**, meaning in principle that the polluter should pay the cost of **pollution** (as well as avoid merely transferring this cost to another location). Currently, both the convention and protocol will be in force in parallel for some time, with the protocol gradually becoming the primary international legal instrument as more and more parties ratify it (34 parties as of 2008). *See also* HAZARDOUS WASTE.

**CONVENTION ON WETLANDS OF INTERNATIONAL IMPORTANCE ESPECIALLY AS WATERFOWL HABITAT.** The Convention on Wetlands was signed in Ramsar, **Iran**, in 1971 and entered into force in 1975. This international treaty, known as the Ramsar Convention on Wetlands, had 158 contracting parties by 2008. It defines wetlands broadly, including natural marshes, lakes, rivers, mangroves, and **coral reefs** as well as fishponds, rice paddies, reservoirs, and salt pans. The primary purpose is to conserve and protect wetlands, including flora and fauna (especially waterfowl) relying on wetlands. It does so by encouraging governments to follow a principle of "wise use," establish nature reserves, fund research, train personnel, and cooperate across jurisdictions. Wise use of wetlands is defined as "their sustainable utilization for the benefit of humankind in a way compatible with the maintenance of the natural properties of the ecosystem." The convention also created the List of Wetlands of International Importance (each party must contribute at least one listing). Today, there are over 1,600 entries on the list, covering around 150 million hectares. Each year, on 2 February, the date of the adoption of the convention, the Ramsar Secretariat also helps to celebrate World Wetlands Day. *See also* BIODIVERSITY; CHINA, PEOPLE'S REPUBLIC OF.

**CORAL REEFS.** A mix of living coral and skeletal material, coral reefs are found in shallow, mostly clear tropical waters. About 100 countries have them; one of the best known is **Australia**'s Great Barrier Reef. Significant sources of animal and plant **biodiversity**, these fragile ecosystems support over one-quarter of all known marine life and are often called the rainforests of the sea; as a result, various governments and environmental groups are working to save them. Still, many (e.g., those on **Indonesia**'s coastline) remain under grave threat from recreational divers (who can disturb and damage them), destructive **fishing** techniques (such as using explosives or cyanide), **pollution** (such as **oil** and pesticides), and **climate change** (which, for example, is warming waters that can cause coral to expel algae and turn white—called bleaching). Some scientists are now projecting that if trends continue, most of the world's remaining coral reefs will die or fundamentally change over the next few decades. *See also* CONVENTION ON WETLANDS OF INTERNATIONAL IMPORTANCE ESPECIALLY AS WATERFOWL HABITAT.

**CORPORATE SOCIAL RESPONSIBILITY (CSR).** Corporate social responsibility, or CSR, is a business approach that not only assumes companies have a duty to protect social and environmental values but that it generally makes good business sense to do so. It is not the same as charity work: rather, it presumes everyday business activities should reflect these values. Many firms explain this in terms of meeting a "triple bottom line," with economic, social, and environmental accounting. Such accounting requires firms to be conscientious producers, at times voluntarily going "beyond compliance" with existing laws (especially in developing countries with low standards).

The phrase *corporate social responsibility* began to spread in the 1970s and 1980s in response to calls for stronger national and international regulations (such as a **United Nations** code of conduct) on multinational corporations. Corporations began to stress the need for voluntary regulatory measures, or **industry self-regulation**. In the 1990s CSR solidified as standard policy for multinational corporations with the strengthening of global environmentalism and under pressure from a growing antiglobalization campaign. Today just about every large multinational corporation declares a CSR policy for shareholders and the public. Advocates of CSR see this as a practical and effective way to shift the globalization of capitalism toward more **sustainable development**. Critics attack CSR as disingenuous public relations to conceal business as usual—what some call **greenwash**. *See also* ACCOUNTABILITY (AA); COALITION FOR ENVIRONMENTALLY RESPONSIBLE ECONOMIES (CERES); ECO-CERTIFICATION; ECO-EFFICIENCY; EQUATOR PRINCIPLES; GLOBAL COMPACT; WORLD BUSINESS COUNCIL FOR SUSTAINABLE DEVELOPMENT (WBCSD).

**COSTANZA, ROBERT (1950–).** Robert Costanza is cofounder and past president of the **International Society for Ecological Economics (ISEE)** and was chief editor of the society's journal *Ecological Economics* from its first issue in 1989 until 2002. In 1997 Costanza put the value of the world's ecosystem services at about US$33 trillion a year, an often-cited estimate. Until 2002, he was the director of the University of Maryland Institute for Ecological Economics. He is currently director of the Gund Institute for Ecological Economics at the University of Vermont.

**COSTA RICA.** With the world's highest species density and 5 percent of the world's **biodiversity**, Costa Rica has set aside almost a quarter of its lands and forests for environmental protection. Since the mid-1990s the government has been compensating landowners for **reforestation** and forest conservation (as part of its payments for environmental services initiatives). The Sistema Nacional de Áreas de Conservación de Costa Rica (SINAC, or National Conservation Areas System) includes many biological reserves, forest reserves, **national parks**, protected zones, and wildlife refuges. The government also coordinates tree planting—with a plan, for example, to plant 7 million trees in 2008.

Over the last few decades energy, resource, and environmental issues have fallen under the purview of several government agencies, with the Ministry of Energy and Mines created in 1980; the Ministry of Industry, Energy, and Mines in 1982; the Ministry of Natural Resources, Energy, and Mines in 1988; and most recently the Ministry of the Environment and Energy (MINAE) in 1995. Along with MINAE, the government established an overarching environmental law, national and regional environmental councils, and a national technical secretary for the environment.

It ranks fifth on the 2008 Environmental Performance Index (run by Yale and Columbia Universities), the highest rank of any developing country. **Ecotourism** comprises a significant part of its economy. Renewable sources generate over 80 percent of Costa Rica's energy, and in 2007 the government announced plans to become the first carbon-neutral country (by 2021). It has also incorporated environmental concerns into its trade relations, including the 2001 Canada-Costa Rica Agreement on Environmental Cooperation (a side agreement to the Canada-Costa Rica Free Trade Agreement).

Costa Rica has many civil society and environmental advocacy organizations. These include the Centro Científico Tropical (Tropical Science Center), created in 1962 to focus on biodiversity research and protection, and the Instituto Nacional de Biodiversidad (INBio, or National Biodiversity Institute), established in 1989 to research and manage biodiversity. *See also* RENEWABLE ENERGY.

**CRITICAL MASS.** Emerging in San Francisco in the early 1990s, Critical Mass is a decentralized, leaderless, and memberless global cycling movement. It has little organizational structure other than arranging for a time (often the last Friday of every month) and place for bicyclists to gather for a ride through a city, often, although not always, following a spontaneous route (these occur around the world with little coordination and with different degrees of planning). Noncompetitive and festive events, these rides aim to raise awareness by bringing together enough cyclists to create a "critical mass" able to disrupt traffic and draw attention to the dangers of riding bicycles in cities designed for **automobiles** (and the corresponding need for more environmentally friendly transportation). In some cases, these rides occur on other celebratory environmental days, such as **Earth Day** (22 April). On occasion, Critical Mass events involve altercations between cyclists blocking traffic and annoyed drivers; the resulting publicity, as some cycling organizations lament, does little to advance the interests of those wanting to cycle safely in cities.

**CUBA.** The decline of the **Soviet Union** in the late 1980s contributed to a fall in **oil** supplies in Cuba, along with decreased aid (including agricultural products, fertilizers, pesticides, and animal feed) from its former Communist supporter. This caused economic and production troubles in Cuba, but spurred positive environmental changes. The government, for example, promoted urban agriculture after the decline of food markets in the early 1990s, and local governments allowed the use of state-owned vacant land in Havana for community gardens. Basic Units for Cooperative Production, created in 1993 to restructure state-run farms, were used for organizing some of the urban agricultural activities. In 1996, Havana passed bylaws that only **organic food** could be produced in the city.

Domestic oil exploration, initiated after the fall of the Soviet Union, is ongoing. In 2006, test drilling took place in the North Cuba Basin. Cuba also has large reserves of nickel and is a producer of cobalt, a nickel **mining** by-product.

The 1990s also came with an increase in nongovernmental activity, including the establishment of the organizations ProNaturaleza (Sociedad Cubana para la Protección del Medio Ambiente, or Cuban Society for the Protection of the Environment) and the Fundación de la Naturaleza y el Hombre (Foundation of Nature and Humanity). On its website, **World Wildlife Fund (WWF)**-Canada says that "Cuba is currently the only country on the globe to meet WWF's criteria for **sustainable development**, minimizing its **ecological footprint** while preserving a healthy standard of living." WWF-Canada does see ongoing challenges to environmental protection, however, and is currently working on conservation projects in Cuba, including a program to phase out marine turtle harvesting.

Cuba incorporated the Rio Earth Summit resolutions into its constitution in 1992 and created a National Environmental Strategy in 1997. With the transition in leadership from Fidel to Raúl Castro in 2008, however, Cuba's future environmental trajectory is now less certain.

## – D –

**DALY, HERMAN (1938–).** Professor Herman Daly at the University of Maryland is one of the best-known ecological economists. A former senior economist at the World Bank, his critiques of the environmental effects of trade have been especially influential. One of his most influential books was *Steady-State Economics* (1977). *See also* ECOLOGICAL ECONOMICS.

**DDT.** *See* DICHLORODIPHENYLTRICHLOROETHANE (DDT).

**DEEP ECOLOGY.** The term *deep ecology* was coined by Arne Naess (1912–) in a 1973 article titled "The Shallow and the Deep, Long-Range Ecology Movement: A Summary," in a journal Naess founded called *Inquiry*. Naess, arguably the most influential Norwegian philosopher of the 20th century, is professor emeritus at the University of Oslo. After publishing this article he became a leading intellectual figure in what some now call the deep ecology movement. One of the aims of deep ecology is to critique materialism, consumerism, and capitalism. It strives as well to integrate religious and philosophical traditions into ecological reasoning and ethics. Followers move beyond a simple focus on solving particular environmental problems by going "deeper," taking a holistic and relational approach, seeing, for example, humans as one part of nature. Such an approach requires a questioning of the purpose of life and fundamental values.

Shallow ecology sees humans as separate from nature, producing superficial analysis by assuming nature is comprised of separate, discrete "things." This shallow approach also accepts a world order with unjust and unsustainable outcomes—one that prioritizes economic growth and draws down natural resources to feed excessive consumption. Unlike deep ecology, a shallow ecology approach proposes solutions like **recycling** and more efficient production rather than fundamental changes to basic principles and practices.

For followers of the deep ecology movement, the destruction of nature becomes equal to the destruction of humanity. Here, humans should not exploit nature except to satisfy essential needs, striving instead for a sustainable existence. Supporters assume, too, that all life has the same inherent value. A radical wing of deep ecology calls for a revolution—a few even advocate violence—to reestablish the harmony between people and nature lost in modern times. For Naess, however, deep ecology is a moral philosophy of reimagining the place of humans in the global environment, one best achieved through ecocentric values, Gandhian nonviolence, cultural diversity, and simple living. Critics see the ideas of philosophers like Naess as naïve or reckless and the "solutions" of more radical "claimers" to a deep ecology philosophy as dangerous or even misanthropic.

**DEFORESTATION.** Defined in basic terms as the permanent loss of forest cover, deforestation is one of the greatest stresses on the global environment. By some estimates, more than half of the earth's original forests are now gone, most of them disappearing during the 20th century. Every year the area of forests continues to decrease by millions of hectares, with the biggest losses in Asia, Africa, and South America. The loss of forests as a sink for carbon (trees store and absorb carbon dioxide) contributes to **climate change**. Logging, decaying wood, and forest fires also release carbon, adding further to **greenhouse gases**.

Worldwide, deforestation now accounts for one-quarter of anthropogenic emissions of carbon dioxide. Deforestation is also a significant cause of soil erosion, flooding, and **biodiversity** loss, especially in the tropics. In developed countries with temperate forests, **reforestation** and stricter environmental management over the last half century have slowed some of the environmental damage: here, the total forest area is now growing, although generally not with complex forests, but with tree plantations. The overall rate of tropical deforestation remains high, with rates in countries like **Indonesia** and

**Brazil** particularly so. In these places the process of deforestation often begins with destructive logging. Loggers open the canopy, leaving forests drier; littered with debris; and more accessible to developers, plantation owners, ranchers, and swidden (sometimes called slash-and-burn) farmers. Burning is the cheapest way to clear these degraded forests: out-of-control fires, such as the **Indonesian forest fires of 1997–1998**, are a common result.

For centuries the debate over how, and to what extent, to preserve forests has been at the heart of environmentalism. Still, unlike most environmental issues, no international agreement exists for forestry. Efforts to develop one failed at the 1992 **United Nations Conference on Environment and Development**. Since then a series of international meetings have been held to discuss the possibility of negotiating such an agreement, but so far no formal negotiations have begun. Countless numbers of environmental **nongovernmental organizations**—like **Greenpeace**, the **World Wide Fund for Nature/World Wildlife Fund (WWF)**, and the **Rainforest Action Network**—are currently campaigning to save forests. Many do not support the idea of negotiating an international treaty, worrying producers would dominate the process and seeing too much diversity of causes and solutions to deforestation for a treaty to work effectively. Some of these groups instead call for local bans on logging, timber exports, and clearing land for ranches and plantations. Others, such as the **Forest Stewardship Council**, are working with timber companies and governments to establish programs to certify internationally traded products from forests managed in a sustainable way. *See also* BISHNOIS OF RAJASTHAN; CHIPKO MOVEMENT; EASTER ISLAND; ECOFORESTRY; ENVIRONMENTAL KUZNETS CURVE (EKC); GREEN BELT MOVEMENT; ILLEGAL LOGGING; MARSH, GEORGE PERKINS; PHILIPPINES, THE; THAILAND.

**DESERTIFICATION.** Desertification, defined as a process, involves incremental decreases in the productive capacity of arid, semiarid, and dry subhumid ecosystems. Defined as a result, desertification is the creation of desert-like conditions following degradation of non-desert land. Causes vary, but two of the most significant and common are climatic changes and human activity. Overexploitation and inappropriate land use in dry ecosystems are two primary ways humans cause desertification. More specifically, grazing livestock, logging, collecting firewood, and tilling and irrigating land for agriculture can damage or destroy the flora keeping soil in place.

French scientist and explorer Louis Lavauden coined the term *desertification* in 1927; André Aubreville popularized it in 1949. The drought in western Africa from 1968 to 1973, which killed 200,000 people and millions of animals, launched desertification onto the international agenda. In 1974, the **United Nations** General Assembly called for an international conference on desertification. The first UN Conference on Desertification was held in Nairobi, **Kenya**, in 1977. The 1992 **United Nations Conference on Environment and Development** put forth a new integrated approach to combat desertification, which led to the 1994 **United Nations Convention to Combat Desertification** (which came into force in 1996). As of 2008, there were 193 parties to this convention. The year 2006 was the International Year of Deserts and Desertification; the UN designates 17 June as the World Day to Combat Desertification. *See also* NIGERIA; SUB-SAHARAN AFRICA.

**DICHLORODIPHENYLTRICHLOROETHANE (DDT).** Dichlorodiphenyltrichloroethane, more commonly known as DDT, is a synthetic pesticide effective against mosquitoes that spread malaria and lice that transfer typhus. The chemist Paul Hermann Müller (1899–1965) of Switzerland was awarded the 1948 Nobel Prize in Physiology or Medicine for saving millions of lives by discovering in 1939 the "high efficiency" of DDT as an insecticide. Since then scientists have learned that DDT can build up in animals (including humans), becoming toxic and causing cancer. **Rachel Carson**'s bestselling 1962 book, *Silent Spring*, was one of the first to alert the public to the deadly effects of pesticides like DDT, leaving many in the **United States** seeing the acronym as little more than an industrial poison. The United States banned DDT in 1972.

Today, many countries ban or significantly restrict its use. The **Stockholm Convention on Persistent Organic Pollutants**, which went into force in 2004, has also put in place an international treaty to begin to control the production, use, and trade of DDT. This convention still allows DDT to control malaria, however, a disease that continues to kill millions of people every year. *See also* ENVIRON-

MENTAL DEFENSE; PERSISTENT ORGANIC POLLUTANTS; PLASTIC; SYNTHETIC CHEMICALS.

**DRIFTNETS.** In the 1980s, driftnets on the high seas were spanning tens of kilometers. Generally, trawlers would set these near the ocean's surface to drift with the wind and currents, indiscriminately catching everything, including noncommercial species, commercial species below the minimum size for markets, as well as dolphins, sharks, and turtles. Also, pieces of the nets were routinely lost, further killing and harming sea life. By the end of the 1980s, a worldwide environmental campaign to ban these nets was gaining strength, especially in the tuna industry (responsible for drowning at least 100,000 dolphins a year). Facing a consumer backlash, by the beginning of the 1990s, many of the world's largest tuna canning companies—such as StarKist Seafood, Chicken of the Sea, and Bumble Bee Seafoods—stopped buying tuna caught in driftnets and began to market "dolphin-safe" tuna. In 1991, the General Assembly of the **United Nations** passed a moratorium on the use of large-scale driftnets on the high seas (effective from 1992). Illegal driftnet **fishing** still occurs, but driftnets now kill far fewer dolphins each year.

## – E –

**EARTH DAY.** Gaylord Nelson, **United States** Democratic senator from Wisconsin, was the first to call publicly for an Earth Day. The first Earth Day was held on 22 April 1970 and was modeled after the nonviolent Vietnam War protests. Across the United States around 20 million people rallied as part of an "environmental teach-in," one of the largest organized public demonstrations in American history and a defining moment in American environmentalism. Earth Day was an outgrowth of increasing environmental concern in the United States in the 1960s, in part as bestselling books like **Rachel Carson**'s *Silent Spring* and **Paul Ehrlich**'s *The Population Bomb* raised public awareness. In the wake of the 1970 Earth Day, the U.S. government created the United States Environmental Protection Agency and took steps to pass and strengthen environmental legislation. In 1990, Earth Day became a global event. The Earth Day Network, the organizing body for Earth Day, estimates 1 billion people marked Earth Day in 2007.

Earth Day is sometimes confused with an international celebration to mark the spring equinox in the Northern Hemisphere (around 21 March) and reconfirm the need to care for the global environment; it is also called Earth Day and was also first held in 1970. On occasion Earth Day is also confused with **World Environment Day**.

**EARTH FIRST!** A radical environmental movement, Earth First! is comprised of small groups that take direct action to protect natural environments. Pioneered in 1979–1980 by American environmental activists David Foreman, Mike Roselle, Howie Wolke, Ron Kezar, and Bart Koehler, it promotes the values of biocentrism through grassroots education, litigation, and creative civil disobedience. Early acts by Earth First! in the **United States** included what the group called ecotage, acts of environmental sabotage such as tree-spiking (driving nails into trees to make it dangerous to cut into them). In 1989, the U.S. government charged five members, including Foreman, with planning to destroy an electrical transmission tower in Arizona. All, except Foreman who was not directly involved, received jail time in federal prison. Foreman was placed on probation for five years for distributing copies of his book *Ecodefense: A Field Guide to Monkeywrenching*.

By 1990, many of the founders of the U.S. group had quit the organization, some of whom founded the less radical environmental group *The Wildlands Project*. Today, besides in the United States, Earth First! also has chapters in **Great Britain**, **Canada**, **Australia**, the **Philippines**, and the Czech Republic, among others. Participants share a common goal of taking direct action to defend the remaining natural areas from humans. Many Earth First! activists have been influenced by the writings of Edward Abbey (*The Monkey Wrench Gang*), the **deep ecology** philosophy, and anarchist political philosophy.

**EARTH LIBERATION FRONT (ELF).** Founded in **Great Britain** in 1992, the Earth Liberation Front (ELF) is a "leaderless" resistance to capitalism and environmental destruction comprising secret cells of individuals willing to resort to sabotage with precautions to avoid harming people or animals (such as burning down vacant housing developments or closed car dealerships), a practice some call ecotage. Today, ELF is a small global movement whose members on occasion cooperate with the Animal Liberation Front. Its capacity to function and expand has been severely constrained after the United States Federal Bureau of Investigations (FBI) classified the ELF in 2001 as a domestic terrorism threat and members as **ecoterrorists**. *See also* ECOTERRORISM.

**EARTH NEGOTIATIONS BULLETIN (ENB).** *See* INTERNATIONAL INSTITUTE FOR SUSTAINABLE DEVELOPMENT (IISD).

**EARTH SUMMIT.** *See* UNITED NATIONS CONFERENCE ON ENVIRONMENT AND DEVELOPMENT (UNCED).

**EASTER ISLAND.** Among those who see humanity on a path toward ecological collapse, the history of Easter Island is a common metaphor for the planet's future. Located in the southeastern Pacific (around 2,300 miles/3,700 kilometers from **Chile**), its name in English derives from the first recorded visit by Dutch explorer Jacob Roggeveen on Easter Sunday in 1722. As Jared Diamond describes vividly in his bestselling 2005 book *Collapse*, Roggeveen was amazed to find hundreds of giant stone statues (called *moai*) with many erected on massive stone platforms (called *ahu*). Yet, at the same time, the small island was in environmental ruins, without a single tree over 10 feet tall; by then, the Polynesian population had crashed from a peak of between 1,400 and 1,600, with the remaining people struggling to survive. For centuries, large trees were cut down to drag and lift the massive stones to build ever-bigger monuments to the gods, causing **deforestation** and contributing to the loss of wild food, a decline in seaworthy canoes for **fishing**, a decrease in wood for cooking and heat, high rates of soil erosion, and a fall in crop yields. Starvation became widespread; military factions overthrew the chiefs and priests; civil wars erupted; and, to survive, people began to hide in caves and turned to cannibalism.

Critics of the use of Easter Island as a metaphor for today's escalating global crisis argue that its extreme isolation means it is a unique historical case, unlike modern societies able to trade and bring in new natural resources, people, and technologies.

**EASTERN GARBAGE PATCH.** Hundreds of kilometers north of Hawaii, the Eastern Garbage Patch (also called the Great Pacific Garbage Patch) is a "dead" zone of the vast Pacific Ocean now filled with floating **plastic** waste: everything from grocery bags to cigarette lighters to foam cups. Covering an area some estimate to be larger than half of the continental **United States** (although estimates vary considerably), it is located within the North Pacific Gyre, a 26-million-square-kilometer clockwise vortex of calm winds and slow-moving water. The Garbage Patch, the nonprofit Agalita Marine Research Foundation estimates, now contains more than five kilograms of plastic per square kilometer: an amount six times the concentration of zooplankton in this region. Usually no deeper than 10 meters below the surface, much of this plastic waste has broken down into tiny pellets that can resemble food to jellyfish and lantern fish (a major source of food for dolphins, sharks, tuna, and whales). Many environmentalists stress the ecological and health consequences of so much plastic entering the world's food chains; many also see this as a metaphor for the consequences of throwaway capitalism and the shadow effects of consumption.

**ECO-CERTIFICATION.** Eco-certification assesses business processes and/or products to evaluate whether these conform to a particular environmental standard. It is a voluntary mechanism relying on the market to promote **corporate social responsibility**, accountability, and **sustainable development**. Conformance can be determined in three ways: an internal audit (self-certification), an industry association audit, or an independent verifier (third-party certification). Typically, eco-certified organizations or products receive an **eco-label** to inform consumers, although not all eco-certification programs have an eco-label (e.g., **International Organization for Standardization [ISO]**) 14001). The first eco-label certification program was **Germany**'s Blue Angel program created in 1977. Other product certifications now include: Green Seal (**United States**), Eco Mark (**Japan**), Eco-label (European Union), NF Environnement (**France**), Nordic Swan (Scandinavia), and the Environmental Choice/EcoLogo Program (**Canada**).

Beyond ISO 14001 and the European Union's **Eco-management and audit scheme (EMAS)**, an increasing number of eco-certification programs now audit overall business processes. These include the international **Forest Stewardship Council (FSC)** and **Marine Stewardship Council** programs as well as numerous **organic food** and **coffee** certification programs. Eco-certification standards tend to fall into two categories: systems standards or performance standards. A systems standard (e.g., ISO 14001) specifies the elements of a required management system, whereas a performance standard specifies outcome goals and objectives (e.g., FSC). Sometimes, as more eco-certification schemes enter the marketplace, these begin to compete for legitimacy, as in the case of sustainable forestry standards with the FSC and the **Programme for the Endorsement of Forest Certification (PEFC)**. The Global Ecolabelling Network (GEN) was founded in 1994 to facilitate the harmonization of eco-certification labeling programs.

**ECO-EFFICIENCY.** Industry coined the term *eco-efficiency* in the period leading up to the 1992 **United Nations Conference on Environment and Development**. It describes a business strategy where companies maximize resource efficiencies and minimize ecological impacts to produce more competitively priced goods and services (generating more with less). The idea is to create both economic and environmental benefits by integrating environmental values into business practices. Economic benefits can include fewer risks, lower costs for environmental cleanups, and larger market shares by improving performance and image. Environmental benefits can arise as more efficient firms use less energy and natural resources and produce less waste per unit of output. Proponents of eco-efficiency, such as **ecological modernization** theorists, see this as a way to reframe environmental stewardship so it becomes a standard corporate tool to try to gain a competitive advantage. Here, environmental management becomes a business opportunity rather than a cost; thus, going "beyond compliance" with environmental regulations becomes part of normal corporate operating procedures (often under a more general rubric of pursuing **corporate social responsibility**).

Proponents of eco-efficiency see this as one of the most significant business strategies to achieve **sustainable development**. Businesses that adopt an eco-efficient approach will eventually drive other firms into bankruptcy, leaving behind a global network of corporations able to produce more durable and recyclable products, and willing to set ambitious long-term environmental goals, such as zero-emission production. Critics charge that eco-efficiency is merely a repackaging for consumers of long-standing business efforts to maximize profits and minimize financial costs and therefore overstates the environmental benefits (as well as justifies weak government regulations).

**ECOFEMINISM.** Ecofeminist thought began to develop in the 1970s, emerging alongside and as part of protests for peace, labor rights, and animal liberation, as well as environmental and women's movements. In 1974, Françoise d'Eaubonne coined the term *ecofeminism*, or what some call *ecological feminism* (uniting environmentalism and feminism). It is an intellectual movement connecting the patriarchal oppression of women (often including other groups, too) with human domination and exploitation of the natural world.

Ecofeminists stress the interconnections between all forms of oppression: for example, racism, heterosexism, and ageism. Many see misogyny as rooted in the opposition and separation of nature and culture. Many also see women as central to ecological thought because women are "closer" to nature, be it by natural/innate connections (sometimes labeled as *radical ecofeminism*) or by cultural/historical developments (sometimes labeled as *materialist/constructivist ecofeminism*). For these thinkers ecological change affects women more than men; thus, with more at stake, women are often central to efforts to stop environmental degradation (at least compared to other movements). Examples include **Love Canal,** the **Chipko Movement**, and the **Green Belt Movement.** Prominent thinkers in this tradition include Carol J. Adams, Irene Diamond, Ynestra King, Carolyn Merchant, Maria Mies, Gloria Orenstein, and **Vandana Shiva**. *See also* ENVIRONMENTAL JUSTICE.

**ECOFORESTRY.** This term stands for ecologically based or ecocentric forestry. Its origins go back over a hundred years: early notions, for example, are found in debates between **John Muir**, the founder of the **Sierra Club**, and **Gifford Pinchot**, head of the United States Forest Service from 1905–1910. The primary aim of ecoforestry is to harvest—and then care for—natural forests in ways that allow self-regulating and self-renewing processes to maintain **biodiversity** and ecological integrity (such as for soils and watersheds). Today, in contrast to maximizing output and profits through industrial forestry, ecoforestry avoids practices such as clear-cutting, plantations, or pesticides, and instead aims to harvest forests selectively more along the lines of a 19th-century family homestead. *See also* SUSTAINABLE FOREST MANAGEMENT; SUSTAINABLE YIELD.

**ECO-LABELING.** Eco-labeling uses a label or logo to inform consumers that a product has met certain environmental standards. Generally, it is voluntary and certified by third parties (usually either a government or a **nongovernmental organization**). The first eco-labeling scheme was in **Germany** in 1977—called the Blue Angel program. Schemes in **Canada**, **Japan**, and the **United States** followed in the late 1980s, and the idea spread in the 1990s. Today, at least 30 national governments are employing labeling schemes. The **International Organization for Standardization** has also created eco-labeling standards.

Many environmentalists support eco-labeling, but only when the criteria are clear and the outcomes improve environmental performance; otherwise, they worry it can become a sophisticated form of **greenwash**. Some economists also argue eco-labels can distort trade with only marginal benefits for protecting environmental values. In particular, because they are most common in developed countries, eco-labels can function as a barrier to trade with disproportionate costs for export-oriented economies in the developing world. In response, to promote principles of equivalency and mutual recognition for eco-labeling, some within the environmental movement are working to harmonize procedures to measure and assess environmental impacts across jurisdictions.

**ECOLOGICAL ECONOMICS.** An interdisciplinary field of inquiry integrating ecology and economics, ecological economics combines economic theory with ideas from thermodynamics, systems theory, and ecology. It assumes that economies function within physical environments (rather than outside as is common in other economic approaches). Thus, an economy is not an isolated, self-sustaining system but relies on—and is limited by—flows of energy, materials, and ecosystem services.

Many ecological economists build on these assumptions to argue that a rising global population with rising per capita consumption is increasingly putting the earth above its biological **carrying capacity**. **Nicholas Georgescu-Roegen**'s pioneering research on the concept of *entropy* influenced this field; so have the writings of **Kenneth Boulding** and **Herman Daly**. The books of **E. F. Schumacher**, especially the bestseller *Small Is Beautiful* (1973), also shaped this field. Another important leader in this field is **Robert Costanza** who cofounded the **International Society for Ecological Economics (ISEE) in 1989**, which publishes the peer-reviewed academic journal *Ecological Economics* (first volume, February 1989).

Supporters see this field as one on the cutting edge of critical economic inquiry into understanding the root causes of environmental degradation and the growing global crisis. Critics, including many in the field of inquiry commonly called environmental economics, argue ecological economists tend to underestimate the power of ingenuity and technology to substitute for resource scarcity and natural capital (which explains why everything from food to energy has managed to keep up with exponential population growth).

**ECOLOGICAL FOOTPRINT.** William Rees and Mathis Wackernagel developed the concept of an ecological footprint to measure the environmental impact of human lifestyles. It calculates the average amount of productive land and water necessary to sustain current levels of consumption and waste. The measure concentrates on the impacts of food, water, housing, transportation, and consumer goods and services. An individual's footprint is the total area in global hectares (one hectare of average biological productivity) required to support his or her lifestyle. The latest data set (2003) puts the average footprint at 2.2 global hectares per person. Sharp differences, however, exist across the globe. Across Africa it is about 1.1 hectares per person (with a low in Somalia of 0.4) and in **China** it is 1.6. In contrast, it is 5.6 in **Great Britain** and 9.6 in the **United States**. The concept is now common in educational programs, environmental campaigns, and the Western media. Critics argue it is more of a political tool to raise environmental consciousness than an accurate scientific measure, as it underestimates the potential of new technologies and the value of international trade and financing.

**ECOLOGICAL MODERNIZATION.** Ecological modernization theory is a strand of environmental thought drawing primarily on the environmental and economic histories of Western Europe after World War II. German political scientist Martin Jänicke coined the term *ecological modernization* in the late 1970s, although many see German sociologist Joseph Huber as the founder of the "theory" for his writings in the 1980s. Many other social scientists (at first from Western Europe, then later from many other developed countries) added further to the empirical and conceptual foundations of this theory. The gist is straightforward: putting in place stricter environmental regulations does not need to impede economic or social development and with appropriate policies can even increase the competitiveness of industry. The theory assumes a restructuring of global capitalism and that the institutions of modernity can relieve ecological pressures (rather than cause environmental crises) and allow sustainable economic growth. States can do this in particular by transforming the ecological impact of production and consumption. This requires governments to guide markets and promote innovative technologies to increase efficiency, use less energy, deplete fewer resources, and recycle waste and thus produce greener economic growth. Governments need as well to create incentives for firms to go beyond compliance—that is, go beyond the legal environmental rules in various jurisdictions. Here, states need to develop a policy framework so firms see protecting the environment not as a cost, but as a business opportunity to improve competitiveness.

Some critics accuse proponents of ecological modernization of Eurocentrism—of describing the institutional practices of countries like the Netherlands, **Germany**, and **Great Britain** rather than developing a real theory exportable to poor countries. Other critics stress that the theory underestimates the power of structural inequalities in the current world order. Still others contend that the theory only captures a slice of the process of global change, highlighting the progress in wealthy states while overlooking the escalating global environmental crisis. *See also* DEEP ECOLOGY; ECO-EFFICIENCY; ENVIRONMENTAL KUZNETS CURVE (EKC); *THE LIMITS TO GROWTH*; SIMON, JULIAN.

**ECO-MANAGEMENT AND AUDIT SCHEME (EMAS).** The European Union's eco-management and audit scheme—commonly called EMAS—is a voluntary program for regular site audits by independent, accredited experts of an organization's impacts on the environment. It was introduced in 1993 and opened for participation in 1995. It aims to enhance the credibility of organizations that go beyond minimum legal compliance and strive to improve environmental performance on a continual basis. Registered organizations can use the EMAS logo to demonstrate a commitment to environmental goals. The scheme initially targeted the industrial sector but now includes the service sector. It goes beyond the requirements of the **International Organization for Standardization** as participating organizations must not only implement an environmental management system complying with ISO 14001 but also publish a performance statement verified by an external assessor. *See also* ECO-CERTIFICATION; ECO-LABELING.

**ECOSYSTEM MANAGEMENT.** Ecosystem management has multiple definitions. At a general level, it is a systems approach to resource management that integrates ecological, economic, and social goals into land-use decisions and practices. Many definitions stress that the aim is to sustain ecological integrity (not just species) while still meeting economic needs and societal values. This assumes each generation should manage renewable natural resources so succeeding generations will have comparable resources: in this way it is a means for achieving **sustainable development**. Key themes to achieve this include balancing human and ecological needs; managing systems rather than components; defining management areas ecologically rather than politically; assessing longer time horizons; and employing an **adaptive management** approach. The origins are complex and involve multiple inputs; one source in the **United States** is the discussions in the 1920s and 1930s among ecologists and conservationists about the need for nature reserves of sufficient size to conserve wildlife species and **biodiversity**. The Central and Eastern European origins of the concept emerged more through the discipline of landscape ecology after World War II.

**ECOTAGE.** *See* EARTH FIRST!; EARTH LIBERATION FRONT.

**ECOTERRORISM.** The United States Federal Bureau of Investigation (FBI) defines ecoterrorism within its domestic terrorism unit as the criminal use or threatened use of violence by a subnational group in the name of an environmental cause. The FBI estimates ecoterrorists caused hundreds of millions of dollars of property damage over the last decade. Some environmentalists contest this definition of ecoterrorism, seeing it as government-speak to scare the public into thinking of radical environmentalism as terrorism. Some of these radical environmentalists, such as former **Greenpeace** founder **Paul Watson** (now leader of the Sea Shepherd Conservation Society), turn the definition of ecoterrorism inside-out, defining it as acts by governments and corporations that terrorize species and the earth. *See also* EARTH LIBERATION FRONT.

**ECOTOURISM.** Definitions vary, but generally ecotourism aims to limit the footprint of tourists on local ecosystems and communities. Sometimes called responsible tourism, it assumes that with controls tourism can infuse local economies with valuable foreign exchange, which can then finance **sustainable development** and ease pressures on governments to export agriculture crops and natural resources to maintain basic services and service foreign debts. In practice, the concept does not always take on these meanings, however, as creative marketers use it to draw tourists into remote and exotic places to experience nature (with, in effect, ecotourism becoming little more than a way to promote adventure tourism to tropical rainforests, glaciers, or **coral reefs**). *See also* COSTA RICA.

**ECO-WARRIOR.** The term *eco-warrior* generally refers to someone who is willing to protect the environment with radical acts like ecosabotage or tree-spiking. The Canadian environmentalist **Robert "Bob" Hunter**, a cofounder of **Greenpeace**, is often credited with coining the term. American environmentalist David Foreman, cofounder of the radical environmental organization **Earth First!**, popularized the term with his 1991 book *Confessions of an Eco-Warrior*. Today, the term is often diluted to refer to activists campaigning with tactics ranging from rallies to filing legal appeals. *See also* SWAMPY (DANIEL HOOPER).

**EHRLICH, PAUL R. (1932–).** A professor in the Department of Biological Sciences at Stanford University in California, Paul Ehrlich is best known for his analyses of the impact of population growth on the health of the global environment. His most famous book, *The Population Bomb*, was published in 1968, selling millions of copies. Following in the tradition of **Thomas Malthus**, Ehrlich foresaw a collapse of the global environment under the pressures of exponential population growth on a planet with finite resources. For people, such a collapse would mean widespread famine, social instability, and a dieback of the population. To avoid this future, Erlich advocated strict controls on population growth, such as **China**'s One Child Policy. Environmentalists like Ehrlich are sometimes called neo-Malthusians, a line of reasoning more popular in the late 1960s and 1970s than today, in part because many of the predictions of doom have failed to happen.

**EMISSIONS TRADING.** Two types of market-based instruments for environmental policy include taxing **pollution** and trading pollution permits (which includes emissions trading). Many in the environmental movement now see emissions trading (with a cap on the amount of pollution) as a practical—and potentially effective—way to handle complex environmental problems such as **climate change**. Advocates see the trading or buying of pollution credits, such as for carbon, as more flexible and cost-effective than government regulations, with more capacity to account for significant differences in abatement costs across many sources and jurisdictions.

The concept of emissions trading goes back to the late 1960s (including, for example, the work of **Herman Daly**). Since then the number of specific schemes has been growing steadily. The **United States** introduced credit-based emissions trading schemes in the 1970s and 1980s as part of air quality policy. A 1990 amendment of the U.S. Clean Air Act established a cap-and-trade system (in effect since 1995) for sulphur dioxide emissions, a major cause of **acid rain**. The **Kyoto Protocol to the United Nations Framework Convention on Climate Change** established an "emissions trading mechanism." The European Union (EU) also has an Emissions Trading Scheme for **greenhouse gases** that became operational in 2005 (covering sources accounting for nearly half the EU's overall emissions of carbon dioxide). In 2008 the government of British Columbia became the first in **Canada** to introduce cap-and-trade legislation for large emitters, with the goal of reducing the province's greenhouse gas emissions by one-third by 2020. *See also* CARBON TAX.

**ENDANGERED SPECIES.** A species is "endangered" when its population is so low it could soon become extinct over all (or at least most) of its natural range. Biologists sometimes distinguish between three levels of threat: local extinction, where a species no longer lives in its original habitat but exists elsewhere (sometimes referred to as "extirpated"); ecological extinction, where so few are left that the species can no longer carry out its natural role (e.g., as predator or food) in its ecosystems (sometimes called "functional extinction"); and biological extinction, where the species no longer exists. Related, a "threatened" species is one that is still abundant, but declining numbers suggest it might become endangered in the near future unless something is done.

The current rate of biological extinction for animal and plant species is 50–100 times higher than natural ones. **Climate change** is one of the greatest threats to species: an increase of just 0.8–2.0 degrees Celsius (1.4–3.6 degrees Fahrenheit), for example, could "commit" a quarter of plant and animal species to extinction by 2050. Other causes of rising numbers of endangered species include **deforestation**, poaching, alien species, **pollution**, land clearance, soil erosion, and trade in endangered species, to name just a few.

The international community, to control trade in endangered species, negotiated the 1973 **Convention on International Trade in Endangered Species of Wild Fauna and Flora (CITES)**. At the 1992 **United Nations Conference on Environment and Development**, over 150 countries also signed the **Convention on Biological Diversity** to protect **biodiversity**, including endangered species. **Nongovernmental organizations** such as the **International Union for Conservation of Nature (IUCN)** and **World Wide Fund for Nature/World Wildlife Fund (WWF)** have also played important roles in efforts to protect endangered species. *See also* ENVIRONMENTAL INVESTIGATION AGENCY (EIA); ILLEGAL LOGGING; IVORY TRADE; NATURE CONSERVANCY.

**ENVIRONMENTAL CITIZENSHIP.** No single definition of environmental citizenship exists, but the basic idea is to bring the environmental rights and responsibilities of individuals into citizenship. Such approaches identify the role of attitudinal change in bridging self-interest and environmentally responsible actions of consumers. Promoting environmental citizenship has been gaining in popularity among governments and environmentalists as a way to engage civil society and promote sustainability. It is also a way to highlight that relying on taxes and financial incentives is not the only means to motivate changes in individual environmental behavior.

**ENVIRONMENTAL DEFENSE.** Part of a wave of **nongovernmental organizations** forming in North America and Europe in the 1960s and early 1970s, Environmental Defense was founded in the **United States** in 1966 (and incorporated in 1967) by scientists concerned about the effects of **dichlorodiphenyltrichloroethane (DDT)** on wildlife on Long Island, New York. Until 1998, it was known as the Environmental Defense Fund (EDF), and on occasion people would confuse it with the **Sierra Club**'s Legal Defense Fund. Now headquartered in New York City, Environmental Defense has over half a million members and offices in seven U.S. states (as well as one office in Beijing). It is currently running four main campaigns: **climate change**, species **preservation**, human health, and oceans and marine life. Its primary strategy for change relies on collecting strong scientific evidence to work with business and communities on market-based solutions for environmental protection, and, if necessary, take its case through the U.S. courts. Some critics feel Environmental Defense has caved to business interests by advocating market-based compromises; supporters, however, see it as one of the most practical and effective "scientific" advocacy organizations working for cleaner and safer environments in the United States.

**ENVIRONMENTAL ECONOMICS.** See ECOLOGICAL ECONOMICS.

**ENVIRONMENTAL IMPACT ASSESSMENTS.** This is a management technique to predict and assess the environmental consequences of a proposed project. Proponents see this as an essential tool to mitigate environmental damage of development as well as block destructive activities. Most environmentalists see environmental impact assessments as necessary, although most agree they are an imperfect tool, prone to underestimating long-term spillovers on ecosystems. Critics argue that without systematic government and societal input and controls, there is a high degree of uncertainty in many of the estimates and scenarios and corporations can manipulate these to get a green light for business as usual.

**ENVIRONMENTAL INVESTIGATION AGENCY (EIA).** Founded in 1984, the Environmental Investigation Agency (EIA) is a **nongovernmental organization** with offices in London and Washington, D.C. Its mission is to investigate international "crimes" against the environment. Its investigators go undercover to document illegal activities through film, photographs, and scientific evidence. Campaigns include exposing trade in **endangered species**, poaching, **illegal logging**, and illegal trade in ozone-depleting substances. More specifically, the EIA has gone undercover in **Indonesia** to document illegal logging, in Sri Lanka and the Maldives to trace illegal trade in marine turtle shells, and in **Japan** to expose the killing of porpoises.

**ENVIRONMENTAL JUSTICE.** The concept of environmental justice brings together movements for social justice and environmentalism. Some analysts see it as arising out of the **United States** in the 1980s, although it is in many ways a result of countless struggles worldwide for environmental rights. The environmental justice movement highlights socioeconomic and political processes creating—or reinforcing—unequal distribution of environmental harms, such as the dumping of **hazardous waste** from wealthy neighborhoods or countries into poor and marginalized ones. Causes of environmental crises, according to environmental justice theorists, lie not only in the global economy but also in factors such as systemic racism, gender discrimination, and a neocolonialist global system. One solution to enhance environmental justice is to end (or at least confront) environmental racism, a term that more specifically refers to how racism can cause discriminatory environmentalism, where environmental laws, industrial locations, cleanup or phaseout efforts, representation on environmental agencies, and environmental priorities favor one group (usually a majority) at the expense of another (usually a minority). *See also* ECOFEMINISM.

**ENVIRONMENTAL KUZNETS CURVE (EKC).** The Environmental Kuznets Curve (EKC)—in the shape of an inverted U—graphs the relationship between rising **pollution** (y-axis) and rising per capita incomes (x-axis) during the process of industrialization: a relationship similar to the one between income inequality and per capita income, first proposed by 1971 Nobel Prize–winner Simon Kuznets. The EKC shows that pollution (such as **smog**, mercury, and lead) rises in the early stages of development as governments pursue economic growth, but then begins to decline once per capita income reaches high enough levels (in the past generally between US$5,000 and US$8,000 per year).

This inverted U occurs for several reasons. It happens because citizens demand better living conditions. It occurs because corporations and governments now have the financial and institutional capacity to respond effectively. And it arises because growing economies naturally shift from heavy industry to service and information industries. The EKC generally relies on data for industrial pollution rather than depletion of natural resources, although a few studies have found a correlation between lower rates of **deforestation** and higher incomes in Asia, Latin America, and Africa. **Japan**'s history of industrial pollution in the 1960s and 1970s—going from one of the world's most polluted countries with few environmental controls to one of the cleanest with relatively strong environmental measures—matches the EKC especially well.

Many environmentalists see valuable lessons to be learned from the EKC. For advocates, it shows the need for economic growth and higher per capita incomes to advance environmentalism. Many advocates further contend that it is possible to "tunnel" through the middle of the inverted U in countries with low per capita incomes, raising per capita incomes with less environmental damage. This can be done through eco-markets, free trade, new technologies, appropriate policies, and international organizations. Critics counter that the EKC is a fallacy, more ideology than reality, allowing states to justify pollution during the early stages of industrialization. It fails as a theory for issues like municipal waste, **biodiversity** loss, and carbon dioxide emissions. It ignores, too, that a decline of particular pollutants in one country may occur because dirty industries move overseas, improving local conditions in wealthy states but causing global conditions to deteriorate.

**ENVIRONMENTAL RACISM.** *See* ENVIRONMENTAL JUSTICE.

**ENVIRONMENTAL SECURITY.** The concept of environmental security only began to draw widespread interest after the end of the Cold War in the 1990s (building on a few earlier essays). Security theorists had long recognized the significance of the conflict environment (whether at sea or on land, on hills or on mountains). But, after the Cold War, some analysts began to advocate broadening the security discourse to include nontraditional security threats, ranging from earthquakes to resource scarcity to environmental degradation.

Definitions of environmental security have proven contentious, and official statements, policy, and international agreements have provided disparate understandings. Three main understandings tend to reappear: a **deep ecology** emphasis on global ecological security; a human security emphasis on social justice; and a national security emphasis on the propensity, or not, of resource scarcity and environmental degradation to cause violent conflict. *See also* FINLAND.

**EQUATOR PRINCIPLES.** The Equator Principles, a voluntary initiative launched in 2003 by leading financial institutions with support from the World Bank, establish benchmarks to raise the standard of social and environmental risk assessment in project financing. Revised principles became effective from July 2006. These principles include appropriate consultation with affected stakeholders and management of impacts on wildlife and indigenous peoples. Institutions that adopt these principles, known as Equator Principles Financial Institutions (EPFIs), must put in place internal policies and processes consistent with the principles, agreeing that "negative impacts on project-affected ecosystems and communities should be avoided where possible, and if these impacts are unavoidable, they should be reduced, mitigated and/or compensated for appropriately." As of late 2008, 63 financial institutions had adopted the principles as part of a broader commitment to **corporate social responsibility**. EPFIs from the **United States** include the Bank of America, Citigroup, JPMorgan Chase, and Wells Fargo. Ones from **Great Britain** include Barclays PLC, HSBC Group, and Lloyds TSB. Ones from **Japan** include Mizuho Corporate Bank and the Bank of Tokyo-Mitsubishi UFJ. Supporters see the Equator Principles as a practical and effective way to advance the goals of corporate social responsibility. Critics see them as yet another example of the increasing amount of **greenwash** coming out of the corporate world.

**E-WASTE.** *See* HAZARDOUS WASTE.

**EXTENDED PRODUCER/PRODUCT RESPONSIBILITY (EPR).** Extended producer/product responsibility, or EPR, is a policy instrument where governments place responsibility for postconsumer waste on producers. EPR principles were formalized in the early 1990s with the help of the Organisation for Economic Co-operation and Development (OECD). It is a market-based approach to **sustainable development,** internalizing the costs of waste into the production process, and thus creating incentives for producers to shift to more environmentally friendly designs and manufacturing processes. Design changes can reduce material inputs and increase reusability and recyclability. EPR uses a life-cycle analysis of the environmental impacts of a product, from inception and production (upstream) to use and disposal (downstream). The idea is to shift the traditional balance of responsibilities relating to waste management from municipalities and taxpayers to manufacturers and consumers. In this sense it is an extension of the **polluter pays principle**. EPR can include rules to require manufacturers to take back used goods, economic instruments (deposit/refund schemes), and performance standards.

The most successful example of an EPR policy is the German Green Dot System (Duales Systeme Deutschland), which has significantly decreased packaging waste in **Germany**. In contrast, in North America EPR still tends to focus on end-of-life management (i.e., industry funding for municipal **recycling** programs) or on reducing toxins in products. Some industries have developed voluntary **product stewardship** systems to avoid regulation, although environmentalists are often critical of the lack of targets, transparency, and accountability, and various studies suggest industry-led EPR programs are only effective when supported by government regulation.

Some producers express concerns about the potential negative impacts of EPR policies on trade and competition. Other issues include the risk of free-riding, orphan products (i.e., where the producer no longer exists), and existing/preexisting products. Nevertheless, EPR appeals to environmentalists with both conservative and liberal political leanings. On the one hand, it removes waste management from the general tax base and uses market mechanisms to achieve change. On the other hand, it places responsibility on producers and consumers—that is, on the polluters.

*EXXON VALDEZ* **OIL SPILL.** On 24 March 1989, the *Exxon Valdez* **oil** tanker grounded on Bligh Reef in Prince William Sound, Alaska. The resulting oil spill was the largest in the history of the **United States** and one of the world's worst environmental accidents at sea, polluting the sound and over 550 kilometers of the Alaskan shoreline with 11 million gallons (41 million liters) of unrefined crude oil. The spill killed tens of thousands of migratory birds as well as countless marine organisms. The year after the disaster, the U.S. Congress passed the Oil Pollution Act.

Exxon ended up spending billions of dollars on the cleanup and settling lawsuits. Today, those lobbying for stricter environmental rules to govern international transportation continue to point to the *Exxon Valdez* as an example of the ecological and financial dangers of shipping oil.

## – F –

**FAIR TRADE.** This approach to trading aims to establish more equal transactions between buyers and suppliers to support community development through access to international trade. It relies on direct trade with producers to guarantee a minimum price and thus ensure more stable incomes and fairer prices, even when world market prices are falling. It can also involve other support for producers, such as social premiums to support better labor conditions, low-interest credit in times of hardship, and up-to-date market information.

The idea of trading fairly has a long history in bartering between neighbors and communities. The modern-day fair trade movement first began to take shape during the 1960s around the import of Third World handicrafts into Europe. It soon spread to agricultural products—first **fair trade coffee** and tea, then sugar, bananas, nuts, dried fruits, and wine, among many others. The movement did not take off as a major economic force, however, until fair trade labels and certification programs took hold after the 1990s.

Today, some key fair trade organizations include Fairtrade Labelling Organizations International (FLO), International Fair Trade Association (IFAT), Network of European Worldshops (NEWS!), and the Fair Trade Federation. Proponents of fair trade see it as a realistic and effective way for consumption in the First World to promote development in the Third World. Critics see it as little more than a token, doing more to relieve the guilt of the wealthy "cappuccino class" than promote better environmental and social conditions in developing countries.

**FAIR TRADE COFFEE. Fair trade** in **coffee** began in the 1960s as part of the fair trade movement in Europe. It spread into North America in the 1980s as small-scale roasters started importing directly from cooperatives at above-market prices. It remained a niche market until the late 1990s, when certification programs began to expand its potential to reach mainstream markets.

The world's largest coffee chain, Starbucks, started serving fair trade coffee in 2000 as part of its policy of **corporate social responsibility**. Its purchases grew quickly, from just under 650,000 pounds in 2001 to over 12 million pounds of fair trade certified coffee today—in 2006, Starbucks' purchases accounted for approximately 10 percent of global fair trade certified coffee imports. Supporters of fair trade stress how quickly sales are now rising for products like coffee, although, as many critics point out, these still comprise a small percentage of total consumption of natural resources from the Third World.

**FAJARDO MENDO, PABLO.** *See* GOLDMAN ENVIRONMENTAL PRIZE.

**FARMED MEAT.** Records suggest per capita meat consumption in most traditional agricultural societies was rarely above 5–10 kilograms a year. Today, consumption of farmed meat is one of the greatest strains on the global environment. Global per capita meat consumption has more than doubled since 1950: from 17 to over 40 kilograms. And, as per capita consumption continues to increase, the number of pigs (now at 1 billion), cattle (now at 1.3 billion), sheep and goats (now at 1.8 billion), and chickens (now at 17 billion) continues to rise, a trend that will continue for some time. Most countries are still well behind leaders like the **United States**, now consuming over 125 kilograms a year and rising.

Industrial meat farms emit significant **greenhouse gases** (belching and flatulent livestock, for example, account for about 16 percent of global methane emissions, especially ones fattened on artificial feed containing things like corn, soy, and antibiotics). Since the 1960s various **nongovernmental organizations** have campaigned to raise awareness about the environmental consequences and inhumane conditions of meat farms. But, compared to campaigns for whales or seals or elephants, these have gained little traction among states, corporations, and the general public. *See also* INTERNATIONAL CONVENTION FOR THE REGULATION OF WHALING; SEALING.

**FIJI.** *See* MELANESIA.

**FINLAND.** Although Finland's economy has many energy-intensive industries, with substantial coniferous taiga forests, many lakes, and little arable land, the government has kept a strong focus on the environment. In 2004, it initiated a national strategy to adapt to **climate change**; it also includes **environmental security**, with particular attention to climate change threats, as part of its comprehensive security and defense strategy. The Ministry of the Environment oversees environmental issues, in conjunction with the Ministry of Agriculture and Forestry and state-run Regional Environment Centers. The Ministry of the Environment also runs a research wing, the Finnish Environment Institute; meanwhile, Metsähallitus, a state-owned enterprise, is responsible for Finland's **national parks** and most of its nature reserves. During Finland's presidency of the European Union in 2006, its environmental focus was on air quality, **biodiversity**, climate change, marine life, and waste management.

Finland is part of the Helsinki Commission (HELCOM), the governing organization of the Helsinki Convention (Convention on the Protection of the Marine Environment of the Baltic Sea Area) of 1974. It is also a member of the Arctic Council, created in 1996 by Finland, **Canada**, Denmark, **Iceland**, Norway**, Russia**, **Sweden**, and the **United States** to promote cooperation on **Arctic** issues, including the environment.

The government has also established the Finnish Forest Certification Council and System as a branch of the **Programme for the Endorsement of Forest Certification** (PEFC) schemes. In addition, although schemes run alongside, the Finnish Association for Nature Conservation (the largest environmental **nongovernmental organization** in Finland), the Finnish Nature League, and **World Wide Fund for Nature (WWF)**-Finland are all members of the **Forest Stewardship Council**. The Green League, Finland's main **green party**, registered as a political party in 1988, although previously various green candidates had run in elections without establishing a formal party (although some cooperated as a list of candidates).

**FISHING.** The seven largest marine fishing states are **China**, Peru, the **United States**, **Japan**, **Chile**, **Indonesia**, and **Russia**, which account for roughly half of the global catch. Worldwide, about 95 percent of the fish catch occurs within the 200-mile Exclusive Economic Zones under national jurisdiction. Countries with "distant-water" fishing fleets such as Russia, Japan, **Spain,** Poland, **South Korea**, and **Taiwan** are responsible for the majority of the catch in international waters.

The 1982 UN Agreement for the Implementation of the Provisions of the **United Nations Convention on the Law of the Sea** relating to the Conservation and Management of Straddling Fish Stocks and Highly Migratory Fish Stocks sets out principles and international standards for the conservation and management of straddling and migratory fish stocks. In 1995, the **United Nations** adopted an international agreement on straddling and highly migratory fish stocks to implement these principles and international standards, which entered into force in 2001. By 2005, only the European Union and 5 (Norway, Russia, United States, Iceland, and **India**) of the 20 most important fishing states had ratified, leaving out key fishing states such as Peru, Chile, **Thailand**, **Mexico,** Malaysia, and **Vietnam**. The treaty, moreover, only applies to about 20 percent of the global fish catch.

Estimates of remaining fish stocks vary widely and are hard to verify. Nevertheless, many marine biologists now agree that overfishing, **pollution**, and **climate change** mean many commercial species are in crisis, with stocks crashing. Over the last half century, for example, the stocks of large predatory fish—including cod, flounder, marlin, swordfish, and tuna—have fallen by at least 90 percent. The once seemingly infinite northern cod are now endangered. Still, even as stocks fall, and even with international agreements on fish stocks now in place, the global marine catch remains far above the 1950 total of 16 million tons annually, and currently sits at above 80 million tons, an amount most environmentalists see as many times above a sustainable catch.

**FOOD NOT BOMBS.** Comprising dispersed, small, independent, consensus-oriented groups of volunteers, the Food Not Bombs movement aims to promote social justice, more equitable and less wasteful consumption, and sustainability by serving free vegan and vegetarian food to the hungry and poor. Volunteers do this in part as a protest against war, capitalism, and poverty; and in part to reduce waste with a practical approach to alleviating hunger, especially among the homeless (whenever possible, the free food comes from surplus stock from bakeries, fruit and vegetable markets, and grocery stores that would otherwise be thrown away). The movement started in Cambridge, Massachusetts, in the early 1980s, spread to San Francisco in the late 1980s, then went worldwide, with over 400 loosely tied and fluidly organized chapters today (with about half of them outside of the **United States**). Many of these "environmental" groups overlap with movements against globalization and war and for animal rights and vegetarianism. *See also* NONGOVERNMENTAL ORGANIZATIONS (NGOs).

**FOREMAN, DAVID (1947–).** *See* EARTH FIRST!; ECO-WARRIOR.

**FOREST STEWARDSHIP COUNCIL (FSC).** The Forest Stewardship Council, or FSC, is a nonprofit international organization founded in 1993, with funding primarily from the **World Wide Fund**

**for Nature/World Wildlife Fund (WWF).** It was originally based in Oaxaca, **Mexico**, but later moved to Bonn, **Germany**. Its mandate is to improve forest management by more effectively taking into account long-term economic, social, and environmental impacts. Its members include forest industries, indigenous peoples, certification bodies, community groups, and environmental organizations. Today, the FSC has more than 550 members from 67 countries, with its decision-making bodies providing equal representation for developed and developing countries.

The FSC is supporting the development of local, national, and regional environmental standards for forest management. Its primary function, however, is to accredit and monitor organizations that certify products are from "a well-managed forest"—defined as one that meets the FSC's Principles and Criteria of Forest Stewardship. FSC representatives also monitor certified forests to ensure compliance. According to the FSC, its logo on a wood product is designed to provide a "credible guarantee" to the consumer that they are buying timber products from a sustainable source. Its label is gaining increasing market strength, and large retailers like Home Depot are now selling significant quantities of FSC-certified wood.

The FSC is an example of a growing trend among environmentalists since the early 1990s: to try to change corporate behavior by influencing consumer demand with voluntary eco-labels. *See also* DEFORESTATION; ECO-CERTIFICATION; ECO-LABELING; SUSTAINABLE FOREST MANAGEMENT.

**FOSSIL FUELS.** *See* COAL; NATURAL GAS; OIL; PEAK OIL.

**FRANCE.** France has a long history of national environmental legislation. An 1810 decree created the category of "licensed sites," requiring permission for highly polluting and hazardous operations. A 1917 act created the Licensed Sites Inspectorate. In 1930, the National Heritage Act allowed for the **preservation** of architectural and natural sites on aesthetic, historic, or scientific grounds, but it was not very effective with respect to environmental protection. Early attempts to establish nature parks included Fontainebleau in 1861 (near Paris), but all of today's nine **national parks** were created since 1963.

The Environment Ministry was established in 1971. The 1976 Nature Conservation Act provides a legal basis for protection of the natural environment, although it is rather general, and implementation has been difficult. Specific measures include **environmental impact assessments** and the authorization of public interest environmental litigation by state-recognized environmental groups, as well as the creation of nature reserves. France has many specific environmental laws: one example is the 1975 Waste Act. European legislation also supplements France's environmental legislation, including the 1979 European Birds Directive, the 1992 Habitats Directive, and the 1993 Landscapes Act, which supports the preservation of the aesthetic quality of urban and rural areas.

Moreover, France has a long history of regulating freshwater for everything from fisheries to agriculture. Regulation of fisheries goes back to an 1829 statute on fish protection, under the *code rural*—still used in court actions today. The 1964 and 1992 Water Acts, and over 20 pieces of European legislation, also form a legal basis for water management. The 1964 Water Act, for example, created the "river basin" as the key unit with respect to water protection. Municipalities (of which there are over 36,000) also hold key management and implementation responsibilities in this area and are strongly represented on basin committees, as are state and industrial interests. These committees set charges for matters like water consumption and **pollution** (in line with the environmental taxation framework).

Environmental taxation in France relies in part on the **polluter pays principle**. The key agency is the Agence de l'Environnement et de la Maîtrise de l'Energie (ADEME), or the Environment and Energy Efficiency Agency, which was established in 1990. This agency receives public funding and taxes charged on practices such as landfill waste disposal, use of **oil**, industrial air pollution, and noise from airports. Tax revenue is partly returned to industry to subsidize environmental measures.

French environmentalism was primarily about conservation until the 1950s. The radicalism of the 1960s was a turning point, with environmentalism beginning to reflect a broader critique of consumer society. The "Vanoise affair" was the first major mobilization of this new environmentalism (arising over a proposal to build a ski resort in Vanoise National Park in 1969). The movement generated more than 500,000 protest letters and managed to stop the project. Another key issue mobilizing environmentalism at this time was **nuclear power**. The antinuclear movement began in the early 1970s, prompted by the 1974 Mesmer Plan, which aimed to provide 70 percent of France's electricity through nuclear power by 1985. Clashes at a demonstration in Malville in 1977 led to a split in the antinuclear movement between environmentalists and the extreme left (Trotskyites and Maoists) over the use of political violence. A major victory for the antinuclear movement was the cancellation of the Plogoff nuclear plant project in 1981.

The first environmental candidate stood in the 1973 legislative elections. In 1974, presidential candidate René Dumont, running on an environmental platform, gained 1.3 percent of the first-round vote. From the beginning there were tensions within the environmental movement between those who wanted to build centralized parties and structures (the organizers) and those who wanted to engage in more direct action (radicals). A split also developed between those wanting to develop an independent and exclusively environmental party without a close affiliation with either the Left or Right, and those wanting to form a common oppositional social movement.

These two strands eventually united to create Les Verts (The Greens) in 1984. In 1986, Antoine Waechter won the leadership, and succeeded in pushing through a policy of full independence from other parties (neither right, nor left). In 1989, Les Verts elected a record number of candidates in the municipal and European elections. Political support for this party, however, was undercut by other environmental politicians like Brice Lalonde, who became state secretary for the environment in François Mitterrand's Socialist government in 1988. Politically oriented environmentalists agreed to run a single campaign in 1993; despite running high in the polls, however, the party did not manage to elect a member of parliament.

In 1995, Dominique Voynet ran for president of Les Verts and launched a new strategy of alliance with the Socialist Party. In 1997, the Left won the legislative elections, including eight seats (for the first time) in the National Assembly for Les Verts. Voynet was appointed minister of environment and town and county planning in the Socialist government. As part of government, Les Verts succeeded in stopping the Super-Phoenix and Le Carnet nuclear plants (which they had failed to block earlier) and took on an important role in the Kyoto Conference on **climate change**. Les Verts was set back in the 2007 French presidential election, however, when Voynet achieved just 1.57 percent of support in the first round, the party's worst result. *See also* BOVÉ, JOSÉ.

**FREON.** *See* CHLOROFLUOROCARBONS (CFCs).

**FRIENDS OF THE EARTH.** In 1969, **David Brower** founded the environmental **nongovernmental organization** Friends of the Earth after resigning as executive director of the **Sierra Club**. With its headquarters in San Francisco and advocacy staff in Washington, D.C., the organization quickly became influential in the **United States**, during the 1970s leading campaigns against the construction of supersonic transport and for restoration of the Florida Everglades.

In 1972, most of the Washington advocacy staff resigned after disagreements arose over the organization's structure and Brower's style of leadership. They founded the Environmental Policy Center and shortly afterward the Environmental Policy Institute (the two groups formally merged in 1977). Opposed by Brower and the activist wing, in 1985 the board of Friends of the Earth decided to restructure and move its headquarters to Washington, D.C. Bower resigned and moved fully to the Earth Island Institute based in San Francisco (which he had founded in 1982).

In 1989, Friends of the Earth merged with the Oceanic Society and the Environmental Policy Institute, effectively reuniting with the group from the 1972 split. They resolved to pursue global environmental issues. Despite this turmoil, membership in Friends of the Earth went from 7,000 in 1970–1971 to 35,000 in 2002–2003. In 2005, Friends of the Earth expanded again with a merger with the Bluewater Network. The U.S. branch of Friends of the Earth was also instrumental in fostering Friends of the Earth International, now the world's largest network of grassroots organizations with over 70 national organizations, over 5,000 local groups, and about 2 million members and supporters.

# – G –

**GAIA HYPOTHESIS. James Lovelock** developed the Gaia hypothesis in the 1970s, with his 1979 book *Gaia: A New Look at Life on Earth* helping to popularize it. Since then Lovelock and many others (notably, microbiologist Lynn Margulis) have further refined and tested the hypothesis, with some now calling it a theory with predictive power. Today, the idea of Gaia (named after the Greek Earth goddess) continues to challenge many of the assumptions underlying environmental policies and institutions. It understands the earth as a living, self-regulating, and adaptive superorganism. No single organism makes life on earth possible, and no organism, not even humans, can disturb the earth without severe consequences, as Gaia adapts to sustain the whole system.

Many scientists reject the Gaia hypothesis as more fantasy than empirical reality. Many environmentalists also refer to Gaia more as a metaphor than a theory or hypothesis. They talk about the earth as alive to stress the vulnerability and interdependence of life on the planet. They also do so to stress the need for a more holistic and spiritual understanding of the "global environment." In many cultures this more general idea, however, predates Lovelock by at least several centuries. In the late 18th century, for example, the Scottish naturalist James Hutton—a founding figure of modern geology—was writing that the earth was a "living world."

**GANDHI, MOHANDAS KARAMCHAND (MAHATMA) (1869–1948).** Born in **India**, Mahatma Gandhi completed a law degree in England in 1891, before moving to **South Africa** in 1893. He led a nonviolent campaign in South Africa against discrimination against Indians, before returning to India in 1914 where he was a leader in the struggle for Indian independence from the British. He is best known for his method of nonviolent resistance, called Satyagraha or "devotion to truth," which has inspired human rights, civil society, and environmental movements worldwide. A vegetarian, Ghandi was a proponent of simple living in harmony with local conditions, and both his life and writings have inspired many strands of environmental thought. He was assassinated by a Hindu extremist.

**GENETICALLY MODIFIED ORGANISMS (GMOs).** The first genetically modified (GM) plants were grown experimentally in 1988. By 2003, in the **United States**, one-third of all corn and three-quarters of cotton and soybeans were GM crops. In **Canada**, around 70 percent of canola farms now contain genetically modified organisms (GMOs). **Argentina** and **China** also have extensive GM plantations. GM crops are particularly controversial in Europe, and **Japan** also bans several GM crops as well as long-grain rice imports from the United States (which contain GMOs).

Supporters stress the value of engineering crops like corn and cotton to reduce the need for pesticides and herbicides as well as to increase yields to feed the burgeoning global population (now at 6.7 billion and on its way to 9–10 billion by 2050). Critics worry about the long-term consequences of altering nature without a full understanding of how this will affect ecosystems with complex feedbacks (such as pesticide-producing GM crops possibly leading to a new generation of superpests). Some in the environmental movement also question the morality of putting patents on life forms, as well as worry that GMOs will push even more farmers into producing cash crops for export in the developing world. In 2002, several African nations refused to take food aid (corn) from the United States because of a lack of guarantees that it was GMO free. *See also* BOVÉ, JOSÉ; FRANCE; SHIVA, VANDANA; SPAIN; THAILAND.

**GEORGESCU-ROEGEN, NICHOLAS (1906–1994).** A Romanian economist, Nicholas Georgescu-Roegen was a founding thinker in the field of **ecological economics** and thermoeconomics (which applies the principles of thermodynamics to the study of economics). His 1971 book *The Entropy Law and the Economic Process* has been especially influential.

**GEOTHERMAL ENERGY.** Geothermal energy relies on the earth's natural heat to produce power. Humans have always known about this source of energy: from hissing steam vents, erupting geysers, boiling mud pots, and bubbling hot springs. The first attempt to generate electricity from geothermal steam was made in Italy in 1904. Today, it is possible to drill thousands of meters into the earth to release high-pressure steam able to drive large turbine generators.

Normally, economically extractible heat (four kilometers or less) concentrates where hot or molten rocks are at relatively shallow depths. One example of an area with intense thermal activity is the "ring of fire" around the Pacific Ocean.

The world's largest producer of geothermal electricity is the **United States**, followed by the **Philippines** and **Indonesia.** Geothermal energy also plays a significant role in Iceland, where close to half of primary energy is geothermal power. Overall, however, geothermal power generates less than 1 percent of the world's energy.

The environmental movement has tended to support efforts to tap geothermal power as the ecological consequences are much less than alternatives like **coal**, **natural gas**, and **oil**. Typically, a geothermal plant releases only 1–3 percent of the carbon dioxide emissions of a **fossil fuel** plant. Nevertheless, some concerns do exist, such as the impact of the power plants on land stability and surrounding ecosystems.

**GERMANY.** Germany has a long tradition of environmental legislation. One of the first was an 1845 statute regulating industrial processes likely to cause air **pollution** in Prussia. The foundation of the current era was put in place following reforms by Willy Brandt's center-left coalition in 1969. This produced the 1970 Immediate Program for Environmental Action. Most crucially, a 1972 amendment to the Basic Law (the constitutional document) increased the competency of the federal state (called the Bund) over environmental policy. It gave concurrent legislative power in waste management, air pollution control, noise abatement, protection from radiation, and criminal law relating to environmental protection matters. It gave the Länder (the federal units) competence only after the Bund became involved.

The federal Environmental Agency was founded in 1974; still, with the government facing an **oil** crisis and economic recession, environmental policy was not a top political priority from 1974–1978. From 1979–1989, a grassroots environmental movement began to strengthen. The German Green Party was founded in 1979–1980 and was first elected to the Bundestag in 1983. In 1986, the Environmental Agency was subsumed under a more powerful Federal Ministry for the Environment, Nature Conservation and Nuclear Safety. From

1990–1994, however, environmentalism again slid down the list of national priorities as debates over the financing of German reunification took center stage.

Today, Germany's environmental policy rests on three key principles: the **precautionary principle**; the **polluter pays principle**; and the cooperation principle. Of lesser importance are the common burden principle and the international cooperation principle. Although environmental policy is largely federal, the Länder are still highly influential. The Länder are represented in the Bundesrat and can vote on most federal legislation. They retain some competency over environmental policy when the Bund does not become involved. And the Bund depends on the Länder for implementation of most environmental laws (municipalities are also key to implementation). The result is cooperative federalism and joint decision making in developing environmental policy.

Typically, policies favor command-and-control approaches, rather than market instruments, to internalize environmental costs. The style of German environmental policy is highly legalistic, with detailed standard setting. Usually, statutes take the form of "framework legislation," with specific standards set by regulators in the federal bureaucracy and published as ordinances. That said, there is generally significant consultation with stakeholders.

**GLASS.** Glass is made from natural resources such as silica sand, soda ash, and limestone. In theory, it is possible to recycle it indefinitely, as its production does not create significant waste. Some countries in Europe are now **recycling** over 85 percent—and in many countries recycling rates are climbing. Most glass containers, for example, now contain up to 35 percent of postconsumer glass. This uses less energy than quarrying and reduces landfill waste (it takes 1 million years for glass to break down naturally).

But, as some environmentalists stress, recycling glass can involve "downcycling," where each recycling time diminishes the quality as broken glass contaminates the process (often, poorer quality glass becomes filler for construction sites or roads). The solution is to sort glass by color, but this requires a committed public and first-rate collection programs. Some glass is also more difficult to recycle, such as cathode ray tubes (CRTs) in televisions and computer monitors, which contain multiple layers of chemically treated glass. One solution to such complex recycling is for governments to impose **extended producer responsibility** for disposal.

**GLOBAL COMPACT.** The **United Nations** launched the Global Compact in 2000 to encourage corporations to pursue responsible citizenship by aligning operations with 10 "universally accepted principles" for human rights, labor, the environment, and anticorruption. Today, it includes about 5,000 participants, including over 3,700 businesses in at least 120 countries. Participation is purely voluntary, and there is no capacity to monitor or enforce compliance. Once a year, however, the UN expects each member to submit a case study of how they are implementing the principles. Members are also supposed to commit to these principles in their mission statements, newsletters, and annual reports.

Advocates of the Global Compact see it as a way to encourage **corporate social responsibility** and global citizenship. Critics contend it is yet another feel-good measure that helps corporations to **greenwash** business as usual. *See also* PRECAUTIONARY APPROACH/PRINCIPLE; RESPONSIBLE CARE®.

**GLOBAL ENVIRONMENT FACILITY (GEF).** The Global Environment Facility, or GEF, is an international organization involving three implementing agencies: the World Bank, the United Nations Development Programme, and the **United Nations Environment Programme**. It disburses grants and provides technical assistance to cover the additional costs for developing countries of projects with a global environmental goal, such as preventing **climate change**, ozone loss, **persistent organic pollutants**, or **biodiversity** loss. Beginning as a pilot program in 1991, GEF is now one of the world's biggest sources of financing for global environmental projects in the Third World, distributing more than US$7.4 billion in grants and US$28 billion in cofinancing from other sources.

Some **nongovernmental organizations** have been highly critical of GEF's policy of focusing funds on covering the incremental cost of the global reach of projects; others have been unhappy with the significant influence of the World Bank over policy and approaches. Reforms to the governance of GEF, however, have helped to mute criticism and integrate civil society groups into its decision-making structure and projects. *See also* CHINA, PEOPLE'S REPUBLIC OF; VIETNAM.

**GLOBAL REPORTING INITIATIVE (GRI).** Created in 1997, the Global Reporting Initiative (GRI) is a joint venture between the **Coalition for Environmentally Responsible Economies (CERES)** and the **United Nations Environment Programme**. It brings together over 100 organizations, including corporations, **nongovernmental organizations**, consultant organizations, and universities. The objective is to strengthen the comparability and credibility of sustainability reporting by encouraging companies to report on social and environmental performance with the same degree of rigor (including preparing for audits) as with financial performance.

To support this, the GRI has developed specific reporting guidelines for the industry sector. By 2003, 325 companies had relied on the guidelines to issue reports; today, over 1,500 are now using some form of triple-bottom-line accounting (economic, social, and environmental) in line with the guidelines. Such companies include 3M, AT&T, General Motors, Ford, Shell, DuPont, McDonald's, Dow Chemical, Nike, Canon, Electrolux, Ericsson, and France Telecom. This initiative is one of an increasing number in a global movement to promote corporate social and environmental responsibility. *See also* CORPORATE SOCIAL RESPONSIBILITY.

**GLOBAL WARMING.** *See* CLIMATE CHANGE.

**GM CROPS.** *See* GENETICALLY MODIFIED ORGANISMS.

**GOLDMAN ENVIRONMENTAL PRIZE.** Founded in 1990 by Richard and Rhoda Goldman, the Goldman Environmental Prize is now the world's largest prize to honor grassroots environmentalists in Africa, Asia, Europe, Islands and Island Nations, North America, and South and Central America. Six prizes worth US$150,000 each are awarded annually. Recipients include **Wangari Maathai** of **Kenya** (1991), **Ken Saro-Wiwa** of **Nigeria** (1995), Marina Silva of **Brazil** (1996), and Alexander Nikitin of **Russia** (1997).

The 2008 winners were Pablo Fajardo Mendo and Luis Yanza of Ecuador, Marina Rikhvanova of Russia, Ignace Schops of Belgium, Feliciano dos Santos of Mozambique, Jesús León Santos of **Mexico**, and Rosa Hilda Ramos of Puerto Rico. Fajardo and Yanza won for leading a community-based class action lawsuit (possibly the world's largest ever) against the company Texaco for dumping millions of gallons of crude **oil** and billions of gallons of wastewater into the Ecuadorian **Amazon** from 1964 until the end of 1990. Rikhvanova won for leading an environmental movement to protect Lake Baikal in **Siberia**—the oldest and deepest lake in the world, which the **United Nations Educational, Scientific and Cultural Organization (UNESCO)** declared a World Heritage Site in 1996—from construction of an oil pipeline and a uranium enrichment facility. Schops won for his work bringing together industry, governments, **nongovernmental organizations**, and local communities to raise the funds and build a consensus to establish the first and only **national park** in Belgium—the Hoge Kempen National Park, which opened in 2006—a process the **International Union for Conservation of Nature (IUCN)** hopes to use to create more national parks worldwide. Santos won for his use of traditional music, through his band Massukos, to raise environmental awareness and promote innovative solutions to managing water and sanitation in Mozambique (such as using composting toilets able to turn human waste into valuable fertilizer). León won for leading a democratic movement of farmers in the Mixteca region of Oaxaca, Mexico, to adapt traditional Mixteca indigenous practices to restore ecosystems (planting, for example, more than 1 million native trees and building irrigation systems to prevent soil erosion). Ramos won for leading an environmental movement to hold industry responsible for polluting the low-income neighborhood Cataño (within greater San Juan, Puerto Rico), then lobbying the United States Environmental Protection Agency to use the millions of dollars of **pollution** fines to protect the Las Cucharillas Marsh beside Cataño.

**GORE, AL (1948–).** Born in Washington, D.C., Albert Arnold "Al" Gore Jr. was the 45th vice president of the **United States**, serving President Bill Clinton from 1993–2001. After losing the 2000 presidential election to George W. Bush, Gore returned to his earlier work of raising awareness about global environmental problems. In 2007, Gore was awarded the Nobel Peace Prize for his efforts to publicize and solve the problem of **climate change** (he won along with the Intergovernmental Panel on Climate Change). The documentary film *An Inconvenient Truth* (which won two Academy Awards), the accompanying book (which became a bestseller), and a worldwide speaking tour were core to his strategy of raising global consciousness about climate change.

**GREAT BRITAIN.** Great Britain's **green party** (the first in Europe) was founded in 1973 under the name PEOPLE, becoming the Ecology Party in 1975 and the Green Party in 1985. In the 1990s, it split into the Green Party of England and Wales, the Scottish Green Party, and the Green Party in Northern Ireland.

The Department for Environment, Food and Rural Affairs, known as Defra, is the primary government department responsible for environmental management. The Environment Act was passed in 1995, which established the Environment Agency for England and Wales and the Scottish Environment Protection Agency. The current strategy for **sustainable development** for the United Kingdom was launched in 2005. Great Britain is also party to numerous international environmental treaties, including the **Kyoto Protocol**, which it ratified in 2002. It has now met its Kyoto Protocol target of reducing emissions by 12.5 percent from 1990 levels and is currently aiming for a domestic goal of a 20 percent reduction by 2010.

Great Britain has a long history of environmentalism. Early conservation efforts included a network of nature reserves initiated in 1912 through the Society for the Promotion of Nature Reserves. This organization became the Society for the Promotion of Nature Conservation in 1976, the Royal Society for Nature Conservation in 1981, and the Royal Society of Wildlife Trusts in 2004. The oldest conservation organization, the Open Spaces Society, was founded in 1865. Many others have formed since then. A few examples include the **World Wide Fund for Nature (WWF)**-UK in 1961 (the first national organization in the WWF network); WaterAid in 1981 (an international **nongovernmental organization** focused on water and sanitation); and **Reclaim the Streets** in 1991. Two significant environmental issues in Great Britain are **genetically modified organisms** and pesticides, with strong consumer support for strict regulations on both. In 1997, the Genetic Engineering Network was established. In 2002, coordination of the Pesticide Action Network Europe was transferred to London from **Germany**.

**GREAT PACIFIC GARBAGE PATCH.** *See* EASTERN GARBAGE PATCH.

**GREEN ARCHITECTURE.** Green architecture is also called sustainable architecture or green building. Broadly, it aims to use fewer natural resources and energy and build into, rather than on top of, nature. Thus, architects need to see structures as part of an ecosystem rather than as isolated units. Such ideas have a long history but did not begin to gain ground until the 1970s, partly as the **oil** crisis in the early 1970s spurred interest in improving energy efficiency. Publications, such as the journal *Architectural Design*, began to track and promote green designs, such as using traditional or recycled materials and designing ecologically sound buildings. Today, green architects work to improve the efficiency of heating, water circulation, ventilation, and power. Other aspects include sustainable use of resources and long-term planning to allow buildings to adapt to new uses. One example of a certification program to promote sustainable architecture is LEED (Leadership in Energy and Environmental Design). *See also* TAIWAN.

**GREEN BELT MOVEMENT. Wangari Maathai** founded this women's civil society organization in 1977 to reverse **deforestation** in **Kenya**, which was causing soil erosion and water shortages as well as creating a shortage of wood, a primary source of energy for 90 percent of rural villagers and low-income city residents. The movement relies on women to plant tree seedlings in both rural and urban green belts. It depends on donations to purchase seedlings and compensate workers (who receive a small amount of money for each tree that survives).

So far the Green Belt Movement in Kenya has planted more than 30 million trees. This tree-planting also provides opportunities for the movement to advocate for good governance, environmental stewardship, peaceful democratic change, and the protection of human rights. "The planting of trees is the planting of ideas," explains Maathai. "By starting with the simple act of planting a tree, we give hope to ourselves and to future generations."

The Green Belt Movement has inspired similar movements in at least a dozen other countries. Maathai won the 2004 Nobel Peace Prize, an honor enthusiastically applauded by those who believe grassroots environmentalism is an effective way to promote world peace. *See also* ECOFEMINISM; NONGOVERNMENTAL ORGANIZATIONS (NGOs); REFORESTATION.

**GREENHOUSE GASES.** Greenhouse gases in the atmosphere, such as carbon dioxide, methane, and nitrous oxides, keep the earth warm by trapping heat. These gases are necessary to sustain life; more, however, is not better as the trapped heat can cause a warming of the planet's surface. Using a vivid metaphor, some compare the process to rolling up a car window on a hot day. Greenhouse gases occur both naturally and as a result of human activity. The amounts of human-induced greenhouse gases have been rising steadily over the last three decades. For example, global output of carbon dioxide from just consuming fossil fuels now exceeds 27 billion metric tons a year, up from 18 billion in 1980. Over the last decade the emphasis of much of global environmentalism has been shifting toward addressing ways to slow or halt the amounts of greenhouse gases drifting into the atmosphere. The most significant international agreement to address the main greenhouse gas—carbon dioxide—is the **Kyoto Protocol to the United Nations Framework Convention on Climate Change**. *See also* AUTOMOBILES; BIOFUELS; CARBON TAX; CITIES FOR CLIMATE PROTECTION (CCP); CLIMATE CHANGE; COAL; DEFORESTATION; EMISSIONS TRADING; FARMED MEAT; INDONESIA; NATURAL GAS; PEAK OIL; SIBERIAN PERMAFROST.

**GREEN PARTY.** Using the word *green* to describe a political party dates to 1978 when a group of environmentalists listed their candidates under a "Green List" in German local elections. Many analysts, however, see the United Tasmania Group in **Australia** (1972) as the world's first green party and the PEOPLE/Ecology Party in **Great Britain** (1973) as the first green party of Europe (even though initially these parties did not use the word *green* for the name of the party). Definitions and emphases vary across countries and time, but generally green parties tend to support a platform around environmental sustainability, social justice, participatory/grassroots democracy, nonviolence, opposition to nuclear technology, and local communities and economies.

The German Green Party was officially formed in 1979–1980; in 1983, with a list of members that included **Petra Kelly,** it became the first new party to enter the German Parliament in 60 years. Over the next decade the German Greens slowly consolidated (with some setbacks, such as the 1990 elections) and by the 1990s were represented in most provincial parliaments. Green parties have also emerged in many other countries and have entered parliament in countries like Belgium, Italy, and **Sweden**. Compared to these places, however, the political victories and influence over public policy of the German Greens put them in a different category. In contrast, the Green Party of the **United States** has had little political success or influence, which is sometimes attributed to the presence of energetic apolitical environmental organizations, the two-party system, the political culture, and lack of a system of proportional representation, as in **Germany**. *See also* BRAZIL; CANADA; FINLAND; FRANCE; RUSSIA; SPAIN.

**GREENPEACE.** The first recorded use of the name Greenpeace was in the *Vancouver Sun* on 15 February 1970, describing plans of the Don't Make a Wave Committee to sail the vessel *Greenpeace* to Amchitka, Alaska, to stop a nuclear test by the **United States**. Before long, it was one of the best-known environmental activist groups, generating worldwide publicity for its campaigns to halt nuclear testing, **whaling**, and **sealing** off the east coast of **Canada**. Groups with the same name began to spring up around the world, and Greenpeace International was officially founded in 1979 from a half-dozen loosely connected groups.

Today, Greenpeace has more than 2.8 million members in more than 40 countries. Greenpeace does not accept corporate, government, or political party funds and fundraising continues to rely on individual donations. It engages in nonviolent civil disobedience and confrontation, research, treaty negotiation participation, market pressure, clean alternative development, public education, and engagement with legislatures. Four main goals currently define Greenpeace: protect **biodi-**

**versity**; prevent land, air, and water **pollution**; end nuclear threats; and promote peace, disarmament, and nonviolence. The focus of current campaigns include halting **climate change**, protecting old-growth forests, stopping the whale hunt, encouraging sustainable trade, and eliminating toxic chemicals. *See also* BRENT SPAR; ECOTERRORISM; GREENWASH; HUNTER, ROBERT "BOB"; NONGOVERNMENTAL ORGANIZATIONS (NGOs); *RAINBOW WARRIOR*.

**GREEN REVOLUTION.** The phrase *Green Revolution*—reportedly coined by William Gaud (a former director of the **United States** Agency for International Development) in a 1968 speech—describes the changes after World War II to increase agricultural output with high-yield seeds, fertilizers, pesticides, irrigation, and advanced machinery. The result was a substantial increase in the output of crops such as wheat, maize, and rice in developing countries like **Mexico**, **India**, and the **Philippines**. Supporters see this as evidence of the power of human ingenuity and technological innovation to overcome food shortages even when populations are growing quickly. For some, too, it confirms the tendency of environmentalism to exaggerate problems: such as the principle, first put forth by **Thomas Malthus** in a 1798 essay, that mass starvation must one day ensue because population, left unchecked, will increase exponentially while food production can only increase arithmetically.

Critics of the Green Revolution counter by pointing to the impact of irrigation systems on declining freshwater supplies, the **pollution** from fertilizers and pesticides, and the loss of **biodiversity** due to the planting of millions of hectares of monocultures. Some environmentalists, too, stress how the shift to industrial agriculture tends to favor plantation owners and multinational corporations while turning subsistence farmers into low-paid laborers with a less nutritional diet and less satisfying work.

**GREEN TAXES.** *See* CARBON TAX.

**GREENWASH.** The term *greenwash*, which combines the words *green* and *whitewash*, refers to the efforts of corporations to portray more responsible environmental images when in fact practices remain business as usual. Corporate efforts to improve environmental images took off in the late 1980s and early 1990s with the rise in environmental awareness among governments and consumers. More and more firms began to adopt voluntary green codes of conduct, pursue more environmentally benign production methods (**eco-efficiency**), and stress environmental concern in their advertising and public relations. The term *greenwash* gained currency shortly before the 1992 **United Nations Conference on Environment and Development** when **Greenpeace** published *The Greenpeace Book of Greenwash*.

Today, **nongovernmental organization** activists critical of corporate "green talk" are most likely to use this term as a pejorative way of suggesting firms are trying to fool consumers and "hijack" environmentalism for the pursuit of profits or competitive advantage. The nongovernmental organization CorpWatch, for example, gives bimonthly "Greenwash Awards" to offending companies.

**GUERRILLA GARDENING.** Guerrilla gardening is a diffuse movement where people illegally plant seeds or seedlings in urban spaces, such as on vacant lots, back alleys, traffic medians, and commercial land. The majority of guerrilla gardeners are in Europe, especially in **Great Britain**. Many portray guerilla gardening as a revolution or a war, taking action in secret and at night, using language like "troop digs" and "peace talks." The movement, however, calls for nonviolent direct action for inner-city renewal rather than violent uprisings; some members are also now working openly with locals. Most guerrilla gardeners are pursuing both symbolic and practical goals. They target industrialization, commercialization of nature, capitalist food production, unequal land ownership, and the disappearance of public green spaces. And they see it as a way to preserve **biodiversity**, engage in hands-on change, and reconnect to nature through personal stewardship of public space. An example of a major event was May Day (1 May) 2000, when the grassroots group **Reclaim the Streets** organized hundreds of guerrilla gardeners to dig up London's Parliament Square and plant flowers and vegetables.

The phrase *guerrilla gardening* goes back to the 1970s, although the movement only gained significant numbers of followers in the last two decades. In many places the practice has a long history, however, with people without land planting food for sustenance on another person's property. Today, guerrilla farming for sustenance still continues in many developing countries.

## – H –

**HAECKEL, ERNST (1834–1919).** Holding doctorates in medicine and zoology, the German Ernst Haeckel coined the terms *Darwinism* and *ecology* (along with many other terms). Haeckel was highly influential in his time, his works in support of Darwinism outselling Darwin's original *On the Origin of Species*. He also helped to establish the field of oceanography, consulting on the first noncommercial exploration of the deep sea, the Challenger Expedition of 1873–1876. Later, Haeckel's scientific reputation would suffer when he admitted falsifying data, but his reputation in the art world remained strong as a result of his work of naturalist illustration, *Art Forms in Nature*. One of his many quotes, "politics is applied biology," would also become notorious in Nazi propaganda.

**HARDIN, GARRETT JAMES (1915–2003).** Hardin authored "The **Tragedy of the Commons**" (*Science*, 1968), one of the most cited academic articles of all time. Born in Dallas, Texas, he obtained his Ph.D. in microbiology from Stanford University in 1941. He was professor of human ecology at the University of California, Santa Barbara, until retiring in 1978. He remained active in academic life, however, for another two decades, authoring 27 books and over 350 articles during his career.

A central figure in the field of human ecology, Hardin focused much of his research on human overpopulation and degradation of ecosystems. His publications included the controversial "Living on a Lifeboat" (in *BioScience* in 1974), which uses the metaphor of a lifeboat to argue that for humanity to survive it is the ethical duty of the people in stable and wealthy countries to let the poor of the world fend for themselves, otherwise everyone will drown because of insufficient space (**carrying capacity**) in the lifeboats (wealthy states).

Hardin's views were contentious throughout his long career. In 1997, he wrote an open letter to the American Civil Liberties Union arguing that, because of the ecological cost to society, having children should not be an individual right (even though he had four children). He was also a member of the Hemlock Society for the right to assisted suicide. His spouse, Jane, suffered from Lou Gehrig's disease, and shortly after their 62nd wedding anniversary, they committed suicide together.

**HAZARDOUS WASTE.** Hazardous waste includes toxic chemicals, infectious waste, and radioactive material. Characteristics include ignitability, corrosivity, reactivity, and toxicity. Developed countries are the biggest producers of hazardous waste. As a global issue, managing hazardous waste took on greater urgency in the 1980s as First World states began exporting increasing amounts to the Third World. Large numbers of **nongovernmental organizations**, including ones like **Greenpeace**, as well as many states began to call for a ban (or at least clear restrictions) on trade in hazardous waste. An international treaty—called the **Basel Convention**—was negotiated in 1989 and entered into force in 1992 to better control the movement and disposal of hazardous waste across borders. Partly as a result, by the mid-1990s the export of toxic waste to the Third World was declining.

Today, a growing issue is electronic waste, or e-waste. The amount of e-waste is increasing at a rate of 3–5 percent a year, almost three times faster than municipal waste. In many places it is now equal to roughly the amount of **plastic** packaging waste—or about 5 percent of total municipal solid waste. Much of the e-waste from North America is being exported to Asia. *See also* NUCLEAR POWER/ENERGY.

**HOLLING, C. S. "BUZZ" (1930–).** Crawford "Buzz" Holling, received his B.A. and M.Sc. from the University of Toronto in 1952 and his Ph.D. from the University of British Columbia in 1957. Currently, he is Emeritus Eminent Scholar and Professor in Ecological Sciences at the University of Florida after a career that saw him contribute to modern predator-prey theory, **panarchy** theory, and the resilience of nonlinear ecological systems. Holling also initiated the Resilience Alliance, a semiformal global group designed to share environmental knowledge and maintain links between theory, empirical reality, and policy institutions. He was the founding editor in chief (until 2001) of the online open-access journal *Conservation Ecology*, now called *Ecology and Society*.

**HUNTER, ROBERT "BOB" (1941–2005).** Born in **Canada**, journalist Bob Hunter was a cofounder of **Greenpeace**, serving as president of the Greenpeace Foundation from 1973–1977. *Time* magazine chose him as one of the top-ten "eco-heroes" of the 20th century. A writer with a flair for original prose, Hunter is widely credited with coining the terms *eco-warrior*, *mindbombs*, and *rainbow warriors*.

**HYBRID AUTOMOBILES.** In 1881, Gustave Trouvé of **France** built a three-wheel electric automobile able to travel at about 12 kilometers per hour. In 1899, an electric vehicle set the world speed record. By 1900, the market for **automobiles** was almost equally divided between steam, electricity, and gasoline; however, 1900 to 1912 became the golden age of electric vehicles, which were quieter and easier to start than automobiles with a handcrank. The first mass production of a hybrid car, combining electric and gasoline propulsion systems, was the "Woods Gasoline-Electric" in 1916.

By the early 1920s, however, electric vehicles virtually disappeared as automobiles powered by a gasoline engine began to take over markets. Interest in electric cars reappeared in the 1960s as air **pollution** worsened in many industrialized cities. General Motors, for example, built an experimental hybrid car in 1969.

Mass production of hybrids, however, did not begin until 1997 with the launch of Toyota Prius. Ten years later all of the major automakers were investing in hybrids, with these vehicles now comprising a small but increasing share of the global market. Many environmentalists support hybrid automobiles as a small step toward more **sustainable development**, although few would see this as a long-term solution for addressing the global environmental impact of the more than 800 million automobiles and commercial vehicles now on the world's roads. *See also* RENEWABLE ENERGY.

**HYDROELECTRICITY.** *See* RENEWABLE ENERGY.

– I –

**ICLEI: LOCAL GOVERNMENTS FOR SUSTAINABILITY.** ICLEI is an international association of local governments (as well as national and regional local government associations) committed to **sustainable development**. Its membership includes more than 800 cities, towns, counties, and associations. A World Secretariat oversees the ICLEI (hosted by the City of Toronto since 1991). The organization has grown from 2 offices in 1991 to 16 today.

The idea to create an international network to coordinate local responses to global environmental management came from a 1989 meeting of 35 local governments from **Canada** and the **United**

**States** to discuss **ozone depletion**. With support from the International Union of Local Authorities and the **United Nations Environment Programme**, ICLEI was founded as the International Council of Local Environmental Initiatives in 1990. The name was changed in 2003 to ICLEI: Local Governments for Sustainability to better reflect current environmental problems. At the same time, the organization shifted its mandate, mission, and charter to focus on sustainability. One of its important campaigns is **Cities for Climate Protection**.

**ILLEGAL LOGGING.** Examples of illegal activities in the forest industry range from timber smuggling, to logging protected species, to logging in nature reserves. Regions with widespread illegal logging include the **Amazon** Basin, Central Africa, Southeast Asia, and **Russia**. Estimates of the extent of illegal logging are difficult to confirm: still, in some cases, as in **Indonesia**, many analysts now agree it comprises well over half of total timber production.

Poor villagers are often blamed for illegal logging, but just as often, national or multinational forest companies either pay locals a wage or agree in advance to buy the lumber. Also, in some cases these same firms are bribing government and military officers. Illegal logging can generate income for *some* local people; however, this involves many costs, including lost income from forest products, lost job opportunities, less government revenue, threats to physical security, loss of access to forest resources, forest degradation, corruption, and lack of respect for laws.

The **United Nations Convention on International Trade in Endangered Species of Wild Fauna and Flora** is one of the international legal instruments intended to prevent illegal trade in timber. Another important international legal instrument is the **Convention on Biological Diversity**. Also important is the International Tropical Timber Organization (established in 1986). Voluntary certification under the **Forest Stewardship Council** is yet another mechanism to try to rid the global market of illegal lumber.

The collective goal of these institutions and agreements is to ensure that all of the tropical timber in international trade is from sustainably managed forests; however, critics argue these global efforts are failing to meet this aim. Some critics go further and see this international system as encasing a vast network of illegal loggers, many working openly, in legitimacy. *See also* DEFORESTATION.

**INDEX OF SUSTAINABLE ECONOMIC WELFARE (ISEW).** Ecological economists **Herman Daly** and John Cobb created this index for the **United States** in 1989. It builds on Manfred Max-Neef's "threshold hypothesis"—that costs exceed benefits when macroeconomic systems expand beyond a certain threshold. Since then researchers have applied the Index of Sustainable Economic Welfare (ISEW) to many other countries. It is designed to provide a more comprehensive indicator of economic welfare than standard national accounting systems, such as gross national product (GNP) and gross domestic product (GDP). Although the formula varies slightly, generally it is computed as follows: ISEW = personal consumption weighted by income inequality + domestic labor + nondefense-related public expenditure – defense-related private expenditure – the difference between expenditure on consumer durables and service flow from consumer durables – costs of environmental degradation – depreciation of natural resources + capital adjustments.

Advocates also see ISEW as a way to demonstrate that continued growth is unsustainable. Other related measures include the Genuine Progress Indicator, the Sustainable Net Benefit Index, the Gross National Happiness, the Happy Planet Index, and the widely used Human Development Index of the United Nations Development Programme.

**INDIA. Mohandas Gandhi** was an influential thinker and activist in the emergence of the modern environmental movement in India. In his first book, *Hind Swaraj* (Indian Home Rule), published in 1909, Ghandi rejected industrialization as the way forward for India. This reflected his "back-to-the-land" ethos, offering an alternative: minimizing consumption, reusing materials, and relying on agricultural villages. His legacy inspired many local environmental movements in India, including the Narmada Bachao Andolan (Save the Narmada Movement), led by Medha Patkar with the aim of stopping construction of the Sardar Sarovar dam, one of the dams in the **Narmada Dam** project; the **Chipko Movement**, begun in 1973 when villagers in a Himalayan village began hugging local hornbeam trees to halt logging; and the Appiko Movement, begun in 1983 in the tradition of the Chipko Movement, with villagers in southern India struggling to save their forests (*appiko* is the local term for hugging).

India has a long history of grassroots and community environmentalism and activism. More formal environmental organizations are also now common. A few examples include the Indian Environmental Society, a **nongovernmental organization** founded in 1972 with a focus on education, policy, and environmental and resource management (together with the Ministry of Environment and Forests, the Indian Environmental Society set up the National Green Corps in 2001 to promote environmental awareness among children); TERI, the Energy and Resources Institute set up in 1974 to advance research and development; the Centre for Science and Environment (CSE), which Anil Agarwal founded in 1980 to promote knowledge-based activism; and Navdanya, started in 1991 by **Vandana Shiva** to counter corporate control of agricultural and genetic resources (especially by the multinational company Monsanto).

The Indian government's five-year economic plans have increasingly taken environmental concerns into consideration. The Fourth Plan (1969–1970 to 1973–1974) was the first with an **environmental impact assessment**; the Sixth Plan (1980–1985) included an entire chapter on environment and development. This did not, however, prevent India from experiencing one of the world's worst environmental disasters, the 1984 **Bhopal gas leak**, where toxic gas at a pesticide plant run by Union Carbide India (a subsidiary of Union Carbide in the **United States**) killed thousands of people.

Today, the Ministry of Environment and Forests (MOEF) is the key bureaucratic actor, having succeeded the National Committee on Environmental Planning (NCEP), which was set up in the 1970s. Important environmental legislation includes the Forest Conservation Act of 1980 (amended by Act 89 of 1988); the Water (Prevention and Control of Pollution) Act of 1974; the Air (Prevention and Control of Pollution) Act of 1981, subsequently amended in 1987; the Environment (Protection) Act of 1986; and the National Environment Tribunal Act of 1992.

**INDONESIA.** An archipelago of some 17,000 islands, Indonesia, with the world's largest system of **coral reefs** and sweeping rainforests, is home to about 17 percent of the world's plant and animal species. The economy depends in large part on natural resources, especially agriculture, forestry, **mining, oil**, and **natural gas**. In recent years it has also been expanding its production of **biofuels**, from both bioethanol (e.g., sugar and cassava) and biodiesel (e.g., crude palm oil and *Jatropha curcas*). The country has hydroelectric potential, but this is largely undeveloped.

**Deforestation** and air quality are two of its biggest environmental problems. Indonesia is one of the world's largest emitters of **greenhouse gases**, in part because of massive and regular forest fires, high rates of deforestation, and rising consumption of fossil fuels. From 1995 to 2001, for example, the number of **automobiles** and commercial vehicles almost doubled. The government has put in place some regulatory programs to combat **pollution**, including the Blue Sky Program, an air quality program established in 1992. However, in 2002, then president Megawati Sukarnoputri transferred environmental responsibilities to the Office of the State Minister for the Environment and disbanded the Environmental Impact Control Agency, but did not establish legal enforcement powers, resulting in weak regulatory institutions.

Moreover, the currency and economic crash from the 1997–1998 Asian financial crisis was a significant setback for environmentalism, as the government put aside regulations on industry to promote economic recovery, as natural resource and agricultural exports soared to earn foreign exchange, and as enforcement of environmental laws slipped as officers looked for ways to earn a decent living. During the financial crisis, Indonesia was also battling extensive forest fires and severe droughts.

The fall of President Suharto's dictatorship in 1998 did little to improve environmental management. In the case of forestry, Suharto's legacy of unsustainable logging, distribution of timber concessions to reward allies and appease opponents, and dismal enforcement and widespread corruption left the sector in ruins. If anything, deforestation rates are even worse today (now around 2 million hectares a year), with **illegal logging** and timber smuggling rampant as villagers demand a share of the profits and as logging companies exploit broken monitoring and enforcement systems. Some progress has been made to improve forest management, including new laws (that at least on paper are better). Various regional efforts have also been put in place to improve forest management, such as the World Bank's East Asia and Pacific Forest Law Enforcement and Governance initiative, started in 2001 at the East Asia Ministerial Conference in Bali, and the 2002 ASEAN Agreement on Transboundary Haze Pollution (in force from 2003).

Indonesia also participates in many international environmental initiatives. It ratified the **Kyoto Protocol** in 2004 (signed in 1998) and hosted the 2007 United Nations Framework Convention on Climate Change Conference (UNFCCC COP13) in Bali. Initially focused on supporting Clean Development Mechanism (CDM) projects under the Kyoto Protocol, Indonesia recently shifted to supporting projects to promote Reduced Emissions through Avoided Deforestation and Degradation (REDD). These are also supported by **Australia** through its Global Initiative on Forests and Climate and its Kalimantan Forests and Climate Partnership. Indonesia is also part of a planned World Bank pilot project for a Forest Carbon Partnership Facility.

Indonesia's nongovernmental sector has been growing and strengthening since the fall of President Suharto. Founded in 1980, the Indonesian Forum for Environment (WALHI, or the Wahana Lingkungan Hidup Indonesia) did function during Suharto's reign, as a network of **nongovernmental organizations** and community-based associations and also as a member of **Friends of the Earth** International. The fall of Suharto, however, has allowed WALHI more scope to criticize government policies and influence civil society. Today, WALHI has over 400 member organizations. *See also* INDONESIAN FOREST FIRES, 1997–1998.

**INDONESIAN FOREST FIRES, 1997–1998.** Fires on the outer islands of **Indonesia** during 1997–1998 burned as much as 10 million hectares of forests and peat moss, covering Indonesia, Malaysia, and **Singapore** in a smoky haze. Environmentally, this was one of the worst fires in recent history. Over that time, these fires accounted for over one-fifth of the world's carbon dioxide emissions. They did irreparable damage to **biodiversity** and ecological integrity in the region and caused health problems for millions of people. As well, these fires revealed to a global audience the dangers of destructive logging and land clearing in tropical countries. Firms intentionally lit many of the fires to clear land for palm oil plantations (using fires is cheap and fertilizes the soil). Much of the forestland that burned was previously logged and degraded, leaving it dry, littered with debris, and susceptible to so-called controlled fires getting out of control. *See also* DEFORESTATION.

**INDUSTRY SELF-REGULATION.** Industry self-regulation is an alternative to direct governmental command-and-control regulation. It can involve government on a continuum from voluntary self-regulation to mandatory self-regulation. Two basic strategies tend to shape corporate strategies to self-regulate: the first emphasizes internal regulation, auditing, and control; the second emphasizes obligations arising from a set of corporate values, sometimes called a corporate code of conduct, developed after consulting with stakeholders. Critics argue that self-regulation allows industry to appear to be regulating environmental matters without taking any meaningful action. Moreover, some critics add, it allows some firms a free ride while allowing others too much influence over regulations. Supporters see this as a highly efficient and effective way to bring corporations into environmentalism. An example of industry self-regulation is **Responsible Care®** in the chemical industry. *See also* CORPORATE SOCIAL RESPONSIBILITY (CSR).

**INTERGOVERNMENTAL PANEL ON CLIMATE CHANGE (IPCC).** *See* CLIMATE CHANGE.

**INTERNATIONAL CENTER FOR ENVIRONMENT AND DEVELOPMENT (ICED).** *See* TOLBA, MOSTAFA KAMAL.

**INTERNATIONAL CONVENTION FOR THE REGULATION OF WHALING.** Signed in 1946, the Whaling Convention, based upon the principles of an earlier agreement in 1937, was set up to manage the **whaling** industry through conservation of stocks. Fifteen countries signed the 1946 convention; today, there are 80 signatory states to the convention (since its inception, seven countries have withdrawn from the convention).

The convention also set up the International Whaling Commission (IWC) of which membership requires formal acceptance of the 1946 convention. The convention requires the IWC to base decisions on scientific advice. The Schedule to the Convention governs how signatory states can conduct whaling. It specifies allowable catches, seasons, and limits (regulating whales by species, size, breeding status, and age), and also establishes sanctuaries and boundaries. The schedule requires, among other things, states to report whale catches.

**INTERNATIONAL INSTITUTE FOR ENVIRONMENT AND DEVELOPMENT (IIED).** Founded in 1971, the International Institute for Environment and Development, or IIED, is an international policy research institute and **nongovernmental organization** based in London. Its work focuses on sustainable and equitable global development. Earthscan Publishing was originally under its auspices and it published the *World Resources Report*. It was also an originator of the Participatory Rural Appraisal (PRA) method of development. Starting in 1973, IIED was led by **Barbara Ward**; during her tenure (until her death in 1981), the organization grew rapidly. After her death, IIED turned its smaller office in the **United States** into the **World Resources Institute**, which took over the publication of the *World Resources Report*. Today, the organization remains active in promoting **sustainable development**, striving in particular to support vulnerable groups in the development process.

**INTERNATIONAL INSTITUTE FOR SUSTAINABLE DEVELOPMENT (IISD).** Established in 1990, the International Institute for Sustainable Development, or IISD, is a nonprofit international policy research organization based in Winnipeg, **Canada**, to support **sustainable development** globally. It arose out of Canada's response to the 1987 **World Commission on Environment and Development**. It is funded by the Canadian International Development Agency, the International Development Research Centre, Environment Canada, and the government of Manitoba. It also receives funding from international sources (including **United Nations** agencies) as well as governmental project funding. Today, it has a team of about 150 people working in some 30 different countries. It focuses in particular on supporting transparent and effective international negotiations. It publishes the *Earth Negotiations Bulletin* (ENB), which provides independent reporting on international environmental negotiations (partly relying on Ph.D. candidates, thus supporting new and more-informed research on international environmental law and politics).

**INTERNATIONAL ORGANIZATION FOR STANDARDIZA-TION (ISO) 14000, 14001, AND 26000.** The International Organization for Standardization (ISO), with a central secretariat in Geneva, is the world's largest developer of international standards. These include technical ones for manufacturing as well as ones for environmental management. The ISO is a **nongovernmental organization** without legal power to enforce the implementation of standards. Instead, it develops standards through consensus and voluntary participation among member countries (numbering over 155). Today, it is one of the biggest global voluntary initiatives involving industry, with the **World Trade Organization** officially recognizing ISO standards and labels.

ISO 14000 is a series of voluntary environmental standards. These include ones for auditing, performance, labeling, and, most significantly, the ISO 14001 Environmental Management System (EMS) Standard. This standard is the only one to allow for certification from an external authority. To be eligible, a community or organization must comply with the local environmental laws where they operate. Also, they must implement practices and procedures for a system of environmental management: one with a policy to minimize harm, prevent **pollution**, and continually improve environmental performance.

The ISO is establishing ISO 26000 as a voluntary "guidance standard" for social responsibility. It will be published in 2010 and will be consistent with the ISO 14001 Environmental Management System Standard. Unlike ISO 14001, the ISO 26000 will not include requirements and will thus not be a certification scheme.

**INTERNATIONAL SOCIETY FOR ECOLOGICAL ECONOMICS (ISEE).** Founded in 1989, the the International Society for Ecological Economics (ISEE) is a nonprofit, **nongovernmental organization** dedicated to advancing the understanding of the field of **ecological economics**. It assists members and societies by publishing a journal and books as well as holding meetings and coordinating common interests. The first president was **Robert Costanza**; Peter May was the president in 2008–2009.

**INTERNATIONAL UNION FOR CONSERVATION OF NATURE (IUCN).** Established through the **United Nations Educational, Scientific and Cultural Organization (UNESCO)** in 1948 as the International Union for the Protection of Nature, the organization was renamed the International Union for Conservation of Nature and Natural Resources in 1956. It was referred to as the World Conservation Union from 1990–2008, but now goes by the name International Union for Conservation of Nature (IUCN). In response to early criticism of its First World image, the International Union for Conservation of Nature began to conceive conservation in relation to the needs of the developing world, articulating in 1980 a World Conservation Strategy that put it at the forefront of the **sustainable development** movement.

Today, it is the world's largest and oldest conservation network. Headquartered in Gland, Switzerland, IUCN has over 1,100 staff in 62 offices worldwide. Its members include over 1,000 governmental and **nongovernmental organizations** (including corporations and communities) and more than 10,000 volunteer experts. Its mission is to promote conservation, **biodiversity**, and sustainable resource use through scientific research, education, field projects, political dialogue, and practical solutions for improving development and environmental management. IUCN has six commissions: **ecosystem management**; education and communication; environmental, economic, and social policy; environmental law; protected areas; and species survival. To date, it has assisted over 75 countries to implement national strategies for conservation and biodiversity. *See also* SOUTH AFRICA; WORLD WIDE FUND FOR NATURE/WORLD WILDLIFE FUND (WWF).

**INTERNATIONAL WHALING COMMISSION (IWC).** *See* WHALING.

**INVESTOR NETWORK ON CLIMATE RISK (INCR).** *See* COALITION FOR ENVIRONMENTALLY RESPONSIBLE ECONOMIES (CERES).

**IRAN.** Politics and natural resources are closely linked in Iran, which still has large undeveloped reserves of **oil** and **natural gas**. In 1951,

Iran nationalized oil, a decision that strained relations with **Great Britain** and the **United States**, and may have contributed to the coup in 1953. The 1980–1988 Iran-Iraq war, following the Islamic/Iranian revolution of 1978, was in part a struggle over control of the oil fields.

The Supreme Council for the Protection of Environment, initially created as the Iranian Wildlife Association in 1956, oversees environmental legislation in Iran. Passed in 1972, the Environment Protection and Enhancement Act was amended in 1992. With support from the United Nations Development Programme, Iran also developed the Strategic Environmental Assessment and Environmental Impact Assessment programs. The Iranian government also manages a significant conservation program, and, as of 2003, the government had protected more than 11 million hectares of land, including 16 **national parks**.

The current government sees reducing urban air **pollution**, especially in the capital Tehran, as a high priority. As a first step, in 1983 traffic was restricted in the city center. Subsequent actions have included dedicated bus lanes, converting vehicles to compressed natural gas and liquefied petroleum gas, and conducting a 1995–1997 study for an Integrated Master Plan for Air Pollution Control (funded by **Japan**).

In 1998, the Department of the Environment created the Participation Bureau to provide legal and logistical assistance to **nongovernmental organizations (NGOs)**. Over 460 environmental NGOs, according to the bureau, were created from 1998 to 2003.

**ISRAEL.** To restrict the hunting of wildlife, Israel passed the Wildlife Protection Law in 1955, which later became the mechanism for meeting commitments under the **Convention on the International Trade in Endangered Species**. Israel passed its first laws for **national parks** and protected areas in 1963, updating these in 1992, 1998, and 2005. The government also created the Nature and Parks Protection Authority in 1998, and, as of 2002, it was responsible for 186 national parks and reserves. The Coastline Protection Law went into force in 2004, marking the first national framework to protect the coast.

In 1973, the government established the Environmental Protection Service to consolidate responsibility for environmental management and in 1988 created the Ministry of the Environment, which became the Ministry of Environmental Protection in 2006. A Greening Government initiative was started in 2001 to decrease waste in government offices.

In 1990, the **nongovernmental organization** Israel Union for Environmental Defense was founded to strengthen environmental legislation in Israel. Today, the government is aiming to increase the waste **recycling** and recovery rate to 50 percent by 2010. The framework for recycling was established through the 1993 Collection and Disposal of Waste for Recycling Law and developed through further legislation, including the 2001 Bottles and Beverage Container Deposit Law and a 2007 law for recycling vehicle **tires**. In 2007, an explosion at the Makhteshim Agan chemical plant in Ramat Hovav, an industrial zone and **hazardous waste** disposal site, sparked concerns over hazardous materials in the area.

A country with few energy sources, Israel is focused on researching and developing **solar energy**. Water resources are also scarce in Israel, motivating efforts to develop desalination and wastewater recycling technology. Management of freshwater is also linked to peace processes in Israel. In 1992, the Multilateral Working Group on Water Resources was created to advance the Middle East peace process. A 1994 Treaty of Peace with Jordan included water transfer quotas by Israel to Jordan, from the Yarmouk and Jordan Rivers and from the Sea of Galilee. The 1995 Agreement on Cooperation in Environmental Protection and Nature Conservation between Israel and Jordan (Environmental Agreement) also included water-sharing arrangements for the Jordan River.

**IUCN.** *See* INTERNATIONAL UNION FOR CONSERVATION OF NATURE (IUCN).

**IVORY TRADE.** The term *ivory* usually refers to elephant tusks but can also refer to the teeth and tusks of other animals (including hippopotamus, walruses, warthogs, and whales). Ivory has a long history of use for carvings, jewelry, art, trophies, musical instruments, and signature seals. By the 1970s, elephant populations were at risk from overhunting and poaching for ivory, especially in places where hunters were using automatic weapons. In 1976, the **Convention on International Trade in Endangered Species of Wild Fauna and**

**Flora (CITES)** listed Asian elephants in Appendix I (species threatened with extinction), which bans international trade for commercial purposes. Throughout the 1980s, the much larger population of African elephants continued to decline, with legal hunters and poachers killing hundreds of thousands for the ivory trade. In 1989, CITES added African elephants to Appendix I (effective January 1990). Partly in response to the now full ban on international trade in elephant ivory, trade in hippo ivory increased, and in 1995 CITES listed the common hippopotamus in Appendix II (species at risk of extinction unless trade is controlled).

Between 5 and 10 million elephants roamed Africa in the 1930s. By 1977 the numbers were down to about 1.3 million. Twenty years later less than half of these remained. Still, the 10th CITES Conference in 1997 decided to shift the African elephant populations of Botswana, Namibia, and Zimbabwe from Appendix I to Appendix II—a decision that allowed trade in existing ivory stocks. In 1999, these states exported raw ivory to **Japan**, historically one of the largest importers, "on a one-time basis." In 2000, **South Africa**'s elephant population was also moved to Appendix II. This is allowing for more opportunities to raise revenues, which supporters see as essential for protecting the remaining elephant herds. Critics counter, however, that lifting the universal ban on trade in elephant ivory is allowing poaching to increase in places like Zambia, **Kenya**, Central African Republic, Mozambique, Ghana, and Congo, in part because of the difficulty of verifying the country of origin and legal status of traded ivory. In 2004, the parties to CITES agreed to an action plan to dismantle the unregulated trade in African ivory (of the approximately 40 countries with populations of wild elephants, only Angola is not a party to CITES). Today, many African countries—especially in Southern Africa—do a reasonable job of protecting savannah elephants. Still, every year poachers continue to kill thousands of African elephants for ivory, especially ones living in places like the Congo Basin rainforests.

– J –

**JAPAN.** Rapid economic growth after World War II left Japan heavily polluted by the 1960s. Beginning in the 1960s, partly in response to environmental scandals and citizen pressure, the government began regulating **pollution**. In the 1960s, an environmental office was created as part of the Ministry of Health and Welfare. The government also passed the Basic Law for Environmental Pollution Control in 1967. Its scope was fairly limited, however, only stating a need to aim for environmental protection consistent with maintaining a healthy economy. Also, there were no provisions to enforce the law. In 1970, however, the Japanese Diet held a special session—the Pollution Diet—that saw 14 laws passed to regulate specific forms of pollution. The new laws also made it a crime to spread pollution that damaged human health.

By the early 1970s, affected citizens were bringing pollution cases to the courts, where they won four flagship cases that increased the pressure on the government to step in and regulate the environment. Known as the Big Four, these cases included three involving heavy metal poisoning (two about mercury and one about cadmium), while the fourth concerned asthma from sulfur dioxide and nitrogen dioxide. The environmental movement remained largely at the grassroots level, focusing on litigation, local assemblies, and local elections. Initially, business opposed environmental regulations, worrying they would stall economic development, but later switched tactics and cooperated with the government to control pollution and promote energy efficiency. From the 1970s onward, the focus of Japanese environmental policy also began to move away from *kogai* (pollution) and toward *kankyo* (environment).

Progress was dramatic. By the 1980s, Japan had gone from one of the world's most polluted countries to one of the cleanest in the developed world. Since then, Japan has continued to strengthen environmental regulations. In 1993, the Japanese Diet passed the Basic Environmental Law. The 1993 law brought together the environmental efforts of the government under one umbrella; previously these were dispersed throughout various government agencies. As required by the 1993 Environmental Law, in 1994, Japan started drafting the Basic Environmental Plan. In 2001, Japan's Environment Agency (created in 1971) became the Ministry of Environment. Japan has also hosted significant international environmental meetings, including the negotiations for the **Kyoto Protocol** in 1997 and the Third World Water Forum in Kyoto in 2003. Meanwhile, since the late

1980s, the number of environmental **nongovernmental organizations (NGOs)** has been growing, such as the founding of a **Greenpeace** office in 1989, while some of the older ones have been strengthening such as **World Wide Fund for Nature (WWF)**-Japan founded in 1971 and **Friends of the Earth**, Japan, founded in 1980. The Japanese government has also become more willing to invite NGOs to participate in consultations and on decision-making bodies. Legislative changes, such as the 1998 Non-profit Organization Law, have also made it easier for NGOs to operate. Compared to the groups in Europe, **Australia**, and North America, however, Japan's NGOs still have smaller budgets, societal participation, and influence; civil society input into environmentalism in Japan still tends to come more from grassroots citizen protests over particular environmental threats or problems, a tradition that goes back to at least the Meiji era (1868–1912) with protests over pollution from **mining**.

Today, Japan is one of the world's environmental leaders for domestic **recycling**, waste disposal, and management of **greenhouse gases** and is at the forefront of efforts to develop stricter international environmental laws for **climate change**. At the same time, however, on some issues—notably **whaling**, tropical **deforestation**, consumption of marine products, and trade in **endangered species**—Japan is still highly criticized by environmental groups such as Greenpeace. Japan has many environmental citizen groups, but compared to ones in Europe or North America, these rely less on formal structure and fundraising campaigns and more on community participation. Overall, in 2008, Japan ranked 21st on the Environmental Performance Index (run jointly by Yale and Columbia Universities). *See also* MINAMATA DISEASE.

## – K –

**KAZAKHSTAN.** *See* ARAL SEA.

**KELLY, PETRA (1947–1992).** Petra Kelly was one of the founders of the West German Green Party in 1979, a party she described as a coalition of grassroots groups espousing nonviolent resistance to war and ecological destruction. She served as party chairperson from

1980 to 1982. In 1982, Kelly was awarded the Right Livelihood Award (sometimes called the Alternative Nobel Prize). The next year she was elected to the German parliament, one of 28 Green members of Parliament elected that year. An author and prolific speaker, Kelly became an international figure over the next decade, working to integrate the concerns of ecology, peace, feminism, and human rights. She also helped to raise the worldwide profile of the German Green Party, with other green parties emulating its successful strategies and philosophies. In 1992, she was shot and killed in unclear circumstances. *See also* GERMANY; GREEN PARTY; SPAIN.

**KENYA.** Kenya puts considerable emphasis on managing **biodiversity**. This includes establishing **national parks**; most wildlife, however, live outside of these parks, so Kenyans have also been experimenting with promoting **ecotourism** and private initiatives to protect biodiversity. Efforts include reintroducing some species: for example, in July 2001, the Kenya Wildlife Service relocated 56 elephants to the Meru National Park.

**Pollution** of freshwater from domestic, agricultural, and industrial sources is one of Kenya's most significant problems. Mombasa's sewer system, for example, serves less than one-fifth of the population—with sludge from septic tanks and latrines flowing into local waterways. Major lakes such as Nakuru and Bogoria suffer from heavy metal poisoning (from industrial and agricultural runoff and sewage). Part of Lake Victoria in Kenyan territory—a crucial water resource for East Africa—is also polluted and suffers from invasive alien species.

The Kenyan Water Act of 2002 governs water management. Kenya also has a Water Resources Management Authority and a National Water Resource Management Strategy (the first draft was completed in 2004). To collect more water, National Museums of Kenya is introducing large-scale rainwater harvesting, even in the capital, Nairobi. In addition to domestic policies, Kenya, along with Uganda and Tanzania, established the Lake Victoria Environmental Management Project (LVEMP) in 1995 to encourage **sustainable development** of the lake basin.

Kenya has also enacted the Environmental Management and Coordination Act in 1999. This created new guidelines for **environmental**

**impact assessments** (EIAs), including provisions to take traditional knowledge into account and assess the impact of projects on local communities and cultures.

Kenya has been influential in developing global environmentalism. It was among the first countries to agree to "debt-for-nature" swaps in the late 1980s. The idea is to exchange cancelled external debt for more conservation programs (thus reducing debt, which in turn reduces pressure to export natural resources to earn the foreign exchange necessary to service foreign debts). Kenya's **Green Belt Movement** and **Wangari Maathai** have also been at the forefront of innovative ideas for advancing environmentalism in the Third World.

**KOREA, NORTH.** The government of the Democratic People's Republic of Korea (DPRK, or North Korea) has taken formal measures to protect the environment. For example, Cabinet Decisions 57 and 86 in 1972 and the Law on the Forest of DPR Korea of 1992 (revised in 1999) were adopted to restore degraded forests. The government has proclaimed 2 March as Tree Planting Day and developed the Ten-Year Plan for Afforestation/Reforestation. Other measures include the Law of the Land of 1977, the main legal framework for land management and **sustainable development** of land resources. The government also has laws to protect **biodiversity**, including the 1998 National Biodiversity Strategy and Action Plan of the DPR Korea as well as national public awareness campaigns to help implement environmental laws (such as the Land Development Campaign in the spring and autumn of 1996).

Another example of a formal government measure is the 1997 Law on Water Resource (amended in 1999) to protect water resources and promote sustainable development. The government also began a project in 2000 to build a canal between Gaecho and Taesong lakes to help address water shortages for irrigation.

These formal government measures only reveal a small part of the story of environmentalism in North Korea. Grassroots environmentalism has little scope or influence in a country with a totalitarian-Communist government poised for war. Predictably, environmental conditions are deteriorating in North Korea. The country suffers from increasingly severe droughts and shortages of fresh and clean water (industrialization has left many water sources polluted and depleted).

Air quality continues to worsen as the country relies on **coal** for its energy. Remaining forests and biodiversity are also under pressure from **deforestation**, forest fires, **logging**, insect damage, and encroaching farmland. Soil erosion is also getting worse, partly because of deforestation and partly because so much mountainous terrain has been converted into agricultural "land."

**KOREA, SOUTH.** The Japanese occupation (1910–1945) and the Korean War (1950–1953) devastated much of the natural environment in South Korea (officially, the Republic of Korea). Beginning in the 1960s, a central goal of government policy became rapid industrialization—with social and environmental concerns generally subordinate. Air quality in all major cities began to deteriorate; increasing numbers of people began to suffer chronic respiratory diseases. **Acid rain** became common. In 2003, the capital city of Seoul, for example, had the worst air quality among countries in the Organisation for Economic Co-operation and Development (OECD). Another serious problem by this time was water **pollution**, with industrial processes contaminating freshwater and maritime areas. More progress has been made on other environmental issues. For example, in 1985, South Koreans produced on average 2.2 kilograms of waste per day, compared to 1.0 kilogram in **Japan** and 0.9 of a kilogram in **Great Britain**. Ten years later per capita household waste in South Korea was down to 1.1 kilograms per day.

South Korea's first environmental law was the 1961 New Forest Law to promote **reforestation**. The government soon passed the Anti-Public-Nuisance Control Law of 1963 (outlining goals for pollution controls). It did not create any administration or mechanisms to enforce these goals, however. A more far-reaching effort to improve environmental management began with the establishment of the Pollution Control Division within the Bureau of Sanitation of the Ministry of Health and Social Affairs in 1973. The first comprehensive legislation was the 1977 Environmental Preservation Act. The same year the government also passed the Marine Pollution Preservation Act. The administrative structure remained weak; however, it would gradually strengthen over the next few decades.

To some extent these changes in the 1970s arose out of citizen activism beginning with the 1966 anti–air pollution protests in Pusan around an **oil**-fired power station. Local residents were demanding financial compensation for damage to their properties and health, rather than protesting about specific environmental concerns. Such activism increased in the 1970s, although it continued to focus on antipollution demonstrations, which tended to be local and temporary, and was never able to organize effectively on a national level. The New Constitution of 1980 enshrined environmental protection as a right of citizens (Article 35). In 1986, the government passed the Solid Waste Management Act. During the 1980s, the government did take some concrete steps to improve environmental management, though it generally resisted implementing controls on industry or development. In 1990, the government created a Ministry of Environment (MoE).

Over the next few years major revisions were made to environmental law in South Korea, including the Natural Environment Preservation Act and the Resource Recycling Act of 1992. Enforcement has been hampered, however, in part because Korean law does not permit litigation by citizens as a means of dispute resolution. Nevertheless, government support for environmental management has been slowly strengthening over the last four decades. Expenditures for pollution abatement and control, for example, grew from 0.011 percent of gross national product in 1974 to 0.25 percent in 1992 (OECD countries were between 0.5 and 1.6 percent). Funding has subsequently increased—from 0.5–1.0 percent of gross domestic product in the early 1990s to 2 percent in 2007.

**KYOTO PROTOCOL TO THE UNITED NATIONS FRAMEWORK CONVENTION ON CLIMATE CHANGE.** The Kyoto Protocol is the main legally binding international agreement to address **climate change**. Signatories settled on this protocol at the third session of the Conference of the Parties (COP3) of the United Nations Framework Convention on Climate Change (UNFCCC), held in Kyoto, **Japan**, in December 1997. (The nonbinding UNFCCC was signed at the **United Nations Conference on Environment and Development** in 1992.) The rules did not allow the Kyoto Protocol to enter into force until at least 55 parties—accounting for at least 55 percent of the 1990 carbon dioxide emissions of signatories in Annex I (mostly developed countries)—had ratified it. This made it difficult for the agreement to go into force without the **United States**, which accounted for over 36 percent of these emissions. Nevertheless, the Kyoto Protocol did end up going into force in 2005 without support from the United States (which withdrew in 2001) after **Russia**, which accounted for 17.4 percent of 1990 emissions, ratified and pushed the total over 55 percent. Today, there are over 160 parties to the protocol, accounting for over 60 percent of the total emissions for Annex I countries.

The Kyoto Protocol requires Annex I countries (which includes Russia) to reduce emissions of six **greenhouse gases**, in aggregate, by 5.2 percent below 1990 levels for the 2008–2012 commitment period. Specific targets vary. The European Union's target is 8 percent below 1990 levels; the U.S. target is 7 percent; and the target for Japan and **Canada** is 6 percent. Russia agreed to stabilize emissions at 1990 levels. **Australia**, however, is allowed to increase emissions by 8 percent above 1990 levels. Some developing countries, such as **India** and **China**, also agreed to voluntary, nonbinding reduction targets.

States supporting the Kyoto Protocol, notably in the European Union and Japan, see it as a significant step toward reducing greenhouse gases. More critical states, notably the United States, see it as an ineffective instrument to deal with climate change, with the potential to damage economies (and thus lower governmental capacity to manage environmental affairs). These critics call for a market approach, relying on better technologies rather than mandatory (and arbitrary) targets to reduce greenhouse gases. Many **nongovernmental organizations (NGOs)** are highly critical of relying on markets and technologies, seeing it as business as usual with a twist of environmentalism. Many NGOs are equally critical of the Kyoto Protocol, an agreement many see as premised on insufficient emissions targets and inadequate penalties for noncompliance.

**KYRGYZSTAN.** *See* ARAL SEA.

## – L –

**LAKE BAIKAL.** *See* SIBERIA.

**LEADED GASOLINE.** In 1921, a team of scientists led by **Thomas Midgley Jr.** discovered the value of putting tetraethyl lead into gasoline to reduce engine knock (or pinging) and thus increase the power and efficiency of the combustion engine in **automobiles**. A few scientists, such as Yandell Henderson at Yale University, called for precaution to prevail over profits, arguing it was foolhardy to put a known poison into an increasingly common product. Still, after a brief sales pause from 1925–1926 to perform some rather perfunctory tests on the effects of leaded exhaust on laboratory animals, the leaded gasoline industry grew quickly. By the 1930s, 90 percent of the gasoline in the **United States** was leaded; by then, overseas markets were also developing.

Over the following decades few would question the safety of leaded gasoline until geochemist Clair Patterson (famous for dating the earth at 4.55 billion years old) published findings showing unnaturally high levels of lead in humans in the northern hemisphere. The cause, he argued, was primarily leaded gasoline, and he called for a quick phaseout. The subsequent phaseout was much slower than he was hoping; but, after many delays and setbacks, by the late 1980s the environmental movement in the United States had managed to phase out leaded gasoline. (This phaseout was spurred along by a growing body of scientific evidence of the harmful health effects, especially for children, of low, but regular, dosages of lead; it was aided as well by the U.S. government's decision, in an effort to improve air quality, to require all new cars sold after 1975 to have catalytic converters, which require unleaded gasoline to function properly.)

The phaseout of leaded gasoline in the United States did not include a phaseout of lead additive exports or overseas leaded gasoline facilities. Consumption of leaded gasoline in fact went up in many countries (especially in the Third World) as the U.S. lead additive industry searched for ways to regain lost revenue from declining sales in the United States (sales were also down in many other wealthy countries, such as **Japan** and **Canada**). By the end of the 1990s, for example, almost all of the gasoline in **sub-Saharan Africa** was still leaded. Following the 2002 **World Summit on Sustainable Development**, however, significant progress was made as a global environmental partnership involving the **United Nations Environment Programme**, the World Bank, aid institutions, governments, corporations, **nongovernmental organizations**, and local communities was created to accelerate change, so by 2006 sub-Saharan Africa became the first developing region to phase out leaded gasoline.

**LEED (LEADERSHIP IN ENERGY AND ENVIRONMENTAL DESIGN).** *See* GREEN ARCHITECTURE.

**LEÓN SANTOS, JESÚS.** *See* GOLDMAN ENVIRONMENTAL PRIZE.

**LEOPOLD, ALDO (1887–1948).** Born in Iowa, Aldo Leopold graduated from the forestry school at Yale University in 1909 and then joined the United States Forest Service in Arizona and New Mexico. Many consider Leopold the father of wildlife management in the **United States** (as well as a prominent advocate of environmental ethics). He influenced, for example, the 1924 decision to manage the Gila National Forest in New Mexico as a wilderness area (the first time the designation was made). In 1928, Leopold left the Forest Service to become an independent consultant; in 1933, he then joined the faculty at the University of Wisconsin–Madison as a chaired professor of game management in the Department of Agricultural Economics. That same year he published the first textbook on wildlife management. In 1935, Leopold helped found the **Wilderness Society** in the United States. That year he also bought a run-down farm, planted trees, and restored the prairie land; he then documented the changes in flora and fauna for a second book manuscript. He died just days after hearing this manuscript was accepted for publication. The book, *A Sand County Almanac*, went on to sell millions of copies and shape the emergence of the environmental movement in the 1950s and 1960s.

***THE LIMITS TO GROWTH.*** The bestselling 1972 book, *The Limits to Growth*, brought worldwide attention to the idea that economic growth had limits because resources—and the earth itself—were finite. Authored by **Donella H. Meadows**, Dennis L. Meadows, Jørgen Randers, and William W. Behrens III, this book has sold 20–30 million copies. Using computerized modeling, the authors simulate future trends in industrialization, human population growth, natural resource depletion, malnutrition, and **pollution**. Based on these trends, the authors predicted the earth's limits would be reached within 100 years. *Limits to Growth: The 30-Year Update* was published in 2004.

*Himalayan Town of Palampur Advertises a Carbon Sequestration Zone (2007).*

*A Goat Forages in Plastic Garbage in Conakry, Guinea (1990). Plastic shopping bags were adopted in developing countries, including across Africa, in the late 1980s and early 1990s. The immediate effect was waste that would not biodegrade. Previously, shopkeepers and stalls provided alternative means to carry goods, from plant leaves to pages from old schoolbooks to package foods and other products. Goats would eat the waste, or it would biodegrade. Today a widespread problem exists with plastic waste in developing countries. In Guinea, where this photo was taken, a goat eats in the garbage pile. Often, piles of rubbish like this one are set alight to clear up the unsightly mess, which releases toxins into the air.*

*Leaded Gasoline for Sale in One-Liter Vodka Bottles, Guinea (1990). This photo shows a typical "gasoline station" in Guinea in the early 1990s. Old one-liter liquor bottles would hold the gasoline, so buyers would know they were getting a liter if they paid for a liter. Because gasoline is relatively expensive people would often only purchase one or two liters at a time.*

*Advertisement for Corporate Social Responsibility, San José Airport, Costa Rica (2005). Because Costa Rica exports tropical fruits and because it is an "eco-tourist" destination, it is not surprising to see this advertisement of adherence to ISO 14001 environmental management standards in the airport.*

*Burning a Field in Guinea to Clear It for Farming, a Common Practice in Most West African Countries (1990).*

*Emissions from a Factory near Hamilton, Ontario, Canada (2006).*

*A Rickshaw Ride in Delhi, India, Where Many People Travel without Using Fossil Fuels (2006).*

*Bicycle Taxi in Paris, France (2008).*

*Delhi Bus Advertises Its Clean Fuel (2006). Since the early 2000s all buses in New Delhi have been converted to use "compressed natural gas" as a clean fuel in the transit system—and many vehicles advertise this fact. Air pollution levels have improved as a result of these regulations.*

*Clear-Cut Forest in Washington State, near Mount Rainier (2008).*

# EARTH is a CLOSED SYSTEM in which several general "rules" consistently apply:

1. EVERYTHING IS CONNECTED to everything else.
2. EVERYTHING GOES SOMEWHERE . . . nothing goes away.
3. There is NO SUCH THING AS A FREE LUNCH . . . every action has a price.
4. MOTHER NATURE KNOWS BEST . . . having had 4 1/2 billion years to work things out.

GLOBAL PATTERNS

Atmosphere and ocean are closely linked. Changes in

*Educational Sign at Haystack Rock on the Oregon Coast, United States (2008). When the tide is low, you can walk out to this gigantic rock and see a wide variety of birds and sea life (such as puffins and starfish). This sign diffusing ecological economic ideas was part of an educational display on the beach at low tide.*

*Litter and Waste Mar the View of Mountains from Lake Nicaragua, Nicaragua (2005).*

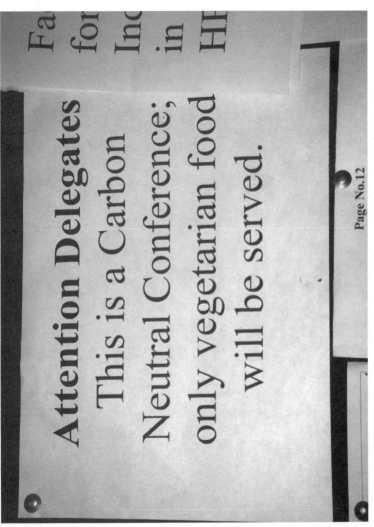

Carbon Neutral Climate Change Conference in Palampur, India (2007).

*Helltox Insecticide in Guinea (probably containing DDT) (1989).*

*Advertisement for Consuming Locally Grown Food, Ghana (2005). This billboard is advocating for the consumption of local rice grown in Ghana. Supported by Oxfam, this advice is part of a broader movement for "food sovereignty" that gives communities and countries the right to choose whether or not to engage in international trade for the purposes of meeting food security. These issues are currently under discussion and debate between rich and poor countries in the Doha Round of trade talks at the World Trade Organization. This billboard was not far from another equally large billboard advertising an American brand of imported rice.*

*Community Chemical Shop Sign, Accra, Accra, Ghana (2005).*

**LIVING PLANET INDEX.** Originally a collaborative project of the **United Nations Environment Programme**'s World Conservation Monitoring Centre and the **World Wide Fund for Nature/World Wildlife Fund (WWF)**, the Living Planet Index is now run by the WWF with support from the Zoological Society of London. It is a statistical measure of trends in global **biodiversity**, tracking over 1,000 vertebrate species (amphibians, birds, fish, mammals, and reptiles). It generates separate indices for freshwater, marine, and terrestrial species, then averages these into an aggregated index. The assumption is that even though vertebrates comprise just a fraction of species, trends here are telling for overall biodiversity. The index suggests that the biodiversity of natural ecosystems is crashing at unprecedented rates, with a decline of over 30 percent since 1970. For many environmental **nongovernmental organizations**, measures such as this one are essential to counter the tendency of governments to measure (and thus understand) everything in economic terms—relying, for example, on measures such as gross domestic product.

**LOMBORG, BJØRN (1965–).** Bjørn Lomborg, as an associate professor in the Department of Political Science at the University of Aarhus, Denmark, rocketed to infamy among environmentalists with the 2001 English translation of his book *The Skeptical Environmentalist*. This book—with over 500 pages, reams of statistics, and nearly 3,000 footnotes—was hailed by the popular media as a groundbreaking refutation of environmentalism. It became a worldwide bestseller, and Lomborg became a hero for those skeptical about the supposed "environmental crises" all around them. The statistical evidence was, according to Lomborg, irrefutable: the world was not running out of natural resources or energy, and the so-called environmental problems were more about media-hype and nongovernmental antics than the "real state of the world."

Since 2001, Lomborg's career has been turbulent. Many ecologists roundly criticized *The Skeptical Environmentalist*, including in the well-known magazine, *Scientific American*. As a worldwide backlash gained momentum, the Danish Committees on Scientific Dishonesty, under the Danish Ministry of Research and Information Technology, investigated and found his book was "objectively dishonest" and "clearly contrary to the standards of good scientific practice" for knowingly selecting biased data. The ruling, however, also declared that because Lomborg was not a "scientist," the book was not a case of "scientific dishonesty." Lomborg filed a complaint about the handling of his case. The Ministry of Research determined that the Committees on Scientific Dishonesty did not properly document its findings and the ruling was "dissatisfactory" and "emotional." Despite numerous critics, Lomborg continues to receive many honors and recognition. In 2004, *Time* magazine listed him as one of the world's 100 most influential people. In 2005, the magazines *Foreign Policy* and *Prospect* ranked him as the 14th most influential active public intellectual. *See also* CLIMATE CHANGE.

**LONDON CONVENTION.** *See* CONVENTION ON THE PREVENTION OF MARINE POLLUTION BY DUMPING OF WASTES AND OTHER MATTER.

**LOVE CANAL.** Love Canal, in Niagara Falls in the U.S. state of New York, was the site of one of the worst **hazardous waste** disasters of the 1970s. William T. Love began digging this canal at the beginning of the 20th century to install a hydroelectric facility between the upper and lower Niagara River. His project collapsed in 1910, however, and in the 1920s the now mile-long ditch became a municipal and chemical dumpsite. A few decades later Hooker Chemical and Plastics Corporation (later Occidental Petroleum) bought the property, and by 1952, the firm had dumped over 20,000 tons of toxic wastes into the ditch (including at least 200 different chemicals, many carcinogenic).

In 1953, Hooker Chemical sold the land to the Niagara Falls Education Board for US$1. Shortly afterward the city of Niagara Falls began to build an elementary school on top of the site, and construction of a neighborhood began as well. By the 1970s, chemicals were seeping into yards and basements, with fumes and puddles of chemicals forming during heavy rains. Evidence began to mount, linking the site to birth defects, poisonings, and cancers. In 1978, faced with a grassroots movement generating nationwide publicity, the U.S. government evacuated homeowners closest to the site. Two years later more families were relocated. The same year the U.S. Congress created a superfund to make polluters more responsible for (and help finance) the cleanup of hazardous waste sites. Today, Love Canal is widely considered a seminal event for the **environmental justice** movement in the **United States**. *See also* ECOFEMINISM.

**LOVELOCK, JAMES (1919–).** James Ephraim Lovelock is best known for developing the **Gaia Hypothesis**, which assumes the earth is a living organism. Trained in chemistry, medicine, and biophysics, he has spent much of his working career as an independent scientist, visiting and teaching at various universities. In 1974, Lovelock was elected a fellow of **Great Britain**'s Royal Society. In 1990, he received the order of Commander of the Order of the British Empire. His career is an example of the influence of independent scientists and writers, who, especially after the 1960s, have been using the power of bestselling books and lecture tours to challenge the direction of global environmentalism with provocative ideas outside the mainstream of academia.

**LOVINS, AMORY B. (1947–).** Born in Washington, D.C., Amory Lovins is a consultant and experimental physicist educated at Harvard and Oxford universities. He is currently the chairman and chief scientist of the Rocky Mountain Institute, an entrepreneurial nonprofit organization that he founded in 1982 with his former wife, L. Hunter Lovins. The Rocky Mountain Institute focuses on advancing the resource productivity of sectors such as **automobiles**, real estate, electricity, water, and semiconductors.

Lovins' many books include *Winning the Oil Endgame*: *Innovation for Profits, Jobs, and Security* (2004); *The Natural Advantage of Nations: Business Opportunities, Innovation and Governance in the 21st Century* (2005); and *Small Is Profitable: The Hidden Economic Benefits of Making Electrical Resources the Right Size* (2002). He has received many awards and prizes, including a Right Livelihood Award (also called the Alternative Nobel Prize) in 1983, the Onassis Foundation's first DELPHI prize (one of the world's premier environmental awards) in 1989, and *Time* magazine's Heroes for the Planet Award in 2000.

# – M –

**MAATHAI, WANGARI MUTA (1940–).** Born in **Kenya**, Wangari Maathai trained in biology and veterinary science before becoming a professor at the University of Nairobi in the 1970s. During her time as chair of the National Council of Women of Kenya (1981–1987), Maathai founded the **Green Belt Movement** to plant trees as a way to protect the environment, promote grassroots activism, and improve the lives of women. By the mid-1990s, this movement had already planted over 20 million trees. In 2004, Maathai was awarded the Nobel Peace Prize for her "contribution to **sustainable development**, democracy and peace," the first time the Norwegian Nobel Committee recognized local environmental activism as a means of enhancing world peace. Today, Maathai and the Green Belt Movement continue to inspire other grassroots environmental movements throughout the developing world. *See also* REFORESTATION.

**MADRID PROTOCOL.** *See* ANTARCTICA.

**MALTHUSIANS.** *See* MALTHUS, THOMAS ROBERT.

**MALTHUS, THOMAS ROBERT (1766–1834).** Born just south of London near Dorking, Surrey, Thomas Malthus studied mathematics at Cambridge University before being ordained as an Anglican parson. In 1805, he became a professor of political economy and history at the East India Company College in Hertfordshire (about 20 miles from central London). Today, Malthus' ideas continue to influence environmentalism through *An Essay on the Principle of Population*. First published in 1798, further editions would follow, with the sixth and final one appearing in 1826. This essay put forth a seemingly inevitable principle: Left unchecked, population increases exponentially. At the same time, food production can only increase arithmetically. Thus, without controls, the laws of math mean famine will inevitably cause a dieback of an exploding human population. Today, environmentalists like **Paul Ehrlich** who accept this logic are commonly called Malthusians or neo-Malthusians. *See also* GREEN REVOLUTION.

**MANSER, BRUNO (1954–2000).** Born in 1954 in Basel, Switzerland, Manser worked in the Swiss Alps before moving to Sarawak, Malaysia, in 1984. For the next six years he traveled with the nomadic Penan people, helping to organize protests against logging. In 1990, after years of evading authorities in Sarawak, who had declared him an enemy of the state, Manser returned to Europe, where he continued to publicize the plight of the Penan and the consequences of tropical logging for indigenous peoples. In 1992, he published the book *Voices from the Rainforest*. Manser also helped to found a non-profit organization in Switzerland—Bruno Manser Fonds—which still advocates today for the Penan people and forests of Sarawak.

An adept campaigner, Manser gained worldwide publicity with, for example, hunger strikes and parachute jumps. In one daring stunt in 1999, taking only a truce offer of a forest reserve for the Penan, he entered Sarawak by paragliding onto the front lawn of the chief minister, a politician with close ties to the logging industry. Manser was promptly arrested and deported. The next year he illegally returned to the rainforests to again live with the Penan and has been missing since May 2000. He was officially declared missing and presumed dead in 2005. *See also* DEFORESTATION.

**MARINE STEWARDSHIP COUNCIL (MSC).** Headquartered in London, the Marine Stewardship Council (MSC) is a nonprofit organization dedicated to the sustainable use of marine fisheries. Building on the example of the **Forest Stewardship Council (FSC)**, Unilever, the world's largest seafood buyer, and the **World Wide Fund for Nature/World Wildlife Fund (WWF)** established the MSC as a joint initiative in 1997. Unilever did this in part to protect declining fish stocks as well as green its corporate image.

The MSC became a fully independent organization in 1999. It accredits independent certifiers to assess whether a fishery meets the MSC standard. Fisheries that do can put the MSC logo on their products to inform consumers. The standard requires sufficient fish stocks for a sustainable fishery as well as rules and procedures to minimize the impact of **fishing** on the marine environment (e.g., on seabirds and marine mammals).

As of November 2008, 35 fisheries producing more than 300 seafood products had been certified to the MSC environmental standard. Supporters see the MSC as a practical and effective way to move toward sustainable fishing. Critics see it as far too little, far too late, allowing a few consumers to feel responsible while industrial overfishing continues to deplete the oceans of commercial species like the northern cod (now endangered). *See also* ECO-CERTIFICATION; ECO-LABELING.

**MARRAKECH PROCESS.** The Marrakech Process is designed to draft a 10-Year Framework of Programmes on sustainable consumption and production. It has three primary goals: to assist efforts to green national economies; to support more sustainable business practices; and to encourage consumers to live more sustainably. It is aiming to meet the objectives of the Johannesburg Plan of Action set out in the 2002 **World Summit on Sustainable Development**. The **United Nations Environment Programme** and UN Department of Economic and Social Affairs are the lead agencies; national governments, development agencies, and **nongovernmental organizations** are active participants. Countries will negotiate the draft Framework at the 19th session of the **UN Commission on Sustainable Development** in 2011.

**MARSH, GEORGE PERKINS (1801–1882).** George Perkins Marsh was multitalented: fluent in many languages, he was a congressman, a diplomat to Europe, a linguist, a manufacturer, a lawyer, a newspaper editor, a sheep farmer, a mill owner, a businessman, an inventor, and one of the founders of the Smithsonian Institution. Many consider him America's first environmentalist. Marsh was one of the first to argue that the collapse of past civilizations was partly because of environmental degradation. Foremost here was **deforestation**, which Marsh saw as contributing to significant secondary impacts such as soil erosion and water turbidity. His book *Man and Nature; or, Physical Geography as Modified by Human Action* (1864) provided the justification for the Forest Reserves Act, the foundational legislation for modern national forests in the **United States**. Marsh also argued that decisions need to account for the environmental consequences of actions, although he did advocate taming the wilderness and asserting human command over nature.

*Man and Nature* also inspired the Arbor Day movement in the United States during the late 1800s, a holiday set aside for planting trees (the first was in Nebraska on 10 April 1872, although the state did not proclaim Arbor Day a legal holiday until 1885, changing the date to 22 April).

**MEADOWS, DONELLA (1941–2001).** In 1968 Donella (Dana) Meadows received a Ph.D. from Harvard in biophysics. As part of an international research and policy group called the Club of Rome, she worked on the Massachusetts Institute of Technology team that programmed the computer model "World3." It simulated future trends for industrialization, population growth, natural resource depletion, malnutrition, and **pollution**. This was the basis for the book *The Limits to Growth* (1972), of which she was the lead author. This book predicted that, without significant changes, the earth would reach its limits within 100 years. In language accessible to the general public, it declared, "The most probable result will be a sudden and uncontrollable decline in both population and industrial capacity"—a conclusion appearing to verify the earlier ones of scholars like **Paul Ehrlich.**

*The Limits to Growth* went on to sell 20–30 million copies in at least 37 languages. Many attacked it as exaggerated pseudoscience. Meadows, in her later speeches and writings, saw such vitriolic criticism as a result of the near-religious belief in economic growth. In a work called *The Limits to Growth Revisited*, she summed up her frustrations as follows: "A book called *The Limits to Growth* could have been filled with nothing but blank pages, and some people would still have thought it was an anti-capitalist plot or an anti-Communist or an anti-Keynesian or an anti-Third World one. They never saw the book for its cover."

In 1981, she and her husband at the time—Dennis Meadows—founded the International Network of Resource Information Centers (INRIC) to promote the exchange of systems-oriented analysis and activism. In 1996, she founded the Sustainability Institute to research ecosystems and demonstrate ways of sustainable living—a **nongovernmental organization** she liked to call a think-do-tank. Humbly, she often described herself as just a writer and a farmer, but many see her as a founding intellectual and activist of global environmentalism, along with prominent thinkers like **Rachel Carson**. From 1972 until her sudden death from meningitis, she taught environmental studies at Dartmouth College.

**MELANESIA.** The Melanesian islands are located northeast of **Australia** in the South Pacific. This region includes the countries of Papua New Guinea, the Solomon Islands, the Santa Cruz Islands, Vanuatu, New Caledonia, and Fiji. The islands are primarily volcanic and continental, which are more amenable to human settlements than atolls and raised limestone islands, which are common in the South Pacific.

Principles of sustainability were common in the traditional practices and rules in Melanesian societies. Many societies depended on maritime resources vulnerable to overexploitation; moreover, many could not turn to the land for alternative food because of limited space and poor quality soil for farming (one exception is Papua, the largest island).

Today the Pacific island economies depend primarily on resource extraction (such as **logging**, **mining**, and **fishing**). Timber companies from Malaysia, for example, operate significant logging operations in Papua New Guinea and the Solomon Islands, exporting logs and lumber to countries like **Japan** and **China**. Papua New Guinea also has large copper and gold mines, while Fiji mines gold and New Caledonia holds large deposits of nickel and chromium. (The Solomon Islands and Vanuatu also contain bauxite, nickel, and copper, but so far these remain generally untapped). **Biodiversity** losses from mining, logging, and fishing are often significant, as up to 80 percent of plant and animal species are commonly endemic to these islands.

Environmental policies using the language of **sustainable development** are now widespread across the Pacific island region. Implementation of environmental regulations is weak, however, across the entire region. Many factors explain this, including a lack of environmental monitoring capabilities and skilled practitioners, boom-and-bust resource economies, the burdens of servicing heavy foreign debts, political instability, and the power of multinational investors (known to bribe officials and smuggle out resources). Local and international **nongovernmental organizations** advocating for environmental protection have gained a higher profile in recent years, although these still wield relatively little influence.

At the same time regional environmental cooperation in the South Pacific is strengthening, most notably with respect to the antinuclear movement and marine resource management. The South Pacific Regional Environment Programme (SPREP), emerging from a small program called the South Pacific Commission in the 1980s, is now a major intergovernmental organization aiming to protect and manage environmental and natural resources. It coordinates the implementation of regional treaties including the Convention for the Protection of the Natural Resources and Environment of the South Pacific Region (SPREP/Noumea Convention), the Convention on Conservation of Nature in the South Pacific (Apia Convention), and the Rarotonga South Pacific Nuclear Free Zone Treaty (NFZT). Meanwhile, regional organizations include the South Pacific Conference, the South Pacific Forum, the Forum Fisheries Agency, the Secretariat for the Pacific Community, the South Pacific Applied Geoscience Commission, and the Regional Seas Programme. The Strategic Action Programme for the International Waters of the Pacific Small Island Developing States was developed in 2001. In 2002, South Pacific states agreed as well to a Pacific Islands Regional Ocean Policy (PIROP).

**MENDES, CHICO (1944–1988).** Chico Mendes (Francisco Alves Mendes Filho) was a rubber tapper from the western Brazilian **Amazon**, working to extract rubber as well as to harvest nuts, fiber, and food. Using nonviolent techniques, he organized his fellow tappers in the 1970s and 1980s to defend the forests from destructive loggers and cattle ranchers clearing land for pasture. In 1985, with international support for his cause rising, he founded the National Council of Rubber Tappers. In 1988, the son of a cattle rancher assassinated Mendes, turning him into a martyr for environmentalism. Seeing the global anger over his death also influenced the decision by the Brazilian government to offer to host the 1992 **United Nations Conference on Environment and Development** in Rio de Janeiro. In addition, the Brazilian government set aside an extractive forest reserve for rubber tappers. Today, the courage of Mendes continues to inspire peaceful movements against commercial logging and land clearing across the tropical world. *See also* BRAZIL; REFORESTATION.

**MEXICO.** From the 1940s to 1980s, development in Mexico focused on industrialization and natural resource exports; environmental concerns were addressed mainly in the context of public health, through the Health Secretariat. Constitutional reforms in the 1980s resulted in new administrative and judicial institutions for environmental protection. The Mexican government created the Secretaría de Desarrollo Urbano y Ecología (SEDUE, or Secretariat of Urban Development and Ecology) in 1982, passed new environmental laws in 1982 and 1988, and established its National Water Commission in 1989. Further structures were established in the early 1990s, including the National Ecology Institute, the Attorney General for Environmental Protection, a National Water Law, and the Secretariat of Social Development (replacing SEDUE). In 2000, the Mexican government established the Secretariat of the Environment and Natural Resources to replace several earlier versions of environmental departments; it also transferred some resource responsibilities to the Secretariat of Agriculture, Livestock, Rural Development, Fisheries, and Food.

Along with new legislation and structural reforms, the government has also been establishing voluntary regulation programs for industry. During the 1990s alone, Mexico created at least 10 programs, involving close to 600 firms. The central program, the National Environmental Auditing Program, also called the Clean Industry Program, was set up in 1992. It required firms to pay for independent third-party audits in exchange for a certificate to exempt them from regulatory inspections for two years (firms could also use the certificate for marketing). The program started with 77 participants; by 2005 it had over 3,000.

Mexico also has an active civil society promoting conservation and environmental protection. The Mexican Fund for the Conservation of Nature, established after the 1992 Earth Summit, is a private conservation organization initially under the auspices of the **World Wide Fund for Nature/World Wildlife Fund (WWF)**. It works collaboratively on environmental projects, including with the United States Agency for International Development (USAID) and the **Nature Conservancy**.

**MIDGLEY, THOMAS JR. (1889–1944).** In 2003, Thomas Midgley Jr. was inducted into the American National Inventors Hall of Fame in Akron, Ohio. A prolific inventor, holding over 100 patents, Midgley is best remembered today for two discoveries with damaging ecological consequences lasting far past his lifetime. The first was his discovery in 1921 of the power of tetraethyl lead as an additive to reduce engine knock (the beginning of the **leaded gasoline** industry). The second was his 1928 discovery of a stable, nontoxic, and nonflammable refrigerant for refrigerators: the seemingly safe and innocuous chemical compounds called **chlorofluorocarbons (CFCs)**, which scientists, a half century later, discovered were depleting the ozone layer. *See also* OZONE DEPLETION.

**MILLENNIUM DEVELOPMENT GOALS.** Arising out of the **United Nation**'s Millennium Summit in 2000, the eight UN Millennium Development Goals are designed as a "blueprint" for states, UN agencies, and international development organizations. These include (all by 2015) reversing the spread of HIV/AIDS and malaria, halving extreme poverty and hunger, providing universal primary education, and achieving environmental sustainability. Most supporters now agree achieving all of these goals is impossible; still, the hope is some, if not most, will be met and for the others these will inspire change to support the needs of the world's poorest people.

**MINAMATA DISEASE.** Minamata disease, named after Minamata Bay in **Japan** where it was first officially "discovered" in villagers in 1956, is a neurological condition caused by methyl mercury poisoning. People in Minamata were poisoned after eating the local seafood, which was contaminated with methyl mercury discharged by the Chisso industrial plant upriver from Minamata Bay. In the 1950s and 1960s, hundreds of people were paralyzed and died, and hundreds more were born with birth defects and brain damage. In Japan, the publicity, lawsuits, and citizen protests in the 1960s and 1970s spurred an environmental cleanup as well as legislation to control industrial **pollution**. Globally, environmentalists continue to point to Minamata disease as an especially horrific example of the dangers of unregulated industrialization and uncontrolled economic growth.

**MINDBOMBS.** The term *mindbombs* was coined by **Robert "Bob" Hunter** to refer to activist campaigns that use the media to blast global consciousness with images, sounds, and language reflecting environmental values.

**MINING.** Minerals are a nonrenewable resource. Thus, to some degree, mining always damages the ecosystem. The environmental debate revolves around best practices: how to minimize consequences and when to close (or not begin) mining. Particular issues include water **pollution**, large volumes of waste, mine closure plans and site rehabilitation, energy use, toxic materials, and threats to **biodiversity**. Storing mine tailings is especially critical as these can contain heavy metals and poisons such as cyanide (used to extract gold). Mining can also create conflict within or between local communities, including indigenous groups, over access to surrounding natural resources and resulting wealth. One example is the conflict around diamond mining in Africa. Thus, many **nongovernmental organizations** call for extensive community consultation and participation in the environmental assessment of mining.

Currently, no comprehensive international agreement is in place for mining or mineral resources. The global mining industry has begun, however, to adopt voluntary codes of conduct under policies of **corporate social responsibility** as communities, governments, and environmental activists demand more accountability. Since 2000, many multinational mining companies, for example, have voluntarily followed the **United Nations Environment Programme (UNEP)** and the International Council on Mining and Metals (ICMM)'s "International Cyanide Management Code for the Manufacture, Transport, and Use of Cyanide in the Production of Gold." Similarly, since 2002 many multinational diamond miners follow an international voluntary certification system for "conflict diamonds" called the Kimberley Process Certification Scheme.

Such codes, however, tend to lack compliance mechanisms and allow nonsignatory companies to ignore them. Also, as mining often occurs in developing countries with less capacity to regulate industry, international mining companies tend to maintain lower standards here than at home. Again, various international initiatives are underway to address these double standards, such as enhancing local capacity with funding from institutions like the World Bank.

**MONTREAL PROTOCOL ON SUBSTANCES THAT DEPLETE THE OZONE LAYER.** The 1987 Montreal Protocol is an international agreement to address stratospheric **ozone depletion**. The 1985 Vienna Convention for the Protection of the Ozone Layer was the framework for negotiating the Montreal Protocol. An Ozone Secretariat in Nairobi, **Kenya** (at the **United Nations Environment Programme**), is responsible for both the Vienna Convention and Montreal Protocol.

The Montreal Protocol is one of the most successful international environmental agreements ever negotiated. Entering into force in 1989, it was quickly amended in 1990 and 1992 to make it even more comprehensive and now has had a total of seven revisions. Financial assistance for phaseouts in developing countries was also made available through the Multilateral Fund for the Implementation of the Montreal Protocol (established in 1990). As of 2008, 192 parties had ratified the agreement, and, with high compliance levels, it has contributed to a worldwide phaseout of over 95 percent of ozone-depleting substances.

These ozone-depleting substances include **chlorofluorocarbons (CFCs)**, halons, carbon tetrachloride, methyl bromide, methyl chloroform, and hydrochlorofluorocarbons (HCFCs). Some significant problems still remain. For example, in some cases CFCs and HCFCs have been replaced by hydrofluorocarbons (HFCs), a **greenhouse gas** that contributes to **climate change**.

**MUIR, JOHN (1838–1914).** Born in Dunbar, Scotland, John Muir became a central figure in the history of American conservation. Muir saw creation and man as belonging to nature, rather than man presiding over nature. His critique of anthropocentrism was radical for the time of the industrial revolution of the 19th century, as was his call to protect nature for its own sake. A nature lover, Muir explored the North American and European wilderness, especially the southwest **United States**, writing and publishing naturalist articles in American literary magazines. Two of his best-known campaigns were in California, for the Sierra Nevada and Yosemite National Park. His Sierra campaign led to the founding of the **Sierra Club** in 1892 (he was president until his death). Muir is also credited with influencing President Theodore Roosevelt's conservation programs and the **national parks** movement.

– N –

**NAESS, ARNE.** *See* DEEP ECOLOGY.

**NANOTECHNOLOGY.** Engineering nanomaterials is one of the newer technologies to spark intense debates between those who see it as a way to improve the quality of life and those who call for more precaution to account for the uncertainty of the long-term environmental consequences. Critics are calling for a range of measures: from consumer labeling to complete bans. Nanomaterials are tiny, engineered substances—from just 1 to 100 nanometers in size. Engineering such tiny particles is hard to even imagine: one nanometer equals a mere billionth of a meter (it takes 100,000 nanometers to reach the diameter of a human hair). Scientists are now able to arrange metals and other compounds the size of a nanometer into shapes that often look like rods or spheres—thus creating stronger and more durable materials with innovative properties.

The nanotechnology industry is rapidly expanding, and over 500 consumer products now contain nanomaterials, including food, food packaging, cosmetics, wrinkle-free clothing, stain-resistant fabric, sunscreen, cleaning products, and tennis rackets. Critics worry these tiny nanomaterials will escape into the environment as products break down, then leach into tissues, cell membranes, and food chains, perhaps acting in ways similar to carcinogens like asbestos. At a minimum, critics are calling for a **precautionary approach** to prevent the industry from incorporating nanotechnology into US$1 trillion worth of consumer products by 2015 (which the industry says it is on track to do). This would avoid risking a repeat of past ecological disasters from introducing technologies into the global environment without adequate understanding or government regulations, such as putting lead into gasoline in the 1920s and **chlorofluorocarbons (CFCs)** into refrigerators in the 1930s. *See also* LEADED GASOLINE.

**NARMADA DAM.** The Narmada Dam project involves building a series of large, medium, and small hydroelectric dams on the Narmada River and its tributaries in **India**. Prime Minister Jawaharlal Nehru floated the idea in the 1940s, but it did not take hold until the late 1970s as the country looked for ways to produce electricity as well as irrigate drought-prone areas. In the 1980s increasing numbers of environmental and human right groups opposed construction. Facing a growing backlash, in 1990 the World Bank withdrew from the project. The Indian government has persisted, however, and the project continues to move ahead even in the face of ongoing grassroots protests and worldwide criticism. *See also* THREE GORGES DAM.

**NATIONAL AUDUBON SOCIETY.** The National Audubon Society is an American nonprofit environmental organization dedicated to conserving natural ecosystems, focusing in particular on protecting and studying birds in natural habitats. Established in 1905 from local Audubon clubs that emerged in the late 1800s, it is one of the world's oldest conservation organizations. The society is named in honor of John James Audubon, an ornithologist who painted, described, and catalogued the birds of North America. Today, the Audubon Society has more than 500,000 members and over 500 local chapters across the **United States**. Members participate in public education and advocacy to promote nature conservation. Local chapters organize bird watching and conservation activities. Audubon also works with a network of partner organizations to protect birds and nature in other countries. It is an example of the ongoing global influence of the earliest wave of U.S. environmentalism.

**NATIONAL PARKS.** As of 2005, about 12 percent of the earth's land area was set aside for environmental protection as nature reserves, parks, wildlife refuges, or wilderness. No consistent global definition is in place for a "national park," though much of this area is tundra, desert, or other extreme environments. Out of the 12 percent, at most 7 percent is strictly protected. In contrast, some conservation biologists see a need to set aside at least 20 percent to protect global **biodiversity**. Moreover, many national parks and nature reserves in the developing world are not actually protected, with **illegal logging**, **mining**, and poaching just some of the many pressures authorities either allow or are unable to prevent.

**NATURAL GAS.** Current trends suggest natural gas will soon surpass **coal** as the world's second largest energy source after **oil**. Reserves currently sit at around 180 trillion cubic meters—able to last 60 years at current production levels. But most analysts predict levels will continue to rise, with worldwide consumption doubling by 2030, making it the fastest growing major source of primary energy.

The development of the natural gas industry in the first half of the 20th century took place mostly in the **United States**, with North America's share of the global consumption of natural gas sitting at 90 percent in 1950. Today, however, North America accounts for less than one-third of global consumption with countries like **Japan** and **Russia** now significant consumers. To diversify its energy portfolio, Japan invested in natural gas and became the largest importer of liquefied natural gas (natural gas that is liquefied to reduce its volume) by the end of the 1970s. Russia is currently the largest producer of natural gas and has the largest reserves.

Natural gas is often called "clean" because it releases less pollutants and carbon dioxide than oil for the same amount of energy. However, methane—a main component of natural gas—is a **greenhouse gas** with more than 20 times the warming effects of carbon dioxide.

**NATURAL RESOURCES DEFENSE COUNCIL (NRDC).** Founded in 1970 by law students and attorneys working in the **United States**, the Natural Resources Defense Council (NRDC) has been especially influential in drafting, shaping, and changing environmental laws in the United States. Today, with 1.2 million members and a staff of over 300 lawyers, scientists, and policy analysts, NRDC is involved in a wide range of campaigns, including ones regarding **climate change**, environmental health, **China**, toxic chemicals, oceans, and wildlife.

**NATURE CONSERVANCY.** Founded in 1951 in the **United States** (with roots going back to 1915), the Nature Conservancy uses a nonconfrontational approach to promote conservation of plants, animals, and nature. Its primary strategy is to acquire land by direct purchase or through land management agreements, leases, and easements. Today, with more than 1 million members, it has managed to set aside millions of hectares of land in the United States, **Canada**, Latin America, and the Caribbean. It directly manages more than 1,600 nature preserves.

A secondary strategy to protect **biodiversity** was its Natural Heritage Inventory Program (started in 1974), a scientific database of rare and **endangered species** and ecosystems, which employed hundreds of scientists and information managers. In 2000, this program was turned into the Association for Biodiversity Information, a nonprofit conservation organization later renamed NatureServe (headquartered in Arlington, Virginia). Today, NatureServe coordinates a network of natural heritage programs/biological inventories. By sharing objective scientific data on biodiversity with all stakeholders (such as governments, indigenous groups, conservation organizations, corporations, and the general public), NatureServe tries to ensure informed decisions regarding the impacts of development on endangered species and ecosystems.

**NEW CALEDONIA.** *See* MELANESIA.

**NEW ZEALAND.** New Zealand contains a large number of unique native species. Environmental problems include **biodiversity** loss, soil erosion (50 percent of land area shows some signs), **deforestation** (less than one-quarter of original indigenous forest cover was left by the early 1980s), and waste management.

Land and forest degradation dates back to the resource industries and farming practices of the earliest European settlers. A tradition of conservation, however, also dates back to these colonial days, as administrators put in place policies to protect the scenic beauty and manage resources more efficiently and effectively. The Forests Act of 1874—to deal with deforestation—was later repealed because of worries it would hamper economic development. Other acts were soon passed, however, including the State Forests Act of 1885 and the Land Act of 1892 (to preserve government-owned land). The first **national park** was created in 1887, the second in 1900. Many acts would follow over the next century, including the Soil Conservation and Rivers Control Act of 1941 (dealing with erosion and flooding); the Nature Protection Council in 1950; and the Water and Soil Conservation Act of 1967.

The modern environmental movement began in the 1960s with growing grassroots support to better protect and manage the environment. The Values Party (created in 1972) was one of the first green parties globally. Key issues over the next few decades included air **pollution** and public health, the use of Lake Manapouri (in the late 1960s) to produce hydroelectric power, a plan to clear-cut 340,000 hectares of forest in South Island (abandoned in 1975 after a public outcry), and French nuclear testing in the Pacific (which hit the news worldwide after the sinking of the *Rainbow Warrior* in 1985).

Institutional reforms in the 1980s altered the framework for environmental protection. Key among these was the reconstitution of local government and the increasing acceptance of economic incentives and market instruments as tools to implement policy. As a result, local capacities have taken on an increasingly important role in environmental management. The city of Christchurch, for example, declared itself a "Clean Air Zone," with the local government investing to control air pollution from open fires. Also key was the initiation of the Resource Management Law Reform in 1988, leading to the Resource Management Act of 1991. This act incorporates a principle of sustainability and brings together most of the previous environmentally related legislation (replacing 57 existing laws and reducing 800 units of government to 93).

Other important changes since then include the New Zealand Forest Accord of 1991, which was signed by major forest companies and environmental groups. Industry agreed to no longer replace indigenous forests with exotic plantations; environmentalists agreed to support exotic forests as an alternative to logging of native forests.

Today, New Zealand has 14 national parks and 20 forest parks, covering about 4.7 million hectares, or 17.5 percent of the total land area.

**NIGERIA.** In 1977, the Nigerian government created the state-run Nigerian National Petroleum Corporation. Today, Nigeria is Africa's largest **oil** producer and the world's eighth largest exporter of crude oil, with about 95 percent of export revenues coming from oil.

The oil industry has been a major source of environmental degradation and human rights violations. For example, in the early 1990s, the Movement for the Survival of the Ogoni People (MOSOP) led a nonviolent campaign against environmental damage from multinational oil companies, especially Shell Oil, in the Niger Delta. After large protests in 1993, Shell suspended operations; then in 1995, to the outrage of human rights and environmental groups worldwide, the government executed a founding member of MOSOP, **Ken Saro-Wiwa**, along with eight others. Since then the struggle against oil production in the Niger Delta has been ongoing, with some tactics now violent, including kidnappings and militant takeovers of facilities by rebel groups such as the Movement for the Emancipation of the Niger Delta.

Over the last two decades the Nigerian government has reorganized its bureaucracy to support more **sustainable development**. It established a Federal Environmental Protection Agency in 1988, which was later replaced by the Federal Ministry of the Environment in 2000. Jurisdiction over environmental regulation also falls under state control and in the mid-1990s each state established a State Environmental Protection Agency. Nigeria also participates in regional environmental initiatives. It helped to create the Niger River Commission (CFN, or Commission du Fleuve Niger) in 1964, and the subsequent Niger Basin Authority (ABN, or l'Autorité du Bassin du Niger) in 1980. In 1968, it also joined the African Convention on the Conservation of Nature and Natural Resources.

Highly affected by **desertification**, Nigeria started the Arid Zone Afforestation Project (AZAP) in 1976. It ratified the **United Nations Convention to Combat Desertification** in 1997 and created the Department of Drought and Desertification Amelioration in the Ministry of the Environment in 2000. **Nongovernmental organizations** have also been active in promoting forest conservation. For example, the Forestry Association of Nigeria initiated a National Tree Planting Campaign in 1970; in 1982, the Nigerian Conservation Foundation was formed to promote conservation (in particular forest resources).

**NIMBY.** An acronym meaning "not in my backyard," NIMBY describes a common sentiment within many communities to oppose locating nearby certain kinds of projects on environmental and safety grounds—such as garbage dumps, incinerators, freeways, and power plants—while supporting (or at least accepting) the project may need to go ahead in someone else's backyard. For some analysts, this helps to explain why environmental conditions are often worse in communities with more minorities or higher rates of poverty, as NIMBYism tends to shift costs onto the least powerful groups in society.

**NONGOVERNMENTAL ORGANIZATIONS (NGOs).** Over the past few decades nongovernmental organizations, or NGOs, have been driving agents of environmental action and education. As more groups were emerging and strengthening in the 1960s and 1970s in countries like the **United States** and **Great Britain**, environmental NGOs began to spread into both developing and developed countries, from **India, Kenya, Mexico**, and the **Philippines**, to **Australia, Finland, Japan**, and **Spain**, and today these NGOs exist in every country covering just about every environmental issue.

The organizational characteristics of environmental NGOs range from leaderless movements and loose networks (e.g., **Critical Mass,** the **Earth Liberation Front**, and **Reclaim the Streets**) to highly ordered and structured organizations (e.g., the **Nature Conservancy**). The focus, tactics, and mandates vary considerably, too, from organizations established to protect individual species (e.g., **Brazil**'s Tartarugas Marinhas, or Sea Turtles organization) or sectors (e.g., forestry, with the **Forest Stewardship Council, Programme for the Endorsement of Forest Certification,** and **Sustainable Forestry Initiative**), to groups pushing for environmental laws and regulations for broad issues (e.g., **Environmental Defense** and the **Natural Resources Defense Council**), to those advocating conservation and large scale environmental action (e.g., the **World Wide Fund for Nature/World Wildlife Fund**). Some are primarily think tanks with a focus on research (e.g., **Resources for the Future**); others work as advocates, consultants, and lobbyists (e.g., **World Resources Institute** and the **Sierra Club**); while others focus on grassroots action (e.g., **Food Not Bombs** and the **Green Belt Movement**). NGOs also span from local and national groups (e.g., the U.S.-based **National Audubon Society** and **Wilderness Society**) to international organizations and networks (e.g., the **International Union for Conservation of Nature, Greenpeace**, and the **Third World Network**)—as well as everything in between.

Some organizations that started as local or national efforts have expanded their activities to address global issues (e.g., **Conservation International** and **Friends of the Earth**, both of which began in the United States). Changes in government or government policies have allowed NGOs to emerge in some countries, such as Mikhail Gorbachev's glasnost policy in **Russia**, the fall of the **Soviet Union**, and **China**'s shift toward a more open economy in the mid-1990s. NGO networks also span national borders, with many working on regional or international issues, and with many in developed countries supporting and funding efforts for conservation in developing countries. Examples of this include Norway's Bellona Foundation, which advocates for better nuclear waste management in Russia.

Some NGOs oppose and take direct action against governments and corporations (e.g., **Earth First!**), while others cooperate in formal and informal partnerships (e.g., the **Marine Stewardship Council** and the **Singapore** Environment Council). A few NGOs arise out of the business world itself, such as the **World Business Council for Sustainable Development**. These alliances between NGOs and industry have contributed to developing environmental laws, **eco-certification** programs, voluntary environmental initiatives, **corporate social responsibility**, and protected areas; some activists, however, see many of the efforts as **greenwash** that does little to advance true environmental protection. *See also* CENTER FOR INTERNATIONAL ENVIRONMENTAL LAW (CIEL); COALITION FOR ENVIRONMENTALLY RESPONSIBLE ECONOMIES (CERES); ENVIRONMENTAL INVESTIGATION AGENCY (EIA); INTERNATIONAL INSTITUTE FOR ENVIRONMENT AND DEVELOPMENT (IIED); INTERNATIONAL INSTITUTE FOR SUSTAINABLE DEVELOPMENT (IISD); INTERNATIONAL ORGANIZATION FOR STANDARDIZATION (ISO); INTERNATIONAL SOCIETY FOR ECOLOGICAL ECONOMICS (ISEE); RAINFOREST ACTION NETWORK (RAN); UNION OF CONCERNED SCIENTISTS; WILDLIFE CONSERVATION SOCIETY; WORLDWATCH INSTITUTE; WWOOF.

**NORWAY.** *See* BRUNDTLAND, GRO HARLEM; WHALING.

**NUCLEAR POWER/ENERGY.** A highly controversial form of energy, nuclear power is billed by some as a "green" and "sustainable" energy source, while others label it a "dangerous" and "costly" (economically and environmentally) option. It is created by extracting energy from atomic nuclei of uranium atoms, using nuclear fission (the most common method), nuclear fusion, or radioactive decay. The heat produced by splitting the atoms converts water into steam, which then spins a turbine or generator to produce electricity. Nuclear power accounts for over 15 percent of the world's total electricity.

Advocates of nuclear energy stress its potential to reduce air **pollution** and **greenhouse gas** emissions (and thus mitigate **climate change**). They also argue that with proper procedures and safety protocols, it is possible to isolate and safely store the small amount of remaining nuclear waste. Critics counter by raising safety and environmental concerns about the production of nuclear power, as well as the disposal of radioactive waste, pointing to accidents such as the 1979 **Three Mile Island Nuclear Accident** in the **United States**, and the 1986 **Chernobyl Nuclear Meltdown** in the Ukraine (at the time, part of the **Soviet Union**). Environmentalists, such as those in **France** in the 1970s, have organized large protests against nuclear power. Most **green parties**, too, oppose nuclear technology. Several **nongovernmental organizations**, including **Greenpeace**, also campaign actively against nuclear power. Nuclear power generation often sparks particularly strong reactions because of its close association for many people with nuclear weapons.

The siting of nuclear reactors and waste disposal facilities reveals a **NIMBY** (not in my backyard) attitude in many communities: some citizens are willing to tolerate (or even support) the idea of using nuclear power, but are reluctant to bear the risks themselves. The input of uranium for power generation also raises environmental concerns, as open-pit **mining** is often used to extract the ore, which tends to be found in low concentrations (**Canada**, **Australia**, and Kazakhstan account for over half of the world's uranium production).

Early international agreements to address nuclear issues include the 1960 Paris Convention on Third Party Liability in the Field of Nuclear Energy and the 1963 Vienna Convention on Civil Liability in the Field of Nuclear Energy. More recent agreements on nuclear issues include the 1994 Convention on Nuclear Safety, the 1996 Comprehensive Nuclear Test Ban Treaty, and the 1997 Convention on Supplementary Compensation for Nuclear Damage. *See also* CONVENTION ON THE CONSERVATION OF ANTARCTIC MARINE LIVING RESOURCES (CCAMLR); RUSSIA.

– O –

**OIL.** As the world's largest source of energy, oil—its production and consumption—dominates current transportation, industrial, and agricultural systems. The oil industry represents a powerful economic sector and is a valuable export commodity for many countries, including **Argentina**, **Nigeria** (Africa's largest oil producer), Norway, **Russia**, and **Iran**. Demand for energy is unlikely to decrease—the

Energy Information Administration of the **United States** projects that global energy demand will rise by 50 percent by 2030—and most analysts project oil consumption will increase significantly unless major advances occur in **renewable energy** technology and incentives shift the world economy away from its current dependence on fossil fuels. Environmental concerns and energy security could encourage such a shift: **Sweden**, for example, has announced bold plans to phase out oil by 2020.

Many environmental **nongovernmental organizations (NGOs)**, such as the **Rainforest Action Network** (with its Freedom from Oil Campaign) and **Greenpeace**, see reducing oil consumption as essential to preventing a global environmental disaster. Along with emissions from **coal** and **natural gas**, **greenhouse gas** emissions from burning oil as gasoline in automobiles and in industrial production contribute significantly to **climate change**; some groups focus on encouraging public transit and cycling (e.g., **Critical Mass**) and reducing the dominance of cars in cities (e.g., **Reclaim the Streets**), while others promote new technology, such as **hybrid automobiles**.

Oil spills from transportation and storage facilities also cause environmental degradation, with notable examples including the grounding of the *Torrey Canyon* in 1967, the *Exxon Valdez* **oil spill** in 1989, and the controversy over the decommissioning of the **Brent Spar** in 1995. Activists have pushed to hold corporations accountable for oil spills and dumping, as with the efforts of Pablo Fajardo Mendo and Luis Yanza in Ecuador, who were among the winners of the **Goldman Environmental Prize** in 2008. Oil exploration also poses environmental risks to sensitive ecosystems, and some international steps have been taken to protect particularly vulnerable regions. The Environmental Protocol to the Antarctic Treaty (the Madrid Protocol), for example, stopped oil and mineral exploration in **Antarctica**. Oil is also one of the six most critical environmental problems in the **Arctic**, as identified by the Arctic Council (created in 1996 by **Finland**, **Canada**, Denmark, Iceland, Norway, **Russia**, Sweden, and the United States).

The oil crisis of the 1970s spurred efforts to promote energy efficiency, leading to developments in **green architecture** and **eco-efficiency** to conserve resources. Prices of oil are volatile, but have risen consistently in recent years, with increases seen every year between 2001 and 2008. Some environmentalists see high oil prices as a positive trend that could lead to less dependence on oil; some encourage **carbon taxes** as part of a strategy to increase consumer prices further.

Initially seen by some environmentalists as a "silver bullet," replacing oil with **biofuels** has become one of the most contentious strategies to reduce the global dependence on oil. Many are now concerned with the consequences for food prices for the world's poorest people. Also, the greenhouse gas emission reductions from biofuels depend on production methods and land conversion that may cause **deforestation** of primary forests as countries like **Indonesia** develop even more palm oil plantations. *See also* CUBA; PEAK OIL; SIBERIA; STRONG, MAURICE.

**ORGANIC FOOD.** Sales of organic food have been rising steadily in North America and Europe as consumers look for healthy ways to avoid pesticides, **synthetic chemicals**, and **genetically modified organisms**. Definitions of *organic* vary somewhat—even within countries. The United States Department of Agriculture's National Organic Program, for example, allows for three other uses of organic besides "100% organic." Retailers can label products *organic* when at least 95 percent of the ingredients are organic; use the phrase *made with organic ingredients* when the product contains at least 70 percent organic ingredients and no sulfites; and use the term *organic* when listing ingredients for products made with less than 70 percent organic ingredients.

In recent years sales of organic fruits and vegetables have been doing especially well in Europe and North America; although rising, sales of organic meat comprise a tiny portion of the total meat market (for example, well under 1 percent in the **United States**). *See also* COFFEE; CUBA; WWOOF.

**OUTER SPACE.** By definition, outer space is beyond the earth's atmosphere. No clear physical boundary exists, however, between the atmosphere and outer space. A common demarcation is the altitude limit of aircrafts, but some use the term to refer to space beyond the range of satellite orbits. For environmentalism, outer space represents a particular type of global commons: where the resource is not consumed but rather accessed and explored primarily with technology.

The principle of national sovereignty has never been applied to outer space—significantly, for example, the **United States** did not claim territorial sovereignty over the moon in 1969. The main international organization for space law is the **United Nations** and its Committee on the Peaceful Uses of Outer Space (COPUOS), which became a permanent body of the UN General Assembly in 1959. The United Nations Office for Outer Space Affairs (UNOOSA) assists this committee and serves as its secretariat.

Five treaties govern outer space: the 1967 Treaty on Principles Governing the Activities of States in the Exploration and Use of Outer Space, including the Moon and Other Celestial Bodies (the Outer Space Treaty); the 1968 Agreement on the Rescue of Astronauts, the Return of Astronauts and the Return of Objects Launched into Outer Space (the Rescue Agreement); the 1972 Convention on International Liability for Damage Caused by Space Objects (the Liability Convention); the 1975 Convention on Registration of Objects Launched into Outer Space (the Registration Convention); and the 1979 Agreement Governing the Activities of States on the Moon and Other Celestial Bodies (the Moon Agreement).

For global environmentalism, the picture of the earth from outer space has reinforced the image of the planet as fragile and interconnected. It remains a powerful symbol for global environmental consciousness. One of the most famous pictures was taken by astronauts Neil Armstrong, Michael Collins, and Edwin (Buzz) Aldrin on their way to the moon in 1969.

**OZONE DEPLETION.** In 1970, Paul Crutzen of the Max Planck Institute for Chemistry in Mainz, **Germany**, raised the possibility that nitrogen oxides from fertilizers and supersonic aircraft might be harming the ozone layer 20–50 kilometers above the earth. In 1974, Mario J. Molina and F. Sherwood Rowland put forth the theory that **chlorofluorocarbons (CFCs)** might be drifting into the stratosphere, breaking apart, and causing a chain reaction that would deplete the ozone layer. This would have, Molina and Rowland stressed, catastrophic consequences as the ozone layer is necessary to protect against the harmful effects of ultraviolet radiation from the sun. All three would go on to win the 1995 Nobel Prize in Chemistry.

Today, many see the global effort to phase out ozone-depleting substances as one of the greatest success stories of global environmentalism. Nevertheless, most scientists still expect it will take another half century or so for the ozone layer to recover to 1980 levels. *See also* MIDGLEY, THOMAS, JR.; MONTREAL PROTOCOL ON SUBSTANCES THAT DEPLETE THE OZONE LAYER.

## – P –

**PANARCHY.** Lance H. Gunderson and **C. S. Holling** recoined the term *panarchy* for ecosystem theory. It combines the words *Pan*, the ancient Greek god of nature, and *hierarchy*. They used the term to avoid the colloquial understanding of hierarchy, which suggests a rigid, top-down approach, and create a framework for analyzing changing hierarchical systems (including within and across nature, societies, and institutions) with constantly adaptive cycles of growth, accumulation, restructuring, and renewal. An ecological example of panarchy is a small ground fire that spreads to the crown of a tree, then to a patch in the forest, and then to a whole stand of trees. A societal example is how local activist groups succeed in transforming regional organizations or institutions.

**PAPUA NEW GUINEA.** *See* MELANESIA.

**PASSENGER PIGEON.** The passenger pigeon was once the most common bird in eastern North America, with perhaps as many as five billion birds at the peak. Hunted for food, the number of passenger pigeons declined steadily during the 19th century, then began falling sharply from about 1870–1890. The last passenger pigeon died in a Cincinnati zoo in 1914. Within the environmental movement, the extinction of the passenger pigeon remains a common example (sometimes told as a metaphor) of the potential devastating environmental damage of unthinking development.

**PBDEs.** *See* POLYBROMINATED DIPHENYL ETHERS (PBDEs).

**PEAK OIL.** American geophysicist Marion King Hubbert developed the idea of peak **oil**. In 1949, he calculated the total world oil supply and consumption. In 1956, using a bell-shaped curve, he predicted that in the **United States** oil production would peak and subsequently fall between 1966 and 1972. This occurred in 1970. Later, Hubbert predicted that global oil production would peak in the 1990s, lecturing and writing on how societies needed to prepare for life after petroleum. Inadequate data and flaws in his method explain this inaccurate and pessimistic prediction.

Others have picked up where Hubbert left off and, although this remains a contentious way of analyzing oil supplies, today a wide range of estimates exist for the date when global oil production will peak. The U.S. Department of Energy does not see this occurring before 2025. The International Energy Agency does not expect it before 2030. For critics of this kind of analysis, the inaccurate estimates for global oil supplies demonstrates the tendency of many environmentalists to underestimate the potential of new technologies and knowledge to find or increase supplies of so-called nonrenewable resources. For many environmentalists, this analysis reveals a disturbing trend toward ever-higher consumption of fossil fuels (with ever-higher emissions of **greenhouse gases**) as well as confirms the need to move quickly toward developing clean alternative energy (such as hydroelectric or **wind power**).

**PERSISTENT ORGANIC POLLUTANTS (POPs).** Persistent organic pollutants are a large group of mostly **synthetic chemicals**. The **United Nations Environment Programme** has targeted the so-called "dirty dozen" for global phaseout. These include four originating mainly from industrial processes—polychlorinated biphenyls (PCBs), hexachlorobenzene (HCB), dioxins, and furans—and eight used primarily as pesticides: **dichlorodiphenyltrichloroethane (DDT)**, toxaphene, mirex, heptachlor, chlordane, aldrin, endrin, and dieldrin. The **Stockholm Convention on Persistent Organic Pollutants**, adopted in 2001, is the primary international legal mechanism for phasing these out.

Air and water currents can transport POPs far away from their emission source. Many POPs travel as well through a process of repeated evaporation and redeposit known as the "grasshopper effect." POPs also tend to build up in animals and plants, a process called bioaccumulation. That property of POPs also leads to an increase in concentration of chemicals higher up in the food chain, a process called biomagnification. Environmentalist **Rachel Carson** was one of the first to recognize the potential effects of POPs in wildlife and people, which include reproductive and immune system disorders, neurological and developmental effects, and some cancers.

**PHILIPPINES, THE.** Management of natural resources and the environment is fragmented in the Philippines, with responsibilities split between the national government and local government units. At the national level, responsibility is centered in the Department of Environment and Natural Resources, which oversees the Environmental Management Bureau, the Forest Management Board, the Parks and Wildlife Bureau, the Department of Energy, and the National Water Resources Board.

The presidency of Ferdinand Marcos (1965–1986) did pass some environmental legislation—including the 1976 Water Code of the Philippines, 1977 Philippine Environmental Policy, and 1978 Environmental Impact Assessment System—but pervasive corruption contributed to weak environmental regulation, destructive logging and land use, extensive **deforestation**, and severe soil erosion. In 1989, following devastating floods, the government banned timber exports; however, **illegal logging** was still widespread and rates of deforestation and land degradation stayed high, contributing to more natural disasters, such as mudslides in 2003 on the island of Leyte.

The 1989 Philippine Strategy for Sustainable Development was put in place in 1989 and the Philippine Council for Sustainable Development (PCSD) was created in 1992 following the **United Nations Conference on Environment and Development**. In 1996, the government also established a national **Agenda 21**, to support implementation of Agenda 21 from this summit (although this has not been very effective). The Civil Society Counterpart Council for Sustainable Development was formed in 2001, as the nongovernmental equivalent to the government's PCSD.

The Philippines is one of the world's **biodiversity** hotspots. In an effort to protect this, it ratified the **Convention on International Trade in Endangered Species** in 1981 and the **Convention on Biological Diversity** in 1993. It also created the National Integrated Protected Areas System Act in 1992.

Garbage is one of the biggest urban environmental problems in the Philippines. The government passed the Ecological Solid Waste Management Act in 2000. However, the disposal and **recycling** infrastructure remains inadequate. In 2001, for example, President Gloria Arroyo declared a state of emergency in Metro Manila because of its mounting garbage crisis. Air **pollution** is another serious problem in cities like Manila. The government did pass the Clean Air Act in 1999; and, in 2003, it required emission testing for motor vehicles registration and established hydrocarbon emission standards for motorcycles and tricycles. However, many residents still live in conditions with unhealthy outdoor and indoor air (as well as inadequate sewage and unsafe water).

The Philippines has a vibrant civil society, with active environmental **nongovernmental organizations**. These include the Legal Rights and Natural Resources Center (a member of **Friends of the Earth** International), which started in 1988; and the Fund for Nature of the Philippines, which became a member of **World Wide Fund for Nature/World Wildlife Fund (WWF)** in 1997. WWF has been involved in the Philippines since 1969, when it funded efforts to protect the Philippine eagle. Eagle conservation was promoted by the Monkey-Eating Eagle Conservation Program, established in 1969. The program lost traction, but was sustained by Peace Corps volunteers from the **United States** and rekindled in 1987 when it became the Philippine Eagle Foundation. The Philippines was also the first country in Asia to participate in a WWF debt-for-nature swap, in 1988.

**PHOTOVOLTAIC ENERGY.** *See* SOLAR POWER/ENERGY.

**PINCHOT, GIFFORD (1865–1946).** Born in Connecticut, Gifford Pinchot was the first chief of the United States Forest Service from 1905–1910. He was a pioneer in the American movement to conserve and manage forests, including playing a leading role in developing a national forest policy and promoting more efficient use of forest resources. He later served as governor of Pennsylvania (1923–1927 and 1931–1935). *See also* ECOFORESTRY; WISE USE MOVEMENT.

**PLASTIC.** Plastics are made of petroleum and **natural gas**, both non-renewable resources. Consumer and industrial uses vary from building material to packaging for goods and food to medical equipment. A common classification system to assist with disposal and **recycling** of consumer plastics is to number them from 1 to 7 according to resin type (developed by the Society of the Plastics Industry in the **United States**). Recycled plastic is turned into many products, including pillow stuffing, plastic lumber, textiles, and drainage pipes.

Plastics do not easily degrade, a characteristic that concerns many in the environmental movement. Some plastic debris can photodegrade (break down into small pellets after extended exposure to sunlight), but most does not biodegrade (decompose into organic matter through bacterial digestion). Caught in ocean gyres, two regions of the Pacific Ocean now swirl with millions of tons of plastic: the so-called **Eastern Garbage Patch** off the coast of Hawaii and the smaller Western Garbage Patch off the coast of **Japan** (with a combined area larger than the continental United States). Plastic can harm marine life as it enters the food chain (plastic polymers effectively absorb toxic compounds such as **dichlorodiphenyltrichloroethane [DDT]** and polychlorinated biphenyls [PCBs], which act as endocrine disruptors to species that consume them).

Environmentalists see so much plastic—and the chemicals leaching out—as a threat to human health. One of the worries is phthalates, which are used as plasticizers (softeners) in polyvinyl chloride (PVC) products. In advance of conclusive scientific evidence, for example, the European Union has banned the use of certain phthalates in toys and childcare articles since 1999. Incineration of PVC is also the largest contributor of chlorine into incinerators, which produces significant dioxin emissions. Another worry for human health is **bisphenol A (BPA)**, a chemical that seems to mimic the female hormone estrogen and is common in everything from hard, clear plastic bottles to the lining in canned foods to dental sealants. *See also* OIL.

**POLLUTER PAYS PRINCIPLE.** The polluter pays principle is a principle incorporated into international environmental law and regulatory policies to allocate the cost of environmental damage to those who cause that damage. It relies on markets to achieve better environmental outcomes, where users and producers of products and activities that impose environmental costs on society bear responsibility for those costs (either voluntarily or through government incentives and penalties).

The principle has been adopted into the environmental policies of the Organisation for Economic Co-operation and Development, the European Community, **Vietnam**, and other countries, as well as integrated into international commitments, such as in the declaration at the 1992 Rio Summit, which states that "national authorities should endeavour to promote the internalization of environmental costs and the use of economic instruments, taking into account the approach that the polluter should, in principle, bear the cost of **pollution**, with due regard to the public interest and without distorting international trade and investment."

Its application can include legal penalties for those who cause environmental degradation through industrial and business activities (such as requiring companies to pay for the restoration of rivers downstream of factories, or to pay for cleanup from oil spills) and requirements that producers of goods take responsibility for end-of-life products (part of **extended product responsibility**). Applying the polluter pays principle promotes **environmental justice** by placing the costs of environmental degradation on those benefiting from polluting activities, and it encourages economic efficiency by internalizing the costs of pollution into the production process. *See also* BASEL CONVENTION ON THE CONTROL OF TRANSBOUNDARY MOVEMENTS OF HAZARDOUS WASTES AND THEIR DISPOSAL; CONVENTION ON THE PREVENTION OF MARINE POLLUTION BY DUMPING OF WASTES AND OTHER MATTER; FRANCE; GERMANY; SWEDEN.

**POLLUTION.** A broad term, *pollution* encompasses many forms of contamination, degradation, and modification of natural and built environments. Pollution of natural environments is often described by its location: for example, air pollution (indoor, outdoor, and transboundary), water pollution (freshwater or ocean), and land pollution. It is also described by its form (e.g., **smog**, **oil** spills, **plastics**, and **persistent organic pollutants**), by its severity (e.g., garbage versus toxic or **hazardous wastes**), or by its cause (e.g., industry, **automobiles**, and **mining**). The impacts of pollution are equally far-ranging, and can include degrading habitats, which can threaten **biodiversity**

and harm vulnerable and **endangered species** (including **coral reefs**). It can also affect human health, causing negative impacts on resources and sectors that support human lives and livelihoods (e.g., **fishing**) as well as contribute to **climate change**.

Many **nongovernmental organizations**, including **Greenpeace** and **Resources for the Future**, focus their activities on reducing or controlling pollution. Public awareness, changes in behavior such as **recycling** and minimizing consumption, and corporate accountability for cleaner production methods and **eco-efficiency** are all potential ways to reduce pollution.

Most countries, including **Canada**, **India**, **South Korea**, and **Taiwan**, among many others, have passed legislation to control air and water pollution. However, even with regulations, many—such as **Chile**, **China**, and **Iran**—are still plagued by problems, especially in urban areas. Air pollution is particularly bad in megacities in developing countries, where, for example, many automobiles do not have catalytic converters and two-stroke scooters and motorcycles are common. Forest fires (both intentional and wild) can also contribute to air pollution; countries like **Indonesia**, Malaysia, and **Singapore** are particularly affected by forest fires, and have negotiated a transboundary haze treaty in an effort to tackle the problem.

Many international agreements also focus on reducing pollution, including **the Convention on Long-range Transboundary Air Pollution (CLRTAP)**, the **Convention on the Prevention of Marine Pollution by Dumping of Wastes and Other Matter**, and the **Basel Convention on the Control of Transboundary Movements of Hazardous Wastes and Their Disposal**. Market-based instruments, such as **carbon taxes** and **emissions trading**, are also becoming an increasingly common means to address pollution; these types of policies follow the **polluter pays principle,** which allocates the costs of environmental damage to those who benefit from the activities that cause the pollution.

Delegates at the 1972 **United Nations Conference on the Human Environment** in **Sweden** coined the term *the pollution of poverty*, describing the role they attributed to underdevelopment and poverty in causing environmental degradation. The concept of **sustainable development** arose in response to this (and to broader concerns about poverty and environmental degradation). However, some environmental economists warn that during the early stages of economic development pollution tends to intensify (see, for example, the **Environmental Kuznets Curve**). The **Green Revolution** is one example of where increased production and economic growth in agriculture led to increased pollution, as the development came with intensified use of pesticides and fertilizers. Some environmentalists advocate for development strategies that strive to avoid the pollution that tends to accompany rapid industrialization. *See also* ACID RAIN; ARCTIC; EASTERN GARBAGE PATCH; *EXXON VALDEZ* OIL SPILL; FRANCE; GERMANY; HYBRID AUTOMOBILES.

**POLYBROMINATED DIPHENYL ETHERS (PBDEs).** Polybrominated diphenyl ethers, or PBDEs, are put into consumer items as flame retardants and are now common in pillows, mattresses, rugs, curtains, TVs, and computers. Heralded as an advance in consumer safety in the 1970s, PBDEs raised few environmental or health concerns until scientists in **Sweden** set off alarms in the late 1990s after discovering that PBDEs in human breast milk seemed to be rising in some populations. Tests now confirm that these chemicals, with a chemical structure similar to polychlorinated biphenyls (PCBs) (some call them "chemical cousins") are somehow migrating from these products into people—not, apparently, mainly through food as with other **persistent organic pollutants** like dioxins or PCBs, but by collecting in homes, particularly in air and household dust.

Residents of the **United States** appear to have the world's highest levels of PBDEs (followed by Canadians). Recent tests show residents of North America have 10–40 times higher PBDE levels than residents of **Japan** or Europe. Environmentalists are now campaigning to ban PBDEs, as laboratory experiments on animals suggest they can cause hyperactivity, attention deficit, and low sperm counts. Medical researchers also worry PBDEs may mimic and interfere with human hormones (such as thyroid hormones) and can damage brain development in only trace amounts.

Progress toward eliminating PBDEs is occurring. The Swedish company IKEA was one of the first companies to ban them. Many European governments have now taken steps to eliminate two of the worst formulations of PBDEs: those common in mattresses and those in computer housings and monitors. Some states in the United States have done the same. The U.S. Environmental Protection Agency is also working with major producers such as DuPont to phase PBDEs out voluntarily. Some U.S. manufacturing and retail firms are also taking steps to stop using PBDEs, such as the computer company Dell.

**POLYCHLORINATED BIPHENYLS (PCBs).** *See* PERSISTENT ORGANIC POLLUTANTS (POPs).

**PRECAUTIONARY APPROACH/PRINCIPLE.** Following a precautionary approach requires a strategy to allow science enough time to investigate uncertainties and anticipate risks, while giving policy makers enough clout to prevent risky decisions in the pursuit of profits and markets (such as putting tetraethyl lead into gasoline to create **leaded gasoline**). Such an approach includes a duty of care where the burden of proof about harm rests with those proposing to introduce a substance into the environment. Other caveats may also surround— and either enhance or detract from its power. For example, Principle 7 of the **United Nations Global Compact** refers to the definition of a precautionary approach from the Rio Declaration from the 1992 **United Nations Conference on Environment and Development**, which stresses the need to apply precaution according to state "capabilities" and with "cost-effective measures."

**PRESERVATION.** The concept of preservation developed in the **United States** in the 19th century to convey the idea of protecting nature for its own sake (in contrast to conservation, which at the time put more emphasis on caring for nature for economic or leisure reasons). Many associate the preservation movement with the American naturalist **John Muir** (1838–1914), the founder of the **Sierra Club**, although other forces were important too, such as a growing outdoor movement among upper- and middle-class Americans. Preservationists in the United States were able to mobilize to save some of the California redwoods; they also contributed to the establishment of state and **national parks**, such as Yellowstone National Park (1872) and Yosemite National Park (1890).

**PRODUCT STEWARDSHIP.** Product Stewardship is a voluntary industry strategy to mitigate the negative environmental and health impacts of products (usually chemicals) throughout their life cycle, including research, manufacturing, transportation, storage, consumption, and disposal. Other goals include reducing corporate liability, preventing negative publicity, and earning public trust, as well as preempting legislation. First established by Dow Chemical in 1972, product stewardship is an example of a market-based instrument for environmentalism, where industries self-regulate to internalize some of the costs of **pollution** to promote **sustainable development** and **corporate social responsibility**. As part of a product stewardship strategy, companies sometimes agree to accept back a dangerous product for **recycling.** One high-profile product stewardship program is **Responsible Care®**, established in the 1980s by the chemical industry. Critics see the voluntary nature of product stewardship as insufficient, lacking accountability, and often ineffective without government regulation to enforce and audit implementation. *See also* EXTENDED PRODUCER/PRODUCT RESPONSIBILITY.

**PROGRAMME FOR THE ENDORSEMENT OF FOREST CERTIFICATION (PEFC).** Launched in 1999 by representatives from 11 European countries, the Programme for the Endorsement of Forest Certification (PEFC) Council is a nonprofit **nongovernmental organization** that aims to provide "an assurance mechanism to purchasers of wood and paper products that they are promoting the sustainable management of forests." PEFC is a global umbrella organization comprising 35 independent national forest certification systems. **Canada** and the **United States** joined in 2001. As of 2008, more than 200 million hectares of forest are PEFC certified. Supporters see this as part of a global movement to develop environmental markets, providing consumers with independent guarantees of sustainability. Critics worry that the standards are too low: for example, it permits logging in old-growth and other forest areas with high ecological value. *See also* ECO-CERTIFICATION; SUSTAINABLE FORESTRY INITIATIVE.

**PROXIMITY PRINCIPLE.** *See* BASEL CONVENTION ON THE CONTROL OF TRANSBOUNDARY MOVEMENTS OF HAZARDOUS WASTES AND THEIR DISPOSAL.

## – R –

**RAINBOW WARRIOR.** The *Rainbow Warrior* was one of the vessels that **Greenpeace** International planned to use to disrupt French nuclear tests in the South Pacific in July 1985. Docked at Auckland Harbor in **New Zealand** on 10 July 1985, the ship sank after two devices exploded on board. One of the crew—a Netherlands national—drowned. Five days later, two agents of the Directorate General of External Security, a branch of the French Ministry of Defense, were arrested in New Zealand. The chief justice of the High Court of New Zealand would later sentence each for manslaughter and willful damage. The killing strained relations between New Zealand and **France**; worldwide, the sinking of the *Rainbow Warrior* became a symbol of the courage of environmentalists and a sign of the brutality of those working to subvert the movement. Today, the current *Rainbow Warrior* (acquired by Greenpeace in 1989) continues to ply the world's oceans on behalf of the Greenpeace cause.

**RAINFOREST ACTION NETWORK (RAN).** Founded in 1985 by Randall Hayes, the Rainforest Action Network (RAN) now has staff members in San Francisco and Tokyo, thousands of volunteers, and an annual budget of over US$3 million. Its central goal is to protect rainforests and the rights of those living in these forests, although recently it has also been campaigning to halt **climate change**. Its primary tactic involves direct-action campaigns targeting specific corporations, with the aim of changing purchasing or other behavior.

The first successful campaign was a 1987 boycott of the restaurant chain Burger King, which stopped importing "rainforest beef"—cattle raised on pastures created from cleared rainforest—after sales dropped by 12 percent. Other campaigns have included the Old Growth Campaign (to protect old-growth forests from logging) and the Freedom from Oil Campaign (to reduce **oil**-related conflicts, decrease oil dependence in the **United States**, and mitigate climate change by working with the auto industry to increase fuel efficiency and reduce **greenhouse gases**). The Old Growth Campaign has influenced the purchasing policies of some major retailers, including Kinko's, Home Depot, and Lowe's, all of which have committed to stop buying or selling products made from old-growth timber. RAN's Freedom from Oil

Campaign is targeting the Ford Motor Company, among other major multinational companies. *See also* DEFORESTATION.

**RAMOS, ROSA HILDA.** *See* GOLDMAN ENVIRONMENTAL PRIZE.

**RAMSAR CONVENTION ON WETLANDS.** *See* CONVENTION ON WETLANDS OF INTERNATIONAL IMPORTANCE ESPECIALLY AS WATERFOWL HABITAT.

**RECLAIM THE STREETS (RTS).** Relying on grassroots and spontaneous organization and espousing a principle of nonviolence, Reclaim the Streets (RTS) involves protests opposing corporate capitalism (usually with a specific focus on the societal and environmental damage from the increasing dependency on **automobiles**). It first emerged in London in the fall of 1991 as part of a direct-action movement against automobiles in **Great Britain**.

This group disbanded, but another reemerged in 1994 in the "Battle for Claremont Road," also known as the "No M11" campaign, to protest plans to demolish a residential street in East London to build a thoroughfare. Protestors occupied every vacant house on the street, then turned the neighborhood into a street party. Although this did not stop construction of the thoroughfare, RTS became famous for its street parties—or political raves. Street Party 1 (1995) was held in Camden Town. Street Party 2 (1995) was held at the Angel, Islington (north London). Street Party 3 (July 1996) was much bigger, occupying a stretch of motorway in west London, with over 7,000 participants. Organizers pulled these protests off by using tight security, with only a handful of people knowing a party's location ahead of time.

Shortly after Street Party 3, chapters of RTS began to emerge in the **United States**, with the first in San Francisco when RTS/Bay Area held a street party on Berkeley's Telegraph Avenue in 1998. Today, although this group has done little to slow the growing global dependency on the automobile as the primary form of transportation, this diffuse movement has spread around the world, with occasional protests occurring from **Australia** to **Canada** to **Finland** to **Mexico**. *See also* GUERRILLA GARDENING.

**RECYCLING.** Recycling is a waste-management strategy to reprocess used materials into new products, thus reducing the amount of waste. Proponents contend that it is more ecologically benign than landfills and incineration, depleting fewer resources. Also, it can generate economic benefits, including funds for municipalities from sales, job creation, and new markets from product innovation.

Modern household recycling started in the late 1960s in response to concerns about social equity and **pollution**. Community groups ran early facilities, selling collected materials back to manufacturers. In Western societies, curbside recycling was spreading by the late 1980s. Reasons for these programs vary, but common ones are rising landfill costs, public opposition to incineration and new landfills, escalating amounts of garbage, and strengthening public support for environmentalism. Recycling in industrial processes also occurs, where one industry's waste stream becomes a raw material for a different industry.

Some environmentalists criticize recycling for not challenging unsustainable patterns of production and consumption. Others stress it is at best only a partial solution to the environmental consequences of rising consumption. Often, for example, breaking materials down and remanufacturing them requires chemical and energy inputs and releases toxins. It is common as well to reinforce recycled content with new materials. Most environmentalists, however, support recycling, although many propose a "3 R" waste management hierarchy: reduce, reuse, and as a last resort, recycle. *See also* DEEP ECOLOGY; EXTENDED PRODUCER/PRODUCT RESPONSIBILITY; GLASS; PLASTIC; PRODUCT STEWARDSHIP; TIRES.

**REES, WILLIAM.** *See* ECOLOGICAL FOOTPRINT.

**REFORESTATION.** Forestation includes both afforestation and reforestation. Afforestation involves establishing forest cover in areas without a recent history of forests. Reforestation involves reestablishing forests on degraded forestlands or in areas where forests grew in more recent times. In developed countries, replanting efforts over the last few decades have allowed the total area of temperate forests to expand, although afforested and reforested areas are often less complex forest ecosystems (including many monoculture plantations). Intense logging, fires, and land-clearing in developing countries, however, have left tropical **deforestation** rates far exceeding any gains from afforestation and reforestation. Still, reforestation can provide many benefits in developing countries—for example, slowing soil erosion and **desertification** and providing people with wood and fuel—and it has been an effective strategy for some community-based environmental movements, such as the **Green Belt Movement** in **Kenya**. *See also* ILLEGAL LOGGING.

**RENEWABLE ENERGY.** Renewable energy is, in theory, from inexhaustible sources, unlike, for example, energy from finite sources such as fossil fuels. This includes **solar energy**; **wind energy**; **geothermal energy**; wave, tidal, and ocean thermal; hydroelectricity; and biomass.

Except for hydroelectricity and biomass, in practice, these energy sources are often expensive, unreliable, or available only on a small scale. Worldwide, renewable energy supplies 12–14 percent of the world's total primary energy. Developing countries currently account for three-quarters of renewable energy use globally, principally in the form of biomass or hydropower.

Countries like Austria, **Canada**, **New Zealand**, Switzerland and **Sweden** currently derive over 50 percent of their electricity production from renewables. A few countries, such as Paraguay, Iceland, Nepal, Mozambique, the Democratic Republic of Congo, **Costa Rica**, and Norway meet almost all of their energy needs with renewable energy. The sustainable energy movement, including environmentalists like **Amory B. Lovins**, is calling for more efforts to develop renewable energies like wind and solar power to address threats like **climate change**. *See also* BRAZIL; HYBRID AUTOMOBILES; PHOTOVOLTAIC ENERGY; THREE GORGES DAM.

**RESOURCES FOR THE FUTURE (RFF).** Founded in 1952, Resources for the Future (RFF) is a nonprofit and nonpartisan organization based in Washington, D.C. It was the first think tank in the **United States** to focus exclusively on environmental, energy, and natural resource issues. Today, it contributes in particular to demonstrating the value of economic tools for developing effective policy for exploiting and conserving natural resources. RFF has about 40 researchers in Washington, D.C. Most hold doctorate degrees in economics, but staff expertise also includes engineering, law, ecology, city planning, and public policy. Current research efforts are concentrating on **biodiversity**, **climate change**, **pollution** control, land and water use, **hazardous waste**, energy policy, and environmental issues in developing countries.

**RESPONSIBLE CARE®.** A voluntary commitment by the chemical industry to environmental and social responsibility, Responsible Care® is an environmental management system for chemicals. Companies that commit must continuously improve the health, safety, security, and environmental performance of chemical operations as well as respond to public concerns about the safe management of chemicals. It encourages companies to go above and beyond government requirements. Goals include improving chemical processes, practices, and procedures; reducing waste, accidents, incidents, and emissions; and developing reliable communication with the public. Standards comprise Codes of Management Practice addressing **product stewardship**, community awareness and emergency response, employee health and safety, process safety, and **pollution** prevention. Companies undergo a third-party independent audit for a Responsible Care Management System® (RCMS®) standard or an integrated standard such as the RC14001® American standard (which provides joint certification with the **International Organization for Standardization [ISO] 14001**).

Launched in **Canada** in 1985 by the Canadian Chemical Producers' Association (spurred in part by the chemical accident in 1984 in **Bhopal, India**), Responsible Care® has now been adopted in 53 countries. It is one of the largest and most successful voluntary **corporate social responsibility** initiatives. In 2005, the International Council of Chemical Associations created a Responsible Care® Global Charter to encourage adoption of national Responsible Care® programs and advance the global chemical industry's commitment to **sustainable development** consistent with the environmental principles of the **United Nations Global Compact**. Participation is mandatory for membership in many national chemical industry associations, such as the Canadian Chemical Producers' Association and the American Chemistry Council (formerly the Chemical Manufacturers' Association). *See also* ECO-CERTIFICATION.

**RIKHVANOVA, MARINA.** *See* GOLDMAN ENVIRONMENTAL PRIZE.

**RIO SUMMIT.** *See* UNITED NATIONS CONFERENCE ON ENVIRONMENT AND DEVELOPMENT (UNCED).

**RUSSIA.** The breakup of the **Soviet Union** in 1991 contributed to an economic crisis in the Russian Federation. This added to environmental pressures, especially on water and air quality and **hazardous waste** management.

President Mikhail Gorbachev's glasnost policy mandating a more open and transparent government allowed many environmental **nongovernmental organizations (NGOs)** and civil society groups to form. For example, the Socio-Ecological Union, founded in 1988, persisted after the fall of the Soviet Union and now operates as a network of NGOs across the former Union of Soviet Socialist Republics (USSR). Other environmental groups also began to take shape and gain more influence in the 1990s. For example, the Ecojuris Institute of Environmental Law was founded in 1991 as Russia's first public-interest environmental law firm. By 1998, it had won a Supreme Court case brought against several government proposals, including for development in protected forest areas. Other groups have had some notable achievements, too. For example, the government created a **national park** to protect the Siberian tiger in 2007, in part because of advocacy and pressure by the **World Wide Fund for Nature/World Wildlife Fund (WWF)** and other environmental groups.

Official political participation by environmental activists started in 1991 with the founding of the Interregional Green Party, which started as a local political party in Leningrad (St. Petersburg). In 2005, this party became Zelenaya Alternativa (GROZA), or Green Alternative, a national political movement but not a political party. The political **green party** of Russia, the Russian Ecological Party, or The Greens, was started as the Constructive Ecological Party in 1992.

In 2000, environmental responsibilities were transferred from the State Committee for Environmental Protection to the Natural Resources Ministry. Some environmental NGOs like **Greenpeace** saw this as a troubling move, since the Natural Resources Ministry is focused on resource extraction rather than conservation.

Nuclear waste and safety is a major issue in Russia. A European Commission program to improve nuclear safety across the former Soviet Union, the Technical Assistance to the Commonwealth of Independent States (TACIS) Programme, was launched in 1991. The program was revised in 1998 following a slow start, highlighted by incidents such as an explosion at a plutonium processing facility in Tomsk in 1993. Russia was also criticized following a 1996 exposé on nuclear waste from a nuclear submarine base in the **Arctic** by Alexander Nikitin (a Russian environmentalist and winner of the 1997 **Goldman Environmental Prize**) and the Bellona Foundation (an NGO from Norway).

Russia suffers from many other environmental problems as well. The country has the world's largest **natural gas** reserves as well as substantial **coal** and **oil** reserves. Several ships caught in 2007 in a storm in the straits between the Azov and Black Seas spilled oil, sulfur, and other toxic materials. Recently, the WWF and others have also been raising concerns over environmental damage in Chechnya, following many years of conflict over demands for independence. Environmental concerns in the area include chemical and radioactive **pollution**, leaking oil pipelines, inadequate sewerage systems leading to water contamination, and **illegal logging**.

In 1997, Russia joined the Group of 8 (G8); its presidency in 2006 was focused, in part, on energy. Also in 1997, Russia signed an Agreement on Partnership and Cooperation with the European Union (EU), which includes environmental cooperation concerns. Environmental issues were included in subsequent Russia-EU agreements, including the EU-Russia Strategic Partnership and the EU-Russia Common Economic Space road map. Notably, in 2005, Russia ratified the **Kyoto Protocol**, a landmark event as it allowed the protocol to enter into force (it needed at least 55 countries contributing at least 55 percent of 1990 **greenhouse gas** emissions). *See also* FISHING; NUCLEAR POWER/ENERGY; SEALING; SIBERIA.

# – S –

**SANTA CRUZ ISLANDS.** *See* MELANESIA.

**SANTOS, FELICIANO DOS.** *See* GOLDMAN ENVIRONMENTAL PRIZE.

**SARO-WIWA, KEN (1941–1995).** Kenule (Ken) Beeson Saro-Wiwa was a Nigerian public servant, environmentalist, television producer, and author (with 25 books). The son of a chief of the Ogoni people, in 1990, he helped found the Movement for the Survival of the Ogoni People (MOSOP) to fight with nonviolent tactics for social and ecological justice (especially against the multinational **oil** companies). MOSOP was popular among the Ogoni: for example, more than half of the 500,000 Ogoni people showed up at one protest in 1993. Saro-Wiwa was particularly critical of the oil company Shell and **Nigeria**'s military dictatorship for destroying the environment and threatening the survival of the Ogoni people.

In 1993, four chiefs, including Saro-Wiwa's brother-in-law and a founding member of MOSOP, were murdered during a riot in Ogoni. In October 1995, Saro-Wiwa and eight others were sentenced to hang for inciting the murders. Human rights and environmental groups, along with many governments, condemned the ruling. To the surprise of many observers, despite the international backlash Saro-Wiwa was executed in November 1995, creating an even greater storm of worldwide anger at Nigeria's dictator, General Sani Abacha, as well as at Shell. Today, Saro-Wiwa is honored worldwide as an example of the bravery necessary for environmentalism in corrupt and repressive states propped up by profit-seeking multinational corporations.

**SCHOPS, IGNACE.** *See* GOLDMAN ENVIRONMENTAL PRIZE.

**SCHUMACHER, E. F. (1911–1977).** Born in Bonn, **Germany,** Ernst Friedrich (Fritz) Schumacher left Germany in 1936 for **Great Britain** (where earlier he had been a Rhodes Scholar at Oxford University) to escape Nazism. Unable to find work in his field, he became a farm laborer before being interned for three months during World War II as an enemy alien. Returning to the farm after his internment, Schumacher began to write on the economic prerequisites for lasting peace in Europe. Having gained British citizenship in 1946, he then became an economic advisor to—and was a member of—the British Control Commission, which worked to rebuild the German economy. In the 1950s and 1960s, he was chief economic advisor to the British National Coal Board. In 1955, he traveled to Burma for the **United Nations**, a trip that would inspire his writings on what he called "Buddhist economics," where priority is put on improving human lives with local economies producing goods from local resources for local needs. After a trip to **India** in 1961, Schumacher pioneered the idea of intermediate or appropriate technology: arguing simpler technologies that match the scale of community life were often more efficient and environmentally suitable in rural developing areas. He brought all of these ideas together into his bestselling 1973 book, *Small Is Beautiful: Economics as If People Matter*, which to this day remains highly influential among those who argue for the localization of environmentalism. *See also* ECOLOGICAL ECONOMICS.

**SEALING.** As early as 5000 BC, native people were hunting seals in what is now Atlantic **Canada**. European settlers have hunted harp seals for over 300 years off the coast of Newfoundland and in the Gulf of St. Lawrence. Countries involved over the centuries include **Russia**, **Great Britain**, Norway, Canada, and the **United States**, mostly sealing in Canadian waters but also in the White and Baltic seas, the North Pacific, and the Sub-**Antarctic** Islands. Already, by the end of the 19th century, a dozen species of seals were on the verge of extinction.

Environmentalists and animal rights activists began to protest the hunting of harp seals in eastern Canada in the 1960s, saying it was cruel and unsustainable. Protestors objected in particular to the "slaughter" of "baby" whitecoats—harp pups between 6–12 days old—usually killed with several blows to the skull with a wooden bat or hooked gaff.

Facing a global outcry, the Canadian federal government began to regulate harvesting and impose quotas. But the antisealing campaign continued to gain ground in the 1970s as environmental groups like **Greenpeace** joined forces with animal rights groups like the International Fund for Animal Welfare (IFAW). The activists were creative and bold, confronting hunters and cuddling whitecoats in front of millions of television viewers. During the 1970s, activists became better organized, fundraising for million-dollar budgets, filling conventions with snow-white balloons, and handing politicians petitions with thousands of pages of signatures calling for an end to the hunt.

Over time activists began to focus on disrupting import markets in Europe (the primary market for white fur coats). This strategy eventually produced a dramatic victory when, in 1983, the European

Community imposed a two-year ban on the import of whitecoat pelts. The ban was renewed in 1985 and, with an antisealing campaign to boycott Canadian fish products growing in Europe and the United States, the Canadian government banned the hunt for whitecoats in 1987, in effect ending Canada's commercial seal hunt.

This did not last, however. In the mid-1990s, the Canadian government began to increase the allowable catch for seals older than 12 days, provide subsidies, and develop new markets. Although it was still illegal to kill whitecoats and only small boats and locals could harvest the older seals, the Canadian government was effectively reopening the commercial hunt. Today, sealers are landing around 300,000 harp seals, larger than the hunts of the 1960s, 1970s, and 1980s. The activists are back—angry and vocal—but now with far less influence, partly because the primary markets for seal fur coats are now **China** and Russia.

**SHALLOW ECOLOGY.** *See* DEEP ECOLOGY.

**SHIVA, VANDANA (1952–).** Born in Dehradun, **India**, Vandana Shiva trained as a physicist, receiving a Ph.D. from the University of Western Ontario in 1978 with a dissertation title of "Hidden Variables and Non-locality in Quantum Theory." Returning to India, Shiva did research for the Indian Institute of Management on technology, science, and environmental policy. In 1982, she moved back to her hometown to found her Research Foundation for Science, Technology and Ecology. Since that time she has become one of the world's leading environmental writers and campaigners on issues of **biodiversity**, **genetically modified organisms (GMOs)**, food security, and gender. She helped found the movement Navdanya to protect the diversity of food sources, promote organic farming, and advocate for the rights of farmers in India. She was also a leader in the Neem Campaign and Basmati Campaign, which strove to prevent biopiracy (the appropriation of the rights of indigenous peoples over knowledge, generally using patents). Her books include *The Violence of the Green Revolution*, *Monocultures of the Mind*, *Staying Alive*, and *Biopiracy*.

**SIBERIA.** Strictly speaking, Siberia only encompasses the region extending east of the Ural Mountains up to the western border of the

Russian Far East, which is geographically and economically distinct (mountainous and more sparsely populated). Both regions, however, are generally grouped into what is called Siberia. For centuries this remote and expansive region has been a source of natural resources, and the priorities of faraway governments have tended to override local efforts to promote conservation or sustainable production.

Today, the region continues to supply the global economy with natural resources. It contains vast **oil** and **natural gas** reserves: for example, the eastern Siberian gas fields in Yakutia and around the Lena River and oil and gas fields under Sakhalin Island in the Far East. It also has deep mineral stores, especially in the Far East. Timber is equally vast, with the forests of Siberia and the Far East containing about one-quarter of the global wood inventory.

This has affected the environment in many ways, often negatively. Waterways, such as the Ob River, are contaminated; in many cities, such as Kemerovo Oblast, residents are suffering from high rates of bronchial asthma and lung cancer. **Deforestation** rates are also some of the world's highest. Water and soil quality are much better in the Far East, but even here environmental degradation is severe in many of the places with open pit **mining**. The region also suffers from the legacy of nuclear testing, radioactive waste storage, and plutonium mining during the era of the **Soviet Union**.

Environmental activism in Siberia existed throughout the Soviet period, but was particularly influential during the years of Nikita Khrushchev (1953–1964), following his "opening" of the political system. Students and scientists were at the core of this activism. One example is the Kedrograd movement in the late 1950s to protect Siberian stone pine forests in the Altai. Led by students from the Leningrad forestry academy, it proposed harvesting forest resources without damaging the trees. A second example was the scientific movement in the 1960s to protect Lake Baikal, a **United Nations Educational, Scientific and Cultural Organization (UNESCO)** World Heritage Site and the world's oldest and deepest freshwater lake, from industrial waste, air **pollution**, deforestation, and plans to divert flows for agriculture and hydroelectricity. Today, local environmentalists are joined by international campaigners from groups like **Greenpeace**, with, for example, campaigns to save the boreal forests from logging. *See also* GOLDMAN ENVIRONMENTAL PRIZE; RUSSIA; SIBERIAN PERMAFROST.

**SIBERIAN PERMAFROST.** Some 49 billion metric tons of methane—almost one-sixth of the total stored on land—sits in the northeast Siberian ice complex. Melting permafrost in **Siberia** is now releasing this methane, which has about 20 times the greenhouse effect of carbon dioxide. Some ecologists worry this is producing a self-reinforcing feedback, with warmer conditions producing more methane and more methane accelerating the process of warming. *See also* CLIMATE CHANGE.

**SIERRA CLUB.** The Sierra Club is one of the oldest and largest grassroots environmental organizations in the **United States**. Cofounded in 1892 by preservationist **John Muir**, who became its first president, the Sierra Club originally focused on preserving the forests and ecosystems of the Sierra Nevada. Today, it campaigns on a range of issues from protecting national forests and marine **biodiversity** to promoting **environmental justice**, sustainable consumption, population management, and responsible trade. Headquartered in San Francisco, it has a lobbying office in Washington, D.C. (since 1963), as well as many state and regional offices. It has hundreds of thousands of members in local chapters throughout the United States as well as an affiliate Sierra Club of **Canada**. Members receive the bimonthly magazine, *Sierra*. *See also* NONGOVERNMENTAL ORGANIZATIONS (NGOs); PRESERVATION.

**SIMON, JULIAN (1932–1998).** Simon was a professor of business administration at the University of Maryland and a senior fellow at the Cato Institute. One of his best-known books is *The Ultimate Resource* (1981). Writers like Simon—and more recently **Bjørn Lomborg**—have challenged the pessimistic prediction of a looming "global crisis" common among environmentalists. For these optimists, history is defined primarily by social and economic progress. This history confirms the fallacy of believing in limits to growth, as efficiency gains from ingenuity and technology can in fact allow economic growth to continue forever. Thus, for Simon the current trajectory toward better standards of living can, with balanced responses to the alarmism of environmentalism, also continue indefinitely. Simon's publications have stirred a hornet's nest of environmental critics. His defenders respond by pointing to global trends over the last century like longer life expectancies and higher per capita incomes.

**SINGAPORE.** A small island state with few natural resources, Singapore has a strong administrative framework for environmental governance and legislation. Following independence from Malaysia in 1965 (a short-lived arrangement replacing British rule in 1963), the government created its Ministry of the Environment in 1972. In 2004, this became the Ministry of the Environment and Water Resources (MEWR) with control over the National Environment Agency and the Public Utilities Board. The **National Parks** Board oversees several hundred parks and gardens in the country, along with three nature reserves and one wetland reserve. In 1998, the Interagency Committee on Energy Efficiency was created; it was restructured as the National Energy Efficiency Committee in 2001, then as the National Climate Change Committee in 2006 when Singapore acceded to the **Kyoto Protocol**.

Singapore gives particular attention to developing water technology, first experimenting with water **recycling** in 1974. High costs precluded significant progress until the late 1990s, however, when the Public Utilities Board started the Singapore Water Reclamation Study (known as the NEWater Study).

**Nongovernmental organizations** tend to cooperate closely with government agencies in Singapore. The National Council on the Environment, created in 1990 and renamed the Singapore Environment Council (SEC) in 1995, works with the government to coordinate environmental action. For example, the SEC administers the Singapore Green Labelling Scheme (SGLS), an **eco-labeling** program created in 1992 by the Ministry of the Environment.

Singapore is active in promoting cooperative environmental management in the Asia-Pacific region. It is the headquarters of the Asia-Pacific Centre for Environmental Law, established in 1996 by the National University of Singapore's Faculty of Law, the Commission on Environmental Law of the **International Union for Conservation of Nature (IUCN)**, and the **United Nations Environment Programme**. In 2002, the nongovernmental Environmental Challenge Organisation (ECO) Singapore was founded to support environmental movements in Singapore. It also acts as the Secretariat for the Asia Youth Environmental Network, and helped to found the Asia-Europe Meeting (ASEM) Youth Network for Sustainable Development.

Singapore has some of the world's strictest environmental regulations for **automobiles** and industry (both for waste and emissions). In recent years, however, during drier months a smoky haze from forest fires in **Indonesia** has been drifting over Singapore (as well as Malaysia and **Thailand**) and causing unhealthy levels of air **pollution**; in an effort to stop this, in 2003 Singapore ratified the ASEAN Agreement on Transboundary Haze Pollution. *See also* INDONE-SIAN FOREST FIRES, 1997–1998.

**SINGER, PETER (1946–).** Born in **Australia**, philosopher Peter Albert David Singer was educated at the University of Melbourne and Oxford University. Since 1999, he has been Ira W. DeCamp Professor of Bioethics at Princeton University; since 2005, he has also held a Laureate Professorship at the University of Melbourne. His book, *Animal Liberation* (1975), has been especially influential among those critical of the anthropocentrism of modern environmentalism. He is also considered a leading intellectual within the animal rights movement, although his controversial arguments have also angered many people, such as advocates for the disabled.

**SMOG.** Combining the words *smoke* (from burning **coal**) and *fog*, the word *smog* became common after a London newspaper quoted Dr. Henry Antoine Des Voeux in 1905 describing the London Fog as "smog." Today, smog refers more generally to air **pollution** hanging over cities as a thick haze. First World cities with heavy traffic and a natural tendency to trap pollution—such as London and Los Angeles—still regularly experience smog. On the one hand, air quality in much of the First World tends to be improving with stricter controls on **automobile** and industrial emissions. On the other hand, smog remains severe and is worsening in many cities of the Third World: for example, Beijing, Mexico City, and Tehran.

**SOLAR POWER/ENERGY.** Solar power arises from solar heat and photovoltaic energy. Along with wind energy, solar electricity is one of the fastest growing forms of renewable energy. Around 80 percent comes from photovoltaic energy; solar thermal power plants, almost all in the First World, produce the rest. Solar collectors can also generate heat and hot water for domestic use, common, for example, in **Israel**, Turkey, and Greece.

The capacity to generate solar electricity has been rising quickly over the last decade, roughly doubling every two years since 1996. In 2006, the global capacity reached 5.3 gigawatts (GW), with **Germany** leading the production at 2.5 GW, followed by **Japan** and the **United States**. Many analysts predict solar electricity will continue to grow as a source of power, with production in Europe alone reaching 4.6 GW in 2007.

Photovoltaic energy occurs by converting light directly into electricity. In 1839, French physicist Edmund Becquerel was the first to note the photoelectric effect. Albert Einstein won the Nobel Prize in 1921 for his theories explaining this effect: the basis of modern photovoltaic technology. In 1954, Bell Laboratories developed a silicon photovoltaic cell able to convert enough sunlight to power electrical equipment. The United States space program would later develop photovoltaic cells to power satellites.

Photovoltaic technology involves significant investment and operating costs as a commercial renewable energy source. Some environmentalists see this as a potential solution to provide a limitless source of environmentally friendly energy for the billions of people who currently live in areas without access to electricity. Doubters worry it is too expensive and unreliable (due to the seasonal nature of sunshine and the difficulty of storage) to power the transportation and agriculture infrastructure necessary for reasonable standards of living in these places. Currently, photovoltaic solar energy only accounts for a tiny portion of the world's energy supply, and the focus of industry is on improving the technology to reduce its cost. *See also* RENEWABLE ENERGY.

**SOLOMON ISLANDS.** *See* MELANESIA.

**SOUTH AFRICA.** In 1981, the South African government put in place its National Conservation Strategy. The National Parks Act had already been passed in 1926; today, there are 20 **national parks** managed under the Department of Environmental Affairs and Tourism. Much greater environmental issues, however, include **deforestation**, **mining** degradation, population pressures, scarce water resources, invasive species, and a severe HIV/AIDS epidemic (one of the worst in the world).

Marked by the policy of apartheid from 1948–1994, South Africa established a new constitution in 1996 under President Nelson Mandela, which includes the right to water in the Bill of Rights. The 1997 National Water Policy and 1998 Water Act emphasized sustainability and equity, establishing a water tribunal for dispute resolution and water rights based on permits. In 1997, the government ratified the **Convention to Combat Desertification**, which led to a National Action Programme. In 2001, the government introduced a Free Basic Water policy, which gave each household the right to 6,000 liters of safe and free water per month. South Africa is now, according to the **United Nations** Human Development Report 2006, one of only a few countries that spends less on its military than on water and sanitation.

South Africa is one of the world's largest producers of platinum, gold, and chromium. Diamonds are also important to its economy. In light of concerns over conflict diamonds, the Kimberley Process was started in South Africa in 2000 to create an international certification scheme for rough diamonds.

South Africa has also played an influential role in advancing global environmentalism. The Wildlife and Environment Society of South Africa was founded in 1926 and became one of the founding members of the **International Union for Conservation of Nature (IUCN)**. The **World Summit on Sustainable Development** was held in Johannesburg in 2002, as a follow-up to the Earth Summit held in Rio de Janeiro in 1992.

**SOUTH PACIFIC REGIONAL ENVIRONMENT PROGRAMME (SPREP).** *See* MELANESIA.

**SOVIET UNION (1922–1991).** A tradition of natural history and nature protection societies was in place prior to the 1917 Russian Revolution: in that year, for example, a Conservation Conference to discuss the establishment of **national parks** was held in Petrograd. Still, the 1920s is sometimes called the golden age for Soviet environmentalism as the state put in place legislation to support *zapovedniki*, or protected areas, first set up in the 1890s. These were similar to national parks in the **United States**, although locations were selected more for ecological criteria.

The Soviet Union's (USSR, or Union of Soviet Socialist Republics) first Five-Year Plan of 1929–1933, however, ended this wave of environmentalism, increasing timber production and altering production methods in agriculture and industry. In the 1930s and 1940s, the state did not allow intellectual and political dissent; conservationists were labeled un-Marxist and antirevolutionary. By the end of the 1950s, the protected area had decreased from 12.5 million to 1.5 million hectares. Joseph Stalin's death in 1953 did little to change Soviet environmentalism; not until the 1970s did environmental writings appear in newspapers and magazines. During this time the extent of protected areas also began to rise again. But it was not until Mikhail Gorbachev's glasnost that environmental critics and the environmental movement began to gain strength.

Among the many environmental problems of the Soviet Union were the eutrophication of Lake Baikal caused by effluents of a paper mill; the accident at the **Chernobyl** nuclear plant in 1986; nuclear contamination from the nuclear arms race; air **pollution** in industrial cities; and lead, carbon monoxide, and nitrogen oxide pollution from traffic. In Central Asia, the **Aral Sea**, once the world's fourth largest lake, shrank by half by the early 1990s as authorities diverted its inflows to agriculture and hydroelectricity. *See also* CUBA; NUCLEAR POWER/ENERGY; RUSSIA.

**SPACESHIP EARTH.** The metaphor of spaceship earth became popular in the 1960s as a way to stress the need to respect resource limits and care for onboard systems to enable the earth to continue to support life as it journeys through space and time. Pictures of the earth from space, in particular ones as astronauts went to the moon in the late 1960s, brought home for many people the vulnerability of life on a small planet swirling through a vast universe. Since then the image of the earth from space has been a core symbol of environmentalism, appearing on everything from books to T-shirts to websites. For some people it continues to evoke the need to care for and respect the interconnected life systems of a "spaceship earth." *See also* BOULDING, KENNETH E.

**SPAIN.** Spain's first **national parks** law was passed in 1916, and replaced with new laws to protect national spaces in 1957, 1975, and

1989. The country now has 14 national parks, setting up a new parks network in 2007. The Ministry of Rural, Marine, and Natural Environments is the government department responsible for environmental management.

The Confederation of the Greens, Spain's **green party**, was founded in 1984. **Petra Kelly**, a founder of the German Green Party, was instrumental in its formation; she convened a meeting of Spanish environmental activists in the early 1980s, which led to the Manifesto of Tenerife and the party's creation. Spain also has active **nongovernmental organizations** for the environment, including Amigos de la Tierra España, created in 1979 as part of **Friends of the Earth** International.

Although it is a party to the **Kyoto Protocol**, Spain is struggling to meet its commitments to reduce **greenhouse gas** emissions, and currently emissions far exceed 1990 levels. A new national **climate change** adaptation plan was approved in 2006; however, significant challenges face the country, including a severe drought beginning in 2004 that is undermining hydroelectricity generation.

**Genetically modified organisms (GMOs)** have evoked mixed responses in Spain. It was the only European Union country to allow commercial genetically modified corn crops in 2005; however, four regions and over 30 municipalities have declared themselves GMO-free zones.

**STEADY-STATE ECONOMY.** Economist **Herman Daly** developed the notion of a steady-state economy, building on philosopher John Stuart Mill, who imagined economies becoming mature and one day reaching a steady state. For Daly, in a steady-state economy the inflow and outflow of people and capital are constant at levels sufficient for a satisfying and sustainable life. This does not necessarily mean zero growth in the gross national product, as it is not defined in these terms, but it does require a rate of throughput of matter and energy that is as low as possible.

Such an economy, Daly argues, would not harm the global environment yet would still allow societies to develop and improve human well-being. He has published many articles and books explaining his vision, including *Toward a Steady-State Economy* in 1973 (edited), *Steady-State Economics: The Economics of Biophysical*

*Equilibrium and Moral Growth* in 1977, and *Economics, Ecology, Ethics: Essays Toward a Steady-State Economy* in 1980 (edited).

**STOCKHOLM CONFERENCE.** *See* UNITED NATIONS CONFERENCE ON THE HUMAN ENVIRONMENT.

**STOCKHOLM CONVENTION ON PERSISTENT ORGANIC POLLUTANTS.** The Stockholm Convention was adopted in 2001 and entered into force in 2004 (90 days after the 50th ratification). As of 2008, there were 146 parties. The convention involves multiple strategies for controlling **persistent organic pollutants (POPs)**, toxic chemicals that persist in the environment, accumulate in the fatty tissue of living organisms, and biomagnify through food chains. It covers 12 of the worst POPs arising from pesticides, industrial chemicals, combustion, and incineration. Research over the last few decades has found the "dirty dozen" (which includes **dichloro-diphenyltrichloroethane [DDT]**, polychlorinated biphenyls [PCBs], dioxins, and furans) can, among other things, cause cancer as well as damage liver, nervous, and reproductive systems in wildlife and people. The Stockholm Convention seeks to ban and restrict intentional production of POPs; minimize and eventually eliminate unintentional POPs; manage and dispose of stockpiles safely; control imports and exports of POPs; promote technologies and practices to replace existing POPs; and prevent the creation of new POPs. The rules allow for some exemptions: for example, allowing DDT for disease control until effective replacements become available as well as allowing PCBs in electrical transformers and other equipment until 2025.

Environmentalists have been campaigning to ban these chemicals since the 1960s—spurred in part by **Rachel Carson**'s influential critique of DDT in her book *Silent Spring*. In the 1990s, the Inuit people became an influential moral force in the environmental movement advocating for an international environmental treaty against POPs. These pollutants move on wind and water currents. They also migrate though food chains and as fish, birds, animals, and people travel. In a process sometimes called the "grasshopper effect," POPs can also travel through the atmosphere by a repeated (often seasonal) process of evaporation, deposit, evaporation, and deposit, one that tends to settle POPs in colder climates. The result is that places like the **Arctic** now contain significant amounts of POPs even though the origins are primarily in distant lands, from incinerators in **Japan** to smokestacks in **Mexico**. Tests show, for example, worrying levels of POPs in the blood and breast milk of Inuit women, a fact many advocates of bans and phaseouts see as unfair, unjust, and, for a few, even an environmental violation of human rights. *See also* CANADA; CONVENTION ON LONG-RANGE TRANSBOUNDARY AIR POLLUTION; VIETNAM.

**STRONG, MAURICE (1929–).** Born in **Canada**, Maurice Strong was one of the most influential organizing figures behind the globalization of modern environmentalism. In 1966, he went from president of the Power Corporation of Canada to head of Canada's External Aid Office (which became the Canadian International Development Agency). From 1970–1972, Strong served as secretary-general of the **United Nations Conference on the Human Environment** before becoming the first executive director of the **United Nations Environment Programme** in 1973. He returned to Canada to serve as president of the **oil** company Petro-Canada from 1976–1978, then as chairman of the International Energy Development Corporation and the Canada Development Investment Corporation in the first half of the 1980s. A member of the **World Commission on Environment and Development** from 1983–1987, Strong also became an under-secretary-general of the **United Nations** in 1985. After that, he once again became secretary-general of a major international environmental conference: this time the 1992 **United Nations Conference on Environment and Development**. In 1995, Strong was appointed as a senior advisor to the president of the World Bank, then, before stepping aside, as a senior advisor to Secretary-General Kofi Annan on UN reforms and as a UN envoy to **North Korea**.

**SUB-SAHARAN AFRICA.** The region of sub-Saharan Africa, lying south of the Sahara desert, comprises 48 countries. Since the 1980s, much of this region has been in financial, social, and environmental turmoil. There are many reasons, which vary from place to place, but generally these include the legacy of colonialism, boom-and-bust resource economies, unemployment, AIDS, rapid population growth, wars, droughts, and crop failures. Today, with two-thirds of people in this region relying on natural resources and agriculture for income, it contains the highest proportion of poor people among major world regions.

Just about every ecosystem in this region is in crisis. It suffers from some of the world's highest rates of **deforestation, desertification, biodiversity** loss, and soil erosion. Enforcement of conservation and wildlife is inconsistent, and poaching and **illegal logging** are rampant. Low-technology industry, old transportation systems, and weak enforcement of environmental regulations have left the air in many cities dirty and dangerous; water and sewage systems in many places are unsanitary, too. The need for wood and animal waste for domestic cooking is also degrading forests and contributing to unhealthy indoor air.

At the same time, community environmentalism is strong in some areas. Two examples among many are **Wangari Maathai**'s **Green Belt Movement** to plant trees in **Kenya**, and the activities of **Ken Saro-Wiwa** in **Nigeria**. In recent years, the region has also had notable environmental achievements, such as phasing out **leaded gasoline** in just four years following the 2002 **World Summit on Sustainable Development** in Johannesburg, **South Africa** (becoming the world's first developing region to accomplish this).

Two-thirds of the African continent is desert or drylands, and governments in Africa see desertification as one of the most significant environmental stresses. African states were instrumental in establishing the 1994 **United Nations Convention to Combat Desertification in Countries Experiencing Serious Drought and/or Desertification, Particularly in Africa** (which entered into force in 1996).

**SUSTAINABLE DEVELOPMENT.** The idea of sustainable development can be traced back to the Cocoyoc Declaration, issued in 1974 at a symposium on development and environment hosted by the **United Nations Environment Programme** and the United Nations Conference on Trade and Development in Cocoyoc, **Mexico**. However, the World Conservation Strategy of 1980, published by the **International Union for Conservation of Nature (IUCN)**, is commonly credited with launching the term into the international vocabulary. The publication of the 1987 **World Commission on Environment and Development** report, *Our Common Future* (also known as the Brundtland Report, after its chair **Gro Harlem Brundtland**), brought it to the center of environmental debate. The commission defined sustainable development as "development that meets the needs of the present without compromising the ability of future generations to meet their own needs." This definition was central to the discussions at the 1992 **United Nations Conference on Environment and Development (UNCED)**. Afterward, the United Nations Commission on Sustainable Development (UNCSD) was established to ensure effective follow-up of the conference's resolutions. Sustainable development defined in this way would then shape the mandate and goals of the 2002 **World Summit on Sustainable Development** in Johannesburg, **South Africa**.

Today, this definition remains the most common one among governments, business, and intergovernmental agencies. Here, because poverty is identified as a major cause of environmental degradation, economic growth remains necessary. The main approaches to achieve this form of sustainable development are market-based instruments: for example, green taxes, tradable emissions permits, and **eco-efficiency**.

The term as defined by the Brundtland Commission has many critics. Some contend the concept is ambiguous or vague; others see it as a clever way to legitimize the status quo of continued growth and overconsumption. Ecological economists like **Herman Daly** commonly point to what they see as a contradiction in this definition, arguing that infinite economic growth is physically impossible in a closed ecosystem with finite resources—and that true sustainable development requires "development without growth."

**SUSTAINABLE FOREST MANAGEMENT.** Today, many see sustainable forest management as the forestry component of **sustainable development**. It has a long history, however, going back over a century to the idea of managing a forest in a way that ensures a **sustainable yield** of timber. More recent understandings of sustainable forest management tend to put more weight on nontimber products and services as well as protecting water supplies, **biodiversity**, soil quality, cultural sites, and the well-being of indigenous peoples. Two examples of international initiatives to support sustainable forest management are the International Tropical Timber Organization Guidelines and the **Forest Stewardship Council** Principles and Criteria. *See also* CANADIAN STANDARDS ASSOCIATION, CSA Z809; DEFORESTATION; ECOFORESTRY; ILLEGAL LOGGING; SUSTAINABLE FORESTRY INITIATIVE (SFI).

**SUSTAINABLE FORESTRY INITIATIVE (SFI).** The Sustainable Forestry Initiative (SFI) program, established in 1994 by the American Forest and Paper Association, is a voluntary certification standard to promote **sustainable forest management** and responsible purchasing practices. In 2007, the SFI became a fully independent organization. A board of directors—with representatives from industry, landowners, environmental groups, academia, and the public sector—governs the SFI standard. It now has international recognition through the international **Programme for the Endorsement of Forest Certification (PEFC)** schemes. It is an example of a worldwide trend over the last few decades toward increasing numbers of environmental labeling and certification schemes for forest products. The best-known international program is the **Forest Stewardship Council**.

**SUSTAINABLE YIELD.** A sustainable yield is the rate one can harvest without harming the capacity of the ecosystem to regenerate the same amount in the future. The idea—what some call the maximum sustainable yield—is a common organizing principle for environmental management of renewable resources like forests and fisheries. For forestry, for example, it is the basis for determining guidelines such as the annual allowable cut. Supporters see this as a sensible way to supply resources without damaging ecosystems; however, critics see it as unachievable in practice and thus argue it ends up justifying unsustainable production and overconsumption. *See also* DEFORESTATION; ILLEGAL LOGGING; SUSTAINABLE FOREST MANAGEMENT.

**SUZUKI, DAVID (1936–).** Born in Vancouver, **Canada**, David T. Suzuki is professor emeritus at the University of British Columbia and co-founder of the David Suzuki Foundation. He is one of the world's best-known environmental writers (with over 40 books), activists, and radio and TV personalities (since 1979 hosting the Canadian Broadcasting Corporation's *The Nature of Things with David*

*Suzuki*). For many environmentalists, his career is a prime example of the power of the popular media to translate academic research into a language able to change global environmental consciousness, an idea dating back to the emergence of **Greenpeace** in Vancouver during the 1970s.

**SWAMPY (DANIEL HOOPER) (1974–).** Daniel Hooper, nicknamed "Swampy," rose to fame in the mid-1990s after a protest against yet another new highway through the British countryside. For years activists had been camping along the route, living in tree houses and chaining themselves to concrete blocks. Then, a group including Swampy pioneered a new form of environmental resistance by digging and hiding in tunnels under the excavation site. It would take a week for the British government to find and evict these protestors, with the press relishing in their efforts to dodge radar and diggers. The 22-year-old Swampy was the last to come out, becoming an instant celebrity **eco-warrior**. Afterward, he would appear in tabloids, fashion shots, and on television celebrity panels, and, along with a second tunnel protest to prevent a new runway at the Manchester airport, he managed to bring an intense media spotlight on road building in **Great Britain** in the late 1990s. Many environmentalists still see Swampy as a hero of the direct nonviolent action movement, although he is no longer an active protestor. Critics, however, commonly deride him as a joke—an example of how the media tends to give far too much coverage to the silly antics of a few outliers in the environmental movement.

**SWEDEN.** The Ministry of the Environment is the central agency in charge of the environment, climate, and energy issues in Sweden. The Swedish Environmental Protection Agency, which reports to the Ministry of the Environment, was established in 1967. The Swedish Environment Party/**Green Party**, Miljöpartiet de Gröna, was founded in 1981, first winning seats in Parliament in 1988. Environmental legislation is coordinated through the 1999 Environmental Code, which includes, among other things, a **precautionary principle** and a **polluter pays principle**. Sweden was ranked third in the world on the 2008 Environmental Performance Index (developed by Yale and Columbia universities to assess environmental sustainability).

Sweden has been influential in advancing global environmentalism. In 1972, Stockholm hosted the **United Nations Conference on the Human Environment**, which among many accomplishments launched the **United Nations'** first **World Environment Day**. Since then Sweden has also moved forward negotiations for environmental agreements, such as the 2001 **Stockholm Convention on Persistent Organic Pollutants**.

Sweden has an active civil society around environmentalism. For example, in the late 1960s, soil scientist Dr. Svante Odén helped to raise public awareness about **acid rain** in Sweden. In 1982, the Swedish **nongovernmental organization** Secretariat on Acid Rain was founded, as a partnership including **Friends of the Earth** Sweden, the Swedish Society for Nature Conservation, and the **World Wide Fund for Nature** (**WWF**)-Sweden. Sweden is also home to several environmental research institutions, including the International Institute of Ecological Economics (Beijer Institute), established in 1977; the Stockholm Environment Institute, founded in 1989; and the Stockholm International Water Institute, created in 1991.

Recently, the government has been focusing on promoting **renewable energy**. A **carbon tax** on "domestic travel fuels" (**oil**, **coal**, **natural gas**, and so on) was put in place in 1991, and increased in both 1997 and 2007. In 2003, the government introduced Tradable Green Certificates for renewables in electricity production; in 2005, set a target of 3 percent for renewable fuels in transportation; and in 2006, announced a target date of 2020 to phase out oil consumption.

**SYNTHETIC CHEMICALS.** Synthetic chemistry started in European laboratories seeking to make anaesthetics and disinfectants in the mid-19th century. **Dichlorodiphenyltrichloroethane (DDT)**, for example, was discovered in 1874 but not developed as a pesticide until 1939. At the turn of the 20th century, the production of **oil**-based dyes in **Germany** led the way for the commercialization of synthetic chemicals. Between 50,000 and 100,000 new chemicals were brought into commercial production after the synthetic chemical revolution of World War II. Production kept increasing, and by the end of the 20th century, around 18 million synthetic substances were known to science. Today, about 1,000 new synthetic substances are created every year, with multinational companies like Dow and

DuPont in lead roles. Among the 100,000 chemicals currently in use, fewer than 1,000 have complete toxicological profiles. More than 500 different synthetic chemicals have now been found in human blood, body fat, and breast milk.

Many people believe synthetic chemicals have contaminated the planet, contributing to illness and death in humans and other species. One of the best-known critiques of synthetic chemicals—in particular DDT—is **Rachel Carson**'s 1962 book *Silent Spring*. A number of environmental disasters are also associated with synthetic chemicals, including tragedies such as **Love Canal** and **Bhopal**. Many of these chemicals are persistent, reactive, and oil soluble, allowing them to enter and travel up the food chain through processes known as bioaccumulation and biomagnification. The class of synthetic chemicals with such properties is generally called **persistent organic pollutants**. Another well-known class of synthetic chemicals is **chlorofluorocarbons (CFCs)**, the primary cause of **ozone depletion**. *See also* BISPHENOL A (BPA); HAZARDOUS WASTE; ORGANIC FOOD; POLYBROMINATED DIPHENYL ETHERS (PBDEs).

## – T –

**TAIWAN.** The issues of environmental protection and public health are closely tied in Taiwan, with the Environmental Protection Bureau emerging in 1979 out of the Department of Environmental Health, which the Department of Health set up in 1971. Prior to that, municipal units managed environmental issues. The city of Taipei, for example, integrated its Municipal Cleaning Unit and Sewage Treatment Commission with its Department of Environmental Cleaning in 1968 to manage waste, air, and water **pollution**.

Taiwan established the Environmental Protection Agency in 1987. Since then, it has managed to improve air quality through a mix of policies, such as mandatory use of unleaded gasoline and controls on vehicles and industrial emissions. Nevertheless, a high population density, industrial activity, two-stroke motorcycles and scooters, and dust and pollution from mainland **China** mean residents still suffer from significant exposure to air pollutants. China sees Taiwan as part of its official territory, and thus Taiwan is in an unusual international position. It follows the guidelines of many environmental treaties, such as the **Basel Convention**, the **Montreal Protocol**, and the **Kyoto Protocol**, but is not an official signatory. Taiwan introduced a green building **eco-certification** system in 1999, which is similar to the LEED (Leadership in Energy and Environmental Design) green building rating system in the **United States** and **Japan**'s CASBEE (Comprehensive Assessment System for Building Environmental Efficiency) certification scheme.

The 1980s and 1990s saw many environmental **nongovernmental organizations** emerge in Taiwan, including the Environmental Quality Protection Foundation (1984), the Taiwan Christian Ecological Center (1992), Wetlands Taiwan (1994), the Taiwan Business Council for Sustainable Development (1995), and the Society of Wilderness (1996). The Wild at Heart Legal Defense Association was created in 2003 to provide legal advice on environmental issues; in 2005, it was involved in several cases, including one to stop a hydroelectric power plant because of an incomplete **environmental impact assessment** and falsified data and another to indict the Taiwan Cement Corporation for illegal dumping of waste **oil**.

**TAJIKISTAN.** *See* ARAL SEA.

**TASMANIA WILDERNESS SOCIETY.** *See* WILDERNESS SOCIETY.

**THAILAND.** Thailand has an especially long history of forest management. The Royal Forest Department was created in 1897, and all forests were declared government property in 1899. The Forest Act was passed in 1941 (updating the 1913 Forest Protection Act) and the Forest Industry Organization was created in 1956. The 1960s saw the establishment of protected areas, with the 1960 Wildlife Protection and Preservation Act, the 1961 National Park Act, and the 1964 National Forest Reserve Act. At the same time, however, **deforestation** increased, and replanting and silvicultural practices in logged areas were poor. Political instability after a military coup in 1976 also contributed to deforestation, as forests were cleared to fight rebel groups. Following severe flooding and subsequent landslides in southern Thailand, the government banned commercial logging in natural forests in 1989.

Rapid industrialization and intensive resource consumption over the last few decades have put intense pressure on Thailand's environment. In response, several Thai environmental **nongovernmental organizations** were established in the late 1980s and early 1990s, including the Thailand Environment Institute, which focuses on conservation and environmental certification. The Thai Green Coalition acts as a political advocacy organization for environmental issues; however, there is no official political **green party**. Several important pieces of environmental legislation also passed in the early 1990s, including the Enhancement and Conservation of National Environment Quality Act, an amended Navigation in Thai Waterways Act, the Forest Plantation Act, and the Wild Animals Reservation and Protection Act. Thailand also managed to phase out **leaded gasoline** by 1995, although large numbers of old vehicles, forest fires, factories, and power plants all mean air quality, particularly in urban areas like Bangkok, remains poor. The Asian financial crisis of 1997–1998 also hit the economy hard, adding pressures to earn foreign exchange by exporting natural resources and agricultural products; the 2004 tsunami added further to the hardships of life in many coastal and island communities.

For genetically modified crops the reception has been mixed in Thailand. In 1995, the government allowed **genetically modified** crops in research settings, but in 2001 it put in place a temporary ban on these field trials to ensure proper safeguards were in place. The lifting of this ban in 2007 resulted in a court case against the government.

Thailand also participates in many regional and international environmental agreements, including the ASEAN Agreement on Transboundary Haze Pollution (in force from 2003), the **Kyoto Protocol**, the **Convention on Biological Diversity**, the Convention on Migratory Species, and the **Convention on International Trade in Endangered Species**. Although Thailand (like **China** and Malaysia) is making increasing efforts to join international agreements and improve environmental management at home, Thai companies are continuing to disrupt the environment of neighboring countries such as Burma (Myanmar), for example, by logging old-growth forests and importing timber from unsustainable sources.

**THIRD WORLD NETWORK (TWN).** An international network of nonprofit **nongovernmental organizations**, the Third World Network

(TWN) publishes books and articles, organizes conferences, and facilitates dialogues with international negotiators and processes on issues relating to development and South-North relations. With an international secretariat in Penang (Malaysia), it also has offices in Delhi (**India**), Montevideo (Uruguay), Geneva, and Accra (Ghana). For environmentalism, it has been an influential voice in raising the profile of critical nongovernmental perspectives from within developing countries on issues such as trade, foreign debt, intellectual property rights, **climate change**, biosafety, and human rights.

**THOREAU, HENRY DAVID (1817–1862).** Born in Concord, Massachusetts, the philosopher and author Henry David Thoreau is best remembered among environmentalists for his poetry and contributions to the fields of ecology and environmental history. After graduating from Harvard University and running a school in Concord with his older brother John from 1838 to 1841, he moved in with his mentor, Ralph Waldo Emerson, as a live-in handyman. During this time, Thoreau published his first poems in the transcendentalist journal *The Dial*. In 1845, he convinced Emerson to allow him to build a small cabin on Emerson's property in the woods at Walden Pond, where he wrote his first book, *A Week on the Concord and Merrimack Rivers*. Thoreau began his second book, *Walden*, while there, and, inspired by spending a night in jail for refusing to pay a poll tax, he also wrote one of his most famous works, *Civil Disobedience* (originally published as *Resistance to Civil Government*).

**THREE GORGES DAM.** The Three Gorges Dam, located in the upper Yangtze River of **China**, will be the world's largest hydroelectric dam when completed in 2009. It will generate over 80 billion kilowatt-hours of electricity annually—about 10 percent of China's total capacity when construction began in 1994. Many environmentalists and human rights advocates (as well as a few members of the National People's Congress) have opposed the dam. Filling the gigantic reservoir (which began in 2003) will require relocating 1–2 million people. It will entail, too, the loss of 30,000 hectares of agricultural land. Supporters see this project as **sustainable development**—as a way to produce **renewable energy** and replace **coal** burning in steam power plants. Critics counter that the costs for local peoples and ecologies outweigh the benefits for generating cleaner electricity. *See also* NARMADA DAM.

**THREE MILE ISLAND NUCLEAR ACCIDENT.** The partial meltdown of a core reactor in 1979 at Three Mile Island Nuclear Generating Station in Harrisburg, Pennsylvania, remains the biggest accident in commercial nuclear history in the **United States**. The release of radioactivity did not lead to the immediate deaths of any workers or residents in the area; along with television crews, President Jimmy Carter even visited the control room during the crisis to show it was safe. Still, the accident—caused by maintenance, operational, design, and response errors—undermined American public confidence and strengthened environmental opposition to **nuclear power**. This would reinforce the earlier trend in the United States during the 1970s to scale back plans to expand nuclear power. The cleanup operation at Three Mile Island did not end until December 1993, costing nearly US$1 billion. *See also* CHERNOBYL NUCLEAR MELTDOWN.

**TIPPING POINT.** The tipping point, in ecological terms, occurs when the process of steady change in an ecosystem (for example, a decline in the numbers of a particular species) suddenly begins to accelerate into an uncontrollable change (for example, extinction of a species). This idea is common among those environmentalists who call for tough measures to prevent seemingly separate environmental "problems"—from **deforestation** to **desertification** to **endangered species** to overfishing to **mining** to **climate change** to **ozone depletion** to **persistent organic pollutants**—from aggregating to a point that tips the earth into a global crisis beyond the capacity of humanity to control. (This is not the same meaning as in the bestselling book by Malcolm Gladwell, *The Tipping Point*, published in 2000, which uses the phrase to explain social epidemics.)

**TIRES.** In the **United States** alone, about 300 million tires are discarded every year. More than three-quarters of these are recycled into things like tire-derived fuel, civil engineering applications, and ground rubber. One of the most successful efforts at **recycling** tires comes from using them as subgrade road base.

Tires are difficult to bury in landfills because they work their way back to the surface. Today, over 275 million tires sit in junkyards in the United States. Such stockpiles can threaten people's health and the environment. Tire fires are difficult to extinguish and can last a long time, releasing toxic pollutants. Notable tire fires in U.S. history include a 7-million-tire fire in Virginia in 1983 and a tire fire that lasted 30 days in California in 1999. Tire stockpiles are also breeding grounds for pests (rodents) and diseases, as tires hold water and protect insects (like mosquitoes) from pesticides. Global figures on the number of tires in landfills are difficult to calculate, but most environmentalists see this as an increasing environmental threat in developing countries without the capacity to recycle and monitor landfills. *See also* AUTOMOBILES.

**TOLBA, MOSTAFA KAMAL (1922).** Born in Zifta, Egypt, Mostafa Kamal Tolba graduated from Cairo University in 1943 and received a Ph.D. from Imperial College in 1948. He became internationally known, first as the head of Egypt's delegation at the 1972 **United Nations Conference on the Human Environment** and later as the executive director of the **United Nations Environment Programme (UNEP)** from 1976 to 1992. Tolba was instrumental during the negotiations over the **Montreal Protocol on Substances That Deplete the Ozone Layer**, personally negotiating with delegations to ensure a treaty was reached. After leaving the UNEP, in 1994 he started the International Center for Environment and Development (ICED), a nonprofit organization that funds environmental projects in less-developed countries.

**TORREY CANYON.** The *Torrey Canyon*, a 974-foot (297-meter) **oil** tanker flying a Liberian flag to take advantage of lower income taxes and wage rates, was carrying between 30 and 38 million gallons of crude oil when on 18 March 1967 it ran aground on Pollard's Rock, part of the Seven Stones reef near Cornwall, **Great Britain**. Owned by Barracuda Tanker Corporation, a subsidiary of the Union Oil Company of California, and chartered by British Petroleum, it was the largest recorded shipwreck to date. Attempts to salvage and refloat the tanker using tugs and air compressors were unsuccessful. It broke into pieces and more oil tanks ruptured, causing several oil slicks. The standard practice at the time was to disperse spilled oil with detergent, but the amount of oil overwhelmed this approach so the British government chose to burn the oil off and sink the tanker by dropping bombs and using other weapons. When the spill touched land in Great Britain it stretched 260 square miles (or roughly 670 square kilometers). The number of seabirds killed was probably around 15,000. The disaster drew worldwide publicity to the ecological dangers of shipping oil on the high seas, spurring the growing global environmental movement in the late 1960s. *See also EXXON VALDEZ* OIL SPILL.

**TOURISM.** *See* ECOTOURISM.

**TRAGEDY OF THE COMMONS. Garrett Hardin**'s article "The Tragedy of the Commons" is one of the most influential articles in the evolution of environmentalism. Published in *Science* in 1968, it tells a story of access and collapse of the English commons as an analogy to access and collapse of shared spaces in modern times, such as the high seas, atmosphere, and unregulated forests. It is, Hardin reasons, in the rational self-interest of a herder to breed and graze as many animals as possible on a pasture "open to all." Adding one more animal enhances a herder's personal wealth far more than it degrades the pasture for his herd. Not adding another animal to conserve the grazing land will merely penalize this herder as others add animals instead. Over time, without preventative measures, the logic of each person pursuing such private gain will destroy the pasture.

This same logic and process, Hardin surmises, is true in all commons with rising populations and unrestricted access. "Ruin is the destination toward which all men rush," he writes, "each pursuing his own best interest in a society that believes in the freedom of the commons. Freedom in a commons brings ruin to all." The only way to prevent this collapse, he concludes, is "mutual coercion, mutually agreed upon by the majority of the people affected." To this day Hardin's metaphor continues to hold great sway among environmentalists, who see the pursuit of self-interest (state, corporate, and personal) and open access to common spaces as a core cause of the global ecological crisis. It is also frequently invoked by those who call for a world government to solve crises like **climate change**.

**TURKMENISTAN.** *See* ARAL SEA.

## – U –

**UNION OF CONCERNED SCIENTISTS.** The Union of Concerned Scientists is a nonprofit organization based in the **United States**. It grew out of a December 1968 statement of concern by faculty at the Massachusetts Institute of Technology, including the heads of the biology, chemistry, and physics departments, who were calling for "more responsible exploitation of scientific knowledge" and admonishing government for "an intention to enlarge further our immense destructive capabilities." Signatories wanted to "convey to our students the hope that they will devote themselves to bringing the benefits of science and technology to mankind and to ask them to scrutinize the issues raised here before participating in the construction of destructive weapons systems."

Today, with more than 200,000 members, the organization aims to combine citizen action with reliable and independent scientific knowledge to promote cleaner and safer environments. Recently, it has been active around issues such as global security, **climate change**, clean energy, food, clean vehicles, and invasive species.

**UNITED NATIONS.** The United Nations is the core institution for organizing and coordinating global environmental action among states. Among countless meetings and conferences, three stand out: the 1972 **United Nations Conference on the Human Environment**; the 1992 **United Nations Conference on Environment and Development**; and the 2002 **World Summit on Sustainable Development.** The UN also houses organizations responsible for supporting and improving global environmental management. The **United Nations Environment Programme (UNEP),** which was established following the 1972 UN Conference on the Human Environment, has the most direct mandate. But many others also influence global, national, and local environmental management, including the UN Development Programme (UNDP), the UN Food and Agriculture Organization (FAO), and the UN Population Fund (formerly the **United Nations Fund for Population Activities**). The UN also cooperates closely with powerful organizations such as the World Bank, International Monetary Fund (IMF), and the **Global Environment Facility (GEF)** (which has three implementing agencies: the World Bank, UNDP, and UNEP).

The UN also plays a key role in defining terms and setting agendas for international environmental negotiations and management. In 1983, the UN convened, for example, the **World Commission on Environment and Development**, which in 1987 would put forth a definition of **sustainable development** that to this day still guides most of the world's environmental policies (defined as "development that meets the needs of the present without compromising the ability of future generations to meet their own needs"). The UN also strives to raise environmental awareness through activities such as **World Environment Day**.

UN environmental agreements are also the basis of many of the international rules governing environmental management. Some of the hundreds of agreements include the UN Framework Convention on Climate Change and **Kyoto Protocol to the United Nations Framework Convention on Climate Change**; the UN **Convention on International Trade in Endangered Species of Wild Fauna and Flora (CITES)**; the **United Nations Convention to Combat Desertification in Countries Experiencing Serious Drought and/or Desertification, Particularly in Africa**; the Ramsar Convention on Wetlands; the **Convention on Biological Diversity**; and the **Stockholm Convention on Persistent Organic Pollutants**. *See also* WORLD CHARTER FOR NATURE.

**UNITED NATIONS COMMISSION ON SUSTAINABLE DEVELOPMENT.** *See* SUSTAINABLE DEVELOPMENT.

**UNITED NATIONS CONFERENCE ON ENVIRONMENT AND DEVELOPMENT (UNCED).** The United Nations Conference on Environment and Development (UNCED) was held in Rio de Janeiro **(Brazil)** in June 1992 on the 20th anniversary of the **United Nations Conference on the Human Environment** (Stockholm). Commonly known as the Rio or Earth Summit, it was the largest **United Nations** conference to date, with 178 national delegations, over 1,400 officially accredited **nongovernmental organizations**, and 117 heads of state participating. The Canadian **Maurice Strong** was again secretary-general of the conference (as he was for the 1972 conference in Stockholm). Another 17,000 people also attended a parallel nongovernmental forum.

The official conference produced two documents of particular note: the Rio Declaration on Environment and Development and **Agenda 21** (a 300-page action plan for **sustainable development**). The Rio Declaration lays out 27 principles on the rights and responsibilities of states for environment and development, placing more emphasis on the right to develop than was the case with the Declaration on the Human Environment adopted at the 1972 Stockholm Conference. Rio also opened two conventions for signature: the United Nations Framework Convention on Climate Change and the **Convention on Biological Diversity**. As well, it issued a nonbinding statement of principles for forest management after efforts to sign a legally binding forest treaty failed. Finally, it created the United Nations Commission on Sustainable Development to monitor and evaluate the progress of meeting the objectives set out at Rio.

The 1992 Rio Summit brought global environmentalism to the top of the agendas of world leaders. As at the 1972 conference, contentious debates occurred over the links between environmental change, development, poverty, and South-North inequities. In the end most states endorsed the definition of sustainable development put forth in 1987 by the **World Commission on Environment and Development**: "development that meets the needs of the present without compromising the ability of future generations to meet their own needs." Over the following decades, this concept (and compromise), which assumes that more economic growth is compatible with a better global environment, shifted global environmentalism into a more cooperative stance with corporations and economic interests. The **World Summit on Sustainable Development**, held 10 years later in Johannesburg, **South Africa**, further ensured the supremacy of this concept.

**UNITED NATIONS CONFERENCE ON THE HUMAN ENVIRONMENT.** The United Nations Conference on the Human Environment, held in June 1972 in Stockholm, **Sweden**, was the first international environmental conference for state officials. **Maurice Strong**, a Canadian businessman and environmentalist, was secretary-general of the conference, commonly called the Stockholm Conference. About 1,200 people attended, with delegates from 113 countries and two heads of government: Olof Palme (Sweden) and Indira

Gandhi (**India**). The Communist bloc boycotted the conference, however, to protest the exclusion of East Germany. Three nongovernmental conferences ran parallel to the official one: the Environment Forum (with **United Nations** support); the People's Forum; and the Dai Dong Independent Conference on the Environment (held the week before the official one).

The Stockholm Conference revealed fundamental differences between environmentalism in developed and developing countries. Developing countries were wary that "northern" concerns over **pollution** and nature conservation would trump far greater environmental problems arising from poverty and underdevelopment. "Southern" delegates coined the phrase *the pollution of poverty*, an idea that still runs strong in environmentalism in the developing world. Tensions between the North and South arose too over responsibility, financing, and the inequalities of global capitalism.

The conference produced a Declaration on the Human Environment (including 26 principles), an Action Plan (with 109 recommendations), and a Resolution on Institutional and Financial Arrangements. All of these were nonbinding on signatory states. Significantly, these documents protected the principle of state sovereignty and the right of states to control domestic resources. They did so, however, while recognizing the competing interests of developed and developing countries as well as the responsibility of all states to consider cross-border environmental damage.

The conference did not produce many concrete environmental commitments by states. It did set the stage, though, for further state negotiations as an increasingly significant source of global environmentalism. In addition, it led to the United Nations General Assembly establishing the **United Nations Environment Programme**, which opened in 1973 with its headquarters in Nairobi, **Kenya**, and with Maurice Strong as its first executive director.

**UNITED NATIONS CONVENTION ON THE LAW OF THE SEA (UNCLOS).** Adopted in 1982, the Law of the Sea Treaty—officially the Third United Nations Convention on the Law of the Sea (UNCLOS), after two previous agreements from 1958 and 1960—provides a legal framework for governing the oceans. UNCLOS III, or LOST as some critics call it, took 15 years to negotiate. The process started in 1967 after the Maltese ambassador to the **United Nations** called for an international agreement to protect the oceans. The treaty did not enter into force until 1994, with a subsequent implementation agreement added in 1996. The convention now has 155 parties. It replaced the previous Law of the Sea treaties: the Convention on the Territorial Sea and Contiguous Zone, Convention on the Continental Shelf, Convention on the High Seas, and Convention on Fishing and Conservation of Living Resources of the High Seas.

UNCLOS includes dispute resolution mechanisms, where states failing to resolve contentious issues independently must choose among the International Tribunal for the Law of the Sea, the International Court of Justice, or one of two arbitration tribunals established through the convention. Key provisions of UNCLOS include the establishment of Exclusive Economic Zones (EEZs), regulations over continental shelves, deep seabed **mining**, and rules concerning marine scientific research. EEZs give coastal states rights over resources (from fish to **oil**) in the waters or ocean floor 200 miles from the shoreline. **Climate change** will challenge some of these resource claims as rising sea levels alter EEZs. *See also* FISHING.

**UNITED NATIONS CONVENTION TO COMBAT DESERTIFICATION IN COUNTRIES EXPERIENCING SERIOUS DROUGHT AND/OR DESERTIFICATION, PARTICULARLY IN AFRICA.** The **United Nations Conference on Environment and Development (UNCED)** first initiated negotiations for a treaty on **desertification** in 1972. In 1977, a UN Conference on Desertification agreed on a Plan of Action to Combat Desertification; however, by the early 1990s the **United Nations Environment Programme** had concluded this was insufficient and the problem was intensifying. The UN Convention to Combat Desertification (UNCCD) was adopted in 1994 (entering into force in 1996). Although the convention addresses land degradation globally, it has a specific focus on Africa because two-thirds of the continent is desert or drylands while three-quarters of its agricultural drylands were already degraded to some extent by the mid-1990s. The Regional Implementation Annex for Africa provides a framework for UNCCD activities in Africa.

The UNCCD established two new partnerships in 2008: one with the UN Economic Commission for Africa, for issues including financing and capacity building, and the other for a science program—the Oasis Challenge Program.

The **United Nations** also works to raise awareness of desertification more generally. The year 2006 was the UN's International Year of Deserts and Desertification, and the honorary spokesperson for the year was the Kenyan environmental activist **Wangari Maathai**, a Nobel Peace Prize winner (2004) and leader of the **Green Belt Movement**. *See also* SUB-SAHARAN AFRICA.

**UNITED NATIONS EDUCATIONAL, SCIENTIFIC AND CULTURAL ORGANIZATION (UNESCO).** The **United Nations** Educational, Scientific and Cultural Organization seeks to identify natural and cultural heritage sites of outstanding value around the world, working to preserve and protect these with the assistance of national governments (including emergency assistance to sites in danger). It is guided by the international Convention Concerning the Protection of the World Cultural and Natural Heritage (adopted in 1972), which arose from the merging of two separate, though related, movements: preserving cultural sites and conserving nature.

**UNITED NATIONS ENVIRONMENT PROGRAMME (UNEP).** The United Nations Environment Programme, or UNEP, was set up following the 1972 **United Nations Conference on the Human Environment** with headquarters in Nairobi**, Kenya**, and a global network of regional offices. Responsibility for environmental governance is dispersed throughout the **United Nations**, although the UNEP is the primary environmental agency. Its initial mandate was to educate, inspire, and enable; in the 1990s, it expanded to facilitate coherent implementation of **sustainable development**. It is primarily funded by governments, but also receives funding from **nongovernmental organizations** and businesses.

Most analysts agree it has been successful in establishing a strong base of environmental information and coordinating international environmental negotiations and conventions on issues such as **climate change**, **ozone depletion**, and **biodiversity**. Critics stress its mandate is too vague, with a weak political and financial base compared to other UN agencies, in part because back in 1972 some states worried it might constrain economic growth, consumption, and development.

**UNITED NATIONS FUND FOR POPULATION ACTIVITIES (UNFPA).** Since at least 1798, the year *An Essay on the Principle of Population* by **Thomas Malthus** was published, analysts have been worrying about the consequences of the escalating size of the world's human population. By the 1960s, when **Paul Ehrlich** wrote his best-selling book *The Population Bomb*, many were projecting social and environmental catastrophe unless measures were put in place to slow the growth of the human population (then at over 3 billion and rising fast). To assist national efforts to understand and manage population growth, the **United Nations** created the Fund for Population Activities in 1969 (renamed the UN Population Fund in 1987, although it kept the acronym UNFPA). Today, UNFPA remains the world's largest source of international financing for population programs (both governmental and nongovernmental) with a mandate that includes expanding reproductive choices for individuals and couples as well as working with governments to reduce poverty and promote **sustainable development**.

Despite declining birthrates in many prosperous places and despite the efforts of organizations such as UNFPA, some environmentalists—for example, a faction of the **Sierra Club** in the **United States**—continue to express alarm about the growing world population (now at 6.7 billion and rising by more than 200,000 people a day). Yet many in the environmental movement no longer focus on population growth and instead concentrate on how to best promote sustainable development for a population heading toward a peak of 9–10 billion by 2050.

**UNITED STATES, THE.** Government efforts in the United States to conserve natural resources go back to the earliest colonial settlements. In 1626, for instance, Plymouth Colony passed an ordinance to regulate the timber industry. By the mid-1800s, the public was taking an interest in conservation: **George Perkins Marsh**, for example, published *Man and Nature* in 1864, which called for protection of songbirds and prevention of soil erosion. The United States Commission of Fish and Fisheries was founded in 1871—the first federal agency tasked with conservation of a particular natural resource. Rapid urbanization and industrial growth from 1870 to 1900 caused some serious environmental problems, including water contamination, unsanitary waste disposal, and air **pollution**, prompting civil society groups to emerge around various environmental issues.

A movement to preserve natural areas also gained strength in the 1800s, with public activism leading to the establishment of Yellowstone National Park in 1872, Sequoia and Kings Canyon and Yosemite Parks in 1890, and the Mount Rainier National Park in 1899. This process continued with the Forest Reserve Act of 1891. A true "environmental" movement was emerging by the turn of the 20th century, with markers such the founding of the **Sierra Club** in 1892 by **John Muir**. It was broadly split into two submovements: preservationists (wanting to preserve wilderness areas) and conservationists (wanting to exploit natural resources more sustainably).

Conservationists began to emerge as the dominant camp in the early 1900s. A number of prominent conservation organizations were created in this period: the **National Audubon Society** in 1905; the National Parks Association (now called the National Parks Conservation Association) in 1919; and the Izaak Walton League in 1922. Simultaneously, municipal governments began to introduce regulations to tackle pollution and secure public health, dealing with issues such as sanitation, waste removal, exposure to hazardous substances in workplaces, and so on. The role of the federal government in conservation grew during the Great Depression, with projects such as the Tennessee Valley Authority (1933) and the Soil Conservation Service (1935) (now called the Natural Resources Conservation Service), both of which provided work to unemployed young men.

After World War II ended in 1945, the focus of U.S. environmentalism began to shift away from how to best exploit natural resources and toward more active measures to preserve land for recreational purposes. Environmental problems became a major national issue in the 1960s, with bestselling books such as **Rachel Carson**'s *Silent Spring* (1962) and **Paul Ehrlich**'s *The Population Bomb* (1968) and high-profile environmental disasters such as the **oil** spills off the coast of Santa Barbara, California, in January and February 1969. The federal government passed major environmental legislation during this time, including the first Clean Air Act (1963), the Water Quality Act (1965), the Endangered Species Preservation Act (1966) (an amendment later changed its name to the Endangered Species Conservation Act), and the National Environmental Policy Act

(NEPA) (1970). In this same period, membership in environmental **nongovernmental organizations (NGOs)** grew quickly (tenfold for the Sierra Club between 1952 and 1969 alone).

Environmentalism continued to strengthen during the 1970s, although *not* at the fast pace of the 1960s as other matters, including the oil crisis (1973–1974, 1979–1980), took center stage. The Environmental Protection Agency (EPA) was created in 1970, and Congress passed a number of new bills, such as the Marine Mammal Protection Act (1972) and the Resource Conservation and Recovery Act (1976). At times events did drag environmental issues to the top of the political agenda, most notably, after the **Three Mile Island nuclear accident** in 1979.

The 1980s saw the beginning of an antienvironmental backlash. In 1981, the new administration of Ronald Reagan cut the EPA's budget, personnel, and powers to enforce regulations. This administration then pursued an active and effective policy of obstruction, aiming to weaken governmental regulation generally and environmental regulation in particular. While the Democratic Congress succeeded in blocking Reagan's broader environmental agenda, he was successful in using his discretionary powers as chief executive to weaken regulatory activity throughout the government (the principal strategy was to appoint individuals supporting his environmental agenda to upper- and mid-level positions in the bureaucracy).

The presidency of George H. W. Bush (1989–1993) was less hostile to environmental regulations than his predecessor, presiding over the emergence of the 1990 Clean Air Act Amendments and the 1992 Energy Policy Act, two major pieces of legislation. The early 1990s also saw global environmental problems like **climate change** and **biodiversity** rise to the top of the world agenda (as the 1992 **United Nations Conference on Environment and Development** shows). The Bill Clinton/**Al Gore** administration came to power with strong environmental credentials, but congressional resistance stymied many initiatives during the administration's two terms. Congress, for example, defeated Clinton's proposal to change public lands policies (with the aid of congressional Democrats from western states). The 1995–1996 Republican Congress led by Newt Gingrich was especially hostile to any sort of government regulation. It cut EPA and Interior Department budgets and attempted to change a number of environmental laws, although President Clinton vetoed these attempts. Eventually, the antienvironmentalism of Congress over this time prompted a public backlash (for example, the largest environmental NGOs gathered signatures in support of an Environmental Bill of Rights, which they presented to Congress and the White House). Republicans decided to tone down the efforts to reform environmental policy during the rest of Clinton's term, but congressional resistance continued to prevent significant progress on strengthening environmental measures.

The presidency of George W. Bush returned Republican antiregulatory sentiment to the White House. Democratic control of the Senate in 2001–2002 frustrated early efforts at deregulation. The administration seized on the rolling blackouts in California in early 2001 as an excuse to create a new national energy plan, which relaxed environmental regulations and spurred exploration for energy resources in public lands.

Federal-state relations, fragmented political institutions, and formal division of power across the legislative, executive, and judicial branches of government in the United States makes the formation and implementation of environmental regulations more complex than in many countries. Most federal environmental laws since 1970, for example, require or permit implementation by the states. Also, localism, interest groups, and "horse-trading" in Congress, along with the powers of committees, subcommittees, and particular members of Congress, can further complicate environmental decision making. Because a comparatively high number of points in the policy process exist where actors can block or veto an initiative, broad-based coalitions are often necessary to push through new legislation. The bureaucracy—with the EPA as a lead agency, but with 27 separate federal agencies with significant responsibilities over environmental protection and occupational health—can again make for a very tangled regulatory structure around environmental management.

The judicial branch also influences environmental regulation through its power to interpret legislation and ensure compliance by federal agencies (courtesy of the Administrative Procedures Act, 1946). Litigation has been a crucial tool in the politics of environmental regulation—environmental organizations, businesses, and federal agencies have all gone to court when other avenues fail to produce results. In the 1970s, judicial decisions tended to advance the environmental movement's agenda. Since the mid-1980s, however, the courts have become less friendly to environmental concerns, in part due to judicial appointments by Republican presidents. *See also* EARTH FIRST!; ECOLOGICAL FOOTPRINT; EMISSIONS TRADING; ENVIRONMENTAL DEFENSE; *EXXON VALDEZ* OIL SPILL; LEADED GASOLINE; LOVE CANAL; ORGANIC FOOD; POLYBROMINATED DIPHENYL ETHERS (PBDEs); PRESERVATION; WISE USE MOVEMENT.

**UZBEKISTAN.** *See* ARAL SEA.

– V –

**VIETNAM.** The Vietnam War (1959–1975) caused extensive environmental damage to Vietnam's countryside. The use of herbicides, including the dioxin-containing Agent Orange, by the **United States** defoliated large swaths of forests, destroyed rice crops, and polluted food chains.

Additional land degradation and high rates of **deforestation** followed free-market reforms by the Communist Party in the mid-1980s to promote rapid agricultural and industrial growth. Since the early 1990s, however, environmental management of forests, land, and water has been improving. With support from the **Global Environment Facility** and the United Nations Development Programme, the government conducted a Protected Areas for Resource Conservation landscape ecology pilot project from 1999 to 2004. To coordinate river development, flood control, and information sharing, Cambodia, Lao PDR, **Thailand**, and Vietnam created the Mekong River Commission in 1995, replacing the former Committee for Coordination of Investigations of the Lower Mekong Basin (founded in 1957), which had a rocky history through wars in the region. In 1999, Vietnam also passed a law on water resource management with a **polluter pays principle** (although the government has struggled to implement it). Other specific initiatives also began in the 1990s. In 1992, the Cat Loc Rhino Sanctuary was set up to protect forests for the critically endangered Javan rhino. Various groups, including the **World Wide**

**Fund for Nature/World Wildlife Fund (WWF)**, also began work-ing to protect the forested border region of Cambodia, Vietnam, and Lao PDR, especially for elephants, rhinos, and tigers.

Vietnam's Ministry of Natural Resources and Environment was created in 2002, along with its National Strategy for Environmental Protection. Since then the government has strengthened its **environmental impact assessments,** adopted the Rio Earth Summit Agenda 21 Strategy for Sustainable Development (in 2004), drafted a new na-tional **biodiversity** action plan (in 2006), and drafted a law on energy conservation and efficiency (in 2007).

At an international level, Vietnam has ratified the **Stockholm Convention on Persistent Organic Pollutants** and is now planning a proj-ect for polychlorinated biphenyl (PCB) management and disposal. Re-garding international efforts to protect the ozone layer, Vietnam still uses **ozone-depleting** substances (for insulation foam, refrigerators, air-conditioners, and fire extinguishers for industrial uses), but is in the process of phasing out **chlorofluorocarbons (CFCs)** and halons.

**VOLUNTARY SIMPLICITY.** Voluntary simplicity is a loosely organ-ized social movement that, among other things, calls for decreasing con-sumption in order to live at a more environmentally friendly scale. It is also referred to as simple living, downshifting, downsizing, and simpli-fying. Core values include material simplicity, appropriate living, eco-logical awareness, and personal growth. The phrase is commonly cred-ited to Richard Gregg (from his 1936 essay, "The Value of Voluntary Simplicity"). The movement, however, traces its roots to much earlier, starting with the teachings of Buddha, Christ, and Mohammed, and later to people like **Henry David Thoreau**, Ralph Waldo Emerson, and **Mahatma Gandhi**. In the **United States** the idea of voluntary simplicity spread organically through the 1980s, gaining particular attention in the late 1990s after a series of major American newspapers ran articles on the idea. *See also* ECOLOGICAL FOOTPRINT.

## – W –

**WARD, BARBARA (1914–1981).** A British economist and author, Barbara Ward influenced the early discussion around the concept and definition of **sustainable development**. In 1971, she founded the **International Institute for Environment and Development (IIED)**; after retiring as Schweitzer Professor of Economic Development from Columbia University, Ward served as president of IIED from 1973 and chair from 1980. One of her most influential books was *Only One Earth* (coauthored with René Dubos), prepared for the 1972 **United Nations Conference on the Human Environment**.

**WATT-CLOUTIER, SHEILA.** *See* CANADA.

**WHALING.** Hunting whales for oil and food has a long history, from the Inuit to the Europeans to the Japanese. This disparate hunt, however, did not begin to threaten the survival of whale populations until the 19th and 20th centuries as harvesting became increasingly efficient. The first treaty to manage whaling went into effect in 1931, but this did little to halt the declining populations as whalers continued to take tens of thousands of whales a year. The International Whaling Commission (IWC) was formed in 1946, but again the number of whales continued to decline. In the mid-1960s **Japan** was still hunting close to 27,000 whales a year, and whale meat was the most consumed type of meat in the country.

Animal rights and environmental activists began to campaign to save whales in the 1960s and 1970s. Groups like **Greenpeace** went to sea to thwart whalers. Greenpeace also employed media "**mindbombs**" to change global consciousness about the worth of a "whale," using images and metaphors to reimagine a whale from an animal for food and oil, to a sentient, majestic creature too beautiful to harm. Activists also lobbied states, including those with no history of whaling. With whale numbers continuing to fall, in 1982 the IWC shifted away from trying to manage whales sustainably and declared a moratorium on commercial whaling, effective in the 1985–1986 season. It was supposed to be a temporary moratorium, lifted once the IWC approved the Revised Management Procedure, but the IWC was never able to agree on new procedures, and it has turned into a de facto permanent ban.

Today, the IWC allows limited whaling for indigenous communities (such as the Inuit in Greenland) and for scientific research, but it continues to ban commercial whaling. The debate about the merits of the ban is ongoing in the IWC. In 2006, a resolution was put forth at the IWC to resume commercial whaling, but it did not achieve the necessary three-quarters majority to pass. Critics, in particular Japan and Norway, argue the moratorium is too blunt, ignoring the fact that not all whale species are threatened, and accuse the IWC of caving in to the sentimentality of the Greenpeace mind-set. Pro-whaling states estimate, for example, the population of minke whales at over 700,000 in the southern oceans—enough to sustain some commercial operations; however, this number is contested. Many antiwhaling countries inside the IWC have shifted away from environmental arguments and toward ethical ones to uphold the moratorium.

Despite the IWC moratorium, some countries, notably Japan and Norway, continue to hunt whales. Japan relies on the clause allowing scientific research to continue to hunt hundreds of whales a year (which, under IWC rules, the country must process and distribute as meat). Norway also hunts hundreds of whales every year under IWC rules that allow a country to not comply if it registers an objection to a rule. The commercial whaling that remains, however, is currently not the biggest threat to the survival of whales; rather, it is the disturbance of their habitats from things like **persistent organic pollutants** and **climate change**.

**WILDERNESS SOCIETY.** Two separate environmental organizations operate under this name: one in the **United States**, the other in **Australia**.

The Wilderness Society (U.S.) focuses on science, analysis, and advocacy to protect and restore wilderness areas in the United States. Founded in 1935 with the assistance of conservationists such as **Aldo Leopold**, the organization was instrumental in passing the 1964 U.S. Wilderness Act. Indeed, the organization's executive secretary, Howard Zahniser, was the primary author of the act.

The Wilderness Society (Australia) is a national organization based in communities. It advocates protecting and restoring wilderness and natural areas in Australia. It began in 1976 as the Tasmania Wilderness Society, changing its name in 1984 after a successful campaign to save the Franklin River in Tasmania. It now has campaign centers in every state of Australia. The organization claims its work since 1976 has protected over 8 million hectares of land. *See also* NONGOVERNMENTAL ORGANIZATIONS (NGOs).

**WILDLIFE CONSERVATION SOCIETY.** Headquartered at the Bronx Zoo in New York City, the Wildlife Conservation Society has been working to conserve wildlife and wilderness since 1895. One of the first conservation organizations in the **United States**, today the society operates in over 50 countries across Africa, Asia, and North and Latin America to conserve everything from tigers to butterflies. *See also* NONGOVERNMENTAL ORGANIZATIONS (NGOs).

**WILSON, EDWARD O. (1929–).** Born in Alabama in 1929, Edward O. Wilson is currently Pellegrino University Research Professor Emeritus at Harvard University. At age 13 he discovered the first known colony of fire ants in the **United States** and went on to become one of the world's leading authorities on ants. After uncovering how ants communicate, Wilson became a highly controversial scientist when he began to extend his conclusions about the behavior of ants to the behavior of humans. He is well-known, too, for his scholarly and popular contributions to environmental writings, including his research on conservation and species extinctions. Indicative of Wilson's influence are his more than 75 international awards, including the U.S. National Medal of Science and two Pulitzer Prizes for *On Human Nature* (1978) and *Ants* (1990). *Time* magazine named Wilson one of America's 25 Most Influential People in 1995.

**WIND POWER/ENERGY.** Wind power from turbines is a **renewable energy** that does not emit carbon dioxide or other **greenhouse gases**. Since the 1990s, wind and **solar power** have been two of the fastest growing energy sectors. Global wind power capacity from 1992 to 2003 alone increased 16 times, from 2,500 megawatts (MW) to just over 40,000 MW; by 2007, it was around 94,000 MW. Nearly three-quarters of this capacity was installed in Europe. By then wind power was providing 20 percent of electricity in Denmark and 5 percent in **Germany** and **Spain**. The German state of Schleswig Holstein was meeting 30 percent of its energy needs with wind power. Global capacity is potentially very high. Putting wind farms on one-tenth of the earth's land could, in theory, produce twice the anticipated energy consumption for the year 2020.

Still, although many in the environmental movement see wind power as one of the most effective ways to move away from a dependence on fossil fuels, others (including many outside the movement) oppose expanding capacity because, among other things, turbines kill birds and destroy the visual landscape. In **Great Britain**, for example, a protest movement against wind power has been bolstered by the Country Guardian, an anti-wind lobby group founded in 1991. Globally, environmentalists are split, with groups like **Greenpeace** and **Friends of the Earth** supporting wind power and defending government wind policies often in the face of local anti-wind lobbies in the affected communities. *See also* CLIMATE CHANGE; PEAK OIL.

**WISE USE MOVEMENT.** Used in 1910 by **Gifford Pinchot** to describe his understanding of scientific natural resource management, since the late 1980s the phrase *wise use* in the **United States** has become associated with a loose grassroots movement including farmers, loggers, miners, and property owners who oppose the mainstream environmental movement (in particular, the tendency to create public lands for conservation). Many in the wise use movement, especially political and religious conservatives, see environmental advocacy groups as too "radical," with hidden agendas to exaggerate problems and take over land; instead, they advocate private property and environmental resources going to benefit locals (who, by living off the land, are true "environmentalists"). Ron Arnold, executive vice president of the Center for the Defense of Free Enterprise, has been a critical influence in promoting the wise use movement in the United States.

**WORLD BUSINESS COUNCIL FOR SUSTAINABLE DEVELOPMENT (WBCSD).** First established as the Business Council for Sustainable Development (BCSD) in 1991 by Swiss industrialist Stephan Schmidheiny to participate in the 1992 **United Nations Conference on Environment and Development**, the council merged with the World Industry Council on the Environment in 1995 to become the World Business Council for Sustainable Development (WBCSD). Today, the World Business Council works to promote the role of business in achieving **sustainable development**, promoting the green image of big business while also supporting efforts to promote **corporate social responsibility**. Its main approaches to sustainable development are **eco-efficiency**, global market liberalization, and **industry self-regulation**. It also works with an international network of corporate and **nongovernmental organization** partners, including the **United Nations Environment Programme** and environmental groups such as the **World Wide Fund for Nature/World Wildlife Fund (WWF)**. The WBCSD has been active in international environmental policy, such as negotiating the **Kyoto Protocol**, advocating flexible, market-based instruments.

Activist groups like **Greenpeace** and Corporate Watch see the WBCSD as little more than big **greenwash**. Still, it has gained legitimacy as the voice of big business for international environmental discussions and is a sign of the trend over the last two decades to include big business as an active participant in the global environmental movement.

**WORLD CHARTER FOR NATURE.** Adopted by the **United Nations** in 1982, the World Charter for Nature lays out "general principles," "functions," and "implementation" for judging and guiding human interaction with nature. Principle 1, for example, states, "Nature shall be respected and its essential processes shall not be impaired." Although this document has not translated into many specific and concrete changes, it is an important symbolic declaration of the significance of environmentalism within the United Nations.

**WORLD COMMISSION ON ENVIRONMENT AND DEVELOPMENT.** The World Commission on Environment and Development was established in 1983 by the **United Nations** General Assembly. Chaired by Norwegian Prime Minister **Gro Harlem Brundtland**, it presented its report *Our Common Future* (commonly called the Brundtland Report) to the UN General Assembly in 1987. To this day its definition of **sustainable development**—"development that meets the needs of the present without compromising the ability of future generations to meet their own needs"—remains the consensus one for the international community of states and national governments. Most businesses also accept this definition. Many environmental **nongovernmental organizations** also accept it, although more radical groups see it as a disastrous compromise, allowing business as usual to brand the pursuit of profit, economic growth, and development with the word *sustainable*. More specifically, some groups contest the logical policy arising from the conclusions of the World Commission on Environment and Development: that economic growth is necessary to alleviate poverty (and because poverty causes environmental degradation the pursuit of growth can solve environmental problems).

**WORLD CONSERVATION UNION.** *See* INTERNATIONAL UNION FOR CONSERVATION OF NATURE (IUCN).

**WORLD ENVIRONMENT DAY.** The **United Nations** General Assembly established World Environment Day in 1972 to mark the opening of the **United Nations Conference on the Human Environment**. The **United Nations Environment Programme (UNEP)** was entrusted with its commemoration. Every year, on 5 June, over 100 countries now celebrate World Environment Day to focus attention on the need for collective political action to tackle environmental problems. It provides an opportunity for people around the world to raise ecological awareness with fun activities such as street rallies, green concerts, and tree planting. It also provides an opportunity to encourage states to sign and ratify international environmental agreements as well as state leaders to announce new environmental policies or agencies.

A different city hosts the global celebrations, working with the UNEP to choose a theme. In 2006, the international celebrations for World Environment Day were held in Algiers, Algeria, with the theme Don't Desert Drylands! In 2007, Environment Day was hosted by the City of Tromsø, **Norway**, with the slogan Melting Ice—a Hot Topic? The theme for 2008, in Wellington, **New Zealand**, was Kick the Habit! Towards a Low Carbon Economy. The first theme was a saying still well-known among environmentalists: Only One Earth.

**WORLD RESOURCES INSTITUTE (WRI).** Founded in 1982, the World Resources Institute (WRI) was set up to conduct independent and scientific policy research and analysis on global environmental change and natural resource management. Nonprofit and nongovernmental, WRI was specifically *not* an activist organization like **Greenpeace** or **World Wide Fund for Nature/World Wildlife Fund**

**(WWF)**. Its goal was to ensure its research was hard-hitting and accurate about the changing state of the world's environment, but also politically practical about the development needs of growing human populations so policy makers found the research—and recommendations—relevant. The founding president was James Gustave Speth (serving until 1993), now dean at the School of Forestry and Environmental Studies, Yale University. *See also* INTERNATIONAL INSTITUTE FOR ENVIRONMENT AND DEVELOPMENT (IIED).

**WORLD SUMMIT ON SUSTAINABLE DEVELOPMENT.** The World Summit on Sustainable Development, held in 2002 in Johannesburg, **South Africa**, was an even larger international environmental conference than the **United Nations Conference on Environment and Development (UNCED)** held in Rio de Janeiro 10 years earlier. Over 180 countries sent representatives, although only about 100 heads of state came, fewer than at Rio. In total, there were more than 10,000 delegates, at least 8,000 civil society representatives and 4,000 members of the press, as well as thousands of ordinary citizens. Popularly called Rio+10 or the Johannesburg Summit, it evaluated the progress of **sustainable development** since UNCED. Its mandate also included setting clearer targets to implement the Rio goals.

The two most important publications from the Johannesburg Summit were the Johannesburg Declaration on Sustainable Development (a summary of challenges and general commitments) and the Johannesburg Plan of Implementation to meet these. Both of these are nonbinding agreements. As during the negotiations for the Rio Conference, the most contentious and least settled issue remained financing for sustainable development. Some analysts see the Johannesburg Summit as a success, focusing states on global environmental problems and advancing implementation of sustainable development through voluntary partnerships with corporations and **nongovernmental organizations**. Others see it as an outright failure; just another example of too much rhetoric and not enough action and money. The reality is somewhere in between, with the Johannesburg Summit adding yet another layer of common understanding to international efforts to advance environmentalism globally.

**WORLDWATCH INSTITUTE.** Founded by Lester Brown in 1974, who served as president for 25 years, the Worldwatch Institute (based in Washington, D.C.) conducts independent research on sustainability and social justice. It is funded by donations from private foundations and individuals, as well as sale of its research and some government grants. The current president is Christopher Flavin.

Worldwatch focuses on analyzing environmental, social, and economic trends, from a global and interdisciplinary perspective. It is especially well-known for its annual State of the World reports (first launched in 1984). Critics, such as **Bjørn Lomborg**, argue such "research" is creating a misleading statistical database of the state of the global environment in order to justify and publicize their research. Supporters within the environmental movement see Worldwatch as an essential source of cutting-edge statistics and projections, less encumbered by the conservative tendencies and technical language typical of much of the peer-reviewed scientific literature.

**WORLD WIDE FUND FOR NATURE/WORLD WILDLIFE FUND (WWF).** Founded in London in 1961 as the World Wildlife Fund, the World Wide Fund for Nature (WWF) is now based in Gland, Switzerland (and now tends to just use the acronym WWF, since the organizations in **Canada** and the **United States** did not join the rest of the world in 1986 in changing the name to the World Wide Fund for Nature). The original vision was to raise funds for conservation, working in partnership with the **International Union for Conservation of Nature (IUCN)**. Its mission was to conserve **biodiversity**, promote sustainable use of renewable natural resources, and reduce **pollution** and wasteful consumption. It began to develop its own agenda during the 1960s, moving away from partnerships with the IUCN.

Today, the WWF has close to 5 million regular supporters worldwide and operates in over 90 countries. Its guiding principles are to remain nonpolitical, global, independent, and scientific, building partnerships with local communities, governments, and business. Its work is geared toward conservation projects, including funding thousands of projects, fieldwork, research, policy advice, education, and raising public awareness. It has a reputation within the environmental movement for its partnerships with business (with some seeing these as practical and successful and others as a sell-out). It helped launch, for example, the **Forest Stewardship Council** in 1993. More recently, WWF-**Sweden** has been cooperating with the multinational food firm Tetra Pak on responsible wood purchases and **climate change** policies. WWF-India has been cooperating with the Austrian crystal firm Swarovski to establish a wetlands visitor center in the Keoladeo National Park in **India**. And WWF-Denmark has been cooperating with the pharmaceutical firm Novo Nordisk to reduce carbon dioxide emissions.

**WWOOF.** World Wide Opportunities on Organic Farms, or WWOOF, is a network of national organizations that link travelers wanting to volunteer with organic farms (or smallholdings and gardens) looking for help in exchange for food and accommodation. Beginning in **Great Britain** in 1971, it has evolved into a global "WWOOFing" movement building worldwide networks of "WWOOFers" and farmers around a common vision of sustainable living.

– Y –

**YANZA, LUIS.** *See* GOLDMAN ENVIRONMENTAL PRIZE.

# Bibliography

## CONTENTS

# INTRODUCTION

Thomas Malthus' *Essay on the Principle of Population* (1798) was one of the earliest and most influential publications on environmentalism. Over the next century and a half, many other influential books were published from time to time: ones like Henry David Thoreau's *Walden* (1884) and Aldo Leopold's *A Sand County Almanac* (1949). After the late 1960s, books and articles on environmentalism began to appear with increasing frequency. Today, it is close to impossible to keep up with this ever-expanding academic literature, which spans almost every discipline—including anthropology, architecture, economics, environmental studies, biology, geography, history, human ecology, international relations, law, medicine, occupational health, philosophy, planning, political science, psychology, and sociology.

Many of the most influential books have been lasting bestsellers, crossing disciplines and reaching readers within government and the general public. These include Rachel Carson's *Silent Spring* (1962), Paul Ehrlich's *The Population Bomb* (1968), Donella Meadows et al.'s *Limits to Growth* (1972), E. F. Schumacher's *Small Is Beautiful* (1973), and James Lovelock's books *Gaia* (1979) and *The Ages of Gaia* (1995). A few articles, too, have had stunning intellectual reach, such as Garrett Hardin's "The Tragedy of the Commons" (1968), which drew an analogy of access and historical collapse of the English commons with access and future collapse of modern-day commons (such as the atmosphere or high seas). Now one of the most cited articles of all time, "The Tragedy of the Commons" and the merits of Hardin's analysis are still debated by many scholars, with some seeing much value (e.g., Marvin Soroos, 2005) and others, notably Elinor Ostrom (e.g., in her 1990 book *Governing the Commons*), questioning the logic and accuracy of Hardin's parable.

The debates over the "tragedy of the commons" comprise just a small portion of a vast literature shaping the direction and understanding of environmentalism. Although many overlaps exist, one reasonable way to divide this literature is into six broad categories: global environmentalism, national environmentalism, specific environmental issues, environmental ethics and philosophies, environmental events and influential people, and Internet resources on environmentalism.

Within global environmentalism, many research tracts exist with varying contributions to knowledge. Most of this research assumes environmentalism is a progressive force of global change: a small subset, however, is highly critical, arguing that the research tends to exaggerate environmental problems (often presenting unreliable statistics to "confirm" crises) by underestimating the benefits of technology, ingenuity, capitalism, free markets, and economic growth. In recent years, Bjørn Lomborg has been leading the critical charge since publishing his bestseller, *The Skeptical Environmentalist* (2001). But he is following in the footsteps of others, such as the economist Julian Simon, who published, for example, *The Ultimate Resource* in 1981, and journalist Gregg Easterbrook, who published the bestseller *A Moment on the Earth* in 1995.

For those who believe a global environmental crisis looms (or is already here), much of the literature includes an analysis of the consequences of globalization and global capitalism—with many works focusing on particular aspects, such as the impact of the politics and economics of growth, poverty, consumption, trade, multinational corporations, corporate greenwash, financing, and debt. Typical of the books highly critical of the consequences of globalization is Hilary French's *Vanishing Borders* (2000). Some of these books see potential good from globalization, such as Arthur Mol's *Globalization and Environmental Reform* (2001), but most, such as Gustave Speth's *The Bridge at the Edge of the World* (2008), tend to be critical, with suggestions for ways to reform the global political economy. Other writers concentrate on particular aspects of globalizing capitalism, such as economic growth (e.g., Herman Daly's *Beyond Growth*, 1996), consumption (e.g., my book *The Shadows of Consumption*, 2008), the principle of efficiency (e.g., Thomas Princen's *The Logic of Sufficiency*, 2005), poverty (e.g., Jack Hollander's *The Real Environmental Crisis*, 2003), trade (e.g., Eric Neumayer's *Greening Trade and Investment*, 2001), multinational corporations (e.g., Aseem Prakash's *Greening the Firm*, 2000), and Third World debt (e.g., Susan George's *The Debt Boomerang*, 1992).

A second significant strand of the literature on global environmentalism analyzes the contributions of international agreements, international organizations, nongovernmental organizations, grassroots activism, and shifting forms of global governance more generally. Specialists on global negotiations, such as Pamela Chasek (e.g., *Earth Negotiations*, 2001) and Oran Young (*International Cooperation*, 1994), have advanced our understanding of why and how international environmental norms and rules form, strengthen, and change. Recently, many of these specialists have been working in particular to evaluate the effectiveness of environmental agreements (e.g., Edward Miles et al., *Environmental Regime Effectiveness*, 2001). Other researchers have analyzed the consequences of organizations such as the World Bank (e.g., Tamar Gutner's *Banking on the Environment*, 2002) and nongovernmental organizations like Greenpeace, the World Wide Fund for Nature/World Wildlife Fund (WWF), and Friends of the Earth (e.g., Paul Wapner's *Environmental Activism and World Civic Politics*, 1996). An even larger number of books and articles are now analyzing the nature and influence of emerging forms of global environmental governance (both government based and market based), such as *Earthly Politics* (2004), edited by Sheila Jasanoff and Marybeth Long Martello.

A third strand of the literature on global environmentalism brings in analyses of issues such as history, security, justice, and science to further probe the nature of environmentalism (and ideas such as sustainability and sustainable development). The collection of books is diverse here, including ones like Ramachandra Guha's *Environmentalism* (2000); Thomas Homer-Dixon's *Environment, Scarcity and Violence* (1999); Andrew Dobson's *Justice and the Environment* (1998); and Stephen Bocking's *Nature's Experts* (2004).

Another large body of literature on environmentalism focuses on particular countries or regions. This literature commonly refers to, or is relevant for, understanding global change, but its primary contribution is to understand the nature of environmentalism within particular cultures, political systems, or economic structures. This includes studies comparing histories and policies, as well as ones examining specific places such as Africa (e.g., Gregory Maddox's 2006 book *Sub-Saharan Africa: An Environmental History*); the Antarctica and Arctic (e.g., Marla Cone's 2005 book *Silent Snow*); the Asia-Pacific (e.g., Elizabeth Economy's 2004 book *The River Runs Black*, on China); Europe (e.g., Matthew Auer's 2005 book *Restoring Cursed Earth*, on Eastern Europe and Russia); Latin America (e.g., Kathryn Hochstetler and Margaret Keck's 2007 book *Greening Brazil*); the Middle East (e.g., Mostafa Dolatyar and Tim Gray's 2000 book *Water Politics in the Middle East*); North America (e.g., Robert Gottlieb's 2005 book *Forcing the Spring*); and Oceania (e.g., Judith Bennett's 2000 book *Pacific Forest*). The literature on the United States and Western Europe is particularly extensive here, although in the interests of balanced coverage the following bibliography only provides a sampling.

Much of this global and national literature involves case studies of particular environmental problems. The most extensive body of writing is on climate change, with the amount of research now increasing rapidly. Many books and articles have also been written on air pollution, food, forest management, and ozone depletion. But the coverage of many other issues is extensive, too, including automobiles, biodiversity, endangered species, energy, hazardous chemicals and waste, oceans, persistent organic pollutants, urbanization, water, and whaling (see the bibliography for a sampling). Much of this broader literature also weaves in arguments and concepts from environmental ethics and particular environmental philosophies (e.g., Peter Wenz's 2001 book *Environmental Ethics Today*), although some of this literature is distinct, as is true for many of the bibliographies and autobiographies of environmentalists and the histories of particular environmental disasters (again, see the bibliography for examples).

Popular journals such as *Scientific American* have published some of the most influential environmental thinking (for example, the debate in 1993 between Herman Daly and Jagdish Bhagwati over the environmental consequences of trade). The journal *Nature* has also published articles with profound impacts on global environmental relations—for example, the 1974 article by Mario J. Molino and F. Sherwood Rowland that would lead to an international agreement to ban chlorofluorocarbons (CFCs) and other ozone-depleting substances. A diverse range of other professional journals also publish articles more specifically on environmental problems and the meaning and significance of environmentalism itself. These include *Climate Policy*, *Ecological Economics*, *Environment*, *Environment and Planning (A, B, C, D)*, *Environment and Urbanization*, *Environmental Ethics*, *Environmental History*, *Environmental Politics*, *Environmental Values*, *Global Environmental Change—Human and Policy Dimensions*, *Global Environmental Politics*, the *Journal of Environment and Development*, the *Journal of Environmental Planning and Management*, and *Organization & Environment*.

The Internet, however, holds a significant and growing amount of the world's environmental research, scientific databases, advocacy networks, and knowledge exchanges. As an inexpensive and fast way to reach readers in a large number of countries, over the last decade this has become the primary place that nongovernmental organizations publish and archive information. Increasingly, governments, corporations, and the United Nations are also turning to the Internet to disseminate up-to-date information (and sometimes counter nongovernmental and academic criticism). Academics still tend to publish first and foremost in peer-reviewed university presses and academic journals, but even here the Internet is becoming increasingly important as e-publishing gains ground on standard publishing practices. As computers become cheaper and as the Internet extends further into more developing countries, more and more information is also appearing on grassroots environmentalism in even the remotest regions of the earth.

The list of Internet resources at the end of this bibliography provides a sampling of the very best websites for a range of environmental issues (from air pollution to whaling). It provides as well the websites of many of the international environmental agreements, as these are useful sources of scientific and consensus-based statistics. Finally, it provides the website addresses for over 50 nongovernmental environmental groups and international agencies, as these contain more up-to-date and detailed information about grassroots and global environmental initiatives than is possible to obtain from reading books or articles.

## DIRECTORIES, REFERENCE WORKS, STATISTICS, AND JOURNALS

### Directories and Reference Works

Allaby, Michael A., ed. *The Oxford Dictionary of Ecology*. 3rd ed. Oxford: Oxford University Press, 2005.
Atkinson, Giles, Simon Dietz, and Eric Neumayer, eds. *Handbook of Sustainable Development*. Cheltenham, England: Edward Elgar, 2007.

Betsill, Michele, Kathryn Hochstetler, and Dimitris Stevis, eds. *Palgrave Advances in International Environmental Politics*. New York: Palgrave Macmillan, 2005.

Collin, P. H. *Dictionary of Environment & Ecology*. 5th ed. London: Bloomsbury, 2004.

Dauvergne, Peter, ed. *Handbook of Global Environmental Politics*. Cheltenham, England: Edward Elgar, 2005.

Dryzek, John, and David Schlosberg, eds. *Debating the Earth: The Environmental Politics Reader*. Oxford: Oxford University Press, 1998.

Ekins, Paul, Mayer Hillman, and Robert Hutchinson. *The Gaia Atlas of Green Economics*. New York: Anchor Books, 1992.

Gay, Kathlyn. *Rainforests of the World: A Reference Handbook*. 2nd ed. Santa Barbara, Calif.: ABC-CLIO, 2001.

Gordon, Bruce, Richard Mackay, and Eva Rehfuess. *Inheriting the World: The Atlas of Children's Health and the Environment*. Geneva, Switzerland: World Health Organization, 2004.

Krech, Shepard III, J. R. McNeill, and Carolyn Merchant, eds. *Encyclopedia of World Environmental History*. New York: Routledge, 2004.

Paehlke, Robert, ed. *Conservation and Environmentalism: An Encyclopedia*. New York: Garland, 1995.

Park, Chris. *A Dictionary of Environment and Conservation*. Oxford: Oxford University Press, 2007.

Saunier, Richard E., and Richard A. Meganck. *Dictionary and Introduction to Global Environmental Governance*. London: Earthscan, 2007.

Schreurs, Miranda, and Elim Papadakis. *Historical Dictionary of the Green Movement*. Lanham, Md.: Scarecrow Press, 2007.

Stokke, Olav Schram, and Øystein B. Thommessen, eds. *Yearbook of International Co-operation on Environment and Development*. London: Earthscan, 2003.

Thai, Khi V., Dianne Rahm, and Jerrell D. Coggburn, eds. *Handbook of Globalization and the Environment*. Boca Raton, Fla.: CRC Press, 2007.

Trzyna, Thaddeus C., and Julie Didion, eds. *World Directory of Environmental Organizations*. 6th ed. London: Earthscan, 2001.

Wells, Edward R., and Alan M. Schwartz. *Historical Dictionary of North American Environmentalism*. Lanham, Md.: Scarecrow Press, 1997.

## Statistics

Sacquet, Anne-Marie. *World Atlas of Sustainable Development: Economic, Social and Environmental Data*. London: Anthem Press, 2005.

United Nations Development Programme, United Nations Environment Programme, World Bank, and World Resources Institute. *World Resources*

*2005: The Wealth of the Poor: Managing Ecosystems to Fight Poverty.* Washington, D.C.: World Resources Institute, 2005.

United Nations Environment Programme. *GEO Yearbook 2007.* Nairobi, Kenya: United Nations Environment Programme, 2007.

———. *UNEP Yearbook 2008.* Nairobi, Kenya: United Nations Environment Programme, 2008.

World Bank. *The Little Green Data Book 2007.* Washington, D.C.: World Bank, 2007.

———. *World Development Indicators 2008.* Washington, D.C.: World Bank Publications, 2008.

———. *World Development Report 2006: Equity and Development.* Washington, D.C.: World Bank Publications, 2005.

———. *World Development Report 2007: Development and the Next Generation.* Washington, D.C.: World Bank Publications, 2006.

———. *World Development Report 2008: Agriculture and Development.* Washington, D.C.: World Bank Publications, 2007.

World Resources Institute. *Earth Trends.* http://earthtrends.wri.org/, 2007 (accessed 7 July 2008).

Worldwatch Institute. *State of the World 2008: Toward a Sustainable Global Economy.* New York: W. W. Norton, 2008.

———. *Vital Signs 2007–2008: The Trends That Are Shaping Our Future.* New York: W. W. Norton, 2007.

## Journals

*Climate Policy* (Elsevier).
Focuses on climate change.

*Ecological Economics* (Elsevier).
The journal of the International Society for Ecological Economics.

*Environment* (Heldref).
Analyzes the interface of environment and development.

*Environment and Planning A* (Pion).
Interdisciplinary research on urban and regional environmental issues.

*Environment and Planning B—Planning & Design* (Pion).
Publishes research on formal methods, models, and theories with a focus on the built environment of cities and regions.

*Environment and Planning C—Government and Policy* (Pion).
Interdisciplinary research with a focus on governments and policy from an international perspective.

*Environment and Planning D—Society and Space* (Pion).
Interdisciplinary research with a focus on the interrelationship of social and spatial issues.

*Environment and Urbanization* (Sage).
Analyzes urban and environmental issues, especially in Africa, Asia, and Latin America.

*Environmental Ethics* (Center for Environmental Philosophy).
Interdisciplinary research on philosophical aspects of environmental issues.

*Environmental History* (Copublished by the Forest History Society and the American Society for Environmental History in association with History Co-operative).
Publishes historical research on human interactions with the natural world.

*Environmental Politics* (Taylor and Francis).
Concentrates on environmental movements, political parties, and environmental policy.

*Environmental Values* (White Horse Press).
Provides research on values, environmental policy, and current and future conditions for people and other species.

*Global Environmental Change—Human and Policy Dimensions* (Elsevier).
Interdisciplinary research on global environmental change, covering issues such as economics, equity, health, public policy, risk, science, and international relations.

*Global Environmental Politics* (MIT Press).
Analyzes the connections between political forces and environmental change, particularly the consequences of local-global interactions.

*Journal of Environment and Development* (Sage).
Concentrates on analyses of sustainable development and public policy, including local, regional, and international case studies.

*Journal of Environmental Planning and Management* (Taylor and Francis).
Concentrates on planning and management of the environment.

*Organization & Environment: International Journal for Ecosocial Research* (Sage).
Publishes research on connections between the natural environment and formal and informal organizational patterns.

## GLOBAL ENVIRONMENTALISM (GENERAL WORKS)

### Critiques of Environmentalism

Bailey, Ronald, ed. *Global Warming and Other Eco-Myths: How the Environmental Movement Uses False Science to Scare Us to Death*. Roseville, Calif.: Forum, 2002.

Driessen, Paul. *Eco-imperialism: Green Power, Black Death*. Bellevue, Wash.: Free Enterprise Press, 2003.

Easterbrook, Gregg. *A Moment on the Earth: The Coming Age of Environmental Optimism*. New York: Penguin, 1995.

Lomborg, Bjørn. *The Skeptical Environmentalist: Measuring the Real State of the World*. Cambridge: Cambridge University Press, 2001.

———. *Cool It: The Skeptical Environmentalist's Guide to Global Warming*. New York: Alfred A. Knopf, 2007.

Shellenberger, Michael, and Ted Nordhaus. *Break Through: From the Death of Environmentalism to the Politics of Possibility*. New York: Houghton Mifflin: 2007.

Simon, Julian L. *Population Matters*. New Brunswick, N.J.: Transaction Publishers, 1990.

———. *The Ultimate Resource*. Princeton, N.J.: Princeton University Press, 1981.

———. *The Ultimate Resource 2*. Princeton, N.J.: Princeton University Press, 1996.

Stirling, M. David. *Green Gone Wild: Elevating Nature above Human Rights*. Bellevue, Wash.: Merril Press, 2008.

## Economic Growth, Population, and Consumption

Cohen, Maurie J., and Joseph Murphy. *Exploring Sustainable Consumption: Environmental Policy and the Social Sciences*. Oxford: Pergamon, 2001.

Crocker, David A., and Toby Linden, eds. *Ethics of Consumption: The Good Life, Justice, and Global Stewardship*. Lanham, Md.: Rowman & Littlefield, 1998.

Daly, Herman. *Beyond Growth: The Economics of Sustainable Development*. Boston, Mass.: Beacon, 1996.

———. *Steady-State Economics: the Economics of Biophysical Equilibrium and Moral Growth*. San Francisco, Calif.: W. H. Freeman, 1977.

Daly, Herman, and John Cobb Jr. *For the Common Good: Redirecting the Economy toward Community, the Environment, and a Sustainable Future*. Boston, Mass.: Beacon Press, 1996.

Dauvergne, Peter. *The Shadows of Consumption: Consequences for the Global Environment*. Cambridge, Mass.: MIT Press, 2008.

Davidson, Eric A. *You Can't Eat GNP: Economics as If Ecology Mattered*. Cambridge, Mass.: Perseus Publishing, 2000.

Ehrlich, Paul R. *The Population Bomb*. New York: Sierra Club-Ballantine, 1968.

Ehrlich, Paul R., and Anne H. Ehrlich. *One with Nineveh: Politics, Consumption, and the Human Future*. Washington, D.C.: Island Press, 2004.

Escobar, Arturo. *Encountering Development: The Making and Unmaking of the Third World*. Princeton, N.J.: Princeton University Press, 1995.

Hardin, Garrett. *Living within Limits: Ecology, Economics, and Population Taboos*. Oxford: Oxford University Press, 2000.

Jha, Raghbendra, and K. V. Bhanu Murthy. *Environmental Sustainability: A Consumption Approach*. London: Routledge, 2006.

Kuznets, Simon. "Economic Growth and Income Inequality." *American Economic Review* 45, no. 1 (1955): 1–28.

Malthus, Thomas Robert. *Essay on the Principle of Population*. London: J. Johnson, 1798. www.econlib.orglibraryMalthusmalPlong.html (accessed 7 July 2008).

Meadows, Donella H. "The Limits to Growth Revisited." In *The Cassandra Conference: Resources and the Human Predicament*, edited by Paul Ehrlich and John P. Holdren, 257–70. College Station, Tex.: Texas A&M University Press, 1993.

Meadows, Donella H., Dennis L. Meadows, William W. Behrens, and Jørgen Randers. *The Limits to Growth*. New York: The Club of Rome, 1972.

Meadows, Donella H., Dennis L. Meadows, and Jørgen Randers. *Beyond the Limits: Confronting Global Collapse, Envisioning a Sustainable Future*. White River Junction, Vt.: Chelsea Green, 1992.

Micheletti, Michele, Andreas Follesdal, and Dietlind Stolle, eds. *Politics, Products, and Markets: Exploring Political Consumerism Past and Present*. New Brunswick, N.J.: Transaction Publishers, 2004.

Myers, Norman, and Jennifer Kent. *The New Consumers: The Influence of Affluence on the Environment*. Washington, D.C.: Island Press, 2004.

Porritt, Jonathon. *Capitalism as If the World Matters*. London: Earthscan, 2007.

Princen, Thomas. *The Logic of Sufficiency*. Cambridge, Mass.: MIT Press, 2005.

Princen, Thomas, Michael Maniates, and Ken Conca, eds. *Confronting Consumption*. Cambridge, Mass.: MIT Press, 2002.

Rapley, John. *Understanding Development: Theory and Practice in the Third World*. Boulder, Colo.: Lynne Rienner, 2002.

Sachs, Wolfgang. *Planet Dialectics: Explorations in Environment and Development*. London: Zed Books, 1999.

Schor, Juliet. *The Overspent American: Upscaling, Downshifting, and the New Consumer*. New York: Basic Books, 1998.

Schor, Juliet B., and Douglas B. Holt, eds. *The Consumer Society Reader*. New York: The New Press, 2000.

Schumacher, E. F. *Small Is Beautiful: Economics as If People Mattered*. New York: Harper and Row, 1973.

Southerton, Dale, Heather Chappells, and Bas Van Vliet, eds. *Sustainable Consumption: The Implications of Changing Infrastructures of Provision*. Cheltenham, England: Edward Elgar, 2004.

Vogel, David. *Trading Up: Consumer and Environmental Regulation in a Global Economy*. Cambridge, Mass.: Harvard University Press, 1995.

Woollard, Robert F., and Aleck S. Ostry, eds. *Fatal Consumption: Rethinking Sustainable Development*. Vancouver, B.C.: University of British Columbia, 2000.

## Financing and Debt

Ganzi, John, Frances Seymour, and Sandy Buffett, with Navroz Dubash. *Leverage for the Environment: A Guide to the Private Financial Services Industry*. Washington, D.C.: World Resources Institute, 1998.

George, Susan. *The Debt Boomerang*. London: Pluto, 1992.

————. *A Fate Worse Than Debt*. London: Penguin, 1988.

Gutner, Tamar L. *Banking on the Environment: Multilateral Development Banks and Their Environmental Performance in Central and Eastern Europe*. Cambridge, Mass.: MIT Press, 2002.

Malbasic, Ivona, and Jozsef Feiler, eds. *Heavy Footprint: The World Bank and Environment in Europe and Central Asia*. Budapest, Hungary: CEE Bankwatch Network, 2000.

Rich, Bruce. *Mortgaging the Earth: The World Bank, Environmental Impoverishment, and the Crisis of Development*. London: Earthscan, 1994.

Roodman, David Malin. *The Natural Wealth of Nations: Harnessing the Market for the Environment*. New York: W. W. Norton, 1998.

Schmidheiny, Stephan, and Federico Zorraquín. *Financing Change: The Financial Community, Eco-efficiency, and Sustainable Development*. Cambridge, Mass.: MIT Press, 1996.

## Global Environmental Governance

Adeel, Zafar, ed. *East Asian Experience in Environmental Governance: Response in a Rapidly Developing Region*. Tokyo: United Nations University Press, 2003.

Axelrod, Regina, David Leonard Downie, and Norman Vig, eds. *The Global Environment: Institutions, Law and Policy*. Washington, D.C.: CQ Press, 2005.

Ayre, Georgina, and Rosalie Callway, eds. *Governance for Sustainable Development: A Foundation for the Future*. London: Earthscan, 2005.

Badenoch, Nathan. *Transboundary Environmental Governance: Principles and Practice in Mainland Southeast Asia*. Washington, D.C.: World Resources Institute, 2002.

Bernstein, Steven, and Louis W. Pauly, eds. *Global Liberalism and Political Order: Toward a New Grand Compromise?* Albany: State University of New York Press, 2007.

Biermann, Frank, and Steffen Bauer, eds. *A World Environmental Organization: Solution or Threat for Effective International Environmental Governance?* Aldershot, England: Ashgate, 2005.

Bruch, Carl, Wole Coker, and Chris VanArsdale. *Breathing Life into Fundamental Principles: Implementing Constitutional Environmental Protections in Africa.* Washington, D.C.: World Resources Institute, 2001.

Chambers, W. Bradnee, and Jessica F. Green, eds. *Reforming International Environmental Governance: From Institutional Limits to Innovative Reforms.* Tokyo: United Nations University Press, 2005.

Chasek, Pamela, ed. *The Global Environment in the Twenty-First Century: Prospects for International Cooperation.* New York: United Nations University Press, 2000.

Conca, Ken, and Geoffrey D. Dabelko, eds. *Green Planet Blues: Environmental Politics from Stockholm to Johannesburg.* 3rd ed. Boulder, Colo.: Westview Press, 2004.

DeSombre, Elizabeth R. *The Global Environment and World Politics.* 2nd ed. London: Continuum, 2007.

Dryzek, John. *Politics of the Earth: Environmental Discourses.* 2nd ed. Oxford: Oxford University Press, 2005.

Haas, Peter M., Robert O. Keohane, and Marc A. Levy, eds. *Institutions for the Earth: Sources of Effective International Environmental Protection.* Cambridge, Mass.: MIT Press, 1993.

Hardin, Garrett. "Extensions of 'The Tragedy of the Commons.'" *Science* 280 (1 May 1998): 682–83.

——. "The Tragedy of the Commons." *Science* 162 (1968): 1243–48.

Hempel, Lamont C. *Environmental Governance: The Global Challenge.* Washington, D.C.: Island Press, 1996.

Higgins, Vaughan, and Geoffrey Lawrence, eds. *Agricultural Governance: Globalization and the New Politics of Regulation.* London: Routledge, 2005.

Hirst, Paul, and Grahame Thompson. *Globalization in Question: The International Economy and the Possibilities of Governance.* 2nd ed. Cambridge: Polity Press, 1999.

Jasanoff, Sheila, and Marybeth Long Martello, eds. *Earthly Politics: Local and Global in Environmental Governance.* Cambridge, Mass.: MIT Press, 2004.

Jordan, Andrew, Rüdiger K. W. Wurzel, and Anthony R. Zito, eds. *New Instruments of Environmental Governance? National Experiences and Prospects.* London: Frank Cass, 2003.

Kanie, Norichika, and Peter M. Haas, eds. *Emerging Forces in Environmental Governance.* Tokyo: United Nations University Press, 2004.

Krasner, Stephen D. *International Regimes.* Ithaca, N.Y.: Cornell University Press, 1983.

Le Prestre, Philippe G., ed. *Governing Global Biodiversity: The Evolution and Implementation of the Convention on Biological Diversity*. Aldershot, England: Ashgate, 2002.

Lipschutz, Ronnie D. *Global Environmental Politics: Power, Perspectives, and Practice*. Washington, D.C.: CQ Press, 2003.

Lipschutz, Ronnie D., with Judith Mayer. *Global Civil Society and Global Environmental Governance*. Albany: State University of New York Press, 1996.

Oberthür, Sebastian, and Thomas Gehring, eds. *Institutional Interaction in Global Environmental Governance: Synergy and Conflict among International and EU Policies*. Cambridge, Mass.: MIT Press, 2006.

Ostrom, Elinor. *Governing the Commons: The Evolution of Institutions for Collective Action*. Cambridge: Cambridge University Press, 1990.

Park, Jacob, Ken Conca, and Matthias Finger, eds. *The Crisis of Global Environmental Governance: Towards a New Political Economy of Sustainability*. New York: Routledge, 2008.

Soroos, Marvin. "Garrett Hardin and Tragedies of Global Commons." In *Handbook of Global Environmental Politics*, edited by Peter Dauvergne, 35–50. Cheltenham, England: Edward Elgar Publishing, 2005.

Spaargaren, Gert, Arthur P. J. Mol, and Frederick H. Buttel, eds. *Governing Environmental Flows: Global Challenges to Social Theory*. Cambridge, Mass.: MIT Press, 2006.

Speth, James Gustave, and Peter Haas. *Global Environmental Governance*. Washington, D.C.: Island Press, 2006.

Tilwell, Matthew, and Richard Tarasofsky. *Towards Coherent Environmental and Economic Governance: Legal and Practical Approaches to MEA-WTO Linkages*. Gland, Switzerland: WWF, 2001.

Vogler, John. *The Global Commons: Environmental and Technological Governance*. 2nd ed. New York: John Wiley & Sons, 2000.

Weale, Albert, et al. *Environmental Governance in Europe: An Ever Closer Ecological Union?* Oxford: Oxford University Press, 2000.

Young, Oran R., ed. *Global Governance: Drawing Insights from the Environmental Experience*. Cambridge, Mass.: MIT Press, 1997.

———. *International Governance: Protecting the Environment in a Stateless Society*. Ithaca, N.Y.: Cornell University Press, 1994.

## Globalization

Carrier, James G., ed. *Confronting Environments: Local Understanding in a Globalizing World*. Walnut Creek, Calif.: AltaMira Press, 2003.

French, Hilary. *Vanishing Borders: Protecting the Planet in the Age of Globalization*. New York: W. W. Norton, 2000.

Jorgenson, Andrew, and Edward Kick, eds. *Globalization and the Environment*. Boston, Mass.: Brill, 2006.

Kütting, Gabriela. *Globalization and the Environment: Greening Global Political Economy*. Albany: State University of New York Press, 2004.

Leichenko, Robin M., and Karen L. O'Brien. *Environmental Change and Globalization: Double Exposures*. New York: Oxford University Press, 2008.

Mander, Jerry, and Victoria Tauli-Corpuz, eds. *Paradigm Wars: Indigenous Peoples' Resistance to Globalization*. New expanded ed. San Francisco, Calif.: Sierra Club Books, 2006.

McKibbin, Bill. *Deep Economy: The Wealth of Communities and the Durable Future*. New York: Times Books, 2007.

Mol, Arthur P. J. *Globalization and Environmental Reform: The Ecological Modernization of the Global Economy*. Cambridge, Mass.: MIT Press, 2001.

Paavola, Jouni, and Ian Lowe, eds. *Environmental Values in a Globalising World: Nature, Justice and Governance*. London: Routledge, 2005.

Speth, James Gustave, ed. *Worlds Apart: Globalization and the Environment*. Washington, D.C.: Island Press, 2003.

Vertovec, Steven, and Darrell A. Posey, eds. *Globalization, Globalism, Environment, and Environmentalism: Consciousness of Connections*. New York: Oxford University Press, 2003.

## Histories

Adams, William M. *Against Extinction: The Story of Conservation*. London: Earthscan, 2004.

Bocking, Stephen. *Ecologists and Environmental Politics: A History of Contemporary Ecology*. New Haven, Conn.: Yale University Press, 1997.

Brenton, Tony. *The Greening of Machiavelli: The Evolution of International Environmental Politics*. London: Royal Institute of International Affairs, 1994.

Caldwell, Lynton Keith. *International Environmental Policy: From the Twentieth to the Twenty-First Century*. Durham, N.C.: Duke University Press, 1996.

Diamond, Jared M. *Collapse: How Societies Choose to Fail or Succeed*. New York: Viking, 2005.

Guha, Ramachandra. *Environmentalism: A Global History*. New York: Longman, 2000.

MacDonald, Gordon J. "Environment: Evolution of a Concept." *Journal of Environment & Development* 12, no. 2 (June 2003): 151–176.

Marsh, George Perkins. *Man and Nature; or, Physical Geography as Modified by Human Action*. New York: Charles Scribner, 1864.

Mauch, Christof, Nathan Stoltzfus, and Douglas R. Weiner, eds. *Shades of Green: Environmental Activism around the Globe*. Lanham, Md.: Rowman & Littlefield, 2006.

Peterson del Mar, David. *Environmentalism*. New York: Pearson/Longman, 2006.

## International Organizations

Fox, Jonathan A., and L. David Brown, eds. *The Struggle for Accountability: The World Bank, NGOs, and Grassroots Movements*. Cambridge, Mass.: MIT Press, 1998.

Goldman, Michael. *Imperial Nature: The World Bank and Struggles for Social Justice in the Age of Globalization*. New Haven, Conn.: Yale University Press, 2005.

Kelly, Trish. *The Impact of the WTO: The Environment, Public Health and Sovereignty*. Cheltenham, England: Edward Elgar, 2007.

Le Prestre, Philippe. *The World Bank and the Environmental Challenge*. Selinsgrove, Pa.: Susquehanna University Press, 1989.

Rao, P. K. *The World Trade Organization and the Environment*. London: Macmillan, 2000.

Rechkemmer, Andreas, ed. *UNEO: Towards an International Environment Organization: Approaches to a Sustainable Reform of Global Environmental Governance*. Baden-Baden, Germany: Nomos, 2005.

Sampson, Gary P. *The WTO and Sustainable Development*. Tokyo: United Nations University Press, 2005.

Sampson, Gary, and John Whalley, eds. *The WTO, Trade, and the Environment*. Cheltenham, England: Edward Elgar, 2005.

Young, Zoe. *A New Green Order: The World Bank and the Politics of the Global Environment Facility*. London: Pluto Press, 2003.

## Justice

Adamson, Joni, Mei Mei Evans, and Rachel Stein, eds. *The Environmental Justice Reader: Politics, Poetics, & Pedagogy*. Tucson, Ariz.: University of Arizona Press, 2002.

Anand, Ruchi. 2004. *International Environmental Justice: A North-South Dimension*. Aldershot, England: Ashgate Publishing.

Bauer, Joanne, ed. *Forging Environmentalism: Justice, Livelihood, and Contested Environments*. Armonk, N.Y.: M. E. Sharpe, 2006.

Brechin, Steven, Peter Wilshusen, Crystal Fortwangler, and Patrick West, eds. *Contested Nature: Promoting International Biodiversity with Social Justice in the Twenty-First Century*. Albany: State University of New York Press, 2003.

Bullard, Robert D., ed. *The Quest for Environmental Justice: Human Rights and the Politics of Pollution*. San Francisco, Calif.: Sierra Club Books, 2005.

Cole, Luke W., and Sheila R. Foster. *From the Ground Up: Environmental Racism and the Rise of the Environmental Justice Movement*. New York: New York University Press, 2001.

Dobson, Andrew. *Justice and the Environment: Conceptions of Environmental Sustainability and Dimensions of Social Justice*. Oxford: Oxford University Press, 1998.

Hampson, Ren Osler, and Judith Reppy, eds. *Earthly Goods: Environmental Change and Social Justice*. Ithaca, N.Y.: Cornell University Press, 1996.

Hofrichter, Richard, ed. *Toxic Struggles: The Theory and Practice of Environmental Justice*. Salt Lake City: University of Utah Press, 2002.

Low, Nicholas, and Brendan Gleeson. *Justice, Society and Nature: An Exploration of Political Ecology*. London: Routledge, 1998.

Mutz, Kathryn M., Gary C. Bryner, and Douglas S. Kenney. *Justice and Natural Resources: Concepts, Strategies, and Applications*. Washington, D.C.: Island Press, 2001.

Sandler, Ronald, and Phaedra C. Pezzullo, eds. *Environmental Justice and Environmentalism: The Social Justice Challenge to the Environmental Movement*. Cambridge, Mass.: MIT Press, 2007.

Schlosberg, David. *Environmental Justice and the New Pluralism: The Challenge of Difference for Environmentalism*. Oxford: Oxford University Press, 2002.

Stein, Rachel, ed. *New Perspectives on Environmental Justice: Gender, Sexuality, and Activism*. New Brunswick, N.J.: Rutgers University Press, 2004.

Timmons, Roberts, J., and Bradley C. Parks. *A Climate of Injustice: Global Inequality, North-South Politics, and Climate Policy*. Cambridge, Mass.: MIT Press, 2007.

## Multinational Corporations

Anderson, Sarah, and John Cavanagh. *Top 200: The Rise of Corporate Global Power*. Washington, D.C.: Institute for Policy Studies, 1999.

Barnet, Richard J., and John Cavanagh. *Global Dreams: Imperial Corporations and the New World Order*. New York: Simon & Schuster, 1994.

Beder, Sharon. *Global Spin: The Corporate Assault on Environmentalism*. Melbourne, Australia: Scribe Publications, 1997.

Bruno, Kenny, and Joshua Karliner. *Earthsummit.biz: The Corporate Takeover of Sustainable Development*. Oakland, Calif.: Food First Books, 2002.

Esty, Daniel C., and Andrew S. Winston. *Green to Gold: How Smart Companies Use Environmental Strategy to Innovate, Create Value, and Build Competitive Advantage*. New Haven, Conn.: Yale University Press, 2006.

Garcia-Johnson, Ronie. *Exporting Environmentalism: U.S. Multinational Chemical Corporations in Brazil and Mexico*. Cambridge, Mass.: MIT Press, 2000.

Gedicks, Al. *Resource Rebels: Native Challenges to Mining and Oil Corporations*. Boston, Mass.: South End Press, 2001.

Greer, Jed, and Kenny Bruno. *Greenwash: The Reality behind Corporate Environmentalism*. Penang, Malaysia: Third World Network, 1997.

Hay, Bruce L., Robert N. Stavins, and Richard H. K. Vietor, eds. *Environmental Protection and the Social Responsibility of Firms*. Washington, D.C.: RFF Press, 2005.

Holme, Richard, and Phil Watts. *Corporate Social Responsibility: Making Good Business Sense*. Geneva, Switzerland: World Business Council for Sustainable Development, 2000.

Johnstone, Nick, ed. *Environmental Policy and Corporate Behaviour*. Cheltenham, England: Edward Elgar, 2007.

Kamieniecki, Sheldon. *Corporate America and Environmental Policy: How Often Does Business Get Its Way?* Stanford, Calif.: Stanford University Press, 2006.

Karliner, Joshua. *The Corporate Planet, Ecology and Politics in the Age of Globalization*. San Francisco, Calif.: Sierra Club, 1997.

Korten, David C. *The Post-Corporate World: Life after Capitalism*. San Francisco, Calif.: Berrett-Koehler, 1999.

———. *When Corporations Rule the World*. 2nd ed. San Francisco, Calif.: Berrett-Koehler Publishers, 2001.

Leighton, Michelle, Naomi Roht-Arriaza, and Lyuba Zarsky. *Beyond Good Deeds: Case Studies and a New Policy Agenda for Corporate Accountability*. Berkeley, Calif.: Nautilus Institute, 2002.

Levy, David L., and Peter J. Newell, eds. *The Business of Global Environmental Governance*. Cambridge, Mass.: MIT Press, 2005.

Pearson, Charles, ed. *Multinational Corporations, the Environment, and the Third World*. Durham, N.C.: Duke University Press, 1987.

Prakash, Aseem. *Greening the Firm: The Politics of Corporate Environmentalism*. Cambridge: Cambridge University Press, 2000.

Prakash, Aseem, and Matthew Potoski. *The Voluntary Environmentalists: Green Clubs, ISO 14001, and Voluntary Regulations*. Cambridge: Cambridge University Press, 2006.

Rowell, Andrew. *Green Backlash: Global Subversion of the Environment Movement*. London: Routledge, 1996.

Schmidheiny, Stephan, with Business Council for Sustainable Development. *Changing Course: A Global Business Perspective on Development and the Environment*. Cambridge, Mass.: MIT Press, 1992.

Watts, Phil, and Richard Holme. *Corporate Social Responsibility: Meeting Changing Expectations*. Geneva, Switzerland: World Business Council for Sustainable Development, 1999.

## Negotiations and Agreements

Agarwal, Anil, Sunita Narain, and Anju Sharma, eds. *Green Politics: Global Environmental Negotiations 1*. New Delhi: Centre for Science and Environment, 1999.

Chasek, Pamela. *Earth Negotiations: Analyzing Thirty Years of Environmental Diplomacy*. Tokyo: United Nations University Press, 2001.

Davenport, Deborah Saunders. *Global Environmental Negotiations and U.S. Interests*. New York: Palgrave Macmillan, 2006.

Hatch, Chris, ed. *Environmental Policymaking: Assessing the Use of Alternative Policy Instruments*. Albany: State University of New York Press, 2005.

Kütting, Gabriela. *Environment, Society and International Relations: Towards More Effective International Environmental Agreements*. London: Routledge, 2000.

Miles, Edward L., Arild Underdal, Steinar Andresen, Jørgen Wettestad, Jon Birger Skjærseth, and Elaine M. Carlin. *Environmental Regime Effectiveness: Confronting Theory with Evidence*. Cambridge, Mass.: MIT Press, 2001.

Oberthür, Sebastian, and Hermann E. Ott. *The Kyoto Protocol: International Climate Policy for the 21st Century*. Berlin: Springer, 1999.

Pinguelli-Rosa, Luiz, and Mohan Munasinghe, eds. *Ethics, Equity, and International Negotiations on Climate Change*. Cheltenham, England: Edward Elgar, 2002.

Stokke, Olav Schram, Jon Hovi, and Geir Ulfstein, eds. *Implementing the Climate Regime: International Compliance*. London: Earthscan, 2005.

Susskind, Lawrence. *Environmental Diplomacy: Negotiating More Effective Global Agreements*. Oxford: Oxford University Press, 1994.

Tolba, Mostafa K., with Iwona Rummel-Bulska. *Global Environmental Diplomacy: Negotiating Environmental Agreements for the World 1973–1992*. Cambridge, Mass.: MIT Press, 1998.

Victor, David, Kal Raustiala, and Eugene Skolnikoff, eds. *The Implementation and Effectiveness of International Environmental Commitments: Theory and Practice*. Cambridge, Mass.: MIT Press, 1998.

Weiss, Edith Brown, and Harold K. Jacobson, eds. *Engaging Countries: Strengthening Compliance with International Environmental Accords*. Cambridge, Mass.: MIT Press, 1998.

Wettestad, Jörgen. *Designing Effective Environmental Regimes: The Key Conditions*. Cheltenham, England: Edward Elgar, 1999.

Young, Oran R., ed. *The Effectiveness of International Environmental Regimes: Causal Connections and Behavioral Mechanisms*. Cambridge, Mass.: MIT Press, 1999.

———. *International Cooperation: Building Regimes for Natural Resources and the Environment*. Ithaca, N.Y.: Cornell University Press, 1989.

## Nongovernmental Organizations and Activism

Betsill, Michele M., and Elisabeth Corell, eds. *NGO Diplomacy: The Influence of Nongovernmental Organizations in International Environmental Negotiations*. Cambridge, Mass.: MIT Press, 2007.

Boli, John, and George M. Thomas. *Constructing World Culture: International Nongovernmental Organizations since 1875*. Stanford, Calif.: Stanford University Press, 1999.

Curran, Giorel. *21st Century Dissent: Anarchism, Anti-Globalization and Environmentalism*. New York: Palgrave Macmillan, 2006.

Dale, Stephen. *McLuhan's Children: The Greenpeace Message and the Media*. Toronto, Ont.: Between the Lines, 1996.

Fisher, Julie. *Nongovernments: NGOs and the Political Development of the Third World*. West Hartford, Conn.: Kumarian Press, 1997.

Graham, Kevin. *Contemporary Environmentalists*. New York: Facts on File, 1996.

Keck, Margaret E., and Kathryn Sikkink. *Activists beyond Borders: Advocacy Networks in International Politics*. Ithaca, N.Y.: Cornell University Press, 1998.

Mauch, Christof, Nathan Stoltzfus, and Douglas R. Weiner, eds. *Shades of Green: Environmental Activism around the Globe*. Lanham, Md.: Rowman & Littlefield, 2006.

Nelson, Paul J. *The World Bank and Nongovernmental Organizations: The Limits of Apolitical Development*. London: Macmillan, 1995.

Oberthür, Sebastian, Matthias Buck, Sebastian Müller, Stefanie Pfahl, Richard G. Tarasofsky, Jacob Werksman, and Alice Palmer. *Participation of Non-Governmental Organisations in International Environmental Governance*. Berlin: Ecologic Institute, 2002.

Potter, David, ed. *NGOs and Environmental Policies: Asia and Africa*. London: Frank Cass, 1996.

Princen, Thomas, and Matthias Finger, eds. *Environmental NGOs in World Politics: Linking the Local and the Global*. London: Routledge, 1994.

Taylor, Bron Raymond, ed. *Ecological Resistance Movements: The Global Emergence of Radical and Popular Environmentalism*. Albany: State University of New York Press, 1995.

Taylor, J. Gary, and Patricia J. Scharlin. *Smart Alliance—How a Global Corporation and Environmental Activists Transformed a Tarnished Brand*. New Haven, Conn.: Yale University Press, 2004.

Tesh, Sylvia Noble. *Environmental Activists and Scientific Proof*. Ithaca, N.Y.: Cornell University Press, 2000.

Wapner, Paul. *Environmental Activism and World Civic Politics*. Albany: State University of New York Press, 1996.

## Political Economy

Bates, Robert H. *Open-Economy Politics: The Political Economy of the World Coffee Trade*. Princeton, N.J.: Princeton University Press, 1997.

Boyce, James K. *The Political Economy of the Environment*. Cheltenham, England: Edward Elgar, 2002.

Byrne, John, Leigh Glover, and Cecilia Martinez, eds. *Environmental Justice: Discourses in International Political Economy*. New Brunswick, N.J.: Transaction, 2002.

Clapp, Jennifer, and Peter Dauvergne. *Paths to a Green World: The Political Economy of the Global Environment*. Cambridge, Mass.: MIT Press, 2005.

Gonzalez, George A. *Corporate Power and the Environment: The Political Economy of U.S. Environmental Policy*. Lanham, Md.: Rowman & Littlefield, 2001.

Speth, James Gustave. *The Bridge at the Edge of the World: Capitalism, the Environment, and Crossing from Crisis to Sustainability*. New Haven, Conn.: Yale University Press, 2008.

Stavins, Robert N., ed. *The Political Economy of Environmental Regulation*. Cheltenham, England: Edward Elgar, 2004.

Stevis, Dimitris, and Valerie Assetto, eds. *The International Political Economy of the Environment: Critical Perspectives*. Boulder, Colo.: Lynne Rienner, 2001.

Talbot, John M. *Grounds for Agreement: The Political Economy of the Coffee Commodity Chain*. Lanham, Md.: Rowman & Littlefield, 2004.

Young, Oran R. *Natural Resources and the State: The Political Economy of Resource Management*. Ithaca, N.Y.: Cornell University Press, 1981.

## Poverty

Bass, Stephen, et al., eds. *Reducing Poverty and Sustaining the Environment: The Politics of Local Engagement*. London: Earthscan, 2005.

Dellink, Rob B., and Arjan Ruijs, eds. *Economics of Poverty, Environment and Natural-Resource Use*. New York: Springer, 2008.

Hollander, Jack M. *The Real Environmental Crisis: Why Poverty, Not Affluence, Is the Environment's Number One Enemy*. Berkeley: University of California Press, 2003

Johnson, Pierre Marc, Karel Mayrand, and Marc Paquin, eds. *Governing Global Desertification: Linking Environmental Degradation, Poverty, and Participation*. Aldershot, England: Ashgate, 2006.

Middleton, Neil, and Phil O'Keefe. *Rio Plus Ten: Politics, Poverty and the Environment*. London: Pluto Press, 2003.

World Bank. *Poverty and Environment: Understanding Linkages at the Household Level*. Washington, D.C.: The World Bank, 2007.

## Science and Environmentalism

Bocking, Stephen. *Nature's Experts: Science, Politics, and the Environment*. New Brunswick, N.J.: Rutgers University Press, 2004.

Dessler, Andrew E., and Edward A. Parson. *The Science and Politics of Global Climate Change: A Guide to the Debate*. Cambridge: Cambridge University Press, 2006.

Dimitrov, Radoslav S. *Science and International Environmental Policy: Regimes and Nonregimes in Global Governance*. Lanham, Md.: Rowman & Littlefield, 2006.

Ehrlich, Paul R., and Anne H. Ehrlich. *Betrayal of Science and Reason: How Anti-Environmental Rhetoric Threatens Our Future*. Washington, D.C.: Island Press, 1996.

Harrison, Neil E., and Gary C. Bryner, eds. *Science and Politics in the International Environment*. Lanham, Md.: Rowman & Littlefield, 2004.

Litfin, Karen T. *Ozone Discourse: Science and Politics in Global Environmental Cooperation*. New York: Columbia University Press, 1994.

Rockwood, Larry L., Ronald E. Stewart, and Thomas Dietz. *Foundations of Environmental Sustainability: The Co-Evolution of Science and Policy*. New York: Oxford University Press, 2007.

Young, Christian C. *The Environment and Science: Social Impact and Interaction*. Santa Barbara, Calif.: ABC-CLIO, 2005.

## Security

Ali, Saleem H., ed. *Peace Parks: Conservation and Conflict Resolution*. Cambridge, Mass.: MIT Press, 2007.

Barnett, Jon. *The Meaning of Environmental Security: Environmental Politics and Policy in the New Security Era*. New York: Zed Books, 2001.

Brauch, Hans Günter, et al., eds. *Globalization and Environmental Challenges: Reconceptualizing Security in the 21st Century—Hexagon Series on Human and Environmental Security and Peace*. Vol. 3. Berlin: Springer-Verlag, 2008.

Conca, Ken, and Geoffrey D. Dabelko, eds. *Environmental Peacemaking*. Washington, D.C.: Woodrow Wilson Center Press, 2003.

Dalby, Simon. *Environmental Security*. Minneapolis: University of Minnesota Press, 2002.

Diehl, Paul F., and Nils Petter Gleditsch, eds. *Environmental Conflict*. Boulder, Colo.: Westview Press, 2001.

Homer-Dixon, Thomas F. *Environment, Scarcity and Violence*. Princeton, N.J.: Princeton University Press, 1999.

———. *The Ingenuity Gap: Facing the Economic, Environmental, and Other Challenges of an Increasingly Complex and Unpredictable World*. New York: Alfred A. Knopf, 2000.

Jeffery, Roger, and Baskar Vira, eds. *Conflict and Cooperation in Participatory Natural Resource Management*. Basingstoke, England: Palgrave, 2001.

Manwaring, Max G., ed. *Environmental Security and Global Stability: Problems and Responses*. Lanham, Md.: Lexington Books, 2002.

Ophuls, William. *Ecology and the Politics of Scarcity: Prologue to a Political Theory of the Steady State*. San Francisco, Calif.: W. H. Freeman, 1973.

Page, Edward A., and Michael Redclift, eds. *Human Security and the Environment: International Comparisons*. Cheltenham, England: Edward Elgar, 2002.

Peluso, Nancy Lee, and Michael Watts, eds. *Violent Environments*. Ithaca, N.Y.: Cornell University Press, 2001.

Pirages, Dennis, and Ken Cousins, eds. *From Resource Scarcity to Ecological Security: Exploring New Limits to Growth*. Cambridge, Mass.: MIT Press, 2005.

Sachs, Wolfgang, ed. *Global Ecology: A New Arena of Political Conflict*. London: Zed Books, 1993.

Shiva, Vandana. *The Violence of the Green Revolution*. London: Zed Books, 1992.

Suliman, Mohamed, ed. *Ecology, Politics and Violent Conflict*. London: Zed Books, 1999.

## Sustainability and Sustainable Development

Agyeman, Julian, Robert Bullart, and Bob Evans, eds. *Just Sustainabilities: Development in an Unequal World*. London: Earthscan, 2003.

Baker, Susan. *Sustainable Development*. London: Routledge, 2006.

Bigg, Tom, ed. *Survival for a Small Planet: The Sustainable Development Agenda*. London: Earthscan, 2004.

Bryner, Gary C. *Gaia's Wager: Environmental Movements and the Challenge of Sustainability*. Lanham, Md.: Rowman & Littlefield, 2001.

DeSimone, Livio, and Frank Popoff. *Eco-Efficiency: The Business Link to Sustainable Development*. Cambridge, Mass.: MIT Press, 1997.

Ehrenfield, John R. *Sustainability by Design: A Subversive Strategy for Transforming Our Consumer Culture*. New Haven, Conn.: Yale Press, 2008.

Green, Jessica F., and W. Bradnee Chambers, eds. *The Politics of Participation in Sustainable Development Governance*. Tokyo: United Nations University Press, 2006.

Harcourt, Wendy. *Feminist Perspectives on Sustainable Development*. London: Zed Books, 1994.

Johnston, Josee, Michael Gismondi, and James Goodman, eds. *Nature's Revenge: Reclaiming Sustainability in an Age of Corporate Globalization*. Peterborough, Ont.: Broadview Press, 2006.

Keiner, Marco, ed. *The Future of Sustainability*. Dordrecht, Netherlands: Springer, 2006.

Kelly, Petra. *Fighting for Hope*. Translated by Marianne Howarth. London: Chatto and Windus, 1984.

Munasinghe, Mohan, and Rob Swart. *Primer on Climate Change and Sustainable Development: Facts, Policy Analysis, and Applications*. Cambridge: Cambridge University Press, 2005.

Pearce, David, and Jeremy Warford. *World without End: Economics, Environment and Sustainable Development*. New York: Oxford University Press, 1993.

Redclift, Michael, ed. *Sustainability: Critical Concepts in the Social Sciences*. New York: Routledge, 2005.

Rogers, Peter P., Kazi F. Jalal, and John A. Boyd. *An Introduction to Sustainable Development*. London: Earthscan, 2007.

Strachan, Janet R., et al. *The Plain Language Guide to the World Summit on Sustainable Development*. London: Earthscan, 2005.

World Commission on Environment and Development. *Our Common Future*. Oxford: Oxford University Press, 1987.

## Trade

Anderson, Terry L., and Donald R. Leal. *Free Market Environmentalism*. New York: Palgrave, 2001.

Bhagwati, Jagdish. "The Case for Free Trade." *Scientific American* (November 1993): 42–49.

Burtless, Gary, Robert Z. Lawrence, Robert E. Litan, and Robert J. Shapiro. *Globaphobia: Confronting Fears about Open Trade*. Washington, D.C.: Brookings Institution Press, 1998.

Daly, Herman E. "The Perils of Free Trade." *Scientific American* (November 1993): 50–57.

Deere, Carolyn L., and Daniel C. Esty, eds. *Greening the Americas: NAFTA's Lessons for Hemispheric Trade*. Cambridge, Mass.: MIT Press, 2002.

Esty, Daniel C. *Greening the GATT: Trade, Environment, and the Future*. Washington, D.C.: Institute for International Economics, 1994.

Gallagher, Kevin P. *Free Trade and the Environment: Mexico, NAFTA and Beyond*. Palo Alto, Calif.: Stanford University Press, 2004.

Hogenboom, Barbara. *Mexico and the NAFTA Environment Debate: The Transnational Politics of Economic Integration*. Utrecht, Netherlands: International Books, 1998.

Krueger, Jonathan. *International Trade and the Basel Convention*. London: Earthscan, 1999.

Krut, Riva, and Harris Gleckman. *ISO 14001: A Missed Opportunity for Global Sustainable Industrial Development*. London: Earthscan, 1998.

Low, Patrick. *International Trade and the Environment*. Washington, D.C.: World Bank, 1992.

Neumayer, Eric. *Greening Trade and Investment: Environmental Protection without Protectionism*. London: Earthscan, 2001.

Steinberg, Richard, ed. *The Greening of Trade Law: International Trade Organizations and Environmental Issues*. Lanham, Md.: Rowman & Littlefield, 2002.

Thoyer, Sophie, and Benoît Martimort-Asso, eds. *Participation for Sustainability in Trade*. Aldershot, England: Ashgate, 2007.

Tussie, Diana, ed. *The Environment and International Trade Negotiations: Developing Country Stakes*. Basingstoke, England: Macmillan, 2000.

# NATIONAL ENVIRONMENTALISM

## Comparative Histories and Policies

Adams, W. M. *Green Development: Environment and Sustainability in the Third World*. 2nd ed. New York: Routledge, 2001.

Bryant, Raymond, and Sinéad Bailey. *Third World Political Ecology*. New York: Routledge, 1997.

Burchell, Jon. *The Evolution of Green Politics: Development and Change within European Green Parties*. London: Earthscan, 2002.

Cass, Loren R. *The Failures of American and European Climate Policy: International Norms, Domestic Politics, and Unachievable Commitments*. Albany: State University of New York Press, 2006.

Chasek, Pamela S., David L. Downie, and Janet Welsh Brown. *Global Environmental Politics*. 4th ed. Boulder, Colo.: Westview Press, 2006.

Chatterjee, Pratap, and Matthias Finger. *The Earth Brokers: Power, Politics and World Development*. New York: Routledge, 1994.

Connelly, James, and Graham Smith. *Politics and the Environment: From Theory to Practice*. 2nd ed. New York: Routledge, 2003.

de Bruijn, Theo, and Vicky Norberg-Bohm, eds. *Industrial Transformation: Environmental Policy Innovation in the United States and Europe*. Cambridge, Mass.: MIT Press, 2005.

Desai, Uday. *Environmental Politics and Policy in Industrialized Countries*. Cambridge, Mass.: MIT Press, 2002.

Doyle, Timothy. *Environmental Movements in Minority and Majority Worlds: A Global Perspective*. 2nd ed. New Brunswick, N.J.: Rutgers University Press, 2005.

Dryzek, John, David Downs, Christian Hunold, Hans-Kristian Hernes, and David Schlosberg. *Green States and Social Movements: Environmentalism in the United States, United Kingdom, Germany, and Norway*. New York: Oxford University Press, 2003.

Elliott, Lorraine. *The Global Politics of the Environment*. 2nd ed. New York: New York University Press, 2004.

Griffiths, Tom, and Libby Robin, eds. *Ecology and Empire: Environmental History of Settler Societies*. Edinburgh, Scotland: Keele University Press, 1997.

Grundmann, Reiner. *Transnational Environmental Policy: Reconstructing Ozone*. London: Routledge, 2001.

Harrington, Winston, Richard D. Morgenstern, and Thomas Sterner, eds. *Choosing Environmental Policy: Comparing Instruments and Outcomes in the United States and Europe*. Washington, D.C.: Resources for the Future, 2004.

McBeath, Jerry, and Jonathan Rosenberg. *Comparative Environmental Politics*. Dordrecht, Netherlands: Springer, 2006.

Miller, Marian A. L. *The Third World in Global Environmental Politics*. Boulder, Colo.: Lynne Rienner, 1995.

Muller-Rommel, Ferdinand, and Thomas Poguntke, eds. *Green Parties in National Governments*. London: Frank Cass, 2002.

Nagel, Stuart S., ed. *Environmental Policy and Developing Nations*. Jefferson, N.C.: McFarland, 2002.

Peritore, N. Patrick. *Third World Environmentalism: Case Studies from the Global South*. Gainesville: University Press of Florida, 1999.

Ponting, Clive. *A Green History of the World: The Environment and the Collapse of Great Civilizations*. 1st American ed. New York: St. Martin's Press, 1992.

Schreurs, Miranda A. *Environmental Politics in Japan, Germany, and the United States*. Cambridge: Cambridge University Press, 2002.

Steel, Brent, Richard Clinton, and Nicholas Lovrich. *Environmental Politics and Policy: A Comparative Approach*. New York: McGraw Hill, 2003.

Vig, Norman J., and Michael G. Faur, eds. *Green Giants? Environmental Policies of the United States and the European Union*. Cambridge, Mass.: MIT Press, 2004.

Weidner, Helmut, and Martin Jänicke, eds. *Capacity Building in National Environmental Policy: A Comparative Study of 17 Countries*. Berlin: Springer, 2002.

Wurzel, Rüdiger K. W. *Environmental Policy-Making in Britain, Germany and the European Union: The Europeanisation of Air and Water Pollution Control*. Manchester, England: Manchester University Press, 2002.

## Africa

Adams, Jonathan S., and Thomas O. McShane. *The Myth of Wild Africa: Conservation without Illusion*. Berkeley: University of California Press, 1992.

Bassett, Thomas J., and Donald Crummey. *African Savannas: Global Narratives and Local Knowledge of Environmental Change*. Oxford: James Currey, 2003.

Broch-Due, Vigdis, and Richard A. Schroeder, eds. *Producing Nature and Poverty in Africa*. Uppsala, Sweden: Nordic Africa Institute, 2000.

Clapp, Jennifer. *Adjustment and Agriculture in Africa: Farmers, the State, and the World Bank in Guinea*. New York: St. Martin's Press, 1997.

Dibie, Robert, ed. *Non-Governmental Organizations and Sustainable Development in Sub-Saharan Africa*. Lanham, Md.: Lexington Books, 2007.

Fabricius, Christo, and Eddie Koch, with Hector Magome and Steven Turner, eds. *Rights, Resources and Rural Development: Community-Based Natural Resource Management in Southern Africa*. London: Earthscan, 2004.

Hasler, Richard. *Agriculture, Foraging and Wildlife Resource Use in Africa: Cultural and Political Dynamics in the Zambezi Valley*. London: Kegan Paul, 1995.

Keeley, James, and Ian Scoones. *Understanding Environmental Policy Processes: Cases from Africa*. London: Earthscan, 2003.

Leach, Melissa, and Robin Mearns. *The Lie of the Land: Challenging Received Wisdom on the African Environment*. Westport, Conn.: Greenwood, 1996.

Low, Pak Sum, ed. *Climate Change and Africa*. Cambridge: Cambridge University Press, 2005.

Maddox, Gregory. *Sub-Saharan Africa: An Environmental History*. Santa Barbara, Calif.: ABC-CLIO, 2006.

Rodney, Walter. *How Europe Underdeveloped Africa*. Dar es Salaam: Tanzania Publishing House, 1972.

World Bank. *Sub-Saharan Africa: From Crisis to Sustainable Growth*. Washington, D.C.: World Bank, 1989.

## Antarctica and Arctic

Bargagli, Roberto. *Antarctic Ecosystems: Environmental Contamination, Climate Change, and Human Impact*. Berlin: Springer, 2005.

Cone, Marla. *Silent Snow: The Slow Poisoning of the Arctic*. New York: Grove Press, 2005.

Elliott, Lorraine. *International Environmental Politics: Protecting the Antarctic*. London: Macmillan, 1994.

Herber, Bernard P. *Protecting the Antarctic Commons: Problems of Economic Efficiency*. Tucson: Udall Center for Studies in Public Policy, University of Arizona, 2007.

Joyner, Christopher C. *Governing the Frozen Commons: The Antarctic Regime and Environmental Protection*. Columbia: University of South Carolina Press, 1998.

McMonagle, Robert J. *Caribou and Conoco: Rethinking Environmental Politics in Alaska's ANWAR and Beyond*. Lanham, Md.: Lexington Books, 2008.

Mikkelsen, Aslaug, and Oluf Langhelle, eds. *Arctic Oil and Gas: Sustainability at Risk?* New York: Routledge, 2008.

Osherenko, Gail, and Oran R. Young. *The Age of the Arctic: Hot Conflicts and Cold Realities*. Cambridge: Cambridge University Press, 2005.

Triggs, Gillian, and Anna Riddell, eds. *Antarctica: Legal and Environmental Challenges for the Future*. London: British Institute of International and Comparative Law, 2007.

Wadhams, P., J. A. Dowdeswell, and A. N. Schofield, eds. *The Arctic and Environmental Change*. Amsterdam: Gordon and Breach, 1996.

Wenzel, George. *Animal Rights, Human Rights Ecology, Economy and Ideology in the Canadian Arctic*. London: Belhaven Press, 1991.

Wynn, Graeme. *Canada and Arctic North America: An Environmental History*. Santa Barbara, Calif.: ABC-CLIO, 2007.

Young, Oran R. *Creating Regimes: Arctic Accords and International Governance*. Ithaca, N.Y.: Cornell University Press, 1998.

Young, Oran R., and Gail Osherenko, eds. *Polar Politics: Creating International Environmental Regimes*. Ithaca, N.Y.: Cornell University Press, 1993.

## Asia-Pacific

Barrett, Brendan F. D., ed. *Ecological Modernization and Japan*. New York: Routledge Curzon, 2005.

Broad, Robin, with John Cavanagh. *Plundering Paradise: The Struggle for the Environment in the Philippines*. Berkeley: University of California Press, 1993.

Broadbent, Jeffrey. *Environmental Politics in Japan: Networks of Power and Protest*. Cambridge: Cambridge University Press, 1998.

Bryant, Raymond L. *The Political Ecology of Forestry in Burma, 1824–1994*. London: Hurst & Co., 1997.

Day, Kristen A., ed. *China's Environment and the Challenge of Sustainable Development*. London: M. E. Sharpe, 2005.

Economy, Elizabeth C. *The River Runs Black: The Environmental Challenge to China's Future*. Ithaca, N.Y.: Cornell University Press, 2004.

Fahn, James David. *A Land on Fire: The Environmental Consequences of the Southeast Asian Boom*. Boulder, Colo.: Westview Press, 2003.

Gallagher, Kelly Sims. *China Shifts Gears: Automakers, Oil, Pollution, and Development*. Cambridge, Mass.: MIT Press, 2006.

Hasegawa, Koichi. *Constructing Civil Society in Japan: Voices of Environmental Movements*. Melbourne, Australia: Trans Pacific, 2004.

Imura, Hidefumi, and Miranda A. Schreurs. *Environmental Policy in Japan*. Washington, D.C.: Edward Elgar & the World Bank, 2005.

Kalland, Arne, and Gerard Persoon, eds. *Environmental Movements in Asia*. Richmond, England: Curzon Press, 1998.

Lee, Yok-Shiu F., and Alvin Y. So, eds. *Asia's Environmental Movements: Comparative Perspectives*. Armonk, N.Y.: M. E. Sharpe, 1999.

Ma, Xioaying. *Environmental Regulation in China: Institutions, Enforcement, and Compliance*. Lanham, Md.: Rowman & Littlefield, 1998.

Matsumura, Hiroshi. *Japan and the Kyoto Protocol: Conditions for Ratification*. London: Royal Institute of International Affairs Energy and Environment Programme, 2000.

McKean, Margaret A. *Environmental Protest and Citizen Politics in Japan*. Berkeley: University of California Press, 1981.

Mitsuhashi, Tadahiro. *Environment in Japan*. Tokyo: Foreign Press Center, Japan, 2001.

Najam, Adil, ed. *Environment, Development and Human Security: Perspectives from South Asia*. Lanham, Md.: University Press of America, 2003.

O'Rourke, Dara. *Community-Driven Regulation: Balancing Development and the Environment in Vietnam*. Cambridge, Mass.: MIT Press, 2004.

Sizer, Nigel. *Backs to the Wall in Suriname: Forest Policy in a Country in Crisis*. Washington, D.C.: World Resources Institute, 1995.

## Europe

Andonova, Liliana B. *Transnational Politics of the Environment: The European Union and Environmental Policy in Central and Eastern Europe*. Cambridge, Mass.: MIT Press, 2004.

Auer, Matthew R. *Restoring Cursed Earth: Appraising Environmental Policy Reforms in Eastern Europe and Russia.* Lanham, Md.: Rowman & Littlefield, 2005.

Barry, John, Brian Baxter, and Richard Dunphy, eds. *Europe, Globalization and Sustainable Development.* London: Routledge, 2004.

Bomberg, Elizabeth. *Green Parties and Politics in the European Union.* London: Routledge, 1998.

Carmin, JoAnn, and Stacy D. VanDeveer, eds. *EU Enlargement and the Environment: Institutional Change and Environmental Policy in Central and Eastern Europe.* London: Routledge Press, 2005.

Carter, F. W., and David Turnock. *Environmental Problems of East Central Europe.* London: Routledge, 2002.

Eder, Klaus, and Maria Kousis, eds. *Environmental Politics in Southern Europe: Actors, Institutions, and Discourses in a Europeanizing Society.* Dordrecht, Netherlands: Kluwer Academic, 2001.

Grant, Wyn, Duncan Matthews, and Peter Newell. *The Effectiveness of European Union Environmental Policy.* London: Macmillan Press, 2000.

Hunter, Janet R., and Zachary A. Smith, eds. *Protecting Our Environment: Lessons from the European Union.* Albany: State University of New York Press, 2005.

Jordan, Andrew, ed. *Environmental Policy in the European Union.* 2nd ed. London: Earthscan, 2005.

Jordan, Andrew, and Duncan Liefferink, eds. *Environmental Policy in Europe: The Europeanization of National Environmental Policy.* New York: Routledge, 2004.

Korppoo, Anna, Jacqueline Karas, and Michael Grubb, eds. *Russia and the Kyoto Protocol: Opportunities and Challenges.* London: Chatham House, 2006.

McCormick, John. *Environmental Policy in the European Union.* Basingstoke, England: Palgrave, 2001.

Moe, Arild, and Kristian Tangen. *The Kyoto Mechanisms and Russian Climate Politics.* London: Royal Institute of International Affairs, 2000.

Oldfield, Jonathan D. *Russian Nature: Exploring the Environmental Consequences of Societal Change.* Burlington, Vt.: Ashgate, 2006.

Prendiville, Brendan. *Environmental Politics in France.* Boulder, Colo.: Westview Press, 1994.

Rootes, Christopher, ed. *Environmental Protest in Western Europe.* Oxford: Oxford University Press, 2003.

Weiner, Douglas R. *A Little Corner of Freedom: Russian Nature Protection from Stalin to Gorbachev.* Berkeley: University of California Press, 1999.

Zito, Anthony. *Creating Environmental Policy in the European Union.* Basingstoke, England: Palgrave, 2000.

## Latin America

Carruthers, David V., ed. *Environmental Justice in Latin America: Problems, Promise, and Practice*. Cambridge, Mass.: MIT Press, 2008.

Collinson, Helen, ed. *Green Guerrillas: Environmental Conflicts and Initiatives in Latin America and the Caribbean*. London: Latin America Bureau, 1996.

García Guadilla, María-Pilar. *Environmental Movements, Politics, and Agenda 21 in Latin America*. Geneva, Switzerland: United Nations Research Institute for Social Development, 2005.

Hochstetler, Kathryn, and Margaret E. Keck. *Greening Brazil: Environmental Activism in State and Society*. Durham, N.C.: Duke University Press, 2007.

Jenkins, Rhys, ed. *Industry and the Environment in Latin America*. London: Routledge, 2000.

Roberts, J. Timmons, and Nikki Demetria Thanos. *Trouble in Paradise: Globalization and Environmental Crises in Latin America*. New York: Routledge, 2003.

Silvius, Kirsten M., Richard E. Bodmer, and Jose M. V. Fragaso, eds. *People in Nature: Wildlife Conservation in South and Central America*. New York: Columbia University Press, 2005.

Sklair, Leslie. *Assembling for Development*. San Diego: University of California, Center for U.S.-Mexican Studies, 1993.

Steinberg, Paul F. *Environmental Leadership in Developing Countries: Transnational Relations and Biodiversity Policy in Costa Rica and Bolivia*. Cambridge, Mass.: MIT Press, 2001.

Striffler, Steve. *In the Shadows of State and Capital: The United Fruit Company, Popular Struggle, and Agrarian Restructuring in Ecuador, 1900–1995*. Durham, N.C.: Duke University Press, 2002.

Striffler, Steve, and Mark Moberg, eds. *Banana Wars: Power, Production, and History in the Americas*. Durham, N.C.: Duke University Press, 2003.

Utting, Peter, ed. *The Greening of Business in Developing Countries*. London: Zed Books, 2002.

West, Sarah Elizabeth. *Environmental Issues in Latin America and the Caribbean*. New York: Springer, 2005.

## Middle East

Adaman, Fikret, and Murat Arsel, eds. *Environmentalism in Turkey: Between Democracy and Development?* Hampshire, England: Ashgate Publishing, 2005.

Allan, Tony. *The Middle East Water Question: Hydropolitics and the Global Economy*. London: I. B. Tauris, 2000.

Dolatyar, Mostafa, and Tim S. Gray. *Water Politics in the Middle East*. New York: St. Martin's Press, 2000.

Foltz, Richard C., ed. *Environmentalism in the Muslim World*. New York: Nova Science Publishers, 2005.

Hillstrom, Kevin, and Laurie Collier Hillstrom. *Africa and the Middle East: A Continental Overview of Environmental Issues*. Santa Barbara, Calif.: ABC-CLIO, 2003.

Jabbra, Joseph G., and Nancy Walstrom Jabbra. *Challenging Environmental Issues: Middle Eastern Perspectives*. Leiden, Netherlands: Brill, 1997.

Starr, Joyce, and Daniel Stoll. *The Politics of Scarcity: Water in the Middle East*. Boulder, Colo.: Westview Press, 1988.

Tal, Alon. *Pollution in a Promised Land: An Environmental History of Israel*. Berkeley: University of California Press, 2002.

## North America

Black, Brian. *Nature and the Environment in Twentieth-Century American Life*. Westport, Conn.: Greenwood Press, 2006.

DeSombre, Elizabeth R. *Domestic Sources of International Environmental Policy: Industry, Environmentalists, and U.S. Power*. Cambridge, Mass.: MIT Press, 2000.

Gottlieb, Robert. *Forcing the Spring: The Transformation of the American Environmental Movement*. Rev. ed. Washington, D.C.: Island Press, 2005.

Harrison, Kathryn. *Passing the Buck: Federalism and Canadian Environmental Policy*. Vancouver: University of British Columbia Press, 1996.

Kline, Benjamin. *First along the River: A Brief History of the U.S. Environmental Movement*. 3rd ed. Lanham, Md.: Rowman & Littlefield, 2007.

Leopold, Aldo. *A Sand County Almanac*. New York: Oxford University Press, 1949.

McKenzie, Judith. *Environmental Politics in Canada: Managing the Commons into the Twenty-First Century*. Don Mills, Ont.: Oxford University Press, 2002.

Shabecoff, Philip. *A Fierce Green Fire: The American Environmental Movement*. Washington, D.C.: Island Press, 2003.

Speth, James Gustave. *Red Sky at Morning: America and the Crisis of the Global Environment*. New Haven, Conn.: Yale University Press, 2004.

Switzer, Jacqueline Vaughn. *Environmental Politics: Domestic and Global Dimensions*. Belmont, Calif.: ThomsonWadsworth, 2004.

Thoreau, Henry David. *Walden*. Edinburgh, Scotland: D. Douglas, 1884.

## Oceania

Bennett, Judith A. *Pacific Forest: A History of Resource Control and Contest in Solomon Islands, c.1800–1997*. Leiden, Netherlands: White Horse Press, 2000.

Doyle, Tim. *Green Power: The Environment Movement in Australia*. Sydney, Australia: University of New South Wales Press, 2000.

Emberson-Bain, 'Atu, ed. *Sustainable Development or Malignant Growth? Perspectives of Pacific Island Women*. Suva, Fiji: Marama Publications, 1994.

Filer, Colin, ed. *The Political Economy of Forest Management in Papua New Guinea*. London: The International Institute for Environment and Development and the National Research Institute, 1997.

Garnaut, Ross, ed. *Resource Management in Asia Pacific Developing Countries*. Canberra, Australia: Asia Pacific Press, 2002.

Hamilton, Clive. *Running from the Storm: The Development of Climate Change Policy in Australia*. Sydney, Australia: University of New South Wales Press, 2001.

Hutton, Drew, and Libby Connors. *A History of the Australian Environment Movement*. Cambridge: Cambridge University Press, 1999.

Jost, Christian, ed. *The French-Speaking Pacific: Population, Environment, and Development Issues*. Mount Nebo, Australia: Boombana Publications, 1998.

Rainbow, Stephen. *Green Politics*. Auckland, New Zealand: Oxford University Press, 1993.

Walker, Ken, and Kate Crowley, eds. *Australian Environmental Policy: Studies in Decline and Devolution*. Sydney, Australia: University of New South Wales Press, 1999.

## ISSUES

## Air Pollution

Biermann, Frank. *Saving the Atmosphere: International Law, Developing Countries and Air Pollution*. Frankfurt am Main, Germany: Peter Lang, 1995.

Calhoun, Yael, ed. *Air Quality*. Philadelphia, Pa.: Chelsea House Publishers, 2005.

Gonzalez, George A. *The Politics of Air Pollution: Urban Growth, Ecological Modernization, and Symbolic Inclusion*. Albany: State University of New York Press, 2005.

Kidd, J. S., and Renee A. Kid. *Air Pollution: Problems and Solutions*. New York: Chelsea House, 2006.

Leonard, H. Jeffrey. *Pollution and the Struggle for the World Product*. Cambridge: Cambridge University Press, 1988.

Markowitz, Gerald, and David Rosner. *Deceit and Denial: The Deadly Politics of Industrial Pollution*. Berkeley: University of California Press, 2002.

McGranahan, Gordon, and Frank Murray. *Air Pollution and Health in Rapidly Developing Countries*. London: Earthscan, 2003.

Miller, Debra A., ed. *Pollution*. Detroit, Mich.: Greenhaven Press, 2007.

Sliggers, Johan, and Willem Kakebeeke, eds. *Clearing the Air: 25 Years of the Convention on Long-Range Transboundary Air Pollution*. New York: United Nations, 2005.

Sokhi, Ranjeet S., ed. *World Atlas of Atmospheric Pollution*. London: Anthem Press, 2007.

Vallero, Daniel A. *Fundamentals of Air Pollution*. 4th ed. Amsterdam: Elsevier, 2008.

## Automobiles

Berger, Michael L. *The Automobile Industry in American History and Culture: A Reference Guide*. Westport, Conn.: Greenwood Press, 2001.

Boehmer-Christiansen, Sonja, and Helmut Weidnet. *The Politics of Reducing Vehicle Emissions in Britain and Germany*. London: Pinter and Associated University Presses, 1995.

Dunn, James A. Jr. *Driving Forces: The Automobile, Its Enemies, and the Politics of Mobility*. Washington, D.C.: Brookings Institution Press, 1998.

Freund, Peter, and George Martin. *The Ecology of the Automobile*. Montreal, Que.: Black Rose Books, 1993.

McShane, Clay. *Down the Asphalt Path: The Automobile and the American City*. New York: Columbia University Press, 1994.

Newman, Peter, and Jeffrey Kenworthy. *Sustainability and Cities: Overcoming Automobile Dependence*. Washington, D.C.: Island Press, 1999.

Paterson, Matthew. *Automobile Politics: Ecology and Cultural Political Economy*. Cambridge: Cambridge University Press, 2007.

Porter, Richard C. *Economics at the Wheel: The Costs of Cars and Drivers*. San Diego, Calif.: Academic Press, 1999.

Rajan, Sudhir Chella. *The Enigma of Automobility: Democratic Politics and Pollution Control*. Pittsburgh, Pa.: University of Pittsburgh Press, 1996.

Ryan, Lisa, and Hal Turton. *Sustainable Automobile Transport: Shaping Climate Change Policy*. Cheltenham, England: Edward Elgar, 2007.

Sinclair, Stuart. *The World Car: The Future of the Automobile Industry*. London: Euromonitor Publications, 1983.

Wall, Derek. *Earth First! and the Anti-Roads Movement*. London: Routledge, 1999.

## Biodiversity and Biosafety

Bail, Christoph, Robert Falkner, and Helen Marquard. *The Cartagena Protocol on Biosafety: Reconciling Trade in Biotechnology with Environment and Development*. London: Earthscan, 2002.

Chester, Charles C. *Conservation across Borders: Biodiversity in an Interdependent World*. Washington, D.C.: Island Press, 2006.

Chivian, Eric, and Aaron Bernstein, eds. *Sustaining Life: How Human Health Depends on Biodiversity*. Oxford: Oxford University Press, 2008.

Cooney, Rosie, and Barney Dickson, eds. *Biodiversity and the Precautionary Principle; Risk and Uncertainty in Conservation and Sustainable Use*. London: Earthscan, 2005.

Deke, Oliver. *Environmental Policy Instruments for Conserving Global Biodiversity*. Berlin: Springer, 2008.

Jeffery, Michael I., Jeremy Firestone, Karen Bubna-Litic, eds. *Biodiversity Conservation, Law and Livelihoods: Bridging the North-South Divide*. New York: Cambridge University Press, 2008.

Jeffries, Michael J. *Biodiversity and Conservation*. 2nd ed. Oxford: Routledge, 2006.

Mackenzie, Ruth, et al. *An Explanatory Guide to the Cartagena Protocol on Biosafety*. Gland, Switzerland: The World Conservation Union, 2003.

McManis, Charles R., ed. *Biodiversity and the Law: Intellectual Property, Biotechnology and Traditional Knowledge*. London: Earthscan, 2007.

O'Riordan, Tim, and Susanne Stoll-Kleemann. *Biodiversity, Sustainability and Human Communities: Protecting Beyond the Protected*. Cambridge: Cambridge University Press, 2002.

Shiva, Vandana. *Biopiracy: The Plunder of Nature and Knowledge*. Toronto, Ont.: Between the Lines, 1997.

——. *Monocultures of the Mind: Perspectives on Biodiversity and Biotechnology*. London: Zed Books, 1993.

Wilson, Edward O. *The Diversity of Life*. Rev. ed. New York: W. W. Norton, 1999.

Wood, Alexander, Pamela Stedman-Edwards, and Johanna Mang. *The Root Causes of Biodiversity Loss*. London: Earthscan, 2000.

## Climate Change

Adger, W. Neil, Jouni Paavola, Saleemul Huq, and M. J. Mace, eds. *Fairness in Adaptation to Climate Change*. Cambridge, Mass.: MIT Press, 2006.

Brown, Lester R. *Plan B: Rescuing a Planet under Stress and a Civilization in Trouble*. New York: W. W. Norton, 2003.

DiMento, Joseph F. C., and Pamela M. Doughman, eds. *Climate Change: What It Means for Us, Our Children, and Our Grandchildren*. Cambridge, Mass.: MIT Press, 2007.

Emanuel, Kerry. *What We Know about Climate Change*. Cambridge, Mass.: MIT Press, 2007.

Fisher, Dana R. *National Governance and the Global Climate Change Regime*. Lanham, Md.: Rowman & Littlefield, 2004.

Flannery, Tim. *The Weather Makers: The History and Future Impact of Climate Change*. Melbourne, Australia: Text Publishing, 2006.

Hoffmann, Matthew J. *Ozone Depletion and Climate Change: Constructing a Global Response*. Albany: State University of New York Press, 2005.

Mendelsohn, Robert, and Ariel Dinar. *Climate Change and Agriculture: An Economic Analysis of Global Impacts, Adaptation, and Distributional Effects*. Cheltenham, England: Edward Elgar, 2008.

Newell, Peter. *Climate for Change: Non-State Actors and the Global Politics of the Greenhouse*. Cambridge: Cambridge University Press, 2000.

Page, Edward A. *Climate Change, Justice and Future Generations*. Cheltenham, England: Edward Elgar, 2006.

Paterson, Matthew. *Global Warming and Global Politics*. London: Routledge, 1996.

Rowlands, Ian. *The Politics of Global Atmospheric Change*. Manchester, England: Manchester University Press, 1995.

Soroos, Marvin S. *The Endangered Atmosphere*. Columbia: University of South Carolina Press, 1997.

Stern, Nicholas. *The Economics of Climate Change: The Stern Review*. Cambridge: Cambridge University Press, 2007.

Volk, Tyler. *$CO_2$ Rising: The World's Greatest Environmental Challenge*. Cambridge, Mass.: MIT Press, 2008.

## Forests and Deserts

Barber, Charles Victor, and James Schweithelm. *Trial by Fire: Forest Fires and Forestry Policy in Indonesia's Era of Crisis and Reform*. Washington, D.C.: World Resources Institute, 2000.

Cashore, Benjamin, Graeme Auld, and Deanna Newsom. *Governing through Markets: Forest Certification and the Emergence of Non-state Authority*. New Haven, Conn.: Yale University Press, 2004.

Chomitz, Kenneth M., et al. *At Loggerheads? Agricultural Expansion, Poverty Reduction, and Environment in the Tropical Forests*. Washington, D.C.: World Bank, 2007.

Dauvergne, Peter. *Loggers and Degradation in the Asia-Pacific: Corporations and Environmental Management*. Cambridge: Cambridge University Press, 2001.

———. *Shadows in the Forest: Japan and the Politics of Timber in Southeast Asia*. Cambridge, Mass.: MIT Press, 1997.

Geist, Helmut. *The Causes and Progression of Desertification*. Aldershot, England: Ashgate 2005.

Humphreys, David. *Forest Politics: The Evolution of International Cooperation*. London: Earthscan, 1996.

———. *Logjam: Deforestation and the Crisis of Global Governance*. London: Earthscan, 2006.

Kolk, Ans. *Forests in International Environmental Politics: International Organisations, NGOs and the Brazilian Amazon*. Utrecht, Netherlands: International Books, 1996.

Moran, Emilio F., and Elinor Ostrom, eds. *Seeing the Forest and the Trees: Human-Environment Interactions in Forest Ecosystems*. Cambridge, Mass.: MIT Press, 2005.

Place, Susan E., ed. *Tropical Rainforests: Latin American Nature and Society in Transition*. Rev. ed. Wilmington, Del.: Scholarly Resources, 2001.

Rozario, Paul. *Spreading Deserts*. Chicago, Ill.: Raintree, 2004.

Rudel, Thomas K. *Tropical Forests: Regional Paths of Destruction and Regeneration in the Late Twentieth Century*. New York: Columbia University Press, 2005.

Spray, Sharon L., and Matthew D. Moran, eds. *Tropical Deforestation*. Lanham, Md.: Rowman & Littlefield, 2006.

Tuck-Po, Lye, Wil de Jong, and Abe Ken-ichi, eds. *The Political Ecology of the Tropical Forests in Southeast Asia: Historical Perspectives*. Kyoto, Japan: Kyoto University Press, 2003.

Vandermeer, John H., and Ivette Perfecto. *Breakfast of Biodiversity: The Political Ecology of Rain Forest Destruction*. 2nd ed. Oakland, Calif.: Food First Books, 2005.

## Endangered Species

Baillie, Jonathan E. M., Craig Hilton-Taylor and Simon M. Stuart, eds. *IUCN Red List of Threatened Species: A Global Species Assessment*. Gland, Switzerland: IUCN—The World Conservation Union, 2004.

Broswimmer, Franz J. *Ecocide: A Short History of Mass Extinction of Species*. London: Pluto Press, 2002.

Gunter, Michael M., Jr. *Building the Next Ark: How NGOs Work to Protect Biodiversity*. New ed. Lebanon, N.H.: Dartmouth College Press, 2006.

Hutton, Jon, and Barnabas Dickson, eds. *Endangered Species—Threatened Convention. The Past, Present and Future of CITES*. London: Earthscan, 2000.

McGavin, George C. *Endangered: Wildlife on the Brink of Extinction*. Buffalo, N.Y.: Firefly Books, 2006.

Meacham, Cory J. *How the Tiger Lost Its Stripes: An Exploration into the Endangerment of a Species*. New York: Harcourt Brace, 1997.

Myers, Norman. *The Sinking Ark: A New Look at the Problem of Disappearing Species*. New York: Pergamon Press, 1979.

Reeve, Rosalind. *Policing International Trade in Endangered Species: The CITES Treaty and Compliance*. London: Royal Institute of International Affairs, 2002.

Wijnstekers, Willem. *The Evolution of CITES: A Reference to the Convention on International Trade in Endangered Species of Wild Fauna and Flora*. 7th ed. Geneva, Switzerland: CITES, 2003.

Wilcove, David. *No Way Home: The Decline of the World's Great Animal Migrations*. Washington, D.C.: Island Press, 2007.

## Energy

Bradford, Travis. *Solar Revolution: The Economic Transformation of the Global Energy Industry*. Cambridge, Mass.: MIT Press, 2006.

Goldblatt, David L. *Sustainable Energy Consumption and Society: Personal, Technological, or Social Change?* Dordrecht, Netherlands: Springer, 2005.

Gunkel, Darrin, ed. *Alternative Energy Sources*. Detroit, Mich.: Greenhaven Press, 2006.

Knechtel, John, ed. *Fuel*. Cambridge, Mass.: MIT Press, 2008.

Nersesian, Roy L. *Energy for the 21st Century: A Comprehensive Guide to Conventional and Alternative Sources*. Armonk, N.Y.: M. E. Sharpe, 2006.

Rifkin, Jeremy. *The Hydrogen Economy: The Creation of the Worldwide Energy Web and the Redistribution of Power on Earth*. New York: TarcherPutnam, 2002.

Ristinen, Robert A., and Jack J. Kraushaar. *Energy and the Environment*. 2nd ed. Hoboken, N.J.: John Wiley, 2006.

Skjærseth, Jon Birger, and Tora Skodvin. *Climate Change and the Oil Industry: Common Problem, Varying Strategies*. Manchester, England: Manchester University Press, 2003.

Smil, Vaclav. *Energy at the Crossroads: Global Perspectives and Uncertainties*. Cambridge, Mass.: MIT Press, 2003.

Wolfson, Richard. *Energy, Environment, and Climate*. New York: W. W. Norton, 2008.

## Food

Ali Brac de la Perriere, Robert, and Franck Seuret. *Brave New Seeds: The Threat of GM Crops to Farmers*. London: Zed Books, 2000.

Barrientos, Stephanie, and Catherine Dolan, eds. *Ethical Sourcing in the Global Food System*. London: Earthscan, 2006.

Blatt, Harvey. *America's Food: What You Don't Know about What You Eat*. Cambridge, Mass.: MIT Press, 2000.

Falkner, Robert, ed. *The International Politics of Genetically Modified Food: Diplomacy, Trade and Law*. New York: Palgrave Macmillan, 2007.

Gay, Kathlyn. *Superfood or Superthreat: The Issue of Genetically Engineered Food*. Berkeley Heights, N.J.: Enslow, 2008.

Gordon, Susan, ed. *Critical Perspectives on Genetically Modified Crops and Food*. New York: Rosen Pub. Group, 2006.

Lal, Rattan, et al. *Food Security and Environmental Quality in the Developing World*. Boca Raton, Fla.: Lewis Publishers/CRC Press, 2003.

Martineau, Belinda. *First Fruit: The Creation of the Flavr Savr Tomato and the Birth of Genetically Engineered Food*. New York: McGraw-Hill, 2001.

Pimentel, David, and Marcia H. Pimentel. *Food, Energy, and Society*. 3rd ed. Boca Raton, Fla: CRC Press, 2008.

Schlosser, Eric. *Fast Food Nation: The Dark Side of the All-American Meal*. Boston, Mass.: Houghton Mifflin, 2001.

Shiva, Vandana. *Stolen Harvest: The Hijacking of the Global Food Supply*. Cambridge, Mass.: South End Press, 2000.

Thompson, Paul B. *Food Biotechnology in Ethical Perspective*. 2nd ed. Dordrecht, Netherlands: Springer, 2007.

Thomson, Jennifer A. *Seeds for the Future: The Impact of Genetically Modified Crops on the Environment*. Ithaca, N.Y.: Cornell University Press, 2007.

Weirich, Paul, ed. *Labeling Genetically Modified Food: The Philosophical and Legal Debate*. Oxford: Oxford University Press, 2007.

## Hazardous Chemicals and Pesticides

Carlile, W. R. *Pesticide Selectivity, Health and the Environment*. Cambridge: Cambridge University Press, 2006.

Carson, Rachel. *Silent Spring*. Boston, Mass.: Houghton Mifflin, 1962.

Freeze, R. Allan. *The Environmental Pendulum: A Quest for the Truth about Toxic Chemicals, Human Health, and Environmental Protection*. Berkeley: University of California Press, 2000.

Hough, Peter. *The Global Politics of Pesticides: Forging Consensus from Conflicting Interests*. London: Earthscan, 1998.

Lansdown, Richard, and William Yule. *Lead Toxicity: History and Environmental Impact*. Baltimore: The Johns Hopkins University Press, 1986.

Levine, Marvin J. *Pesticides: A Toxic Time Bomb in Our Midst*. Westport, Conn.: Praeger Publishers, 2007.

McCormick, John. *Acid Earth: The Politics of Acid Pollution*. 3rd ed. London: Earthscan, 1997.

Pretty, Jules N. *The Pesticide Detox: Towards a More Sustainable Agriculture*. London: Earthscan, 2005.

## Hazardous Waste Trade

Clapp, Jennifer. *Toxic Exports: The Transfer of Hazardous Wastes from Rich to Poor Countries*. Ithaca, N.Y.: Cornell University Press, 2001.

Fletcher, Thomas H. *From Love Canal to Environmental Justice: The Politics of Hazardous Waste on the Canada-US Border*. Peterborough, Ont.: Broadview Press, 2003.

Iles, Alastair. *Piling Up E-Wastes in Asia: Impacts and Design Solutions*. Berkeley: University of California, 2004.

Jacott, Marisa, Cyrus Reed, and Mark Winfield. *The Generation and Management of Hazardous Wastes and Transboundary Hazardous Waste Shipments between Mexico, Canada and the United States, 1990–2000*. Austin: Texas Center for Policy Studies, 2001.

Kuehr, Ruediger, and Eric Williams, eds. *Computers and the Environment: Understanding and Managing Their Impacts*. Tokyo: United Nations University Press, 2003.

McCarthy, James. *Recycling Computers and Electronic Equipment: Legislative and Regulatory Approaches for E-Wastes*. Washington, D.C.: Library of Congress Congressional Research Service, 2002.

Omohundro, Ellen. *Living in a Contaminated World: Community Structures, Environmental Risks, and Decision Frameworks*. Aldershot, England: Ashgate, 2004.

O'Neill, Kate. *Waste Trading among Rich Nations: Building a New Theory of Environmental Regulation*. Cambridge, Mass.: MIT Press, 2000.

Pellow, David Naguib. *Resisting Global Toxics: Transnational Movements for Environmental Justice*. Cambridge, Mass.: MIT Press, 2007.

Rahm, Dianne. *Toxic Waste and Environmental Policy in the 21st Century United States*. Jefferson, N.C.: McFarland, 2002.

## Oceans and Fisheries

Bhattacharya, Hrishikes. *Commercial Exploitation of Fisheries: Production, Marketing and Finance Strategies*. New York: Oxford University Press, 2002.

Clover, Charles. *The End of the Line: How Overfishing Is Changing the World and What We Eat*. London: Random House, 2004.

DeSombre, Elizabeth R. *Flagging Standards: Globalization and Environmental, Safety and Labor Regulations at Sea*. Cambridge, Mass.: MIT Press, 2006.

Ebbin, Syma A., Alf Håkon Hoel, and Are K. Sydnes, eds. *A Sea Change: Exclusive Economic Zones and Governance Institutions for Living Marine Resources*. Dordrecht, Netherlands: Springer, 2005.

Ellis, Richard. *The Empty Ocean: Plundering the World's Marine Life*. Washington, D.C.: Island Press, 2003.

Gerdes, Louise I., ed. *Endangered Oceans: Opposing Viewpoints*. San Diego, Calif.: Greenhaven Press, 2004.

Hall, Stephen J. *The Effects of Fishing on Marine Ecosystems and Communities*. Oxford: Blackwell Science, 2000.

Jacques, Peter. *Globalization and the World Ocean*. Lanham, Md.: AltaMira Press, 2006.

M'Gonigle, Michael R., and Mark W. Zacher. *Pollution, Politics and International Law: Tankers at Sea*. Berkeley: University of California Press, 1979.

Mitchell, Ronald. *Intentional Oil Pollution at Sea: Environmental Policy and Treaty Compliance*. Cambridge, Mass.: MIT Press, 1994.

Roberts, Callum. *The Unnatural History of the Sea*. Washington, D.C.: Island Press, 2007.

Seckinelgin, Hakan. *The Environment and International Politics: International Fisheries, Heidegger and Social Method*. New York: Routledge, 2006.

Skjaerseth, Jon B. *North Sea Cooperation: Linking International and Domestic Pollution Control*. Manchester, England: Manchester University Press, 2001.

VanDeveer, Stacy D., and Geoffrey D. Dabelko, eds. *Protecting Regional Seas: Developing Capacity and Fostering Environmental Cooperation in Europe*. Washington, D.C.: Woodrow Wilson International Center for Scholars, 1999.

Webster, D. G. *Adaptive Governance: The Dynamics of Atlantic Fisheries Management*. Cambridge, Mass.: MIT Press, 2008.

## Ozone Depletion

Andersen, Stephen O., and K. Madhava Sarma. *Protecting the Ozone Layer: The United Nations History*. London: Earthscan, 2005.

Benedick, Richard Elliot. *Ozone Diplomacy: New Directions in Safeguarding the Planet*. Enlarged ed. Cambridge, Mass.: Harvard University Press, 1998.

Cagin, Seth, and Philip Dray. *Between Earth and Sky: How CFCs Changed Our World and Endangered the Ozone Layer*. New York: Pantheon Books, 1993.

Molina, Mario J., and F. Sherwood Rowland. "Stratospheric Sink for Chlorofluoromethanes: Chlorine Atom-Catalysed Destruction of Ozone." *Nature* 249 (28 June 1974): 810–12.

Parson, Edward A. *Protecting the Ozone Layer: Science, Strategy, and Negotiation in the Shaping of a Global Environmental Regime*. Oxford: Oxford University Press, 2002.

United Nations Environment Programme. *Environmental Effects of Ozone Depletion and Its Interactions with Climate Change: 2006 Assessment*. Nairobi, Kenya: UNEP, 2006.

Ward, Bud, ed. *Reporting on Climate Change: Understanding the Science*. 3rd ed. Washington, D.C.: Environmental Law Institute, 2003.

## Persistent Organic Pollutants

Downie, David Leonard, and Terry Fenge, eds. *Northern Lights against POPs: Combatting Toxic Threats in the Arctic*. Montreal, Que.: McGill-Queen's University Press, 2003.

Johansen, Bruce E. *The Dirty Dozen: Toxic Chemicals and the Earth's Future*. Westport, Conn.: Praeger, 2003.

Olsen, Marco A. *Analysis of the Stockholm Convention on Persistent Organic Pollutants*. Dobbs Ferry, N.Y.: Oceana Publications, 2003.

## Urbanization

Benton-Short, Lisa, and John Rennie Short. *Cities and Nature (Critical Introductions to Urbanism and the City)*. New York: Routledge, 2007.

Brand, Peter, with Michael Thomas. *Urban Environmentalism: Global Change and the Mediation of Local Conflict*. New York: Routledge, 2005.

Bulkeley, Harriet, and Michele M. Betsill. *Cities and Climate Change: Urban Sustainability and Global Environmental Governance*. London: Routledge, 2003.

Doucet, Clive. *Urban Meltdown: Cities, Climate Change and Politics as Usual*. Gabriola Island, B.C.: New Society Publishers, 2007.

Heberle, Lauren C., and Susan M. Opp. *Local Sustainable Urban Development in a Globalized World*. Aldershot, England: Ashgate, 2008.

Kahn, Matthew E. *Green Cities: Urban Growth and the Environment*. Washington, D.C.: Brookings Institution Press, 2006.

Sheehan, Molly O'Meara. *City Limits: Putting the Brakes on Sprawl*. Washington, D.C.: Worldwatch Institute, 2001.

## Water

Conca, Ken. *Governing Water: Contentious Transnational Politics and Global Institution Building*. Cambridge, Mass.: MIT Press, 2006.

Dombrowski, Ines. *Conflict, Cooperation, and Institutions in International Water Management.* Cheltenham, England: Edward Elgar, 2007.

Finger, Matthias, Ludivine Tamiotti, and Jeremy Allouche, eds. *The Multi-Governance of Water: Four Case Studies.* Albany: State University of New York, 2006.

Gleick, Peter H., et al. *The World's Water 2006–2007: The Biennial Report on Freshwater Resources.* Washington, D.C.: Island Press, 2006.

Goldsmith, Edward, and Nicholas Hildyard. *The Social and Environmental Effects of Large Dams.* Wadebridge, England: Wadebridge Ecological Centre, 1984.

Khagram. Sanjeev. *Dams and Development: Transnational Struggles for Water and Power.* Ithaca, N.Y.: Cornell University Press, 2004.

Leslie, Jacques. *Deep Water: The Epic Struggle over Dams, Displaced People, and the Environment.* New York: Farrar, Straus and Giroux, 2005.

McCully, Patrick. *Silenced Rivers: The Ecology and Politics of Large Dams.* Enlarged and updated ed. London: Zed Books, 2001.

Pearce, Fred. *When the Rivers Run Dry: Water—The Defining Crisis of the Twenty-First Century.* Boston, Mass.: Beacon Press, 2006.

Reisner, Marc. *Cadillac Desert: The American West and Its Disappearing Water.* New York: Viking Penguin, 1986.

Turton, Anthony, and Roland Henwood, eds. *Hydropolitics in the Developing World: A Southern African Perspective.* Pretoria, South Africa: AWIRU, 2002.

Waterbury, John. *The Nile Basin: National Determinants of Collective Action.* New Haven, Conn.: Yale University Press, 2002.

## Whaling

Burns, William C.G., and Alexander Gillespie, eds. *The Future of Cetaceans in a Changing World.* Ardsley, N.Y.: Transnational Publishers, 2003.

Epstein, Charlotte. *The Power of Words in International Relations: Birth of an Anti-Whaling Discourse.* Cambridge, Mass.: MIT Press, 2008.

Estes, James A., et al., eds. *Whales, Whaling, and Ocean Ecosystems.* Berkeley: University of California Press, 2006.

Friedheim, Robert L., ed. *Towards a Sustainable Whaling Regime?* Seattle: University of Washington Press, 2001.

Heazle, Michael. *Scientific Uncertainty and the Politics of Whaling.* Seattle: University of Washington Press, 2006.

Hoyt, Erich. *Marine Protected Areas for Whales, Dolphins and Porpoises: A World Handbook for Cetacean Habitat Conservation.* London: Earthscan, 2004.

Stoett, Peter J. *The International Politics of Whaling*. Vancouver: University of British Columbia Press, 1997.

## ENVIRONMENTAL ETHICS AND PHILOSOPHIES

### Ethics

Attfield, Robin. *Environmental Ethics: An Overview for the Twenty-First Century*. Cambridge: Polity Press, 2003.

Boylan, Michael, *Environmental Ethics*. Upper Saddle River, N.J.: Prentice Hall, 2001.

Des Jardins, Joseph R. *Environmental Ethics: An Introduction to Environmental Philosophy*. 4th ed. Belmont, Calif.: Wadsworth/Thomson Learning, 2006.

Hardin, Garrett. *Exploring New Ethics for Survival: The Voyage of the Spaceship Beagle*. Baltimore, Md.: Pelican, 1972.

———. "Living on a Lifeboat." *Bioscience* 24 no. 10 (1974): 561–68.

Light, Andrew, and Avner De-Shalit, eds. *Moral and Political Reasoning in Environmental Practice*. Cambridge, Mass.: MIT Press, 2003.

Light, Andrew, and Holmes Rolston III, eds. *Environmental Ethics: An Anthology*. Oxford: Blackwell Publishing, 2003.

Newton, Lisa H. *Ethics and Sustainability: Sustainable Development and the Moral Life*. Upper Saddle River, N.J.: Prentice Hall, 2003.

Pojman, Louis P., ed. *Environmental Ethics: Readings in Theory and Application*. 3rd ed. Belmont, Calif.: WadsworthThomson Learning, 2001.

Schmidtz, David, and Elizabeth Willott, eds. *Environmental Ethics: What Really Matters, What Really Works*. Oxford: Oxford University Press, 2002.

Stenmark, Mikael. *Environmental Ethics and Policy-Making*. Aldershot, England: Ashgate, 2002.

VanDeVeer, Donald, and Christine Pierce, eds. *The Environmental Ethics and Policy Book: Philosophy, Ecology, Economics*. 3rd ed. Belmont, Calif.: WadsworthThomson Learning, 2003.

Wenz, Peter S. *Environmental Ethics Today*. Oxford: Oxford University Press, 2001.

Westra, Laura, and Patricia H. Werhane, eds. *The Business of Consumption: Environmental Ethics and the Global Economy*. Lanham, Md.: Rowman & Littlefield, 1998.

### Philosophies

Baber, Walter F., and Robert V. Bartlett. *Deliberative Environmental Politics: Democracy and Ecological Rationality*. Cambridge, Mass.: MIT Press, 2005.

Beder, Sharon. *Environmental Principles and Policies: An Interdisciplinary Introduction*. London: Earthscan, 2007.

Costanza, Robert, John Cumberland, Herman Daly, Robert Goodland, and Richard Norgaard. *An Introduction to Ecological Economics*. Boca Raton, Fla.: St. Lucie Press, 1997.

Dobson, Andrew. *Green Political Thought*. 4th ed. New York: Routledge, 2007.

Dobson, Andrew, and Derek Bell, eds. *Environmental Citizenship*. Cambridge, Mass.: MIT Press, 2006.

Goldsmith, Edward. *The Way: An Ecological World-View*. London: Rider, 1992.

Hay, Peter R. *Main Currents in Western Environmental Thought*. Bloomington: Indiana University Press, 2002.

Hines, Colin. *Localization: A Global Manifesto*. London. Earthscan, 2000.

Kaufman, Frederik A. *Foundations of Environmental Philosophy: A Text with Readings*. Boston, Mass.: McGraw-Hill, 2003.

Lovelock, James. *The Ages of Gaia: A Biography of Our Living Earth*. Rev. ed. New York: W. W. Norton, 1995.

———. *Gaia: A New Look at Life on Earth*. Oxford: Oxford University Press, 1979.

Merchant, Carolyn. *Radical Ecology: The Search for a Livable World*. 2nd ed. New York: Routledge, 2005.

Mies, Maria, and Vandana Shiva, eds. *Ecofeminism*. London: Zed Books, 1993.

O'Connor, James. *Natural Causes: Essays in Ecological Marxism*. New York: Guilford, 1998.

Sessions, George. *Deep Ecology for the Twenty-First Century*. Boston, Mass.: Shambhala, 1995.

Sutton, Philip W. *Explaining Environmentalism: In Search of a New Social Movement*. Aldershot, England: Ashgate, 2000.

Thiele, Leslie Paul. *Environmentalism for a New Millennium: The Challenge of Coevolution*. Oxford: Oxford University Press.

Wackernagel, Mathis, and William Rees. *Our Ecological Footprint: Reducing Human Impact on the Earth*. Gabriola Island, B.C.: New Society Publishers, 1996.

Wilson, Edward O. *The Future of Life*. New York: Alfred A. Knopf, 2002.

Zimmerman, Michael E., et al., eds. *Environmental Philosophy: From Animal Rights to Radical Ecology*. 4th ed. Upper Saddle River, N.J.: Prentice Hall, 2005.

## EVENTS AND PEOPLE

### Environmental Disasters

Bryan, Nichol. *Danube: Cyanide Spill*. Milwaukee, Wis.: World Almanac Library, 2004.

Eckerman, Ingrid. *The Bhopal Saga: Causes and Consequences of the World's Largest Industrial Disaster*. Hyderabad, India: Universities Press, 2005.

Fortun, Kim. *Advocacy after Bhopal: Environmentalism, Disaster, New Global Orders*. Chicago: University of Chicago Press, 2001.

George, Timothy S. *Minamata: Pollution and the Struggle for Democracy in Postwar Japan*. Cambridge, Mass.: Harvard University Asia Center, 2001.

Gibbs, Lois Marie. *Love Canal: My Story*. As told to Murray Levine. Albany: State University of New York Press, 1982.

Gunn, Angus M. *Unnatural Disasters: Case Studies of Human-Induced Environmental Catastrophes*. Westport, Conn.: Greenwood Press, 2003.

Mishima, Akio. *Bitter Sea: The Human Cost of Minamata Disease*. Translated by Richard L. Gage and Susan B. Murata. 1st English ed. Tokyo: Kosei Pub. Co., 1992.

Mould, R. F. *Chernobyl Record: The Definitive History of the Chernobyl Catastrophe*. Bristol, England: Institute of Physics Publishing, 2000.

Niedenthal, Jack. *For the Good of Mankind: A History of the People of Bikini and Their Islands*. 2nd ed. Majuro, Marshall Islands: Bravo Publishers, 2001.

Rees, Joseph V. *Hostages of Each Other: The Transformation of Nuclear Safety since Three Mile Island*. Chicago: Chicago University Press, 1994.

Schweithelm, James. *The Fire This Time: An Overview of Indonesia's Forest Fires in 1997/98*. Jakarta, Indonesia: WWF Indonesia, 1999.

Smith, Jim T., and Nicholas A. Beresford. *Chernobyl: Catastrophe and Consequences*. Berlin: Springer, 2005.

Walker, J. Samuel. *Three Mile Island: A Nuclear Crisis in Historical Perspective*. Berkeley: University of California Press, 2004.

## Biographies and Autobiographies

Axelrod, Alan, and Charles Phillips. *The Environmentalists: A Biographical Dictionary from the 17th Century to the Present*. New York: Facts on File, 1993.

Brown, Michael, and John May. *The Greenpeace Story*. Scarborough, Ont.: Prentice Hall Canada, 1989.

Davidson, Cliff I., ed. *Clean Hands: Clair Patterson's Crusade against Environmental Lead Contamination*. Commack, N.Y.: Nova Science Publishers, 1999.

Faber, Doris, and Harold Faber. *Nature and the Environment*. New York: Charles Scribner's Sons, 1991.

Foreman, Dave. *Confessions of an Eco-Warrior*. New York: Three Rivers Press, 1993.

Hunter, Robert. *Warriors of the Rainbow: A Chronicle of the Greenpeace Movement*. New York: Holt, Rinehart and Winston, 1979.

Lear, Linda. *Rachel Carson: The Life of the Author of "Silent Spring."* New York: Henry Holt, 1997.

Maathai, Wangari Muta. *Unbowed: A Memoir.* New York: Alfred A. Knopf, 2006.

Parkin, Sara. *The Life and Death of Petra Kelly.* London: Harper Collins, 1999.

Pearce, Fred. *Green Warriors: The People and the Politics behind the Environmental Revolution.* London: Bodley Head, 1991.

Revkin, Andrew. *The Burning Season: The Murder of Chico Mendes and the Fight for the Amazon Rain Forest.* Washington, D.C.: Island Press, 2004.

Weyler, Rex. *Greenpeace: How a Group of Ecologists, Journalists and Visionaries Changed the World.* Vancouver, B.C.: Raincoast Books, 2004.

## INTERNET RESOURCES

**Environmental Issues**

*Air Pollution*

Convention on Long-range Transboundary Air Pollution
www.unece.org/env/lrtap
Environment Canada: U.S.–Canada Air
www.ec.gc.ca/pdb/can_us/canus_links_e.cfm
U.S.–Canada Air Quality Agreement
www.ijc.org
U.S. EPA Clean Air Markets: Programs and Regulations
www.epa.gov/air

*Bhopal Disaster*

Bhopal Information Center
www.bhopal.com
Bhopal Medical Appeal
www.bhopal.org
International Campaign for Justice in Bhopal
www.bhopal.net

*Biodiversity and Biosafety*

Action Group on Erosion, Technology and Concentration (ETC)
www.etcgroup.org

Biodiversity Convention
www.cbd.int
Biotechnology Industry Organization (BIO)
www.bio.org
Biosafety Protocol
www.cbd.int/biosafety
Genetic Action Resources International (GRAIN)
www.grain.org
International Service for the Acquisition of Agri-Biotech Applications
www.isaaa.org
Research Foundation for Science, Technology and Ecology (Vandana Shiva)
www.navdanya.org

*Climate Change*

Friends of the Earth Climate Page
www.foe.co.uk/campaigns/climate
Greenpeace International Climate Page
www.greenpeace.org/international/campaigns/climate-change
Kyoto Protocol to the UN Framework Convention on Climate Change
unfccc.int/kyoto_protocol/items/2830.php
Union of Concerned Scientists
www.ucsusa.org
United Nations Framework Convention on Climate Change
unfccc.int/2860.php
WWF Climate Page
www.panda.org/about_wwf/what_we_do/climate_change

*Desertification*

United Nations Convention to Combat Desertification
www.unccd.entico.com
United Nations Convention to Combat Desertification
www.unccd.int

*Endangered Species*

Convention on International Trade in Endangered Species (CITES)
www.cites.org
Convention on the Conservation of Migratory Species of Wild Animals
www.cms.int

World Wide Fund for Nature/World Wildlife Fund (WWF)
www.wwf.org

*Forests and Deforestation*

Center for International Forestry Research
www.cifor.cgiar.org
Forest Ethics—Environmental Corporate Action
www.forestethics.org/index.php
Forest Stewardship Council
www.fsc.org
Forest Stewardship Council United States
www.fscus.org
International Tropical Timber Association
www.itto.or.jp

*Hazardous Chemicals and Pesticides*

Canadians against Pesticides
www.caps.20m.com
Environmental Working Group
www.ewg.org
Pesticide Action Network: North America and International
www.panna.org
Rotterdam Convention on the Prior Informed Consent Procedure for Certain
Hazardous Chemicals and Pesticides in International Trade
www.pic.int
Stockholm Convention on POPs
www.pops.int

*Hazardous Waste Trade*

Basel Action Network
www.ban.org
Secretariat of the Basel Convention
www.basel.int

*Ozone Depletion*

Montreal Protocol on Substances That Deplete the Ozone Layer
http://ozone.unep.org/Publications/MP_Handbook/index.shtml

Vienna Convention for the Protection of the Ozone Layer
http://ozone.unep.org/Publications/VC_Handbook/index.shtml

*Persistent Organic Pollutants*

Greenpeace Chemicals Page
www.greenpeace.org/international/campaigns/toxics/chemicals-out-of-control
International POPs Elimination Network
www.ipen.org
Pesticides Action Network Organophosphate Pesticides Page
www.panna.org/ops
Stockholm Convention on POPs
www.pops.int

*Whaling*

Greenpeace Whales Campaign
www.greenpeace.org/international/campaigns/oceans/whaling
International Convention for the Regulation of Whaling
www.iwcoffice.org/commission/convention.htm
International Whaling Commission
www.iwcoffice.org

## International Environmental Agreements (Opened for Signature/Entered into Force)

African Convention on the Conservation of Nature and Natural Resources (1968/1969)
www.africa-union.org/root/au/Documents/Treaties/Text/Convention_Nature%20&%20Natural_Resources.pdf
Agreement for the Implementation of the Law of the Sea Convention Relating to the Conservation and Management of Straddling Fish Stocks and Highly Migratory Fish Stocks (1995/2001)
www.un.org/Depts/los/convention_agreements/convention_overview_fish_stocks.htm
Antarctic Treaty (1959/1961)
www.ats.aq
Cartagena Protocol on Biosafety to the Convention on Biological Diversity (2000/2003)
www.cbd.int/biosafety/

Comprehensive Nuclear Test Ban Treaty (1996/not in force)
www.ctbto.org
Convention for the International Council for the Exploration of the Sea (1964/1968)
www.ices.dk/aboutus/convention.asp
Convention for the Prohibition of Fishing with Long Driftnets in the South Pacific (Wellington Convention) (1989/1990)
http://untreaty.un.org/English/UNEP/driftnets_english.pdf
Convention for the Protection of the Ozone Layer (Vienna Convention) (1985/1988)
http://ozone.unep.org/Publications/VC_Handbook/index.shtml
Convention on Access to Information, Public Participation in Decision-Making and Access to Justice in Environmental Matters (Aarhus Convention) (1998/2001)
www.unece.org/env/pp
Convention on Biological Diversity (1992/1993)
www.biodiv.org
Convention on Fishing and Conservation of the Living Resources of the High Seas (1958/1966)
http://untreaty.un.org/ilc/texts/instruments/english/conventions/8_1_1958_fishing.pdf
Convention on Long-range Transboundary Air Pollution (1979/1983)
www.unece.org/env/lrtap
Convention on Nuclear Safety (1994/1996)
www-ns.iaea.org/conventions/nuclear-safety.htm
Convention on Persistent Organic Pollutants (Stockholm Convention) (2001/2004)
www.pops.int
Convention on the Ban of the Import into Africa and the Control of Transboundary Movement and Management of Hazardous Wastes within Africa (Bamako Convention) (1991/1998)
www.africa-union.org/root/AU/Documents/Treaties/Text/hazardous wastes.pdf
Convention on the Conservation of Antarctic Marine Living Resources (1980/1982)
www.ccamlr.org
Convention on the Conservation of Migratory Species of Wild Animals (1979/1983)
www.cms.int
Convention on the Continental Shelf (1958/1964)
http://untreaty.un.org/ilc/texts/instruments/english/conventions/8_1_1958_continental_shelf.pdf

Convention on the Control of Transboundary Movements of Hazardous Wastes and their Disposal (Basel Convention) (1989/1992)
www.basel.int

Convention on the High Seas (1958/1962)
http://untreaty.un.org/ilc/texts/instruments/english/conventions/8_1_1958_high_seas.pdf

Convention on the International Commission for the Protection of the Rhine Against Pollution (Berne Convention) (1963/1965)
www.iksr.org

Convention on the International Trade in Endangered Species of Wild Fauna and Flora (CITES) (1973/1975)
www.cites.org

Convention on the Law of the Non-navigational Uses of International Watercourses (1997/not in force)
http://untreaty.un.org/ilc/guide/8_3.htm

Convention on the Prevention of Marine Pollution by Dumping of Wastes and Other Matter (London Convention) (1972/1975)
www.londonconvention.org

Convention on the Prior Informed Consent Procedure for Certain Hazardous Chemicals and Pesticides in International Trade (Rotterdam Convention) (1998/2004)
www.pic.int

Convention on the Protection and Use of Transboundary Watercourses and International Lakes (1992/1996)
www.unece.org/env/water

Convention on the Territorial Sea and the Contiguous Zone (1958/1964)
http://untreaty.un.org/ilc/texts/instruments/english/conventions/8_1_1958_territorial_sea.pdf

Convention on Third Party Liability in the Field of Nuclear Energy (Paris Convention) (1960/1968)
www.nea.fr/html/law/nlparis_conv.html

Convention on Wetlands of International Importance Especially as Waterfowl Habitat (Ramsar Convention) (1971/1975)
www.ramsar.org

Convention Relative to the Preservation of Fauna and Flora in their Natural State (1933/1936)
http://sedac.ciesin.org/entri/texts/fauna.flora.natural.state.1933.html

International Convention for the Conservation of Atlantic Tunas (1966/1969)
www.iccat.int

International Convention for the Prevention of Pollution of the Sea by Oil (1954/1958)
www.imo.org

International Convention for the Protection of Birds (1950/1963)
  http://sedac.ciesin.org/entri/texts/protection.of.birds.1950.html
International Convention for the Regulation of Whaling (1946/1948)
  www.iwcoffice.org/commission/convention.htm
International Plant Protection Convention (1951/1952)
  www.ippc.int
International Treaty on Plant Genetic Resources for Food and Agriculture
  (2001/2004)
  www.planttreaty.org
International Tropical Timber Agreement (1983/1985)
  www.itto.or.jp
Kyoto Protocol to the United Nations Framework Convention on Climate
  Change (1998/2005)
  www.unfccc.int
Montreal Protocol on Substances That Deplete the Ozone Layer (1987/1989)
  http://ozone.unep.org/Publications/MP_Handbook/index.shtml
Protocol on Environmental Protection to the Antarctic Treaty (1991/not in
  force)
  www.ats.aq/e/ats_protocol.htm
Protocol on Heavy Metals to the Convention on Long-range Transboundary Air
  Pollution (1998/2003)
  www.unece.org/env/lrtap (see protocols)
Protocol on Persistent Organic Pollutants to the Convention on Long-range
  Transboundary Air Pollution (1998/2003)
  www.unece.org/env/lrtap (see protocols)
Treaty Banning Nuclear Weapon Tests in the Atmosphere, in Outer Space and
  Under Water (1963/1963)
  www.ctbto.org
United Nations Convention on the Law of the Sea (LOS) (1982/1994)
  www.un.org/Depts/los
United Nations Convention to Combat Desertification in Countries Experiencing Serious Drought and/or Desertification, Particularly in Africa (1994/1996)
  www.unccd.int
United Nations Framework Convention on Climate Change (1992/1994)
  http://unfccc.int

## Nongovernmental Organizations and Global Agencies

African Conservation Foundation
  www.africanconservation.org
African Wildlife Foundation
  www.awf.org

Australian Conservation Foundation
www.acfonline.org.au
Center for International Environmental Law (CIEL)
www.ciel.org
Centre for Science and Environment, India
www.cseindia.org/index.html
Coalition for Environmentally Responsible Economies
www.ceres.org
Conservation International
www.conservation.org
Ducks Unlimited
www.ducks.org
Earth Charter Initiative
www.earthcharter.org
Earth First!
www.earthfirst.org
Earthjustice
www.earthjustice.org
Earthtrust
www.earthtrust.org
Earthwatch Institute
www.earthwatch.org
Environmental Defense Fund (EDF)
www.edf.org/home.cfm
Environmental Foundation for Africa
www.efasl.org.uk
Environmental Investigation Agency
www.eia-international.org
Environmental Performance Index
http://epi.yale.edu
European Centre for Nature Conservation
www.ecnc.nl
Forest Stewardship Council
www.fsc.org
Forests and the European Union Resource Network (FERN)
www.fern.org
Friends of the Earth, U.S.
www.foe.org
Friends of the Earth International
www.foei.org
Global Compact
www.unglobalcompact.org

Global Environment Facility (GEF)
www.gefweb.org
Global Witness
www.globalwitness.org
Green Belt Movement
www.greenbeltmovement.org
Green Cross International
www.greencrossinternational.net
Greenpeace International
www.greenpeace.org/international
ICLEI: Local Governments for Sustainability
www.iclei.org
International Institute for Environment and Development (IIED)
www.iied.org
International Institute for Sustainable Development (IISD)
www.iisd.org
International Rivers Network
http://internationalrivers.org
International Union for Conservation of Nature (IUCN)
http://cms.iucn.org
International Whaling Commission
www.iwcoffice.org
Living Earth
www.livingearth.org.uk
Marine Stewardship Council (MSC)
www.msc.org
National Audubon Society
www.audubon.org
Natural Resources Defense Council
www.nrdc.org
Nature Conservancy
www.nature.org
OCEANA
www.oceana.org
Pesticides Action Network
www.panna.org
Rainforest Action Network (RAN)
www.ran.org
Rainforest Alliance
www.rainforest-alliance.org
Resources for the Future
www.rff.org

Sea Shepherd Conservation Society
    www.seashepherd.org
Sierra Club
    www.sierraclub.org
Union of Concerned Scientists
    www.ucsusa.org
United Nations Development Programme
    www.undp.org
United Nations Environment Programme
    www.unep.org
Wetlands International
    www.wetlands.org
Wilderness Society (Australia)
    www.wilderness.org.au
Wilderness Society (United States)
    www.wilderness.org
Women's Global Green Action Network
    www.wggan.org
World Bank (Environment)
    www.worldbank.org/environment
World Business Council for Sustainable Development
    www.wbcsd.org
World Data Center for Human Interactions in the Environment (Center for International Earth Science Information Network, at The Earth Institute at Columbia University)
    http://sedac.ciesin.org/wdc/about.jsp
World Resources Institute
    www.wri.org
World Wide Fund for Nature/World Wildlife Fund (WWF)
    www.wwf.org
Worldwatch Institute
    www.worldwatch.org

# About the Author

**Peter Dauvergne** is professor of political science and Canada Research Chair in global environmental politics at the University of British Columbia. His research focuses on critical global change theory and environmental theory in international relations. He also has subfield interests in the international political economy of sustainable development and the politics of environmental management in the Asia-Pacific. Dauvergne is a member of the Publications Board of the UBC Press and the founding and past editor (2001–2008) of the MIT Press journal *Global Environmental Politics*. Since joining the University of British Columbia in 2002, he has also served as director of the Environment Program at the Liu Institute for Global Issues (2003–2005) and associate dean in the Faculty of Arts (2006–2008). Dauvergne is currently serving as senior advisor to the university president.

Professor Dauvergne has previously published six books, two monographs, 30 journal articles and book chapters, and over two dozen other publications. His books include *The Shadows of Consumption: Consequences for the Global Environment* (MIT Press, 2008); *Paths to a Green World: The Political Economy of the Global Environment* (MIT Press, 2005, coauthored with Jennifer Clapp); *Handbook of Global Environmental Politics* (Edward Elgar, 2005, edited); *Loggers and Degradation in the Asia-Pacific: Corporations and Environmental Management* (Cambridge University Press, 2001); *Weak and Strong States in Asia-Pacific Societies* (Allen & Unwin 1998, edited); and *Shadows in the Forest: Japan and the Politics of Timber in Southeast Asia* (MIT Press, 1997), winner of the 1998 Sprout Award from the International Studies Association for the best book in global environmental affairs.